Developments in Russian Politics 7

Developments titles available from Palgrave

Alistair Cole, Patrick Le Galès and Jonah Levy (eds)
DEVELOPMENTS IN FRENCH POLITICS 4

Maria Green Cowles and Desmond Dinan (eds)
DEVELOPMENTS IN THE EUROPEAN UNION 2

Patrick Dunleavy, Richard Heffernan, Philip Cowley and
Colin Hay (eds)
DEVELOPMENTS IN BRITISH POLITICS 8

Paul M. Heywood, Erik Jones, Martin Rhodes and
Ulrich Sedelmeier (eds)
DEVELOPMENTSINEUROPEANPOLITICS

Stephen Padgett, William E. Paterson and Gordon Smith (eds)
DEVELOPMENTS IN GERMAN POLITICS 3*

Gillian Peele, Christopher J. Bailey, Bruce Cain and B. Guy Peters (eds)
DEVELOPMENTS IN AMERICAN POLITICS 5

Stephen White, Judy Batt and Paul Lewis (eds)
DEVELOPMENTS IN CENTRAL AND EAST
EUROPEAN POLITICS 3*

Stephen White, Richard Sakwa and Henry E. Hale (eds)
DEVELOPMENTS IN RUSSIAN POLITICS 7*

Of Related Interest

Ian Holliday, Andrew Gamble and Geraint Parry (eds)
FUNDAMENTALS IN BRITISH POLITICS

If you have any comments or suggestions regarding the
above or other possible Developmentstitles, please write to
Steven Kennedy, Palgrave Macmillan, Houndmills,
Basingstoke RG21 6XS, UK or e-mail s.kennedy@palgrave.com

* Rights world excluding North America

Developments in Russian Politics 7

Edited by

Stephen White

Richard Sakwa

and

Henry E. Hale

palgrave
macmillan

This edition published 2010 by
PALGRAVE MACMILLAN

Palgrave Macmillan in the UK is an imprint of Macmillan Publishers Limited, registered in England, company number 785998, of Houndmills, Basingstoke, Hampshire RG21 6XS.

Palgrave Macmillan in the US is a division of St Martin's Press LLC, 175 Fifth Avenue, New York, NY 10010.

Palgrave Macmillan is the global academic imprint of the above companies and has companies and representatives throughout the world.

Palgrave® and Macmillan® are registered trademarks in the United States, the United Kingdom, Europe and other countries

ISBN 978–0–230–22448–3 hardback
ISBN 978–0–230–22449–0 paperback

This book is printed on paper suitable for recycling and made from fully managed and sustained forest sources. Logging, pulping and manufacturing processes are expected to conform to the environmental regulations of the country of origin.

A catalogue record for this book is available from the British Library.

A catalog record for this book is available from the Library of Congress.

10	9	8	7	6	5	4	3	2	1
19	18	17	16	15	14	13	12	11	10

Printed and bound in China

Contents

List of Maps, Tables and Figures

Map

Tables

Figures

Preface

Russia is the world's largest country. It spans two continents and eleven time zones. It has one of the world's biggest economies, and one of its largest concentrations of military might. It is a founding member of the United Nations, with a permanent seat on its Security Council, and a member of the Group of Eight leading industrial nations. So Russia matters, even if it no longer represents an ideological challenge to Western ideals. And for these reasons, who controls this massive territory, with its economic, military and human resources, how its leaders are chosen, and what influences them, and how their decisions influence the world in which we live ourselves, are all matters of global significance.

We bring a new team to explore such issues in this seventh edition, and a new editor: Henry Hale of George Washington University, replacing Zvi Gitelman of the University of Michigan, who has given loyal service to the project since its inception. We welcome some entirely new contributors; previous authors tackle new themes; and long-standing contributors have revised or rewritten. For the most part, this is an entirely new book. But it has the same objectives as its predecessors: to provide at least a basic outline of the contemporary Russian political system while giving more attention to topical issues, and questions of interpretation, of a kind we think will be of interest to other scholars as well as to the university and college students for whom it is primarily intended.

We start, as we must, by placing contemporary Russian politics in a longer-term perspective, and then move to the core institutions of the Russian state: the political executive (including the presidency and the prime minister), the legislature, the electoral system, and the political parties. Further chapters consider the wider relationship between Russians and their government: 'civil society', political communication, and the legal system; and then the nature of Russian federalism, and politics in the eighty-odd republics and regions. We move on to policy formation: in the economy, in society, in foreign affairs and in defence and security. A final chapter places the entire system within wider debates about 'democracy' and human rights; we conclude, as in previous editions, with a guide to further reading and a comprehensive list of references.

We complete this book as a new Russian president moves into the second year of his term of office, with continuing debate in Russia and outside it about the nature of the 'tandem' between Dmitri Medvedev and his predecessor, now prime minister, Vladimir Putin. The balance of opinion in this book is generally cautious about the nature of the change this represents in a system in which the presidency has normally been all-powerful. But we give due attention to the possibility that it may represent a sharing of executive authority of a kind that could eventually lead to a more balanced relationship between the branches of government, and between Russia's politicians and the society over which they rule. If it does, the period on which we focus in this volume will represent a break in long-standing patterns of Russian history of no less importance than the institutional changes that took place when the Soviet system itself came to an end.

STEPHEN WHITE
RICHARD SAKWA
HENRY E. HALE

Notes on Contributors

Alfred B. Evans, Jr is Professor Emeritus of Political Science at California State University, Fresno. His publications include *Soviet Marxism-Leninism: The Decline of an Ideology* (Praeger, 1993), and co-edited volumes on *The Politics of Local Government in Russia* (with Vladimir Gel'man, Rowman & Littlefield, 2004) and *Change and Continuity in Russian Civil Society: A Critical Assessment* (with Laura Henry and Lisa McIntosh Sundstrom, Sharpe, 2006). He is the author of *Power and Ideology: Vladimir Putin and the Russian Political System*, published in 2008 by the Carl Beck Papers of the University of Pittsburgh. His current research deals with the topics of civil society and ideological change in Russia.

Henry E. Hale is Associate Professor of Political Science at George Washington University. His publications include *Why Not Parties in Russia? Democracy, Federalism, and the State* (Cambridge, 2006) and, more recently, *The Foundations of Ethnic Politics: Separatism of States and Nations in Eurasia and the World* (Cambridge, 2008). In 2007–08, he was a Fulbright Scholar in Moscow. His current research focuses on political party development, 'hybrid regimes' that combine democratic and authoritarian elements, and ethnic politics.

Philip Hanson is Associate Fellow of the Russia and Eurasia Programme at Chatham House (the Royal Institute of International Affairs) in London. His books include (co-edited with Michael Bradshaw), *Regional Economic Change in Russia* (Edward Elgar, 2000), and *The Rise and Fall of the Soviet Economy* (Pearson Education, 2003). He has published widely in academic journals including *Economy and Society, Europe–Asia Studies, European Economic Review* and *International Affairs*. He is currently working mainly on contemporary Russian economic policy.

Margot Light is Emeritus Professor of International Relations at the London School of Economics and Political Science. Her publications include *Putin's Russia and the Enlarged Europe* (with Roy Allison and Stephen White, Blackwell, 2006), 'Russia and the War on Terrorism', in *Understanding Global Terror*, edited by Chris Ankersen (Polity, 2007), and 'Russia and the EU: Strategic Partners or Strategic Rivals?', in the *Journal of Common Market Studies* (Annual Review, 2008).

Nick Manning is Professor of Social Policy and Sociology at the University of Nottingham. His publications include *Socialism, Social Welfare and the Soviet Union* (with Vic George, Routledge 1980), *Work and Welfare in the New Russia* (with Ovsei Shkaratan and Nataliya Tikhonova, Ashgate, 2000), *Poverty and Social Exclusion in the New Russia* (edited with Nataliya Tikhonova, Ashgate, 2004), 'Inequality in Russia since 1990' in David Lane (ed.), *The Transformation of State Socialism: System Change, Capitalism, or Something Else?* (Palgrave Macmillan, 2007), and *Health and Healthcare in the New Russia* (edited with Nataliya Tikhonova, Ashgate, 2009).

Gillian McCormack earned her PhD in Communications at Glasgow Caledonian University in 2001, writing a dissertation on the development of the post-Soviet media in Russia. She has worked in media research and development in the former communist world for ten years, for the European Institute for the Media and Internews Russia. She has directed media monitoring missions during elections in countries ranging from Armenia to Nigeria, and most recently for the 2008 elections in Cambodia. She is currently based in Brussels, co-ordinating the training of experts for EU election observation missions.

Michael McFaul is Special Assistant to the President of the United States for Russia and Senior Director for Russia and Eurasia at the US National Security Council. He was formerly Director of the Center on Democracy, Development, and Rule of Law at the Freeman Spogli Institute for International Studies and Professor of Political Science at Stanford University. His publications include, with Anders Åslund, *Revolution in Orange: The Origins of Ukraine's Democratic Breakthrough* (Carnegie, 2006); with Nikolai Petrov and Andrei Ryabov, *Between Dictatorship and Democracy: Russian Postcommunist Political Reform* (Carnegie, 2004); with Kathryn Stoner-Weiss, *After the Collapse of Communism: Comparative Lessons of Transitions* (Cambridge University Press, 2004); with Timothy Colton, *Popular Choice and Managed Democracy: The Russian Elections of 1999 and 2000* (Brookings, 2003); and *Russia's Unfinished Revolution: Political Change from Gorbachev to Putin* (Cornell University Press, 2001).

Jennifer G. Mathers is Senior Lecturer in the Department of International Politics at Aberystwyth University. Her publications include *The Russian Nuclear Shield from Stalin to Yeltsin* (Macmillan, 2000) and the co-edited volume *Military and Society in Post-Soviet Russia* (with Stephen L. Webber, Manchester University Press, 2006). She edits *Minerva Journal of Women and War* and is working on a book manuscript about Russian security in the twenty-first century.

Sarah Oates is Professor of Political Communication in the Politics Department at the University of Glasgow. Her publications include *Television, Democracy and Elections in Russia* (Routledge, 2005) and *Introduction to Media and Politics* (Sage, 2008). Her current research examines terrorist threats and the media in Russia, the United States and Great Britain. She has directed or co-directed a range of projects on the post-Soviet media, including studies of election campaigns, voters, and the media audience in contemporary Russia.

Thomas F. Remington is Goodrich C. White Professor of Political Science at Emory University. Among his publications are two books on the Russian parliament: *The Russian Parliament: Institutional Evolution in a Transitional Regime, 1989–1999* (Yale University Press, 2001) and *The Politics of Institutional Choice: Formation of the Russian State Duma* (co-authored with Steven S. Smith, Princeton University Press, 2001). Other books include *Politics in Russia* (5th edn, Longman, 2007); *Parliaments in Transition* (Barnes & Noble, 1994); and *The Truth of Authority: Ideology and Communication in the Soviet Union* (University of Pittsburgh Press, 1988). His current research focuses on the legislative branch and legislative–executive relations in Russia, and on problems of democracy, governance, and inequality in post-communist states.

Cameron Ross is Reader in Politics in the College of Arts and Social Sciences, University of Dundee. He has published widely in the fields of regional and local politics in Russia. His publications include the edited volumes: *Regional Politics in Russia* (Manchester University Press, 2002), *Russian Politics under Putin* (Manchester University Press, 2004), and with Adrian Campbell, *Federalism and Local Politics in Russia* (Routledge, 2009). His most recent monographs are *Federalism and Democratisation in Russia* (Manchester University Press, 2002), and *Local Politics and Democratization in Russia* (Routledge, 2009).

Richard Sakwa is Professor of Russian and European Politics at the University of Kent at Canterbury and an Associate Fellow of the Russia and Eurasia Programme at the Royal Institute of International Affairs, Chatham House. He has published widely on Soviet, Russian and post-communist affairs. His recent books include *Postcommunism* (Buckingham, Open University Press, 1999); the edited volume *Chechnya: From Past to Future* (London, Anthem Press; Sterling, VA, Stylus Publishers, 2005); *Contextualising Secession: Normative Aspects of Secession Struggles* (Oxford University Press, 2003), co-edited with Bruno Coppieters; *Russian Politics and Society* (London and New York, Routledge, 4th edn, 2008), and *Putin: Russia's Choice* (Routledge, 2nd edn, 2008). His book on *The Quality of Freedom: Khodorkovsky, Putin and the Yukos Affair* was published by Oxford University Press in 2009. He is currently working on *The Dual State in Russia: Factionalism and the Medvedev Succession*.

Darrell Slider is Professor of Government and International Affairs at the University of South Florida in Tampa. He has written extensively on Russian regional politics, elections, and federalism in journals such as *Post-Soviet Affairs*, *Europe-Asia Studies*, *Soviet and Post-Soviet Review*, and *Demokratizatsiya*, and has contributed chapters on these issues to a number of edited volumes. In 2004–5 he was a Fulbright Scholar in Moscow at the Higher School of Economics.

Gordon B. Smith is Professor of Political Science and Director of the Walker Institute of International and Area Studies at the University of South Carolina. His publications include *Reforming the Russian Legal System* (Cambridge, 1996) and *State-Building in Russia: The Yeltsin Legacy and the Challenge of the Future* (Sharpe, 1999). His most recent book is *Russia and its Constitution: Promise and Political Reality* (co-edited with Robert Sharlet, Martinus Nijhoff, 2008). His current research deals with democratisation and the development of rule of law in transitional countries.

Kathryn Stoner-Weiss is Associate Director for Research and Senior Research Scholar at CDDRL. Prior to coming to Stanford, she was on the faculty at Princeton University for nine years, jointly appointed to the Department of Politics and the Woodrow Wilson School for International and Public Affairs. She also served as a Visiting Associate Professor of Political Science at Columbia University, and an Assistant Professor of Political Science at McGill University. Her publications include *Local Heroes: The Political Economy of Russian Regional Governance* (Princeton University Press, 1997) and *Resisting the State: Reform and Retrenchment in Post-Soviet Russia* (Cambridge University Press, 2006), and she is also co-editor (with Michael McFaul) of *After the Collapse of Communism: Comparative Lessons of Transitions* (Cambridge University Press, 2004).

Stephen White is James Bryce Professor of Politics and a Senior Research Associate of the School of Slavonic, Central and East European Studies at the University of Glasgow, and also holds visiting appointments at the Institute of Applied Politics in Moscow and the School of Advanced International Studies at the Johns Hopkins University Bologna Center. His recent publications include *Putin's Russia and the Enlarged Europe* (with Roy Allison and Margot Light, Blackwell, 2006), *Party Politics in New Democracies* (co-edited with Paul Webb, Oxford, 2007), and two edited collections, *Media, Culture and Society in Putin's Russia* (Palgrave Macmillan, 2008) and *Politics and the Ruling Group in Putin's Russia* (Palgrave Macmillan, 2008). He is also chief editor of the *Journal of Communist Studies and Transition Politics*.

John P. Willerton is Associate Professor of Political Science at the University of Arizona, Tucson. He is the author of *Patronage and Politics in the USSR* (Cambridge University Press, 1992) and four dozen articles and chapters dealing with various facets of Soviet and post-Soviet Russian domestic politics and foreign policy. His current research focuses on post-Soviet political elites, the Russian federal executive, semi-presidentialism in France and Russia, and Russia's relations with the Commonwealth of Independent States and former Soviet Union countries.

List of Abbreviations

ABM	Anti-Ballistic Missile
CFE	Conventional Forces in Europe
CIS	Commonwealth of Independent States
CPRF	Communist Party of the Russian Federation
CPSU	Communist Party of the Soviet Union
FAR	Fatherland-All-Russia
FNPR	Federation of Independent Trade Unions of Russia
FSB	Federal Security Service
GDF	Glasnost Defence Foundation
GDP	Gross domestic product
GONGOs	government-organised non-governmental organisations
IMF	International Monetary Fund
KGB	Soviet security police
LDPR	Liberal Democratic Party of Russia
MERT	Ministry of Economic Development and Trade
MFA	Ministry of Foreign Affairs
MVD	Ministry of Internal Affairs
NATO	North Atlantic Treaty Organization
NGOs	non-governmental organisations
ODIHR	Office for Democratic Institutions and Human Rights
OHR	Our Home is Russia
OSCE	Organisation for Security and Cooperation in Europe
OVR	Fatherland-All Russia party
PA	presidential administration
PFIGs	Financial–industrial groups
RF	Russian Federation
RSPP	Russian Union of Industrialists and Entrepreneurs
RSFSR	Russian Soviet Federative Socialist Republic
SPS, URF	Union of Right Forces
USSR	The Union of Soviet Socialist Republics
VKP(b)	All-Union Communist Party (Bolsheviks)
WTO	World Trade Organization

Glossary

advokat	lawyer
arbitrazh	commercial (courts)
deesposbnyi	capable
dedovshchina	bullying
demokratizatsiya	democratisation
doverennye	trusted
Duma	Lower house of Federal Assembly (parliament)
kompromat	smear tactics
krai	territory
perestroika	restructuring
poryadok	order
nomenklatura	list of party-controlled posts
oblast'	region, province
obshchestvennye	social or public (organisations)
okrugs	districts
polpred	presidential envoy
siloviki	security and intelligence officials
soviet	council
ukazy	presidential decrees
uskorenie	policy of acceleration
varyagi	'carpetbaggers', derived from the name given to Vikings
zastoi	stagnation

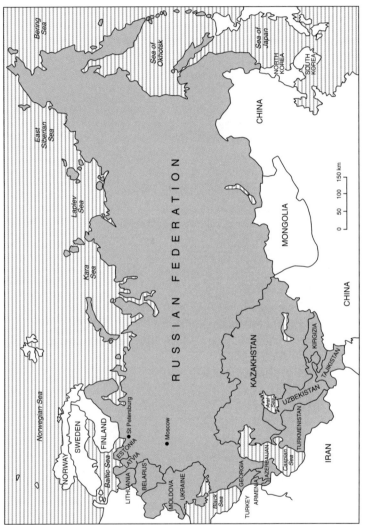

Map 0.1 *Russia and the former Soviet Republics*

Chapter 1

Politics in Russia

RICHARD SAKWA

Two decades after the fall of communism and the establishment of an independent Russia in 1991 the nature of the new political system remains controversial. No one thought it would be easy to create the institutions of representative democracy and the rule of law, together with the mechanisms of market capitalism and national integration, but few could have anticipated quite how difficult these processes would be. The formal establishment of democratic institutions, symbolised above all by the adoption of the constitution in December 1993, was the relatively easy part. Making them work and imbuing them with the spirit of legality, accountability and pluralism is something else. Russia's post-communist development has been marked by some spectacular failures, including armed conflict between the executive and the legislature in 1993 and two wars in Chechnya, yet overall the picture is not quite so bleak as some would suggest. This chapter will present an overview of political developments in the recent past, and suggest some ways of evaluating the contemporary situation.

The Soviet system and its demise

For seventy-four years between 1917 and 1991 the Soviet Union sought to create an alternative social order based on its own interpretation of Marxist thinking combined with a Leninist understanding of the need for a dominant party. The Soviet system endured far longer than most of its early critics thought possible, but ultimately in 1991 came crashing down. The legacy of the failed experiment lives on in Russia today. The *dissolution* of the communist system was accompanied by the *disintegration* of the country. The Union of Soviet Socialist Republics (USSR) was established in December 1922 as a union of allegedly sovereign republics to give political form to the diversity of the new republic's peoples and nations, and this was then given juridical form in the adoption of the Soviet Union's first constitution in January 1924. The system worked as long as long as there was a force standing outside the ethno-federal frame-work; and this force was the All-Union Communist Party (Bolsheviks) (VKP(b)), renamed the Communist Party of the Soviet Union (CPSU) at the Nineteenth Party Congress in 1952. With the launching of *perestroika* (restructuring) by the new General Secretary of the CPSU, Mikhail Gorbachev, in 1985, the Party gradually lost its integrative capacity as its own internal coherence dissolved, precipitating by late 1991 the disinte-gration of the state that it had overseen.

Communism and the Soviet Union

The abdication of Nicholas II in February 1917 brought to an end the Romanov dynasty after more than 300 years in power. During the next eight months Russia tried to fight a war while making a revolution, and although it was notably unsuccessful in the first endeavour it shocked the world with the second. The dominant rule of the Communist Party was established by Vladimir Il'ich Lenin soon after the Bolsheviks came to power in October 1917, and for Lenin (once victory in the Civil War of 1918–20 was assured) development became the priority of Soviet power rather than more general emancipatory goals (the entire sequence of lead-ership from Nicholas II to the present is set out in Table 1.1).

For Joseph Vissarionovich Stalin, who after a struggle following Lenin's death in 1924 achieved dictatorial power, accelerated industriali-sation became the overriding aim, accompanied by the intensification of coercion that peaked in the terror of the 1930s. Victory in the Great Patriotic War of 1941–45 over Nazi Germany and its allies appeared to vindicate all the sacrifices of the early Soviet period, yet the prevalence of terror remained. A first step towards destalinisation was taken following Stalin's death in 1953 by his successor, Nikita Khrushchev, in his 'Secret

Table 1.1   *Soviet and Russian Leaders*

Date	Name of Leader
1894–1917	Nicholas II
1917–24	Vladimir Il'ich Lenin
1924–53	Joseph Vissarionovich Stalin
1953–64	Nikita Sergeevich Khrushchev
1964–82	Leonid Il'ich Brezhnev
1982–84	Yuri Vladimirovich Andropov
1984–85	Konstantin Ustinovich Chernenko
1985–91	Mikhail Sergeevich Gorbachev
1991–99	Boris Nikolaevich Yeltsin
2000–08	Vladimir Vladimirovich Putin
2008–	Dmitri Anatol'evich Medvedev

Speech' of 25 February 1956 at the Twentieth Party Congress. Khrushchev provided a devastating critique of the man – Stalin – but failed to give a systemic critique of how this man had been able to commit so many crimes for so long. During the long reign of Leonid Brezhnev (1964–82) the question of the political renewal of the Soviet system was placed firmly on the back burner. The attempt to renew the communist system by establishing a more humane and democratic form of socialism in Czechoslovakia in 1968 was crushed by Soviet tanks in August of that year. Instead, the last years of Brezhnev's rule gave way to what later was called the period of stagnation (*zastoi*) as the high hopes of the period of *détente* with the West gave way to an intensified and extremely dangerous renewed phase of the Cold War.

Already in 1983 Yuri Andropov, who had headed the KGB since 1967 and then briefly took over as General Secretary of the CPSU between Brezhnev's death in November 1982 and his own death in February 1984, posed the fundamental issue: 'We do not know the country we live in'. Andropov's response was a programme of 'authoritarian modernisation', including the intensification of labour discipline, the struggle against corruption and the restoration of a more ascetic form of communist morality. On Andropov's death the Brezhnevite Konstantin Chernenko managed to claw his way to power for a brief period despite his many illnesses. Chernenko's death in March 1985 finally allowed a new generation to assume the reins of leadership.

Perestroika: from rationalisation to disintegration

The appointment of a reforming General Secretary of the CPSU in March 1985 set in motion changes whose outcome is still not clear. Even though Gorbachev came to power as Andropov's protégé, his programme of reform quickly transcended even a residual notion of 'authoritarian modernisation'. In domestic politics full-scale reforms were adopted, while at the same time he sought to put an end to the Cold War conflict with the West, a struggle that he increasingly considered both futile and damaging for all concerned. Gorbachev came to power with a clear vision that the old way of governing the Soviet Union could no longer continue, but his plans for change swiftly came up against some hard realities. He achieved some significant success in democratising the Soviet system, but by 1991 the communist order was dissolving and the country disintegrating.

On a visit to Canada in May 1983, Gorbachev and the Soviet ambassador, Alexander Yakovlev (who later was to play a large part in shaping the reforms) agreed that 'We cannot continue to live in this way' (Remnick 1993: 294–5). Gorbachev came to power committed to modernising the Soviet system. In the space of six years *perestroika* moved through five main stages: initial attempts to *rationalise* the system moved to a phase of *liberalisation*, and then to *democratisation* (*demokratizatsiya*) that began to transform the society and polity but which provoked the *dissolution* of the foundations of the communist order and culminated in a final stage of *disintegration* of the country itself. Once changes began they could not be limited by regime-led reform, and by 1991 pressure for a radical change of system became overwhelming. The attempt in August 1991 by a group of conservatives to hold back the tide of change precipitated the result that they had sought to avert: the dissolution of the communist system of government and, by the end of the year, the disintegration of the USSR.

Gorbachev did not come to power with a clear set of policies; but he did have an attitude towards change to which he remained loyal to the bitter end. He intended to achieve a modernisation of the communist system through *perestroika*, and within that framework launched what he called a 'revolution within the revolution' to save the system and not to destroy it. Gorbachev understood that the system was suffering from major problems, including declining economic growth rates, social decay, excessive secrecy in scientific and political life, and the degeneration of the ruling elite into an ever more venal and incompetent class. Gorbachev never repudiated the basic idea that the communist system remained a viable and in some respects a superior one to capitalist democracy. His aim was to provide Soviet communism with dynamism similar to that enjoyed by capitalism, but without its defects. He certainly never intended to undermine what was called the 'leading role' of the Communist Party or to destroy the planned economy. *Perestroika*, he insisted, was 'prompted by awareness that the potential of socialism ha[d] been underutilised' (Gorbachev 1987: 10).

In the economic sphere he got off on the wrong foot right away: the policy of acceleration (*uskorenie*) sought to achieve economic transformation and increased output at the same time, and in the event was unable to gain the long-term achievement of either. This was accompanied by an anti-alcohol campaign that deprived the country of nearly one-third of its tax revenues. Soon after came *glasnost'* (openness), intended at first not to be freedom of speech but to be used as a way of exposing the failings of a corrupt bureaucracy, and thus to strengthen the Soviet system. However, *glasnost'* soon became a devastating search for the truth about Leninist and Stalinist repression and took on a life of its own, escaping from the instrumental constraints that Gorbachev had at first intended.

Gorbachev's own views about the past were filtered through a romantic Leninism, believing in an allegedly more democratic and evolutionary late Leninist model of the New Economic Policy of the 1920s. By the end of 1987 *demokratizatsiya* came to the fore, with the gradual introduction of multi-candidate elections accompanied by a relaxation of the Leninist rule against the formation of groups in the Communist Party. Gorbachev's own views at this time were eloquently developed in his book *Perestroika: New Thinking for Our Country and the World* (1987), in which he talked of *perestroika* as a revolution both from above and below. The 'from below' element was by now taking hold in the form of thousands of 'informal' associations, representing the rebirth of an independent civil society. The changes begun by Gorbachev began to outrun his ability to control them. The proliferation of *neformaly* (informals) and an independent press reflected a distinctive type of negative popular mobilisation against the old regime that proved very difficult to channel into positive civic endeavour. The establishment of the Democratic Union on 9 May 1988 marked the beginning of the renewed era of multiparty politics in Russia, but its radical anti-communism signalled that Gorbachev's attempts to constrain and control political pluralism within the framework of 'reform communism' would fail and the communist order would dissolve. In some non-Russian republics the informal movement took the form of popular fronts, with Sajudis in Lithuania one of the largest representing aspirations for national autonomy and, later, independence. Once the genie of political pluralism had been let out of the bottle, it would take on a life of its own.

The high point of Gorbachev's hopes that a humane and democratic socialism could replace the moribund system that he inherited was the Nineteenth Party Conference in June–July 1988, where he outlined a programme of democratic political change and a new role for the USSR in the world. Soon after, institutional changes weakened the role of the party *apparatus*, and constitutional changes in November 1988 created a new two-tier parliament, with a large Congress of People's Deputies meeting twice a year selecting a working Supreme Soviet. The first elections to this body took place in March 1989, and revealed the depths of the unpopularity of party rule. The early debates of the parliament riveted the nation, as problems were openly discussed for the first time in decades. The Congress stripped the Communist Party of its constitutionally entrenched 'leading role' in March 1990, and at the same time Gorbachev was elected to the new post of president of the USSR. His failure to stand in a national ballot is often considered one of his major mistakes. Lacking a popular mandate, he was sidelined by those who did – above all Boris Yeltsin, who became head of the Russian Congress of People's Deputies in May 1990 and then went on to win a popular ballot in June 1991 to become Russia's first president.

What was called the 'nationalities question' now began to threaten the integrity of the country. Although Gorbachev was responsive to calls for greater autonomy by the 15 union republics making up the USSR, he had no time for any talk of independence. Through an increasingly desperate attempt to negotiate a new Union Treaty Gorbachev hoped to transform what was in effect a unitary state into a genuinely confederal community of nations. These hopes were dashed by Lithuania's declaration of independence in 1990, followed by that of Georgia and other republics in 1991. In foreign affairs Gorbachev advanced the idea of 'new political thinking', based on the notion of interdependence and a new co-operative relationship with the West. On a visit to the European Parliament in Strasbourg in September 1988 he talked of the establishment of a 'common European home', but it was not clear what form this would take. By 1989 the Eastern European countries in the Soviet bloc took Gorbachev at his word when he called for change, and from the later months of that year one after another the communist regimes fell. Gorbachev facilitated the unification of Germany, although he is much criticised for failing to guarantee in treaty form the demilitarised status of the eastern part of the new country and of eastern Europe in general.

At home resistance to his aims and his policies grew to the point that a group prepared to seize power in a coup. The specific issue was the planned signing of the new Union Treaty on 20 August 1991, but the plotters were also concerned about economic disintegration and the loss of political control. For three days in August (19–21) Gorbachev was isolated in his holiday home at Foros in the Crimea, while his nemesis, Yeltsin, emerged much strengthened. In the days following the coup Yeltsin put an end to communist rule by banning the party in Russia. Attempts to save the Soviet Union in the last months of 1991 failed. The pressure for increased sovereignty for republics grew into demands for independence, and following the creation of the Commonwealth of Independent States (CIS) on 7–8 December comprising Russia, Ukraine and Belarus, the USSR was clearly on its last legs. The CIS was broadened on 21 December to include most (with the exception of the Baltic republics and Georgia) former Soviet republics. Gorbachev formally resigned as president on 25 December 1991, and on 31 December the USSR formally ceased to exist.

Gorbachev's reform of the Soviet system provoked its demise. The debate over whether the Soviet Union could have been reformed while remaining recognisably communist continues to this day (see for instance Cohen 2004). Gorbachev's *perestroika* clearly showed the system's evolutionary potential, but this was an evolution that effectively meant the peaceful transcendence of the system it was meant to save. The fundamental question remains whether Gorbachev's reforms were a success or a failure. The issue depends on the definition of both. In one sense, they were a triumphant success. By 1991 the country had become relatively democratic, it was moving towards becoming a market economy, the union was changing into a community of sovereign states, and the Cold War had been overcome largely by Gorbachev's efforts. However, the terminal crisis of the system in 1991 revealed deep structural flaws in Gorbachev's conception of reform and in the system's capacity for change while remaining recognisably communist in orientation. Gorbachev remained remarkably consistent in his commitment to a humane democratic socialism with a limited market in a renewed federation of Soviet states. However, his attempts to constrain the process of change within the framework of his preconceived notions soon crashed against some harsh realities: the aspirations for independence in a number of republics, notably of Estonia, Latvia and Lithuania, forcibly incorporated into the USSR by Stalin; the inherent instability of a semi-marketised system – it either had to be one thing or another, a planned or a market economy; and ultimately the lack of popular support for any socialism, irrespective of how humane or democratic it may have been. The attempt to reform the Soviet system brought into the open its many contradictions, and these ultimately brought the whole system crashing down.

Post-communist Russia

Russia entered the twenty-first century and the new millennium a very different country from the one that had entered the twentieth. The tsarist empire had disintegrated, the autocracy had been overthrown, the Soviet communist system had been and gone, and the USSR had also disintegrated leaving fifteen separate republics. Independent Russia was for the first time developing as a nation state rather than as an empire; its economy was severely distorted by the Soviet attempt to establish a planned economy and by the subsequent privatisation of the 1990s with its oligarchs; and the country was engaged in an extraordinary act of political reconstitution intended to establish a liberal democratic system. Democratic politics, defined as the procedural contest for political power and governmental accountability to a freely elected legislature and subordinate to the rule of law, accompanied by a public sphere of debate, criticism and information exchange, had finally arrived in Russia. Whether the so-called transition actually achieved democracy is another question, and one to which we shall return.

Yeltsin: the politics of reform

Russia emerged as an independent and sovereign state in 1991 and since then has been undergoing a complex process of accelerated political change. The Yeltsin administration was committed to Russia becoming a democratic market state allied with the advanced Western nations and integrated into the world economy. There was far less agreement, however, on how these three goals – democratisation, marketisation and international integration – were to be achieved. Bitter debates raged throughout the 1990s over all three, and aspects of these controversies will be discussed in later chapters of this book. On one thing, however, there was broad agreement: the borders of the Russia that emerged as an independent state in 1991 should not be changed, however unfair and arbitrary many considered them to be. Some 25 million ethnic Russians found themselves scattered across the 14 other newly independents states, yet Yeltsin's refusal to exploit the real and imagined grievances of the Russian diaspora to gain cheap political capital must forever stand as one of his major achievements (for a comprehensive review, see Colton 2008). Politics in the post-communist era would be in *Russia*, and not in some mythical re-established Soviet Union in whatever guise.

The nature of these *politics* is less clear. For the first two years following independence Russian politics was wracked by the struggle to adopt a new constitution (Andrews 2002; Sakwa 2008a: Chapter 3). The two-tier parliament that Russia inherited from the Soviet Union was clearly an unworkable arrangement, and ultimately provoked an armed confrontation between the Congress of People's Deputies and the President in October 1993. The constitution was finally adopted in December 1993, and gave Russia a degree of political stability. Although the constitution is a fundamentally liberal document, proclaiming a range of freedoms that would be expected of a liberal democratic state, the balance drawn in the separation of powers between the parliament and president remains controversial. For Fish, Russia's 'low-caliber democracy' is a result of a particular institutional design, namely an excessively strong executive that he and others call 'super-presidential' (Fish 2001b, 2005).

The presidency emerged as the guarantor not only of the constitutional order (as stated in the constitution itself), but also of a reform process that under Yeltsin was driven forward with a single-mindedness that at times threatened to undermine democracy itself (Reddaway and Glinski 2001). This is most vividly in evidence when it came to elections. Fearing that neo-communists and other opponents of moves towards the market and international integration would come to power in the 1996 presidential elections, some in Yeltsin's entourage urged him to cancel them altogether. In the event, although in ill-health, he won a second term and dominated politics to the end of the decade (McFaul 2001).

Although Yeltsin formally remained committed to Russia's democratic development, there were features of his rule that undermined the achievement of his ambition. The first was the unhealthy penetration of economic interests into the decision-making process. Rapid and chaotic privatisation from the early 1990s gave birth to a new class of powerful economic magnates, colloquially known as oligarchs. Their support for Yeltsin's re-election in 1996 brought them into the centre of the political process, and gave rise to the creation of what was known as the 'Family', a mix of Yeltsin family members, politicians and oligarchs. Most notorious of them was Boris Berezovsky, who effectively used political influence as a major economic resource. Many others at this time could exploit insider knowledge to gain economic assets for a fraction of their real worth. It was in these years that the empires of Mikhail Khodorkovsky (pre-eminently the Yukos oil company), Roman Abramovich (with Berezovsky at the head of the Sibneft oil company), Vladimir Potanin at the head of Norilsk Nickel, Vladimir Gusinsky at the head of the Media-Most empire, and many others were built (Fortescue 2006). Their heyday were the years between the presidential election of 1996 and the partial default of August 1998, and thereafter oligarchical power as such waned although as individuals they remained important players.

The second feature was the exaggerated power of the presidency as an institution. Granted extensive authority by the 1993 constitution as part of a deliberate institutional design to ensure adequate powers for the executive to drive through reform, the presidency lacked adequate constraints. Too many decisions were taken by small groups of unaccountable individuals around the president, notably in the case of the decision to launch the first Chechen war in December 1994. We will return to this question below, but associated with that is the third problem, the weakness of mechanisms of popular accountability. Although far from powerless, the State Duma (see Chapter 3) was not able effectively to hold the executive to account. This is related to the weakness of the development of the party system (see Chapter 5). The fourth issue is the question of the succession. While all incumbent leaders try to perpetuate their power or to ensure a transfer to favourable successors, in Yeltsin's case the stakes were particularly high: he feared that a new president could mean a change of system in its entirety, with the possibility of personal sanctions being taken against him and his family. For this reason the Kremlin engaged in a long search for a successor who would be able to ensure continuity and the personal inviolability of Russia's first president (as he liked to style himself) and his associates. They found this guarantee in the person of Vladimir Putin, nominated prime minister on 9 August 1999, acting president on Yeltsin's resignation on 31 December, formally elected for a first term on 14 March 2000 and a second term on 14 March 2004, who then assumed the prime minister's office on 8 May 2008 under the presidency of his chosen successor, Dmitri Medvedev, whose inauguration had taken place the previous day.

Putin: the politics of stability

Putin's accession to the presidency in 2000 did not at first represent a rupture in the constitutional system inherited from Yeltsin, but changes in leadership style, policy orientations and ideological innovations effectively marked the beginning of a distinct era. It is still too early to provide a full analysis of this period or to discern the underlying significance of the events. It is abundantly clear, however, that Putin's programme of 'normal' politics, accompanied by attempts to build a state established on the basis of a modified understanding of the principles of order, represented a new stage in the restless dialectic of continuity and change in Russia's endlessly unforgiving attempts to come to terms with modernity (Sakwa 2008).

Putin's approach was characterised by the pursuit of a politics of stability. The sharp polarisation that attended Yeltsin's rule gave way to an explicitly consensual and 'centrist' approach. The nature of this centrism was not simply an avoidance of the extremes of left and right but was based on a transformative centrism that allowed the regime to reassert its own predominance while allowing the socio-economic transformation of the country to continue. The regime took a relatively pragmatic and technocratic approach that allowed society to get on with its business as long as it did not challenge the leadership's claim that it knew what was best for the country. A relatively coherent and apparently durable new political order began to emerge.

While Putin was undoubtedly a reformer, his approach to change was no longer one of systemic transformation but of system management. His speeches and interventions are peppered with the concept of 'normality'. The concept of normality suggests a certain naturalness of political debate and choice of policy options, relatively unconstrained by the formal imposition of ideological norms. Putin's strategic goal of modernisation of the economy was accompanied by an attempt to consolidate society. Although these goals were not always compatible, a common principle underlay both: the attempt to avoid extremes in policy and to neutralise extremist political actors. Putin's rule was technocratic and based on the exercise of administrative power.

Putin's politics of stability was characterised by the refusal to accept changes to the constitution, the acceptance of the privatisations of the Yeltsin years, and the explicit repudiation of revolution as an effective form of achieving positive political change. This echoed Putin's sentiments voiced in his address on 'Russia at the Turn of the Millennium' at the end of December 1999, where he noted that the communist revolutionary model of development not only had not delivered the goods, but could not have done so (Putin 2000: 212). Although regretting the break-up of the Soviet Union (but not the dissolution of the communist system), Putin never considered the restoration of anything resembling the USSR as remotely possible, let alone desirable. At the heart of Putin's politics of stability was the attempt to reconcile the various phases of Russian history, especially over the last century: the Tsarist, the Soviet and the democratic eras. In the foreign policy sphere Putin insisted that Russia should be treated as a 'normal' great power. He insisted that Russia's foreign policy should serve the country's economic interests, a policy that was evident in debates over the union of Russia and Belarus.

At the heart of Putin's leadership was the reassertion of the constitutional prerogatives of the state (what he called the 'dictatorship of law'), accompanied by the struggle to ensure that that the regime did not fall under the influence of societal actors. In particular, the 'oligarchs' under Yeltsin had exercised what was perceived to be undue influence; this was now repudiated. However, the regime increasingly became insulated from all political actors, including independent political parties and parliament. Accountability mechanisms were weakened, and what was gained in the ability of the government to act as an independent force was lost in its lack of autonomous interaction with society.

An important aspect of Putin's politics was the tension between stability and order. This was a feature of Brezhnev's rule that in the end gave way to stagnation. Stability is the short-term attempt to achieve political and social stabilisation without having resolved the underlying problems and contradictions besetting society. Thus Brezhnev refused to take the hard choices that could have threatened the regime's precarious political stability. Order in this context is something that arises when society, economy and political system are in some sort of balance. To a large extent an ordered society operates according to spontaneous processes, whereas in a system based on the politics of stability administrative measures tend to predominate. As Samuel Huntington (1968) had already noted, political order in changing societies sometimes requires the hard hand of the military or some other force that is not itself subordinate to democratic politics. Putin on a number of occasions explicitly sought to distance himself from this sort of tutelary politics, yet overall the *leitmotif* of his leadership was the technocratic assertion that the regime knows best. To achieve this, a system of 'managed democracy' applied administrative resources to manage the political process, undermining the spontaneous interaction of pluralistic political and social forces. This was in evidence as Putin managed the succession in 2007–08 to allow Medvedev to assume the presidency. The aim was continuity, and this was confirmed by Putin taking up the office of prime minister.

Problems and perspectives

The scope of transformation in post-communist Russia has been unprecedented. A monolithic society was converted into a pluralistic one, a planned economy was reoriented towards the market, a new nation was born, and the state rejoined the international community. None of these processes is complete, and probably by definition never can be. The reform process itself generated new phenomena that raise questions about the received wisdom of the political sciences and economics. There has been rapid divergence in the fate of the post-communist countries, with the majority of Central and East European countries joining the European Union in May 2004 with a second wave in January 2007, while the twelve former Soviet states grouped in the Commonwealth of Independent States (CIS) look ever more different from each other, with some having established more or less functioning democracies while others are firmly locked into authoritarian systems. Russia finds itself somewhere in the middle.

The transition and regime type

The 'third wave' transitions, to use Huntington's (1991) term to describe the mass extinction of authoritarian regimes since the fall of the dictatorship in Portugal in 1974, prompted a renewed interest in problems of democratisation. The fall of communism encouraged political scientists to look again at the theoretical literature on democratisation and to compare the current transitions in the post-communist bloc with earlier transitions in Latin America and Southern Europe. The insights gathered from the study of the democratisation process elsewhere provide a theoretical framework to study the problem of the reconstitution of central political authority on principles of democratic accountability. The degree to which this literature has anything to offer when political regime change is accompanied by economic transformation, state and nation building and societal reconstruction remains a moot point (Bunce 1995).

The view that democracy is the inevitable outcome of post-communist transition is clearly mistaken. There is far too much that is contingent in processes of systemic change to allow any firm teleological view to be convincing. While about a hundred countries have set out on the path of democracy during the 'third wave', at most three dozen have achieved functioning democracies. The contrary view – that the legacy of communist and even pre-communist authoritarian political cultures, economies and social structures doom the attempt to build democracies where there had at best been weak traditions of pluralism, toleration and political competition – is equally wrong. Deterministic views of democratisation leave out of account national political cultures, level of economic development, strategic concerns, leadership choices and elite configurations, economic dependencies and proximity to zones of advanced capitalist democratic development (above all the European Union). Rather than a *teleological* view about the inevitability of democracy, we prefer a *genealogical* approach that takes into account concrete questions of political order, constitutionalism, state-building, social structure and social justice, interacting with the practice of democratic norms and good governance. Despite the best efforts of political scientists, there is no agreement on one single factor that determines the success or failure of a democratisation process.

The relationship between liberalism, democracy and constitutional order remains contested in the post-communist context. Putin's supporters advanced the argument that security should come before democracy. Russia, they suggested, should not be expected quickly to achieve a high-quality democracy, given its authoritarian past, its political culture and the weakness of civil society. Following the Beslan school massacre of 1–3 September 2004, Putin's speech of 13 September announcing a range of reforms to the state system, including the appointment of governors and wholly proportional parliamentary elections, was seen as reflecting this strategy of authoritarian modernisation. The best that Russia can do at this point is to be satisfied with some form of 'managed democracy' – at least, so the supporters of this approach argued. This is not an argument that is satisfactory in the long run. One reason is the lack of contemporary legitimacy for developmental discourses or for those suggesting that 'order' must take priority over democracy. Russians and others who have lived in the shadow of authoritarian regimes are well aware how often the notion of 'order' (in Russian *poryadok*) can be used to subvert political freedom. Unless elites and political leaders strive for genuinely liberal, democratic and constitutional rule, then there is no knowing where the back-sliding will end. This was recognised by Medvedev at the time of his election as Russia's third president in March 2008, when he condemned 'legal nihilism'.

The question of the quality of democracy is particularly acute in Russia, where the very 'givenness' of a structured society is in question. Too often discussions of democratisation assume that once the authoritarian burden is lifted that society will automatically spring back into some sort of democratic shape; although it is usually recognised that in the transition from totalitarianism, society is destroyed to such a degree that it has to become an object of the transition process itself. This tends to justify the displacement of sovereignty from the people to some agency that can carry out the necessary transitional measures. In the Russian case this was the elite group around Yeltsin, and under Putin the institutions of the administrative system.

It is in this context that the notion of 'sovereign democracy' was advanced by Vladislav Surkov, a deputy head of the presidential administration, and others. The debate over sovereignty and democracy and Russia's place in the international system took shape in the months following the Beslan hostage crisis; although certainly not absent earlier, the crisis brought to the fore concerns about territorial integrity and political manageability. This period coincided with solid evidence that the economic situation had improved, with the country registering an average of seven per cent annual growth throughout Putin's presidency, but tailing off rapidly as a result of the economic crisis from 2008. Thus from the first the debate has manifested contradictory aspects: a growing confidence based on domestic economic and political stabilisation and windfall energy revenues, accompanied by a deep-rooted insecurity about Russia's international position and domestic integrity. The term then came to the fore following the 'orange' revolution in Ukraine in late 2004, when a broad popular movement forced a third round run-off presidential contest between Viktor Yushchenko, favoured by the West, and Viktor Yanukovych, the candidate promoted by Russia.

Without going into too much detail, three key aspects can be identified in the 'sovereign democracy' debate. The first focuses on *real sovereignty* for the state. In one of the most considered expositions of the implications of sovereign democracy, Andrei Kokoshin argued that 'real sovereignty' was 'the capacity of a state in reality (and not merely in declaratory fashion) to conduct independently its internal, external and defence policies, to conclude and tear up agreements, enter into strategic partnerships or not'. He held up India and China as exemplars of countries able to uphold real sovereignty in the face of the desovereignisation accompanying globalisation, although he was at pains to stress that he was not defending autarchy or isolation (Kokoshin 2006). The key point was to achieve state sovereignty in the international system, accompanied by what Surkov and others have called the democratisation of international relations (Surkov 2007: 31–32).

The second aspect focuses on domestic concerns and the *sovereignty of experience*. In the aftermath of the Beslan crisis Surkov launched a debate about national priorities, and perhaps even more than that, a new ideology of state development, if not a new state ideology. The latter element was reflected in the debate over the adoption of new school history textbooks, which was imbued with the spirit of 'sovereign democracy', asserting what was considered to be a more balanced approach to Russia's Soviet past. The aim was to build a political system for Russia that claimed to be responsive to its specific needs and national characteristics. Surkov defined sovereign democracy as 'a form of political life of society, under which the authorities, their organs and actions are selected, formed and directed exclusively by the Russian nation in all its variety and completeness so that all citizens, social groups and peoples comprising it achieve material well-being, freedom and justice' (Surkov 2006: 28).

The corollary of this leads to the third aspect, *autochthonous democracy*. This stresses the autonomous character of Russian democratic development. At the heart of the concept is the view that democracy is an evolutionary process, and the revolutionary view of a leap to democracy that was typical of the first post-communist decade is rejected, in keeping with the evolutionary approach espoused by Putin himself. In his address to the Federal Assembly on 25 April 2005, in the wake of the 'orange' revolution, Putin insisted that the strengthening of democracy was the top priority for Russia: 'The main political–ideological task is the development of Russia as a free, democratic country.' Political freedom, he insisted, 'is not just necessary but economically beneficial'. He took issue with the political culture approach, which suggested that the Russian people were somehow not suited to democratic government, the rule of law, and the basic values of civil society: 'I would like to bring those who think like that back to political reality ... Without liberty and democracy there can be no order, no stability and no sustainable economic policies.'

Responding to Western criticism, however, Putin stressed that the 'special feature' of Russia's democracy was that it would be pursued in its own way and not at the price of law and order or social stability: 'Russia ... will decide for itself the pace, terms and conditions of moving towards democracy.' All this would be done in a legal way, warning that 'Any unlawful methods of struggle ... for ethnic, religious and other interests contradict the principles of democracy. The state will react (to such attempts) with legal, but tough, means' (*Rossiiskaya gazeta*, 25 April 2005). Addressing a conference of United Russia activists on 7 February 2006, Surkov drove home the message that sovereign democracy was more than an abstract concept but a basis for action for the long term (Surkov 2006: 43–79).

This was in effect the manifesto of 'sovereign democracy', in the sense that democracy would be developed in Russia at its own pace and in a manner of the country's choosing. While an entirely legitimate approach, there remains the issue of who would be doing the deciding about the pace and type of democratic development, and thus there was the danger once again of the regime substituting for the people. There is a second theme implicit in the message: the autonomy of the regime from society. In that respect, sovereign democracy perpetuates the thinking behind the 'managed democracy' that was characteristic of Putin's first presidential term. Thus for many sovereign democracy was little more than a synonym for managed democracy. It was on these grounds that Medvedev rejected the term, insisting that democracy did not need any qualifying adjectives.

Regime and administered democracy

Democratic political institutions have been created in Russia and function with a degree of autonomy, yet the people remain distant from decision making and the authorities are only weakly accountable to society. Dahl's (1971) polyarchy (contestation and participation) has not yet been established, although Joseph Schumpeter's procedural democracy, defined as the structured competition for votes in exchange for policies, does exist (Schumpeter 1976). A type of co-optive rule has emerged characterised by the interaction of a powerful executive while parliamentary and other elites represent not mass movements but their own interests. This system was given political form by the emergence of a powerful hegemonic party in the form of United Russia, which dominated parliament following the elections of 2003 and 2007. How can we explain the gulf between formal democracy and displaced sovereignty in Russia's 'managed democracy'? To help characterise the present system we will first look at two substantive approaches before providing our own analysis of the system.

Fareed Zakaria (1997: 23) distinguishes between *liberal* democracy, defined as 'a political system marked not only by free and fair elections, but also by the rule of law, a separation of powers, and the protection of basic liberties of speech, assembly, religion and property', what he calls constitutional liberalism, and *illiberal* democracy. In the latter 'Democratically elected regimes, often ones that have been re-elected or reaffirmed through referenda, are routinely ignoring constitutional limits on their power and depriving their citizens of basic rights and freedoms' (p. 23). For Zakaria, the regular staging of relatively fair, competitive, multiparty elections might make a country democratic, but it does not ensure good governance. In practice, even relatively free elections 'have resulted in strong executives, weak legislatures and judiciaries, and few civil and economic liberties' (p. 28). In a later work Zakaria (2003) developed his argument that while constitutional liberalism can lead to democracy, democracy does not necessarily lead to constitutional liberalism. The Central European post-communist states are negotiating the passage to democracy more successfully than the former Soviet states, it is argued, because they went through a long phase of liberalisation without democracy in the nineteenth century that grounded the rule of law and property rights into social practices.

In a similar vein, Guillermo O'Donnell (1994: 59) argued that in weakly established democracies a leader can become so strong that he or she can ignore those whom they are meant to represent. O'Donnell characterises these countries as having 'delegative' rather than representative democracy, with the electorate allegedly having delegated to the executive the right to do what it sees fit, 'constrained only by the hard facts of existing power relations and by a constitutionally limited term of office'. Thus a government emerges that is 'inherently hostile to the patterns of representation normal in established democracies' by 'depoliticising the population except for brief moments in which it demands its plebiscitary support' (O'Donnell 1993: 1367). This sort of democracy is, according to O'Donnell (1994: 59), under-institutionalised, 'characterised by the restricted scope, the weakness, and the low density of whatever political institutions exist. The place of well-functioning institutions is taken by other non-formalised but strongly operative practices – clientelism, patrimonialism, and corruption.' The notion of delegative democracy has a clear application to Russia, and has been used fruitfully in analysing regional politics. However, the concept has limitations when applied to the post-Soviet world. Although the powers of the executive everywhere have been enhanced, these are not classical presidentialist regimes of the Latin American type although they do share some of the characteristics of Latin American *democraduras* ('hard democracies'). Politics in Russia is too unstructured, institutions too fluid, and the personages too constrained by the emerging class system, ethnic contradictions and regional forces to allow the full delegation of authority.

In terms of regime type Russia is a semi-presidential democracy, but this does not tell us much about how the constitution works in practice. The entwining of institutional and personal factors in a weak constitutional order and under-developed civil society gave rise to the dominance of a power system centred on the presidency that relies on administrative ways of managing conflict and of reducing the uncertainty engendered by the electoral process. Decisions and leadership do not emerge out of the untrammelled operation of politics but out of an administrative elite positioned between state and society. This is what we call regime politics.

Russia's fledgling democracy is characterised by the gulf between a system with a constitution to one governed by genuine constitutionalism. According to Max Weber (1995), Russia's 1906 constitution represented sham constitutionalism in that it was not able effectively to establish accountable government. Even less effective in this respect were the various Soviet constitutions (1918, 1924, 1936 and 1977), since they signally failed to define and thus to limit the powers of the leadership. They were pseudo-constitutions since they did not even attempt to fulfil the classic functions of a constitution, let alone foster the practices of constitutionalism (that is, the impartial exercise of the rule of law, limited government and a division of powers). Russia's 1993 constitution finally does what a constitution is supposed to do: establish the basic principles of the polity, define the roles of the institutions of government, and entrench the practice of the rule of law. At the heart of the idea of modern constitutionalism is the separation of powers, and this is indeed embedded in the 1993 document, although this separation is unbalanced in various aspects.

The contrast between the informal relations of power established within the framework of regime politics, on the one hand, and the institutionalised competitive and accountable politics characteristic of a genuinely constitutional democratic state, on the other, is typical of many countries in the post-communist era. In Russia, as elsewhere, particularistic informal practices have been in tension with the proclaimed principles of the universal and impartial prerogatives of the constitutional state. Under Yeltsin personalised leadership came to the fore, with the power system and its oligarchical allies operating largely independently from the formal rules of the political system, whose main structural features were outlined in the constitution. Behind the formal façade of democratic politics conducted at the level of the state, the regime considered itself largely free from genuine democratic accountability and popular oversight. These features, as Hahn (2002) stresses, were accentuated by the high degree of institutional and personal continuity between the Soviet and 'democratic' political systems. This is a finding confirmed by Kryshtanovskaya's and White's study (2003). While a party state ruled up to 1991, the emergence of a presidential state in the 1990s fostered the creation of a system that perpetuated in new forms some of the arbitrariness of the old order. Both the power system and the constitutional state succumbed to clientelist pressures exerted by powerful interests in society, some of whom (above all the so-called oligarchs) had been spawned by the regime itself.

Instead of government being accountable to the representative institutions of the people and constrained by the constitutional state and its legal instruments, the government assumes an independent political existence. It is at this point that a politically responsible and accountable government becomes a regime; formal institutions are unable to constrain political actors and informal practices predominate (North 1990). The outward forms of the constitutional state are preserved, but legality and accountability are subverted. A set of para-constitutional behavioural norms predominate that while perhaps not formally violating the letter of the constitution undermine the spirit of constitutionalism. Para-constitutional behaviour gets things done, but ultimately prove counter-productive because they rely on the personal intervention of leadership politics rather than the self-sustaining practices of a genuinely constitutional system. The regime is constrained by the constitutional state but the system lacks effective mechanism of accountability.

Conclusion

A democratic transition is usually considered to be over when democracy becomes the only game in town and where there is 'definiteness of rules and indefiniteness of outcomes'. According to Kulik (2001) Russia's transition is indeed over, but instead of democratic consolidation Russia's 'managed democracy' has reversed the formula to ensure 'definiteness of outcomes and indefiniteness of rules'. This is true to a degree, but the scope for democratic development in Russia remains open. The government does seek to deliver a set of public goods, and it does not appeal to an extra-democratic logic to achieve them. The regime is legitimate precisely because it claims to be democratic. Putin's government is undoubtedly considered legitimate by the great majority of the Russian people, as evidenced by the outcomes of the 2003–04 and 2007–08 electoral cycles, accompanied by Putin's consistently high personal ratings throughout his two terms. Whether the system is becoming an illiberal or delegative democracy is more contentious. Too much is settled not in the framework of competitive politics but within the confines of the power system, leaving government only weakly accountable to society and its representatives. Nevertheless, the sinews of constitutionality are developing, and politics is not yet entirely subsumed into the administrative order. Just as the price of freedom is eternal vigilance so, too, the struggle for democracy is never a single act but must be advanced daily. This struggle is far from over in Russia.

Chapter 2

Semi-presidentialism and the Evolving Executive

JOHN P. WILLERTON

The spring 2008 presidential election and inauguration of Dmitri Medvedev represented an unprecedented moment in the over thousand-year history of the Russian state, as a politically strong and healthy 55-year-old chief executive willingly turned over formal powers to a similarly vigorous new leader. These events, constituting post-Soviet Russia's second leadership succession, revealed all of the complexities and uncertainties that surrounded Russian politics nearly fifteen years after the adoption of the 1993 democratic constitution. Vladimir Putin, the twice-elected president who was at the height of his power and who was riding public approval ratings in the high 70 per cent range as his term ended, chose to avoid efforts to amend the constitution to permit him a third term, voiced support for a loyal protégé to succeed him, and subsequently agreed to assume the more junior, but highly demanding, position of prime minister. The political significance of these unique developments was subject to varying interpretations, but most observers, Russian and Western, were agreed that Russia was moving onto an uncharted political–institutional course that entailed a new and untried leadership arrangement: a dual-headed executive, with a to-be-constructed and nuanced balancing of decision-making powers and prerogatives between not only the country's two top executive positions, but two capable and ambitious individuals.

The 1993 Russian constitution had formally set up a semi-presidential system entailing a dual-headed executive, with a separation of executive powers between a popularly elected head of state or president and an appointed head of government or prime minister, the latter responsible both to that president and to the national legislature, the State Duma. Yet, looking both at the constitutional particulars and to expectations and experience, post-Soviet Russia had been governed by an all-powerful presidency, a 'hegemonic president', assisted by a weaker and highly malleable prime minister and government. Indeed, the Russian

Federation's (RF) first two presidents, Boris Yeltsin (1991–9) and Vladimir Putin (2000–8), had proven to be forceful leaders who had very much moulded the politics and socio-economic realities of their times. In contrast, the nine men who had served as prime minister during the January 1992–May 2008 period had constituted a varied group in background, orientation, political standing, and bureaucratic savvy, but they had all proven to be subordinate to the president, their tenures, decision-making roles, and policy programmes fully defined by the country's head of state. None of these prime ministers had come into office with strong public support; some had been little known. Only Vladimir Putin had left the prime minister's office with a respectable public approval level (approximately 50 per cent), albeit this was as he assumed the position of acting president on Boris Yeltsin's unexpected retirement on 31 December 1999.

Thus, the 2008 succession raised many questions about the logic of the Russian political system, where power lay, how institutions would operate, and what would be the political–institutional settings from which policy would now arise. As we will see, newly elected President Dmitri Medvedev was not without considerable abilities and experience, even as he assumed office appearing junior to his powerful mentor and new prime minister, Vladimir Putin. Medvedev's own initial high public approval ratings, also in the 70–80 per cent range, and building upon his first round presidential electoral triumph with more than 70 per cent of the popular vote, seemingly placed him on a comparable plane to Putin. The newly Medvedev–Putin tandem communicated a solidarity in both policy preferences and style that suggested a unified presidential–governmental team. It suggested that the Kremlin cohort that had long governed Russia, going back to the Yeltsin presidency and continuing through the eight-year Putin term, would continue. Yet throughout the later 1990s and early 2000s, the ruling Kremlin cohort had evolved, as had the Russian political system and the policy programme. If a putatively democratic system had arisen, and a domestic and foreign policy thrust was in place, they were products of a relatively short period of less than two decades.

The intriguing institutional and personnel changes arising out of Russia's second leadership succession raised uncertainties regarding both the decision-making process and the policy line of the preceding eight years. The ongoing centrality of the federal executive, the president, and the presidential team to Russia's political and economic life is a core feature of contemporary Russian reality. The Yeltsin–Putin team's preference for a strong state, with a powerful federal government led by a strong and multi-faceted executive branch and powerful chief executive, has been fully adopted by the country's elite and populace. The Putin period theory of 'sovereign democracy', grounded in the integrity of the state, a reasserted Russian Eurasian (and global) leadership position, is joined with the concepts of a 'managed democracy' and 'directed economy' that assume a strong state. If a powerful legacy of the Putin presidency was to reassert and advance these systemic and policy ends, then the Medvedev presidency portended their continuing consolidation. Russia's third post-Soviet president promised a fuller realisation of the 'dictatorship of the law' set out in his predecessor's term, pointing to a new strengthening of the courts and the judicial system and a renewed but more serious assault on corruption. He also put renewed emphasis on high-profile domestic socio-economic programmes, the National Priority Projects, which he himself had guided during his predecessor's second term.

After more than sixteen years of an increasingly centralised decision-making system, the evolution of the Russian semi-presidential system into the Medvedev–Putin administration suggested a spreading of decision-making powers across more executive actors. What appeared in the Medvedev presidency to be a modestly reconfigured Kremlin team still entailed a large set of executive institutions and officials, overlapping from the presidential administration into the central government, through the team's platform party, United Russia, into the legislature, and downward into the regions. Questions remained as to the long-term integrity and viability of this extensive conglomeration of political–bureaucratic interests, whether it could move the ambitious agenda set out by President Medvedev and amplified upon by Prime Minister Putin, and what the implications of its successful operation would be for Russia's 'emerging democracy'.

In assessing these questions, we focus here on the federal executive, the president, prime minister and government, examining key institutions, their roles in the Russian polity, and the influential politicians who direct policy making and implementation. We consider the evolving relationship between these federal executive bodies and other actors, federal and subfederal, in the process illuminating the hegemonic decision-making position the executive has carved out for itself. However, to better understand the realities of the contemporary Russian political scene and to appreciate the complexities inherent in continued system building and governance, we must underscore several important considerations that are key to both the operation of the political process and the prospects for democratic consolidation. First, we must distinguish between formal offices such as the presidency and prime ministership and the officials who hold these positions. The constitution invests offices with powers and prerogatives, but these are separate from the abilities, intentions, and potential authority of the individuals who hold such offices. Thus, Dmitri Medvedev, like his predecessor Vladimir Putin, entered the presidency with considerable public support and a commanding first round electoral victory, but he would need time and policy successes to build his authority. Similarly, Putin, bringing significant authority to the presumably junior position of prime minister, could bolster the powers and policy-making possibilities of that more technocratic position, but he could also be drawn into the demands and minutiae of this macro-managerial position that might weaken such authority.

Apart from this, we must distinguish between the formal roles of political positions and the informal arrangements that affect their operation and permit politicians to influence the political landscape. Over the past fifteen years a Kremlin team has dominated the Russian political scene; that team is composed of evolving but identifiable groups, with potentially different interests and perspectives, groups that are constantly manoeuvring around the chief executive and other critical political actors. This dynamic constellation of groups acts as the human conduit through which institutionalised interests and programmatic goals are realised. Finally, we must consider the logic of the Russian institutional design, grounded in a tradition of executive assertiveness and dominance. Perspectives on this design, a semi-presidential system with a hegemonic executive, vary greatly as we distinguish arguments that see the powerful executive (atop a powerful state) either facilitating or obstructing both the construction of viable democratic institutions and the emergence of a more vibrant society. The contemporary shifting and rebalancing of prerogatives and powers between the president and prime minister, presidential administration and government, only contribute additional complexity to this setting.

Putin, Medvedev, and the tradition of a strong executive

Putin took power in the complicated and troubling context of the post-Soviet 1990s, and arguably the most important contribution he made to the ongoing evolution of the Russian polity was to restore the power of the presidency, the executive branch, and the federal state. In personality, style, and policy preferences, he proved able not only in meeting – and exceeding – public expectations, his 50 per cent approval rating at the time of his elevation to the presidency rapidly moving into the 60–70 per cent range. Indeed, he would retain public approval ratings in the mid-to-high 70 per cent range throughout his second term; he left office at a remarkable 84.7 per cent approval level (ITAR-TASS 30 April 2008). Many observers noted Putin's good fortune in the timing of his tenure, with record energy prices significantly boosting an economy that had only emerged from a lengthy depression in Yeltsin's final years. Yet at the heart of Putin's strong leadership was the reality that the institutionalised hege-monic presidency was joined with a decisive, energetic, and highly respected occupant: renewed state power was joined with leadership authority.

Putin's modest background and forceful yet unassuming leadership style fitted with Russian preferences in the emerging democratic era. Born to a working-class family and a product of the post-Stalinist era, Putin had made a career in the Soviet security services that entailed a more elite education, travel and work abroad, and a broader awareness of both the Russian society and the outside world. His life experiences of the late Soviet and immediate post-Soviet periods left him subject to divergent and conflicting influences that were evident both in his rise to power and in his own presidency. As a security agent, Putin was well conditioned to a chain-of-command culture that emphasised loyalty and strict subordi-nation, public order, and commitment to a strong state. Working as a key associate of the reformist St Petersburg mayor Anatolii Sobchak, however, he personally experienced the need for root and branch system change, and became sensitive to bottom-up societal pressures, notions of elite and governmental accountability, electoral procedures, and the messiness of democracy building. Taken in its totality, Putin's life and career experience provided him with a mounting awareness of the complexities of system change and of governmental administration, and not only of commercial life but of civil society.

Perspectives on Vladimir Putin and his eight-year tenure were varied, with especially divergent judgements separating Russian elite and public perspectives from those of many Western observers. At the heart of Russian assessments were widespread elite and public perceptions of significant domestic and foreign policy successes. Other chapters will detail the various socio-economic and other developments of the Putin years, but suffice it to highlight here the considerable national economic growth, the resultant, very evident rise in citizens' standard of living, and Russia's return as a major global player. Putin government initiatives reversed most of the conditions and developments associated with Russia's 'failing state'; the 'failing state' signifying a state that is losing its vibrancy and legitimacy as it fails to carry out the tasks or provide the services to which it is committed (Willerton, Beznosov and Carrier 2005). A combination of factors was responsible for this turnaround, but force-ful political leadership must be included among them. Putin's modest style and 'samurai warrior' personal ethic, his decisiveness from the onset of his presidency to tackle complex problems (such as taking on the influen-tial oligarchs, beginning the process of reining in regional power barons, and crafting an intelligible tax programme), his soon-evident ability to manage the bureaucracy while simultaneously strengthening the state and providing tangible returns to the population, all secured him consistently high marks from an overwhelming majority of Russians. Indeed, the extent of Putin's authority – that is the legitimacy of his governance – was revealed in the second term: his government advanced a number of unpopular reforms that trimmed the welfare state, but Putin's popularity went unaffected. In the judgement of most Russians, on the evidence of the regular surveys conducted by the Levada Centre and other agencies, Putin and his government had delivered on nearly all of the promises set out in the early days of his term (the evidence may be consulted directly at www.levada.ru).

If forceful leadership tied with a strengthened state rested favourably with most Russians, this combination of factors left many Western observers sceptical, their assessments during and after Putin's tenure generally reserved and occasionally highly negative. To many Western observers, the enhanced power concentration and related decision-making 'streamlining' were seen as undercutting democratic impulses. A new corporatism enabling the state to dominate key industries was joined with the state's consolidation of control over the media and its enhanced ability to shape public opinion. Meanwhile, if the oligarchs of the Yeltsin period were reined in and no longer in a commanding position to dominate politics, corruption continued to be widespread and appeared to include elements of the ruling Kremlin team itself. Finally, fledgling impulses for creating a Russian civil society were undercut by the sum impact of the above-noted developments. For many in the West, the bottom line was a new authoritarianism, one that came with a more forceful foreign policy and that was grounded in Russia's re-emergence as a formidable energy-producing power (Goldman 2008).

The disparity in mainstream Russian and Western assessments was enormous, and while we cannot analyse it in detail, it is important to note that Russians and Westerners operated with different world views and reference points for judgement, different preferences and different emphases regarding policies and outcomes, and different understandings of the factors necessary for the successful transformation of Russia and construction of a democratic, free market polity. Perspectives on the 2008 presidential election were a good example of this Russian–Western disparity in assessments. There was little doubt that the popularity of the governing Kremlin team's programme and legacy would highly favour Putin's and the team's candidate, Dmitri Medvedev. The array of opponents was weak, with all observers concluding that Medvedev would easily win the first round and avoid a runoff. Yet the disqualification of two candidates with high international profiles (the one-time prime minister Mikhail Kas'yanov and former world chess champion Garry Kasparov) troubled Westerners, as did various irregularities during the campaign season and in the conduct of the elections. For Westerners, the Kremlin's seeming dedication to retain power reinforced Medvedev's prospects while undercutting the legitimacy of the electoral process. Russians paid less attention to these developments, for instance dismissing Kas'yanov as a shady figure with questionable ties to the Yeltsin past and Kasparov as an eccentric, politically naïve publicity hound. Russians well understood the numerous advantages provided to Medvedev, but they voted for him anyway, and at the high turnout level (of about 70 per cent) seen in earlier elections. They opted for a close confidant and key member of the Kremlin team, a man central to the functioning of the Putin administration, a new leader tapped to maintain that team's governing position while continuing its programmatic thrust.

Putin's successor, Dmitri Medvedev, is a politician who should not be underestimated. While he was young (42) upon assuming high office, he brought a surprisingly impressive résumé to the presidency. Growing up in a family of academics, he had focused on civil law while a student at the prestigious Leningrad State University, ultimately earning a PhD in private law in 1990. A lawyer–academic who worked in the St Petersburg government under the reformist mayor Anatoli Sobchak, Medvedev early in his career developed a close working relationship with Vladimir Putin, initially serving as a legal adviser when Putin was heading a city committee negotiating with foreign businesses. Troubled by the collapse of the USSR and the dilemmas of post-Soviet Russia's 'failing state', both Medvedev and Putin saw a strong state and economic reform – via the market – as keys to Russia's revival. From 1991, when his and Putin's careers first crossed, to his election as RF President seventeen years later, Medvedev served in an impressive array of posts that left him with tremendous organisational experience and policy knowledge. He moved into the federal executive in 1999, shortly after Putin was elevated to the premiership, quickly becoming deputy head of the presidential administration and heading Putin's 2000 presidential campaign. As head of the presidential administration (2003–5), he became well attuned to the intricacies of Kremlin politics. As a first deputy prime minister (2005–8), he oversaw priority projects (agriculture, education, health care and housing) that were at the heart of Russian policy reforms. Meanwhile, chosen to guide (2000–8) and reassert the state's control over Gazprom, the world's most powerful energy conglomerate, he dealt with the important resource questions that have been key to Russia's impressive growth and emergence as an important global economic player. It was during Medvedev's tenure that Gazprom's debts were restructured, its declining production reversed, and its market capitalisation grew from US$9 to $300 billion (as of early 2008). On the international scene, it was Medvedev who negotiated over Russia's energy disputes with Ukraine and Belarus, while in the midst of the 2008 presidential campaign it was Medvedev who flew to Belgrade to offer support to Serbia in the dispute over Kosovo's independence. Medvedev's modest manner and low-key style should not distract the observer from appreciating that he has been ambitious and assertive in promoting his, and Russia's, interests.

Medvedev came into the presidency with a strong electoral victory, but he clearly lacked the standing and authority of his mentor, Vladimir Putin. After Putin identified Medvedev as his successor in December 2007, little was done to alter the institutional arrangements underlying the hegemonic presidency. Moreover, Russians, while expressing strong support for Putin as he left office, overwhelmingly opposed any effort to weaken the federal presidency or transform Russia's semi-presidential system into a parliamentary system with a strong prime minister (Levada Centre survey reported in *Kommersant*, 31 March 2008). With Putin selected to once again hold the prime ministership, decision-making authority now appeared divided between a powerful presidency and a popular prime minister. The challenge before Medvedev was to present himself and move his agenda so as to translate superficial popular support into decision-making authority. Appreciation of these efforts and related issues requires an understanding of the Russian semi-presidential system and illumination of its key institutions and norms of operation.

Semi-presidentialism and institutions of the federal executive

Russia's semi-presidential system is formally grounded in the 1993 Constitution, but its *de facto* logic stems in part from the Soviet experience, where the executive was divided between policy-making bodies housed in the Communist Party apparatus and policy-implementing bodies housed in the Soviet government. In a democratic setting, the semi-presidential system divides political responsibilities between a president (and related institutions), who is head of state and who sets out the broad contours and directions of policy, and a prime minister and government, which are responsible for developing, implementing, and managing policies. In a democratic setting, the prime minister and other ministers who form the government are responsible to both the president and the national legislature. In most modern semi-presidential systems, it is the head of state, the president, who nominates the prime minister, who must enjoy majority support within the legislature. That support is ensured by the president nominating the leader of the majority party or a majority coalition, with the prime minister then forming a government comprised of ministers who must be approved by the legislature. While most modern democracies are either parliamentary (where the prime minister and government arise out of a popularly elected legislature) or presidential (where the top executive, the president, and legislature are separate and elected separately), there is a handful of semi-presidential systems, France and Finland being among the most notable. The logic and organisation of the emerging Russian democratic system are in some ways reflective of the French–Finnish type of semi-presidential system.

The president

A vast array of institutions and officials comprise the federal executive, with the hegemonic presidency at the helm. Informal arrangements, involving various whirlpools of interest, bureaucratic elements, and groupings of personnel also structure the president's decision-making primacy. The federal presidency has been hegemonic not only because its position is legally superior to that of other institutions, but because it has possessed independence and freedom of manoeuvre. Since 1992, the president, through presidential decrees, legislative proposals, and vetoes, has been able to direct the decision-making process. Moreover, he has been able to appoint and guide the work of the prime minister and government, with key cabinet members (such as the foreign, defence, internal affairs, and justice ministers) appointed by and directly accountable to the head of state. He has been supported by a large set of agencies and officials that link him to all federal and major subfederal institutions (see Figure 2.1).

While the Putin government did oversee some institutional changes that further bolstered the president's position (such as in nominating regional governors, rather than allowing them to be directly elected), these changes only modestly expanded the highly advantageous position of the head of state. The 1993 Yeltsin constitution specified that the president 'defines the basic directions of the domestic and foreign policy of the state', while the president also represents the country domestically and internationally (see Articles 80–93). As the head of state and commander-in-chief of the armed forces, the president has the right to declare a state of emergency and martial law, call for referendums, and even suspend the decisions of other state bodies if their actions violate the constitution or federal laws. Changes during the Putin leadership only strengthened the president's ability to direct Russia's centre–periphery relations, this in a country that is as vast as it is varied in its regional and ethnic composition.

Much decision-making initiative comes out of the president's office and the presidential administration, but the president directs the federal government through the appointment and supervision of the prime minister and other ministers. The president, acting through the vast structure of supporting agencies, initiates legislation, reporting annually to a joint

Figure 2.1 *Major institutions of the Putin–Medvedev executive*

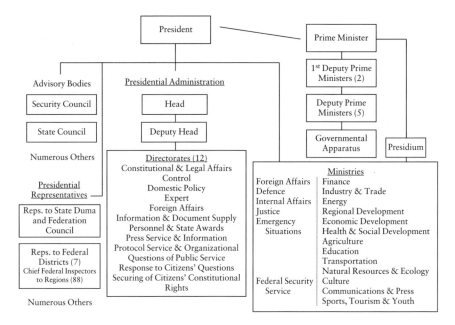

parliamentary session on his government's domestic and foreign policy. Putin used such sessions, as well as annual lengthy press conferences, to good end in promoting his agenda and further consolidating his authority, with every expectation that Medvedev would approach such opportunities similarly. Meanwhile, there are conditions under which the president can dissolve the lower house of the parliament, the State Duma, but these entail unusual circumstances that to date have not materialised. Likewise, the rival legislative branch has the formal ability to remove the president for malfeasance, but the procedures for impeachment are cumbersome and involve numerous federal bodies including the Supreme Court, Constitutional Court, and upper house of the parliament, the Federation Council. Since a two-thirds majority of the full membership of both houses is required to remove a president, the probability of ouster is low by any count; the dominant position of the Kremlin's platform party, United Russia, only further ensures the near-invulnerability of the head of state. The more compelling constraint on a president's tenure in office comes with the constitutionally mandated consecutive two-term limit, with Putin's 2008 decision to step down after two terms, following upon Yeltsin's 1999 decision to retire after nearly two terms, setting a precedent that is unlikely to change. However, the Medvedev-initiated legislation at the end of 2008 to extend the presidential term to six years (it had been four), as from the end of Medvedev's first term, makes this two-term limit a much weakened constraint.

An important, constitutionally permitted, means by which the chief executive can manoeuvre unilaterally is through the issuing of presidential decrees (*ukazy*), which have the force of law. The Constitution (Art. 90) provides the president extensive leeway in issuing decrees to make institutional and policy changes, and while such decrees are inferior to laws, they are binding so long as they do not contradict the Constitution or federal laws. In the face of a massive state bureaucracy, with its numerous and often-conflicting ministries, there is a need for powerful top-down mechanisms such as presidential decrees to direct its activities. While policy-making decrees may be overridden by parliament, a two-thirds vote of both chambers is needed, and this is highly unlikely to occur given the parliament's highly fragmented structure, the weakness of the party system, and the continuing strength of the Kremlin's platform party, United Russia. In the past, most notably during the Yeltsin period, decrees had a significant impact on Russian politics, and Putin relied on them during his first term to advance important initiatives (such as the establishment of the country's seven macro-districts and restoration of the system of presidential envoys, efforts to 'normalise' Chechnya, and energy and economic reforms). Yet as the Putin team further strengthened its position, including within the federal legislature, decrees became less critical and Kremlin initiatives were advanced through legislation. Some late Putin and early Medvedev period decrees involved institutional matters (for instance, further federal governmental supervision of regional officials) that could prove important to the functioning of the Medvedev–Putin team, but the continued dominance of the Kremlin team after the 2008 succession suggested most of its agenda would be advanced via the legislative process.

Presidential administration and advisory bodies

As Figure 2.1 reveals, a vast presidential administration supports the activities of the country's chief executive and supervises the implementation of presidential decisions. Originally built on the organisational resources of the defunct Soviet Communist Party central apparatus, this extensive set of institutions is composed of dozens of agencies and includes approximately 3,000 full-time staff members: a number suggesting it is larger than the comparable support structure of the US president. The 12 directorates that are at the heart of the presidential administration, reorganised during the Putin presidency and continuing under Medvedev, reflect the decision-making and supervisory interests of the federal executive, with the complex and often hidden manoeuvrings of the varied organisations and informal groups of officials constituting a sort of 'checks and balances' system within the federal executive. Since the Russian Constitution is silent on the organisation and functioning of this administration, it is up to each president to structure and manage it according to his own power and policy needs. Elite and public expectations of a chief executive being able to supervise and direct this administration – along with the federal government and the political process overall – are critical to positive evaluations of strong leadership. Putin proved very able in this regard, and while Medvedev appears to have the organisational experience and understanding of the subtleties of Kremlin politics to do likewise, he will need to project the gravitas and build the authority to be successful.

Management of the presidential administration requires a team of reliable subordinates and Medvedev appears to have this, even if his team is composed of associates also closely linked with Vladimir Putin. Critical is the head of the presidential administration, the president's chief of staff as of 2009, Sergei Naryshkin, who oversees both administrative and personnel matters and operates as a sort of *éminence grise* of the federal executive. Medvedev held this post during the middle of the Putin tenure, so he is well tuned to the realities of the presidential administration. Medvedev's own chief of staff, Sergei Naryshkin, is a long-time confidant of both Medvedev and Putin and served for some time on both the presidential administration and prime minister's administrative staff. His experience and connections make him a key figure, not only in linking the President to the extensive set of institutions below, but in connecting the President to the government, Prime Minister Putin, and senior government officials. Other top presidential administration personnel, notably the deputy heads, Vladislav Surkov (first deputy head), Mikhail Gromov, and Aleksandr Beglov, similarly bring significant past presidential administrative experience while having worked directly under both Medvedev and Putin. Finally, dozens of top functionaries who head directorates and agencies beneath these senior officials bring considerable experience and ongoing work relationships with the President and Prime Minister.

Figure 2.1 also indicates that the federal executive includes numerous presidential representatives to most federal and sub-federal organisations, with these representatives serving as liaisons to co-ordinate those bodies' actions with presidential preferences. It also includes numerous advisory bodies that deal with selected policy areas while formally linking the president and his executive team to other institutional actors. These bodies also do not have a constitutional status, they operate at the president's pleasure, and similar to the presidential administration can be reorganised or abolished as the chief executive sees fit. Several of these bodies have now accrued some institutional history, encompass senior officials, and facilitate the president's handling of high-level policy matters. This is true of the Security Council (created 1994), which deals with foreign and security issues and includes the prime minister, relevant ministers, and the heads of the seven federal districts. Its secretary, Nikolai Patrushev, a former intelligence-security official, confidant of Putin, and one time head of the FSB, is an intriguing liaison between Putin and Medvedev as the latter tries to use the Security Council to legitimate his decisions and to influence government actions (especially *vis-à-vis* the Presidium of the Cabinet of Ministers headed by Prime Minister Putin). Meanwhile, the State Council (created in 2000) includes the heads of Russia's 80 or so regions and is the main institutional setting where regional leaders can deal directly with the president. Created to compensate regional leaders for the loss of their seats – and power – in the upper house of the parliament (Federation Council), the State Council addresses centre-periphery and subfederal policy issues through meetings held every three months, a smaller presidium – or governing council – of seven rotating regional leaders, one from each of the federal districts, meeting monthly.

Prime minister and government

The president's power and authority has also been traditionally grounded in his direct influence over the prime minister and cabinet, which form the government and define the 'basic guidelines of the government's activity'. The constitution does not specify which ministries shall be formed, leaving it to the president and prime minister to make the desired choices, but it does identify the policy areas with which the government will deal. The government crafts the federal budget and implements fiscal and monetary policies. It is responsible for the conduct of the economy and has oversight of social issues. The government implements the country's foreign and defence policies, administers state property, protects private property and public order, and ensures the rule of law and civil rights.

At the government's helm stands the prime minister, who is nominated by the president and must be approved by the Duma. While the Duma can remove the prime minister through the passage of two 'no confidence' votes within three months, there are political constraints on the parliament doing so; while the Duma for its part must be dissolved by the president if it does not approve his prime minister designate three times in a row. Traditionally, the prime minister's power is grounded in presidential approval rather than parliamentary support. The position and power of current Prime Minister Putin, however, while formally nominated by President Medvedev and approved by an overwhelming vote of the State Duma (392–56, with only Communist deputies voting against), is grounded in the tremendous authority he brought to the office after eight years in the presidency, not to mention the presence of a vast array of protégés and allies in top governmental and presidential posts.

The prime minister chairs the Cabinet of Ministers, which oversees the state bureaucracy and has both political and law-making functions. Individual ministers set objectives for their ministries, craft their own subordinate bodies' budgets, and oversee policy implementation, but they do not have independent power bases. While most ministers report to the prime minister, five 'power' ministries (Foreign Affairs, Defence, Internal Affairs, Justice, and Emergency Situations) are directly accountable to the president. Putin has further consolidated his power over the ministries through a recently reconstituted Cabinet Presidium, led by the Prime Minister and including the seven first and deputy prime ministers and seven other senior ministers. The Presidium co-ordinates and manages the government's work and, with it including three of the power ministers (foreign, defence, and internal affairs) who report directly to Medvedev, it places Putin in a central executive supervisory role. Presidents Putin and Medvedev exhibited similar preferences in the setting out of ministerial portfolios, with only modest organisational changes coming in May 2008. Putin and now Medvedev have set out a vertical, top-down admin-istration arrangement which Putin claims has as a consequence 'universal elements of management' to streamline the policy process (*Moscow Times*, 16 May 2008). Meanwhile, the 2008 Putin government included two first deputy prime ministers, five deputy prime ministers, and 18 ministers (Table 2.1), an arrangement similar to that of immediate past governments but including a rotation of personnel that has bolstered the real power position of the prime minister. Putin assembled a diverse set of ministers, many drawn from his presidential administration, who were not only competent and reliable managers, but experienced political watchdogs.

The composition of the Putin government included many top officials drawn from Putin's presidential administration and last government. Former Prime Minister Viktor Zubkov, a no-nonsense bureaucrat who had been involved in financial monitoring and tax inspection and who had a reputation as a task-master when he held the top governmental position during Putin's last year as president, was tapped as one of Putin's main assistants as First Deputy Prime Minister. The other First Deputy Prime Minister, Igor Shuvalov, was a Putin confidant who was drawn from the presidential administration and who previously served under Medvedev in supervising the National Priority Projects that were devel-oped from 2005 onwards as a means of focusing government attention on education, health, agriculture and housing. Putin was further assisted by five deputy prime ministers, all of them protégés of the Prime Minister,

Table 2.1 *Leading officials in Putin and Medvedev executive teams*

President	Vladimir Putin (2nd term)	Dmitri Medvedev
Head, Presidential Administration	Sergei Sobyanin	Sergei Naryshkin
Deputy Head	Igor Sechin	Vladislav Surkov (1st Dep.)
	Vladislav Surkov	Aleksei Gromov
		Aleksandr Beglov
Prime Minister	Viktor Zubkov	Vladimir Putin
1st Deputy Prime Minister	Sergei Ivanov	Viktor Zubkov
	Dmitri Medvedev	Igor Shuvalov
Deputy Prime Minister	Aleksei Kudrin	Sergei Ivanov
	Sergei Naryshkin	Aleksandr Zhukov
	Aleksandr Zhukov	Aleksei Kudrin
		Igor Sechin
		Sergei Sobyanin
Leading Ministries & Services		
Foreign Affairs	Sergei Lavrov	Sergei Lavrov
Defence	Anatolii Serdyukov	Anatolii Serdyukov
Internal affairs	Rashid Nurgaliev	Rashid Nurgaliev
Justice	Vladimir Ustinov	Aleksandr Konovalov
Emergency Situations	Sergei Shoigu	Sergei Shoigu
Finance	Aleksei Kudrin	Aleksei Kudrin
Federal Security Service	Nikolai Patrushev	Aleksandr Bortnikov
Industry & Trade	Viktor Khristenko (Industry)	Viktor Khristenko
Energy	Viktor Khristenko	Sergi Shmatko
Regional Development	Dmitri Kozak	Dmitri Kozak
Economic Development	Elvira Nabiullina	Elvira Nabiullina
Health & Social Development	Tatyana Golikova	Tatyana Golikova
Agriculture	Aleksei Gordeev	Aleksei Gordeev
Education	Andrei Fursenko	Andrei Fursenko
Transportation	Igor Levitin	Igor Levitin
Natural Resources & Ecology	Yuri Trutnev	Yuri Trutnev
Culture	Aleksandr Sokolov	Aleksandr Avdeev
Communications & Press	Leonid Reiman	Igor Shchegolev
Sports, Tourism & Youth	–	Vitalii Matko

but with different specialties and political orientations. While we will discuss the informal groups that comprise the Medvedev–Putin team in the next section, suffice it to note here that these first and deputy prime ministers reflected a balance of more 'conservative' (Sergei Ivanov and Igor Sechin, together with Zubkov) and more 'liberal' (Aleksei Kudrin and Aleksandr Zhukov, together with Shuvalov) forces, with the ideologically neutral deputy prime minister Sergei Sobyanin supervising the division of powers among federal, regional, and municipal bodies and overseeing legislative initiatives; a set of responsibilities similar to those Sobyanin assumed when he was Putin's last head of the presidential administration. Meanwhile, a perusal of Table 2.1 reveals that upwards of two-thirds of the ministers within the Medvedev–Putin Cabinet were holdovers from the Putin–Zubkov regime, with five of the six most senior ministers retaining their posts, the sixth entailing the elevation of a Medvedev protégé, Aleksandr Konovalov, to the Ministry of Justice. While acknowledging there are many nuances in fully appreciating this configuration of ministries and inclusion of ministers, we can generalise that experience combined with reliability of membership in the Kremlin team were the key factors explaining the composition of the Putin government.

The Medvedev–Putin (or Putin–Medvedev?) team

Informal politics – the politics of personalities, career networks, regional and sectoral interests, and competing institutions – have been central to the conduct of Russian politics, as they were in Soviet times. The fact that the post-Soviet system is less than a generation old only reinforces this reality. Analysis of informal politics is difficult: definitive evidence is often lacking, with the necessary interpretation always subject to sceptical judgement. We proceed cautiously in assessing contemporary Russia's informal politics, our focus on the elements and logic of an evolving Kremlin team that has governed Russia for more than a decade.

As RF President, Dmitri Medvedev is in a strong institutional position to elevate trusted associates while directing alliances and bridging linkages to other federal and subfederal actors. His past experience in the presidential administration and federal government yielded nuanced knowledge of high-level elite politics and countless personal connections, while his overall training and career reveal regional, institutional, and policy preferences that structure his personnel and decision-making choices. With an educational and early career focus on legal issues, his network of associates includes academics, lawyers, and officials dealing with various aspects of jurisprudence. Not surprisingly, many of the officials linked with Medvedev come from the President's hometown, St Petersburg, and are a component in a group termed the 'St Petersburg lawyers' (Figure 2.2). Justice Minister Aleksandr Konovalov, Supreme Arbitration Court Chair Anton Ivanov, Head of the Federal Bailiffs Services Nikolai Vinnichenko, together with senior Gazprom official Konstantin Chuichenko, are among the President's protégés who have previously studied or worked with him, have ascended to high office with him, and in background and expressed perspectives look to be highly valuable as he promotes his policy and programmatic preferences: fighting crime and corruption, strengthening the law and the court system, while retaining influence over the country's primary income generator,

Figure 2.2   *Major informal groups of the Putin–Medvedev team*

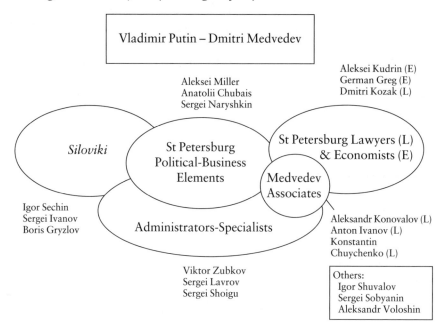

the energy sector. Beyond this group of St Petersburg protégés, other associates who have worked with Medvedev since he came to Moscow in 1999 appear to be allied with him and his causes, among the most influential meriting mention: Presidential Administration Head Sergei Naryshkin, First Deputy Prime Minister Igor Shuvalov, and Deputy Prime Minister and Finance Minister Aleksei Kudrin.

Medvedev and his relatively small cohort (to date) of associates, however, must be nested in the larger and more expansive set of informal groups that are primarily organised around the career and presidency of Vladimir Putin who, in assuming the prime ministership, retained a leading position in the configuration of the federal political elite. As we have noted, Medvedev himself is a protégé of Putin, he rose to federal prominence under Putin, and it was Putin who, with his nomination of Medvedev for the country's highest office, did more than anyone to make Medvedev president. As Figure 2.2 indicates, a complex array of forces have comprised what we see is a Putin-constructed cohort, but what we call the Putin–Medvedev team. Major elements include the *siloviki* (security and intelligence officials), St Petersburg political–business elements, St Petersburg lawyers and economists, and administrators and specialists: they reflect both the career trajectory and presidential history of Vladimir Putin. While Figure 2.2 singles out the modestly sized 'Medvedev associates' cohort, a cohort that is narrowly situated, in fact arguably all of the names listed as examples of the various groupings of the Putin–Medvedev team are Putin protégés, associates, or allies. Indeed, a comparison of Table 2.1 and Figure 2.2 reinforces the fact that the Medvedev team is essentially composed of Putin second-term officials, with some rotation of offices as many who served in the Putin presidential executive moved over with Putin to federal government posts. Even when considering the group identified as 'administrator-specialists', long-term government functionaries or career specialists, we find officials sponsored by the former president who continued in high office under Medvedev (such as former Prime Minister and current First Deputy Prime Minister Viktor Zubkov). Meanwhile, this Putin–Medvedev team that has dominated the Russian political scene since Putin's first term must be nested within the onetime governing team of President Boris Yeltsin, a cohort that came to be known as 'the Family' (since it literally included a few relatives of Yeltsin as well as a large set of trusted protégés) and that included members who continue to influence Medvedev period politics, albeit in the background (such as one-time Yeltsin presidential administration heads Anatolii Chubais and Aleksandr Voloshin, now prominent political-business officials).

Considerations of space preclude a full-blown analysis of all the officials noted in Table 2.1 and Figure 2.2, but the major informal groups listed in Figure 2.2 reflect the diversity of elements comprising the governing team. The so-called 'St Petersburg lawyers and economists' are a highly educated group of academics and specialists, trained and starting their careers in the northern capital, who have been central to the crafting and implementation of Russia's economic and political transformation. Generally educated in the late or immediate post-Soviet period, they ascended to federal importance under Putin, though older figures tied with them were important in the Yeltsin years (such as Anatolii Chubais). Here are officials often focused on the technical complexities of the country's economic and political overhaul, they are generally committed to a market economy, privatisation, careful structuring of the state's role in the country's socio-economic life and full engagement of Russia with the global system, but nested in a democratic political system. This chapter has distinguished another grouping, 'St Petersburg political-business elements', as these officials, also from Putin's hometown, have backgrounds more grounded in practical business experience and politics, but their policy preferences generally have been aligned with those of the St Petersburg lawyers and economists. Overall, while organising officials into these groups, there are differences in background and articulated priorities: we can differentiate the Gazprom executive Aleksei Miller from Anatolii Chubais, Chairman (until 2008) of Russia's national power company, Unified Energy Systems, with the most important part of politician–businessman Sergei Naryshkin's career coming in the presidential administration. Likewise, the policy trouble-shooter, Dmitri Kozak, who has tackled numerous high-profile issues (including problems in the Caucasus and Chechnya) and has served of late as the Regional Development Minister, brings tremendous 'hands on' political experience while Aleksandr Konovalov and Anton Ivanov have more focused institutional–legal interests. In contrast, Aleksei Kudrin and German Gref have been key intellectual forces in the crafting of the Putin (and now Medvedev) domestic economic policies. While there are reported personal–career rivalries among these elements, it is difficult to assess their dynamics, while all of them appear committed to the governing Medvedev–Putin team's power and policy agenda.

The other major group in the governing Kremlin team of the past near decade is the *siloviki* (derived from the Russian word for power), officials from the intelligence–security services who constituted a dominant force during the Putin presidency, and who continue to be well represented at the high level. It is challenging to draw a broad description that accurately captures a common interest or shared set of perspectives for all *siloviki*, but many would conclude they have a natural preference for a strong state and less sensitivity to the nuances of the democratic system. *Siloviki* have presented themselves as disciplined professionals, they are generally highly educated, and some have brought past commercial experience to their government positions. Finally, a view of many in Russia, if not in the West, is that the *siloviki* are generally non-ideological, have a pragmatic law and order focus, and emphasise Russian national–state interests. Setting aside Prime Minister Putin, who has strong connections with all Kremlin informal groups, the *siloviki* do not have a single leader, do not form a cohesive group, and do not promote a common agenda, but they seem to bring the work ethic and skills that have been especially appreciated by one-time President and current Prime Minister Putin. In the Medvedev–Putin regime, long-serving Putin lieutenants, Deputy Prime Ministers Igor Sechin and Sergei Ivanov and State Duma Speaker Boris Gryzlov are among the most prominent *siloviki*, and while their and their allies' collective presence was reduced with the 2008 succession, they constitute a continuing formidable bloc involved in some of the country's highest priority areas (such as energy and the military–industrial complex). Factoring into our discussion such senior ministers as Rashid Nurgaliev (Internal Affairs), Aleksandr Bortnikov (Federal Security Service), and Nikolai Patrushev (Security Council) only drives home this point.

Finally, as Figure 2.2 indicates, all of these groups should be juxtaposed not only to one another, but to the numerous experienced administrators and specialists who hold senior positions within the presidency and government. Many ministers in the Medvedev government are holdovers from the previous regime, and among them are seasoned officials not easily associated with a given career group (such as Zubkov, Foreign Minister Sergei Lavrov, and Emergency Situations Minister Sergei Shoigu). Their credentials and past experience have provided them the personal connections and reputations that make them formidable figures in the governing team. Some bring an organisational prowess that makes them highly valuable to the decisionmaking process (for instance, Sergei Sobyanin). Overall, reviewing Figure 2.2 and Table 2.1, we can see that the constellation of figures responsible for executive branch and federal level policy making is large, multifaceted, and spans both co-operating and competing elements. It reveals the complex interconnection of organisation and personnel considerations. Putative 'conservative' groupings (such as *siloviki* Sechin, Sergei Ivanov, and Patrushev) manoeuvre around 'liberal' groupings (like Shuvalov, Konovalov, and Kudrin), while other influential officials retain their distinguishable positions (among them Zubkov and Sobyanin). If not prone to simple explanation, this constellation of varied actors reinforces the conclusion that a priority concern for all Russian chief executives must be the management of both institutions and personnel. If Vladimir Putin proved highly successful to this end, only time will tell whether Dmitri Medvedev will be likewise.

The executive and governance

As the Medvedev regime moved through its first term, uncertainties surrounded the distribution of power within the federal executive, with President Medvedev consolidating his position and projecting authority as the Putin government demonstrated its capabilities in developing and administering policy. Medvedev assumed a high public profile, whether in well-publicised trips to China and Germany, in his presence at the G8 Summit, or in forcefully setting out Russia's position in the August 2008 Russian-Georgian-South Ossetian war. He was also highly visible in promoting his anti-corruption campaign, pressing for judicial reform, and championing small and medium-sized businesses. It did not take long for a 'Medvedev leadership style' to emerge, characterised in one newspaper as entailing 'predictability, rationality, and composure' (*Komsomol'skaya pravda*, 14–21 August 2008). Meanwhile, Prime Minister Putin was immersed in managing domestic policy administration, from the ongoing transformation of agriculture to tax policies and state regulation of large corporations. The reality of a fluid power relationship between the presidency and government, while new to Russia, was not new to the semi-presidential system, the more mature French and

Finnish systems having experienced changes in the roles of its top executive bodies. Over the past twenty years, France experienced several political cohabitations that entailed complex power relations between competing presidents and prime ministers, while Finland altered its constitutional arrangements to bolster the decision-making position of the prime minister *vis-à-vis* a dominating president. Clearly, the Medvedev first term entailed a new phase in the development of the Russian political system, with the Putin stewardship of the federal government resulting in some shifting of powers, at least some deconcentration of power from the presidency, and a sharing of policy-making functions among a wider array of institutional actors.

Observers could draw very different judgements regarding developments surrounding the 2008 succession and formation of the third post-Soviet administration. Some saw an eight-year incumbent Vladimir Putin retaining power through a shrewd, but legal, sleight of hand by assuming an upgraded prime ministership, that upgrading coming not by constitutional change but by Putin's considerable authority. Others saw Putin helping the designated protégé–successor Dmitri Medvedev to consolidate power so as to continue the Putin–Medvedev team's programmatic agenda. Was the powerful Putin altering the operation of the Russian semi-presidential system to retain effective decision-making primacy, or was Putin laying the institutional–personnel foundation to maintain system–policy stability while withdrawing from the public stage and at best operating as an *éminence grise* in the background? Was the ascending Medvedev motivated to assert his own leadership authority and policy interests, distinguished from those of his mentor-predecessor, or was he motivated to assume more of a caretaker role in pursuing an agenda that would be little more than a derivative of his predecessor's?

Early Medvedev regime posturing and actions suggested the Kremlin team would pursue an agenda similar to that of its predecessor, with attention given to continuing to build the economy and to bolster with investments the areas of the four National Priority Projects that Medvedev himself had previously overseen. Some differing points of accent offered by the Medvedev regime involved the law, court system, and addressing the country's widespread corruption, all areas that Putin had acknowledged had not been adequately addressed by his government. Interestingly, the stabilisation fund (worth US\$158 billion) that had emerged during the Putin second term was reorganised in early 2008 and appeared to offer some of the vast resources needed to address these issues as well as under-funded pensions and state wages. Indeed, these resources would prove especially valuable as the Russian (and global) economy suffered a significant downturn beginning in the second half of 2008. An especially suggestive institutional–personnel–policy trend of the Putin period that was continued under Medvedev involved corporatist approaches to strategic sectors of the economy (including energy, other natural resources, defence, and transportation industries), as the state assumed guiding control over these corporations and inserted leading members of the Kremlin team as chief executives (a so-called 'private–state corporate partnership'). Referring back to our figures and table, note these high-profile Kremlin team figures and the important corporations they headed in the early days of the Medvedev regime: Viktor Zubkov, gas giant Gazprom; Igor Sechin, oil giant Rosneft; Igor Shuvalov, sea shipping company Sovkomflot; Sergei Ivanov, Unified Aircraft Building Corporation, OAK; Sergei Naryshkin, the Channel One television network; and (until 2008) Anatolii Chubais, electricity giant UES, to name a few of the most prominent. Managerial and legal means were replacing the use of force in the Russian struggle for power and property. One sensed that the creeping power of the Kremlin and the state in the country's socio-economic life, a hallmark of the Putin years, was continuing.

Each presidential term has entailed unforeseen developments and policy choices, but we can conclude that post-Soviet Russia's third administration exhibited institutional and personnel arrangements and an articulated policy line that were fairly predictable and intelligible. What is important for the viewer of the evolving Russian system to keep in mind is that all choices and decisions are subject to change, that no institutional structures or configuration of personnel is 'set in stone'. Moreover as Lilia Shevtsova has observed, Russia to date has developed according to the 'law of unintended consequences', so one must be careful not to over-analyse or over-emphasise any single development or action (*The Daily Telegraph*, 20 February 2008). Some observers were already engaging in such over-analysis in the first year of the Medvedev-Putin administration, as supposed differences in public pronouncements by the President and Prime Minister were said to reflect 'disputes' or the tendency of one to be more 'liberal' or the other to be more 'conservative'. Closer to reality was the fact that both Medvedev and Putin were members of the same team, with both the presidential administration and government committed to power and policy coherence. It is clear that Russia today, as in the past, desires what we could term a 'stability of power', and as Russia's richest citizen, billionaire Oleg Deripaska remarked, 'In Russia, in our culture, we need a leader' (AP, 8 May 2008). Russians had such a leader for eight years, and we will need a full four-year presidential term to determine whether Dmitri Medvedev alone, or with his Prime Minister Vladimir Putin, fills that role. Indeed, we will need that four-year term to assess whether, in fact, that 2008 succession was little more than a shifting of formal positions, with a system patron continuing to hold the real reins of power for the foreseeable future. By 2012 we will also learn, with the extended six-year presidential term, whether Dmitri Medvedev opts for a second term and a ten-year tenure, or whether Vladimir Putin returns to the top executive post for a second presidency that could last up to another twelve years. However these personnel matters are sorted out, the federal executive continues to be the pre-eminent force in the Russian polity, and by all indications Russian elites and citizens support this and will ensure its long-term continuation.

Chapter 3

Parliamentary Politics in Russia

THOMAS F. REMINGTON

Changes in the status and role of Russia's parliament reflect the turbulent evolution of the post-communist political system. Mikhail Gorbachev's democratising reforms in the late 1980s transformed the Soviet parliament from a ceremonial adornment of communist rule into an arena of stormy debate and tense political confrontation in the 1990s when Boris Yeltsin was president. In the 2000s, however, under Vladimir Putin's presidency, parliament for the most part reverted to its Soviet-era role as a docile rubber stamp for the leadership's proposals. In this process of transformation are reflected the hopes, contradictions, and failures of democratic reform. Still, while parliament is not the source of political legitimacy and authority for the state in Russia that it is in liberal democracies, neither is it quite the decorative window-dressing that it was in the Soviet era. As at the time of writing, with Dmitri Medvedev having succeeded Putin as president and Putin himself becoming prime minister, parliament remains a site of bargaining and deal making among organised intererests over the distribution of benefits and liabilities while providing the president and prime minister secure support for their legislative agenda. Of particular importance is the dominant position of the United Russia party in parliament: United Russia serves as the mechanism for converting the political needs and ambitions of members of parliament into a solid bloc of voting support for the Kremlin. The transformation of parliament's place over the years since the communist regime ended tells us a great deal about the dynamics of power in Russia.

To understand the contemporary Federal Assembly, it helps to begin with a brief review of the status of elective representative bodies in the Soviet Union. Although they exercised little actual power, they symbolised the idea that the people were sovereign in the state. Legally, the Soviet political system rested on the fiction that state power resided in the hierarchy of *soviets* (soviet means council). Soviets were popularly elected bodies in which, according to Soviet doctrine, legislative and executive power were fused. Each village and town, region and republic, had its nominally elected soviet (elected in the characteristic, uncontested elections for which the regime was famous), while at the apex of the system, the USSR's Supreme Soviet was the equivalent of a parliament for the Soviet Union as a whole. At the same time, it was understood that actual political power lay with the Communist Party of the Soviet Union, which exercised power through the soviets and the executive bodies that were nominally accountable to the soviets. Therefore the few votes that soviets were called upon to take were exercises in the unanimous affirmation of decisions that had been made by the Communist Party. Both Soviet political thought and practice rejected any notion of a separation of powers, and thus reinforced the older Russian tradition of an absolutist state.

This system changed markedly when Mikhail Gorbachev launched his political reforms in the late 1980s. Gorbachev used new expanded parliamentary structures and open elections as instruments for awakening popular political energies. His goal was to channel the country's newly active political life into a new set of legislative structures where he would be able to guide decision making. Gorbachev created a cumbersome four-tiered parliament for the USSR, consisting of a huge, 2250-member Congress of People's Deputies, which elected a smaller, full-time parliament called the Supreme Soviet. In turn, the Supreme Soviet was guided by its Presidium, which was overseen by a Chairman. The first election of deputies to this new parliamentary structure was held in 1989; in 1990, elections were held for the equivalent bodies at the level of the union republics and in regions and towns throughout the Soviet Union.

Gorbachev's strategy was to give *glasnost'*, his policy of open political communication, an institutional base. He sought to incorporate many diverse groups into the new parliamentary arena while ensuring that he would have the ultimate power of decision over policy. But liberalisation of politics under Gorbachev had unanticipated consequences. Not only did it mobilise radical democrats against defenders of the old order, it also encouraged coalitions of democrats and nationalists in the republics, including Russia, to rally around demands for national independence. As a result, the new USSR parliament and its counterparts at lower levels *represented* reasonably well the political divisions existing in the country between defenders and challengers of the old order. But they were woefully unsuited to *deciding* the grave policy questions that the country faced. They lacked even the most rudimentary institutional means to generate and debate coherent alternative policy options. They depended heavily on the executive to set their agendas and guide their decision making. Sessions of the new USSR parliament, and the parliaments in the union republics and lower-level territories, were frequently the sites of passionate but inconclusive debate, dramatic walkouts by embattled minorities, and deep frustration as the deputies found themselves unable to reach majority decisions on difficult issues. Little wonder that they were never able to resolve the most serious crises that the Soviet Union faced.

Gorbachev's awkwardly remodelled parliament did achieve some notable results, passing some major new legislation and stimulating the formation of proto-parties. But faced with the fundamental conflict between radical reformers and hardliners over market-oriented reform, the parliament simply ducked: it created a state presidency for the USSR, a curiosity that was logically incompatible with the principle of CPSU rule. Then it delegated extraordinary powers to President Gorbachev, who fell into a trap of his own making by constantly expanding the nominal powers of the president. What he failed to recognise at the time was that by doing so, he only encouraged the presidents of the union republics to follow suit at their own level of jurisdiction, thus deepening the disintegration of the Soviet state. The more power Gorbachev claimed for himself as president of the USSR, the less power he had in actuality, and the more he undercut the possibility that *any* central level institution – president, parliament or Communist Party – could have held the union together.

Boris Yeltsin and the crisis of 1993

The 1990–3 period was marked by the rise of Boris Yeltsin, who made Russia's parliament his initial base of power. Yeltsin led a coalition of radical democrats and Russian nationalists in a struggle for greater autonomy for Russia within the union. Yeltsin's own position was strengthened, rather than weakened, by Gorbachev's clumsy attempts to undermine him. In 1990, Yeltsin was elected by a narrow margin to the position of Chairman of the RSFSR Supreme Soviet, enabling him to use the parliament as his institutional base for challenging Gorbachev. In spring 1991, Yeltsin rallied a majority of deputies who endorsed his proposal for a powerful, directly elected Russian president. In June 1991, he was elected president of Russia in a nationwide election.

Establishing the presidency, however, led to a contest between the legislative and executive branches. The leadership of the parliament began to challenge Yeltsin for supremacy, claiming that the legislative branch was the supreme seat of state power. Yeltsin claimed that as popularly elected president, he embodied the Russian people's will. The August 1991 coup attempt further solidified Yeltsin's political position. The popular resistance to the coup in Moscow, Leningrad, and other Russian cities, and his own uncompromising opposition, gave Yeltsin a substantial political bonus. Many of his communist opponents in the Russian parliament lost their political bases through a series of presidential decrees which suspended, and later outlawed, the activity of the CPSU and confiscated its considerable property. In October 1991, at the Fifth Congress, Yeltsin sought and received special powers to enact economic reform measures by decree; he won the congress's consent to put off elections of local heads of government until 1 December 1992, and its approval of constitutional amendments giving him the right to suspend the acts of lower authorities in Russia if he found they violated the constitution and to suspend legal acts of the union if they violated Russian sovereignty; and the congress approved his programme for radical economic transformation. A few days later Yeltsin assumed the position of prime minister himself, named a new cabinet dominated by young economists committed to rapid liberalisation, and issued a package of decrees launching the radical 'shock therapy' that is discussed in Chapter 11.

Making full use of his expanded powers, Yeltsin pursued his programme of reform throughout 1992. Although the impetus of 'shock therapy' fizzled out as the year proceeded, opposition to Yeltsin grew, and the majority in the parliament shifted further and further away from him. Yeltsin was also unable to win legislative approval of a new constitution that would formalise his powers *vis-à-vis* the government and the legislative branch. Under the old constitution, however, only the Congress had the power to amend the constitution or adopt a new one. Confrontation between Yeltsin and the Congress-Supreme Soviet intensified. In March 1993 the Congress attempted to remove Yeltsin from power through impeachment but fell slightly short of the required two-thirds majority of its entire membership. Yeltsin responded by holding a popular referendum on support for his policies in April, which gave him a surprisingly strong vote of confidence. However, the constitutional crisis continued to deepen.

Finally, on September 21, Yeltsin issued decrees that lacked constitutional foundation although they offered a political solution to the impasse. He shut down parliament, declared the deputies' powers null and void, and called elections for a new parliament to be held on December 12. He also decreed that there was to be a national vote on the same date on the draft constitution that had been developed under his direction. In the December referendum, Yeltsin's constitution was approved. It has remained in force ever since.

Yeltsin's constitution created a two-chamber Federal Assembly. The upper chamber, the Federation Council, allocated two seats to each of Russia's 89 constituent territories (called 'subjects of the federation'). Under the initial election law that Yeltsin put into effect, half of the 450 seats in the lower house – the State Duma – were to be filled by candidates elected from parties' electoral lists according to the share of votes that party received, so long as it won at least 5 per cent of the party list votes. The other half of the seats were filled by plurality voting in 225 single-member districts. In the first election held under this plan, in 1993, voters were also given the opportunity to elect their two representatives to the Federation Council.

Not surprisingly, Yeltsin's draft constitution provided for a very strong presidency. The president could issue decrees with the force of law, as well as veto laws passed by parliament. Yet the constitution also provided for the 'separation of legislative, executive and judicial powers' (Article 10). Contradictions between the powerful presidentialist elements in the constitution and the principle of separation of powers have been resolved very differently at different times since the adoption of the constitution. Under Yeltsin, the president shared some power with the parliament; since Putin took office, however, parliament has been pushed to the sidelines of the political system. The changes in the balance of power between president and parliament reflect both changes in the organisational arrangements within parliament itself as well as shifts in the larger institutional environment in which parliament and president operate.

The first and second Dumas

One of the most important determinants of the balance of power between president and parliament is the outcome of elections. The first elections held under the new electoral system in 1993 gave no one political party or coalition a majority of seats in the Duma. Winning voting coalitions in the 1994–5 Duma often were formed from the votes of the Communists, Agrarians, and their allies. As a result, parliament fought Yeltsin over much of the legislation he proposed, with the result that Yeltsin sometimes simply bypassed parliament by issuing presidential decrees. Yet both Yeltsin and the parliamentary leadership generally sought to avoid the sort of mutually destructive confrontations that had brought the country to the brink of civil war in 1991 and 1993. Regular bargaining and consultation between the executive and legislative branches succeeded in working out compromises on numerous pieces of legislation.

This pattern continued in the second Duma, which sat from 1996 through 1999. Yeltsin had decreed that the Duma elected in 1993 would serve for only two years and that elections would be held again in December 1995 for a new Duma that would serve a normal four-year term. The December 1995 election was characterised by a huge number of political groups running: 43 parties registered and ran lists – far more than could hope to win seats given the 5 per cent threshold rule for receiving seats. Four parties succeeded in winning seats on the party list ballot, and they divided the 225 proportional representation seats among themselves: the Communists, Vladimir Zhirinovsky's Liberal Democratic Party of Russia, the 'Our Home is Russia' bloc formed around Prime Minister Viktor Chernomyrdin, and the Yabloko bloc led by economist Grigorii Yavlinsky. Of these, the Communists were by far the most successful. Russia's Democratic Choice, which had been the major reform faction in the previous Duma, failed to receive even 4 per cent, and altogether, half of the votes were cast for parties that failed to win any seats on the party list ballot. The Communists were also successful in winning district seats, taking more than 50. Combined with the seats they won through the party list vote, they wound up with one-third of the seats in parliament, the highest share that they or any party had held in the previous Duma.

The Communists and the factions allied with them came close to commanding a majority of seats in the new Duma. The Communists therefore became an indispensable member of many majority coalitions. However, their position was not secure. To win majorities, they generally needed to offer concessions to other factions or to moderate their policy stance. The Communists refrained from seeking full control over the chamber and largely abided by the previous working arrangements in such matters as the distribution of committee chairmanships among factions, and the practice of forming task forces and legislative commissions by recruiting members from all factions. Most important, they retained the rule under which the Duma's steering committee, the Council of the Duma, comprised the leader of every faction, one leader per faction.

Likewise, President Yeltsin devoted considerable effort to bargaining with the Duma over legislation. Both the president and the government maintained permanent representative offices in the Duma, working closely with deputies to ensure the passage of key legislation. Altogether, around one hundred executive branch officials were detailed to liaison duty with the Duma. Much of the bargaining within the Duma and between Duma and the executive took place out of public view; public attention instead tended to focus on the histrionic displays of temper on the floor and high-stakes brinkmanship between president and Duma. One of the most memorable confrontations between the branches came as the Duma tried to remove the president through impeachment. The deputies were well aware that removal of the president by means of impeachment was a long and complicated process of which a two-thirds parliamentary vote was only the first step, and that even if they succeeded in passing a motion to impeach, the odds of actually removing Yeltsin were remote indeed. The action thus served largely symbolic purposes for the parliamentary opposition.

The Communists in the Duma had long tried to put impeachment on the agenda. They finally succeeded in June 1998, when the chamber agreed to form a commission to examine five accusations against Yeltsin: that he had committed treason by signing the agreement in December 1991 to dissolve the Soviet Union; that he had illegally initiated the war in Chechnya in 1994; that he had illegally dissolved the Russian Congress and Supreme Soviet in 1993; that he had destroyed Russia's defence capacity; and that he had committed genocide against the Russian people through the effects of the economic policies of his government since 1992. In March 1999 the commission approved all five charges and submitted them to the full chamber for its consideration. On May 15 the deputies voted on the five charges. None gained the required 300 votes, although the charge that Yeltsin had illegally initiated and conducted military operations in Chechnya came close. Yeltsin used the full range of carrots and sticks at his disposal to avert impeachment, promising material rewards to some deputies in return for their support, and reminding the Duma that he still had other trump cards in his hand.

Yet spectacular as this pyrotechnic display of president–parliament conflict was, it was already a sideshow by 1999. The polarisation between democratic and communist forces, real enough in the early 1990s, had faded in importance by the end of the decade in guiding actual alignments in parliament. Although episodes such as the impeachment vote continued to attract public attention, actual parliamentary politics increasingly came to centre on distributive issues – how government spending should be allocated; on whom the burdens of taxes should be imposed; who should control the privatisation of state enterprises; to whom access rights to the exploitation of lucrative mineral resources should be granted. The Duma became a central arena for wheeling and dealing among powerful organised interests, including firms, business associations, regional governments, federal ministries, and shadowy bureaucratic 'clans' linked to senior figures in the presidency and government. The fine details of legislation were the object of acute interest; vast sums of money were at stake, not a little of which wound up in the pockets of those drafting and voting on the legislation itself (see Barnes 2001).

The high point of parliamentary power occurred after the August 1998 financial crash. Yeltsin tried to bring back Chernomyrdin as prime minister, but the Duma adamantly refused to confirm him. After two tense confirmation votes failed, Yeltsin backed down and appointed Yevgenii Primakov, a centrist acceptable to the Communists. The Duma confirmed him and Primakov formed a government reflective of the balance of power in parliament. With Yeltsin weakened both physically and politically Primakov began making the major decisions on economic policy. This was as close as Russia has yet come to parliamentary government, where the cabinet is made up of the majority coalition in parliament. This phase was short-lived, however. Yeltsin dismissed Primakov in May 1999, on the eve of the impeachment vote in the Duma.

The stormy era of confrontation between president and parliament ended in December 1999. Elections to the third Duma were held on December 19; five days later the second Duma held its final session. On December 31, Yeltsin resigned as president. He was succeeded by his prime minister, Vladimir Putin, whose powerful political appeal had been demonstrated by the remarkable electoral success of the party with which he was loosely affiliated, Unity, in the parliamentary election. Putin's accession to the presidency, combined with the outcome of the parliamentary election of December 1999, produced a fundamentally new dynamic in legislative–executive relations. After January 2000 the Duma was no longer an arena for confrontations between the president and the opposition, but instead became an instrument for legislative endorsement of nearly any initiative offered by the president. This trend grew still more marked following the 2003 presidential election, when the president's allies gained an overwhelming majority in the Duma, and the president had succeeded in taming or suppressing nearly every source of independent political initiative in the country. At the same time, the Duma remained an arena for the resolution of distributive conflicts.

The third, fourth and fifth Dumas

The 1999 election gave the party most closely allied with Putin – Unity – a strong plurality in the Duma. Unity had to work to build majority coalitions that could pass legislation proposed by the president and government. Its success in forming a fairly reliable cross-factional majority coalition reflects the skill with which the presidential administration manipulated parliamentary politics. Table 3.1 shows the strength of parliamentary parties in the third, fourth, and fifth Dumas.

Working in close co-operation with the president's parliamentary managers, Unity assembled a coalition of four parliamentary factions that co-ordinated voting on major legislation proposed by the president and government. Faction leaders could not always enforce party discipline (two of these factions were made up of deputies elected in single-member districts, who had to pay close attention to powerful local interests back home), but by drawing votes as needed from other factions, they ensured that the president's legislative agenda almost never suffered a defeat and the president almost never had to veto legislation passed by parliament. As Table 3.2 indicates, only 76 per cent of the legislation that passed the Duma in third (final) reading was eventually signed by the president in the 1994–5 Duma (sometimes the president only signed after multiple rounds

Table 3.1 *Party factions in 3rd, 4th and 5th Duma convocations*

	3rd Duma (2000–2003)		4th Duma (2003–2007)		5th Duma (2007–2011)	
	Party list vote %	seats in Duma (%)	Party list vote %	seats in Duma (%)	Party list vote %	seats in Duma (%)
Unity/ United Russia*	23.32	18.4	37.4	68	64.3	70
OVR	13.33	10.2				
CPRF	24.29	20.2	12.65	11.56	11.57	13
LDPR	5.98	3.9	11.49	8	8.14	9
SPS	8.52	7.3	3.97	0	0.96	0
Yabloko	5.93	4.8	4.32	0	1.59	0
Motherland/ A Just Russia**	9.04	8.67	7.74	8		

*Unity merged with OVR in 2001 to form United Russia.
**A Just Russia formed in 2006 from the merger of Motherland, the Pensioners' Party, and the Party of Life.

Abbreviations:
OVR = Fatherland-All Russia
CPRF = Communist Party of the Russian Federation
LDPR = Liberal Democratic Party of Russia
SPS = Union of Rightist Forces

Table 3.2 *Passage rates for legislation, Russian State Duma, 1994–2007*

	First convocation: 1994–1995		Second convocation: 1996–1999		Third convocation: 2000–2003		Fourth convocation: 2004–2007	
	No.	As %	No.	As %	No.	As %	No.	As %
Total no. of bills considered in any reading	(na)		2133		2125		2713	
Laws passed (in 3rd reading)	464	100	1045	100	781	100	1087	100
Vetoed by president only	263	29.3	185	18	31	4	7	.64
Vetoed by president + FC			113	11	10	1	3	.28
Signed by president (of those passed in this period)	354	76	724	69	730	93	735	91.9

Source: Based on Analytic Reports of Russian State Duma, various years.

of veto and revision), and only 69 per cent of the legislation passed in the 1996–9 period was signed. But over 90 per cent of the laws passed in the third and fourth Dumas were signed by the president. It is notable that whereas Yeltsin had often resorted to his decree powers to enact major decisions, Putin almost never did: thanks to his commanding base of support in the parliament, he was able to pass a far more sweeping legislative agenda than Yeltsin had proposed. Putin's legislative achievements included significant reductions in taxes, legalisation of a market for transactions in land, foundations for a system of mortgage lending, sweeping changes in the pension system, overhaul of the labour market, major changes to federal relations, substantial liberalisation of the judicial system, and breakups of major national monopolies. Painful as many of these changes were for the deputies to swallow, they ultimately passed them, albeit sometimes in modified form.

The 2003 elections produced a decisive victory for the president's forces and a humiliating defeat for the opposition both on the right and the left. The liberal democratic forces failed entirely to win party list seats and the Communists' share of the party list fell by nearly half, while the party backed by the Kremlin, United Russia (the successor of Unity, which had performed so well in 1999) took more than 37 per cent of the party list vote. Together with deputies elected in single-member districts, United Russia wound up with two-thirds of the seats in the new Duma. Since the advent of democratisation in the late 1980s, no party had ever held so dominant a position in parliament. United Russia used its commanding majority to make sweeping changes to the way parliament was run. They replaced the old power-sharing, proportional arrangements of the previous three Dumas with a new majoritarian system in which their members held nearly all the committee chairmanships and seats on the governing Council of the Duma, and their leader was elected the Duma's chairman. They quickly moved to impose a gag rule on their members, demanding that no member speak to the press without party approval.

But for all their ability to control the Duma, theirs was a pyrrhic victory, because the power to make policy decisions lay in the Kremlin. As total as United Russia's influence was in the Duma, the Kremlin's monopoly on policy making was just as absolute. As a result, United Russia placed itself in a position of complete subservience to the Kremlin for its power and privileges. Its base of support in society is thin, and it has identified itself completely with the interests of office holders rather than offering a clear policy programme. This is a mixed blessing for the Kremlin. The party's effectiveness in delivering reliable majorities in parliament depends on its ability to win elections. Therefore, if the Kremlin were to withdraw its support from the party and its fortunes collapsed, the president and government might not be able to ensure such solid voting support in parliament. President Putin has repeatedly said that Russia needs a capable (*deesposbnyi*) parliament and has tied that to the ability of United Russia to forge consistent, coherent majorities. That is the reason, he explained in October 2007, that he had agreed to head the United Russia list in the forthcoming election (*Rossiiskaya gazeta*, 2 October 2007).

The legislative agenda shifted somewhat between the third and fourth Dumas, reflecting the president's changed priorities. Modernising economic reform took a back seat, while anti-terrorism legislation, generous increases in social spending, and the establishment of a number of new state corporations taking over ownership and control of many of Russia's most significant public and private industries occupied much more of the parliament's time. These pieces of legislation gave deputies, particularly those from United Russia, many opportunities to showcase their effectiveness in bringing benefits back to their home districts and to the powerful business lobbies that backed them. So although they ceded even more power to the executive branch (for example, supporting the law replacing direct elections of governors with a system of presidential nomination and greatly expanding the power of the security police to deal with terrorists), they also reinforced the popularity of United Russia with the electorate.

Preparations for the December 2007 Duma election proceeded amidst great uncertainty about the presidential succession. President Putin resolved many fears and doubts when he announced that he intended to run at the top of United Russia's election list and to stay on in power – but not as president. The presidential administration pulled out all the stops to ensure a smooth and controlled succession. The first step was to guarantee a large victory for United Russia in the Duma election by methods that included manipulation of media coverage, massive funding for United Russia's campaign, disqualification of popular opposition politicians, and outright falsification of voting returns in many districts (Myagkov and Ordeshook 2008). The official results gave United Russia 64.3 per cent of the vote. Because this election was entirely based on proportional representation from party lists (there are no longer any single-member district mandates), and because the threshold to receiving seats was raised from 5 to 7 per cent, only four parties won representation (see Chapter 5). As in the fourth Duma, United Russia took three-quarters of the seats and full control of the Duma: it holds 26 of the 32 committee chairmanships and 8 of the 11 seats on the Duma's steering committee, the Council of the Duma. The party's leader, Boris Gryzlov, was once again elected speaker.

The Federation Council

The president and government enjoy a similar position of dominance in the Russian upper house, the Federation Council. Here, however, executive control is not directly transmitted through the United Russia party.

Like the United States Senate, the Federation Council is designed as an instrument of federalism in that every constituent unit of the federation sends two representatives to it. Thus the populations of small ethnic-national territories are greatly overrepresented compared with more populous regions. Members of the Federation Council were elected by direct popular vote in December 1993 but since the constitution was silent on how they were to be chosen in the future, requiring only that one representative from the executive branch and one from the legislative branch from each region be members of the chamber, new legislation was required to detail how members of the Federation Council should be chosen. Under a law passed in 1995, the heads of the executive and legislative branches of each constituent unit of the federation were automatically given seats in the Federation Council, and this was the system in force between 1996 and 1999. Under President Putin, however, new legislation was passed in 2000 which provided that the governors and legislatures of the regions were to choose full-time representatives to occupy their regions' seats in the Federation Council.

Because the Federation Council has rejected the use of political factions to organise political bargaining, United Russia has only an informal status in the chamber. Nevertheless, the president and government guide its deliberations closely. Under the constitution, some legislation is not required to be considered by the Federation Council, although it can choose to take up any bill it wishes to consider. Actual voting in the Federation Council routinely produces lop-sided majorities favouring the president's position; the chamber spends very little time on floor debate, since the decisions have been agreed upon beforehand in consultations among committee chairs and the president's representatives. Often members of the Federation Council involve themselves in shaping legislation while it is still being considered by the Duma, so that by the time it has passed the Duma it already reflects their interests. Federation Council members also spend a good deal of time in lobbying with federal government agencies on behalf of their home regions or business interests (Remington 2003).

Constitutionally, the Federation Council has important powers. It approves presidential nominees for high courts such as the Supreme Court and the Constitutional Court. It approves presidential decrees declaring martial law or a state of emergency, and any actions altering the boundaries of territorial units in Russia. It must consider any legislation dealing with taxes, budget, financial policy, treaties, customs and declarations of war. In the Yeltsin period, the Federation Council defied the president's will on a number of issues. After President Putin entered office, however, the Federation Council lost the independence it once had enjoyed. Its members, although often caught between the conflicting imperatives of their home regions and the president's domination of the political system, have rarely had much difficulty deciding to take the president's side. The highly centralised nature of the current system means that it is far more costly to members to oppose the president than to side with the president against their home regions.

The legislative process in the Federal Assembly

Basic legislative procedure

The State Duma originates all legislation except in certain areas of policy that are under the jurisdiction of the upper house, the Federation Council. Upon final passage in the State Duma, a bill goes to the Federation Council. If the upper house rejects it, the bill goes back to the Duma, where a commission comprising members of both houses may seek to iron out differences. If the Duma rejects the upper house's changes, it may override the Federation Council by a two-thirds majority. Otherwise it votes on the version of the bill proposed by the commission (see Figures 3.1–3.3). When the bill has cleared both chambers of the Federal Assembly, it goes to the president for signature. If the president refuses to sign the bill, it returns to the Duma. The Duma may pass it with the president's proposed amendments by a simple absolute majority, or override the president's veto, for which a two-thirds vote of the entire membership is required. The Federation Council must then also approve the bill, by a simple majority if the president's amendments are accepted, or a two-thirds vote if it chooses to override him.

State Duma

The steering committee of the Duma is the Council of the Duma. The Council of the Duma makes the principal decisions in the Duma concerning the agenda, and acts on occasion to overcome deadlocks among the political groups represented in the Duma. Until the sweeping changes of 2004, it was made up of the leader of each party faction or registered deputy group regardless of size, and thus served to diffuse political power in the chamber. Since 2004, however, it has been dominated by the United

Figure 3.1   *The legislative process: overview*

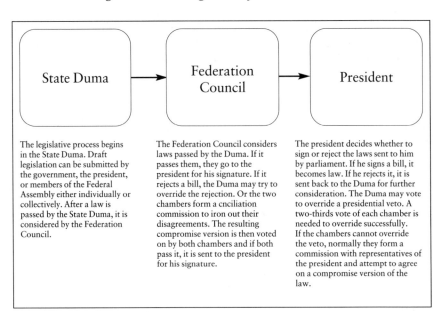

The legislative process begins in the State Duma. Draft legislation can be submitted by the government, the president, or members of the Federal Assembly either individually or collectively. After a law is passed by the State Duma, it is considered by the Federation Council.

The Federation Council considers laws passed by the Duma. If it passes them, they go to the president for his signature. If it rejects a bill, the Duma may try to override the rejection. Or the two chambers form a cnciliation commission to iron out their disagreements. The resulting compromise version is then voted on by both chambers and if both pass it, it is sent to the president for his signature.

The president decides whether to sign or reject the laws sent to him by parliament. If he signs a bill, it becomes law. If he rejects it, it is sent back to the Duma for further consideration. The Duma may vote to override a presidential veto. A two-thirds vote of each chamber is needed to override successfully. If the chambers cannot override the veto, normally they form a commission with representatives of the president and attempt to agree on a compromise version of the law.

Figure 3.2   *The legislative process: bill introduction*

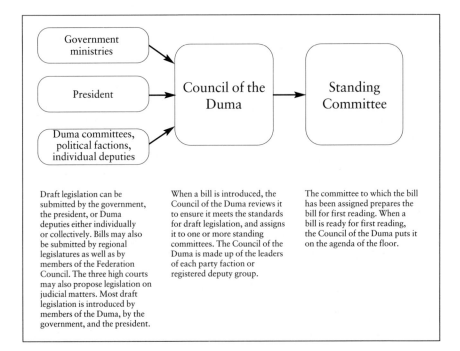

Draft legislation can be submitted by the government, the president, or Duma deputies either individually or collectively. Bills may also be submitted by regional legislatures as well as by members of the Federation Council. The three high courts may also propose legislation on judicial matters. Most draft legislation is introduced by members of the Duma, by the government, and the president.

When a bill is introduced, the Council of the Duma reviews it to ensure it meets the standards for draft legislation, and assigns it to one or more standing committees. The Council of the Duma is made up of the leaders of each party faction or registered deputy group.

The committee to which the bill has been assigned prepares the bill for first reading. When a bill is ready for first reading, the Council of the Duma puts it on the agenda of the floor.

Figure 3.3   *The legislative process: three readings*

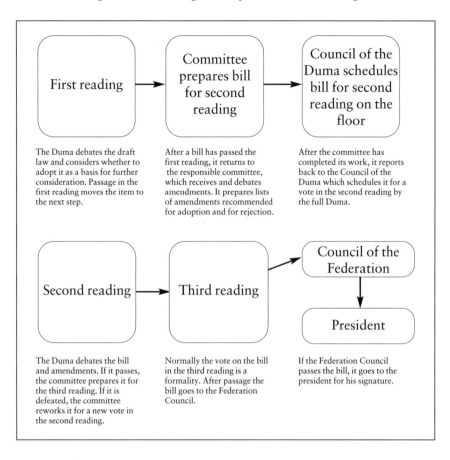

First reading

The Duma debates the draft law and considers whether to adopt it as a basis for further consideration. Passage in the first reading moves the item to the next step.

Committee prepares bill for second reading

After a bill has passed the first reading, it returns to the responsible committee, which receives and debates amendments. It prepares lists of amendments recommended for adoption and for rejection.

Council of the Duma schedules bill for second reading on the floor

After the committee has completed its work, it reports back to the Council of the Duma which schedules it for a vote in the second reading by the full Duma.

Second reading

The Duma debates the bill and amendments. If it passes, the committee prepares it for the third reading. If it is defeated, the committee reworks it for a new vote in the second reading.

Third reading

Normally the vote on the bill in the third reading is a formality. After passage the bill goes to the Federation Council.

Council of the Federation

President

If the Federation Council passes the bill, it goes to the president for his signature.

Russia faction, whose members hold eight out of the eleven seats on the Council.

All deputies in the Duma belong to the political faction tied to the party on whose list they were elected. Under new Standing Rules, they may not change factions (on pain of losing their seat). Each party that has won at least 7 per cent of the party-list vote is entitled to form a faction in the Duma made up of its elected deputies. The factions use the Duma as a means for showcasing their pet legislative projects, giving their leaders a national forum, obtaining crucial organisational support for their party work, and providing service to their constituents. However, only the United Russia faction has any real power to shape legislation. It is so large and diverse that it has subdivided into four internal groupings, organised around common policy interests (such as the interests of the oil and gas industries), or particular leaders. United Russia also uses three political clubs, one with a vaguely pro-market orientation, one broadly social-democratic and the third focused on patriotic and moral concerns, as forums to debate policy.

The Duma also has a system of standing legislative committees to handle legislation in particular issue jurisdictions. Each deputy is a member of one committee. The work of drafting and developing legislation goes on in the committees, and committees report out legislation along with recommendations on amendments that have been proposed. Members join committees according to the issues areas in which they wish to specialise.

Formally, bills are considered in three readings (see Figure 3.3). In the first reading, the Duma simply decides whether or not to approve the bill's basic conception. If it passes, the bill goes back to the committee, which then sifts through the amendments that are offered. When the committee has agreed on its recommended version of the bill, it reports it out again to the floor for a second reading, and the whole chamber decides on which amendments to approve and which to reject. At that point the floor votes on the bill in its entirety, and sends it back to the committee for a final editing and polishing. The third reading gives the Duma's final approval to the bill, after which it goes to the Federation Council.

In recent years, a practice has evolved whereby much of the bargaining over legislation occurs at the so-called 'zero reading' stage. This refers to the consultation between the government and its supporters in the Duma before a bill is ever formally submitted to the Duma. For example, before the government formally introduces the annual budget bill to the Duma, it meets with the United Russia faction leaders, who press for increases in spending in areas that will be politically and electorally useful for it. For example, before the government submitted the 2009 budget, it heard requests from United Russia to add another 20 billion rubles in spending on highway construction, 2 billion on supercomputers, 660 million rubles on preparations to celebrate the 1150th anniversary of the city of Novgorod, and so on. Through the 'zero reading,' deputies in the United Russia faction are able to reward their friends and supporters by such budget revisions – something much easier to do when oil revenues are swelling the budget.

The relationship between the executive and the United Russia party illustrates the dynamics of a dominant party regime. In such a regime, the rulers use the dominant party to control the political process. As in other authoritarian regimes where such a model has been used (as during the era of dominance of the Party of the Institutionalised Revolution in Mexico or that of the United Malays National Organization in Malaysia), the party gives ambitious politicians an opportunity to build political careers. Thanks to their privileged access to the government, elected party politicians can reward the wealthy and powerful interests that back them, steering lucrative contracts or jobs their way. The party operates as a giant national patronage machine. The rulers benefit by ensuring that politicians will be loyal to the authorities rather than competing against it. The party mobilises support for the regime at the elections, and the authorities use all their powers of control over the media, money, election commissions, courts, police and the like, to make sure that opposition parties cannot make serious inroads into the ruling party's dominant status. In parliament, the dominant party organises large, lopsided voting majorities to pass the executive's proposed legislation. In effect, the politicians in the dominant party give up their political voice in return for access to the benefits of office. This allows them to pay back the business interests that have funded their election campaigns.

As a result of the new relationship between parliament and president established under Vladimir Putin and continuing under President Medvedev, almost no legislation that passes the Duma and Federation Council is vetoed. Vigorous debates over legislation continue, but rarely on the floor of either chamber. Bills can be slowed down by disagreements within the executive branch itself (as different ministries lobby for different versions of the legislation) or when the United Russia is given new marching orders by the Kremlin. (For example, in the spring of 2008, a bill making it easy for public officials to sue media organisations for defamation, which passed by a wide margin in first reading, met a crushing defeat in its second reading after President Medvedev told United Russia that he thought the bill excessive and unnecessary; the party's attitude to the bill turned around 180 degrees.)

The 1993 Constitution did not give the Federal Assembly a formal power of 'oversight' over the executive, such as the United States Congress has. Parliament has, however, other formal powers which it can use to monitor and check executive power if it is so inclined and if the executive allows it to do so. One of its instruments is the Audit Chamber, which reviews the accounts of state bodies including federal ministries, regional governments, and even private companies. Another is the practice of inviting government officials to parliament to respond to deputies' questions during 'government hour'. Committees frequently organise hearings to gather public testimony on matters of public policy and assist in developing legislation. Parliament can also conduct investigations of allegations of executive branch misconduct. All of these powers, however, can only be exercised to the extent that parliament chooses to wield them and the executive branch consents to their being used. In the current period, when political power in the state is highly concentrated in the presidential administration, parliament's oversight power has been reduced to virtually nil.

The Federal Assembly in perspective

The ability of a legislature to exercise its constitutional prerogatives depends both on its own internal rules and structures and on features of its institutional environment. One critical aspect of that environment in Russia is the degree to which the president dominates political processes. The 1990s and 2000s present two very different models in this regard. Yeltsin's political and physical weakness, and, undoubtedly, his own fitful but sincere political instincts, allowed parliament to play a stronger role than has been the case under Putin and Medvedev. Although under Yeltsin the balance between the branches was asymmetric, with the presidency still possessing the upper hand over parliament, parliament still managed to check the president's power and influence public policy in a number of significant issue areas. This was because parliament found its own institutional means to overcome fragmentation and to produce majorities on legislative issues, and because the presidential administration and government were often divided, encouraging bureaucratic interest groups to compete for support in parliament.

Putin reversed both patterns. He centralised and disciplined policy making within the executive branch, and reengineered the internal procedures of both chambers of parliament in such a way as to ensure him consistent and reliable majorities. In the Duma this has come about through the domination of parliament by United Russia. In the Federation Council Putin's reforms of 2000 deprived the Federation Council of any political independence, allowing him to shape the chamber's majorities as he chose. Thus neither chamber has the means or inclination to challenge the president. This state of affairs is not necessarily permanent, but a shift to a more balanced relationship between the branches will require significant changes on both sides. The president would need give up much of the informal power he presently possesses, and parliament would need to win an independent political mandate from the electorate.

Putin's move to the prime ministership in 2008 has opened yet a new set of possibilities for the evolution of the regime. It makes it more difficult for the United Russia party to play the familiar role of expressing total loyalty to the president while blaming the government for shortcomings in policy implementation. On the other hand, it requires United Russia to link Putin as prime minister to the parliament, to big business, to regional governors, and to other sources of power. Putin and Medvedev need United Russia and its dominance of parliament just as United Russia depends on the life-support system from the Kremlin. Regardless of how the system of power sharing between president and prime minister works out in the future, the political legacy of Putin is likely to be institutionalised in a party that outlives him.

Over the past fifteen years, parliament's role in the political system has changed fundamentally. In the early 1990s, parliament reflected the sharp polarisation in the country, together with the grave debility of all the central political institutions. No one party held a majority in parliament, and the weakness of parliament and the president forced them to bargain with one another as best they could. After the August 1998 financial crash, another model began to take shape. For a period of several months in late 1998 and early 1999, Russia's political system even gravitated toward a parliamentary system, in that the head of government (at that point Yevgenii Primakov) derived his power from the support of a parliamentary majority rather than from the president. Under Putin, the authorities took pains to construct a lasting dominant party system built around United Russia.

Radical shifts of this kind in the balance of power across the institutions suggest that Russia's political system is likely to evolve still further. If the current dominance of United Russia eventually gives way to a more truly competitive party system, so that political parties in Russia offer alternative visions of policy direction, then parliament will again become a more important arena for deliberation. Likewise, if the mass media, national interest groups, and judicial bodies gain greater independence, they will encourage members of parliament to stake out policy positions independent of the president and to position themselves as counterweights to the executive branch. Finally, if the president himself comes to recognise that a system in which the government is in fact accountable to parliament makes it a more reliable, disciplined, and effective instrument for exercising power, Russia's political system may eventually see a more even balance in the distribution of power between the executive and legislative branches.

Chapter 4

Elections and Voters

MICHAEL McFAUL and KATHRYN STONER-WEISS

Competitive elections were the most dramatic institutional change that distinguished the old Soviet dictatorship from the Russian political system that emerged following the collapse of the Soviet Union in 1991. During the Soviet period, elections occurred on a regular basis, but since the ballot offered no choice between candidates or parties, and Soviet citizens faced sanctions if they did not vote, these elections lacked real political consequences. Beginning in 1989, however, Soviet leader Mikhail Gorbachev introduced reforms that allowed for semi-competitive elections to the USSR Congress of People's Deputies. This reform, in combination with others, brought about a fundamental transformation of the Soviet political system, which eventually led to the collapse of the USSR and the emergence of the Russian Federation as an independent state at the end of 1991.

The function of Russian elections has evolved and changed over time. Since 1993, the formal institutions, rules, and regulations governing the practice of elections in Russia have changed slightly. However, the political implications of elections have changed considerably. If elections in the early 1990s constituted the main political drama of post-Soviet politics, then they most certainly no longer play that role today. In particular, under President Putin (2000–8), the outcomes of elections became more certain, less competitive, and therefore less meaningful in Russian politics. This change occurred in part because Putin was so popular and faced few serious challengers during his time in office. Additionally, Putin's own political 'reforms' – that is, changes in the political system that made Russian politics less pluralist during and following Putin's tenure as President – also contributed to the lessening importance of elections. Since truly competitive elections no longer determine who governs Russia in either the legislative or executive branches, Russia can no longer be considered a democracy (Diamond 2002, 2008 and Freedom House 2008; we consider such issues further in Chapter 15).

Elections as certain procedures with uncertain outcomes

Between June 1991 and December 1993, Russia did not hold elections for national office. In the tumultuous period between August 1991 and the dissolution of the Soviet Union later that year, organising new elections was the last item on Yeltsin's agenda. First and foremost, he concentrated on breaking up the Soviet Union in a peaceful manner, a mammoth project that involved dismantling the Communist Party of the Soviet Union and splitting into pieces the Soviet army and intelligence services while keeping his own Federation from experiencing a similar fate. His other great priority was jumpstarting Russian economic reform. Yeltsin believed that he already had secured an electoral mandate from the people as recently as June 1991. His allies in the Russian Congress were elected in the spring of 1990, just a year earlier. New elections in post-Soviet Russia, therefore, seemed distracting, dangerous, and unnecessary. Yeltsin even postponed local elections scheduled for December 1991.

Yeltsin's failure to secure a new electoral mandate, however, had destabilising consequences for the new state. The combination of major economic dislocation, in part fuelled by Yeltsin's reforms, and poorly defined political institutions created ambiguity, stalemate and conflict both between the federal and sub-national units of the state, and then, more consequentially, between the president and the Congress of People's Deputies. After price liberalisation and the beginning of radical economic reform in January 1992, the Congress, once loyal to Yeltsin, began a campaign to reassert its superiority over the president. The disagreement about economic reform in turn spawned a constitutional crisis between the parliament and the president. With no formal or even informal institutions to structure relations between the president and the Congress, political polarisation not unlike the standoff between Gorbachev and Yeltsin in 1990–1 re-emerged.

In this newly polarised context, both sides claimed to represent the will of the people. In the heat of the stalemate Yeltsin and the Congress agreed to ask the voters directly which political institution and what reforms they supported. In the April 1993 referendum, voters went to the polls to give answers to the following questions:

- Do you trust Russian President Yeltsin?
- Do you approve of the socio-economic policy conducted by the Russian president and by the Russian government since 1992?
- Should a new presidential election be conducted ahead of schedule?
- Should a new parliamentary election be conducted ahead of schedule?

On the first question, despite the serious economic hardship that most people endured at the time, 58.7 per cent of voters affirmed their trust in Yeltsin, compared with 39.3 per cent who did not. Even more amazingly, 53 per cent expressed their approval of Yeltsin's socio-economic policy, while 44.5 per cent disapproved. Regarding questions three and four a plurality (49.5 per cent) supported early presidential elections, while a solid majority (67.2 per cent) called for new parliamentary elections.

These results reflected the highly divided and polarised nature of Russian politics at the time. In essence, voters were being asked their opinion about the revolution midstream in the revolution: half supported it, half did not. This electoral result, therefore, did little to defuse the constitutional crisis in Russia. On 21 September 1993, Yeltsin issued Presidential Decree Number 1400, which dissolved the Russian Congress of People's Deputies and called for a referendum to adopt a new constitution. The Congress rejected Yeltsin's decree as unconstitutional and instead impeached him and appointed his vice-president, Aleksandr Rutskoi, as the new president. In a replay of August 1991, the crisis only ended when one side – Yeltsin's side – prevailed in a military conflict.

The development of more certain rules

After Yeltsin's successful use of force against the Congress, which ended on 4 October 1993, the president sent mixed signals about his commitment to elections and the democratic process. Obviously, the dissolution of the Congress was a blatant violation of both the constitution and the spirit of democracy. The deputies, after all, had been elected by the Russian people. Yeltsin showed the same disregard for the electoral process by dissolving the regional soviets (elected parliaments in Russia's 89 provinces). He also removed three out of eight regional heads of administration who had been elected several months earlier. At the same time, Yeltsin seemed eager to establish new political rules in which elections would play a central role. He published a draft constitution and called for a referendum to approve it in December. After 4 October, Yeltsin also announced that elections for a new bicameral parliament would take place in December.

Without parliament in place, Yeltsin used decrees to establish new electoral laws. As we saw in Chapter 3, he dictated that the new lower house of parliament, the State Duma, would be elected according to a mixed system: half of the 450 seats would be determined by a first-part-the-post system in newly drawn up electoral districts, while the other half would be allocated according to a system of proportional representation. Parties had to win at least 5 per cent of the popular vote to win seats on the proportional representation ballot. (In 2007 this threshold was raised to 7 per cent, as explained later in this chapter.) For the Federation Council, the upper house, Yeltsin decreed that voters in each of Russia's 89 regions would cast two votes for their senatorial candidates on one list. The top two finishers in each region would win. (This too would change to a system of *de facto* appointment under Putin's presidency.)

The December 1993 elections served as the founding elections for Russia's new political system. A majority of Russian voters ratified Yeltsin's draft constitution, giving popular legitimacy to a set of political rules for governing Russia. The new constitution outlined difficult procedures for amendment, meaning that adoption of this constitution was likely to produce a lasting set of political institutions for post-communist Russia. Since 1993, the constitution has not been substantially amended, although there was some discussion about doing so in order to enable Putin to run for a third time as president. The December 1993 vote was also the first election in Russia's brief democratic history in which political parties had the opportunity to participate fully, with proportional representation being an additional incentive for stimulating party participation and development.

The basic rules of the game for elections to the Duma established during this tumultuous period in late 1993 endured for the first four of the (so far) five parliamentary elections. Eventually the newly elected Duma codified Yeltsin's mixed electoral system in to law, meaning that four parliamentary elections (1993, 1995, 1999, and 2003) took place using the same electoral system, while the fifth, in December 2007, was held under a new electoral law that severely circumscribed the number of parties that could gain representation in the Duma. The minimum threshold for parties to gain representation in the Duma was increased to 7 from 5 per cent. This step effectively eliminated small liberal parties, including Yabloko, and the Union of Right Forces (SPS), which had hovered at around the 5 per cent level in the Duma elections of 2003, and who gained more seats through the single mandate races than through proportional representation. In 2007 the single mandate system was eliminated completely such that all Duma deputies are now by law elected only according to party list. As noted later in this chapter, in our discussion of the 2007 parliamentary election results, this served to cement United Russia's dominance of the Duma. Registration requirements for candidates have fluctuated, and become increasingly *ad hoc* such that at the regional and national levels there have been clear efforts to block the participation of candidates deemed undesirable by the Kremlin and local business leaders. Although since 1993, all parliamentary elections occurred as scheduled as prescribed by law and some electoral districts have been redrawn, although not in a radical way, elections have become much less competitive under the system of 'managed' democracy that Putin installed after 2000 in Russia.

The 2000 presidential vote took place three months earlier than planned because Boris Yeltsin suddenly resigned from his office on the last day of the millennium. As prescribed by the law on presidential elections, a new election had to be held three months after Yeltsin's resignation, meaning that the vote was held in March instead of June 2000. All other major rules and practices governing presidential elections, however, have remained stable up to the time of writing. If examining the formal rules and procedures, elections in Russia have become normal, certain events. The predictability of elections and the stability of those institutions run by elected officials in Russia during the last decade stand in sharp contrast to the earlier electoral history from 1989–93, when not a single elected legislative body served out its full term. Formally, the Russian president has the power to disband the Duma under certain circumstances spelled out in the constitution. Since the end of 1993, however, the Russian parliament has never been dissolved.

The Federation Council is the one government body that has experienced volatility in how it is constituted. Originally, as just discussed, deputies to this upper house of parliament were elected in double-mandate districts; in each region in Russia the top two finishers won seats in the Federation Council. After the 1993 vote, however, the rules governing the formation of the Federation Council twice changed dramatically. Before the parliamentary election in 1995, regional executives (presidents in republics and governors in regions and territories) and heads of regional parliaments pushed hard for and succeeded in winning the right for direct elections to their regional offices, followed by automatic appointment to this Federation Council rather than direct elections. Such a formulation gave governors increased local legitimacy and greater autonomy from Yeltsin and Moscow, because elected governors were harder to dismiss than appointed ones. This new formulation also gave governors a direct voice in national legislative affairs, blurring the divisions both between executive and legislative powers and between national and sub-national units of the federal system. This formulation lasted until Vladimir Putin was elected president in the spring of 2000. In one of his first acts as president, Putin pressed for and eventually succeeded in changing the composition of the Federation Council. Instead of elected governors and head of regional parliaments, Putin called on regional executive and legislative heads to appoint representatives to the Federation Council from their regions. In effect, this new procedure for selecting 'senators' made the upper house less powerful, since those serving did not have an electoral mandate. Many members of the upper house had rarely, if ever, visited the regions that they purportedly represented and behaved more like paid lobbyists for their respective provinces, rather than elected representatives.

From uncertain electoral outcomes to one party dominance

From 1993–2007, Russia's electoral rules were relatively certain. Throughout the 1990s, the outcome of these elections, however, remained uncertain. For those interested in the development of Russia's electoral democracy, this was good news, as the presence of stable electoral rules and unpredictable electoral outcomes is the essence of genuine democracy (Przeworski 1991). However, following the Duma elections of 2003, and the increased dominance of Putin's preferred 'party of power', United Russia/Unity, this situation changed notably and dramatically.

The constitutional referendum in December 1993 produced predictable if somewhat contentious results. Not surprisingly, a majority of Russians approved the new constitution. But the vote for the Duma did produce a shocking, unexpected outcome (these and later results are set out in Table 4.1). The pro-reform party affiliated with Yeltsin, Russia's Choice, won only 15 per cent of the popular vote, only a third of what pollsters and analysts had predicted just two months earlier. Even more amazing was the strong showing of Vladimir Zhirinovsky's Liberal Democratic Party of Russia (LDPR), a xenophobic, nationalist organisation that was neither liberal nor democratic. In essence, Russian voters remained divided in rather equal proportions between those who supported Yeltsin's 'reforms' and those that did not. Zhirinovsky's supporters were simply a new, non-communist expression of dissatisfaction with Yeltsin's course. Zhirinovsky's sudden splash created the impression that Russian voters yearned for a fascist resolution to the tumultuous times in which they lived.

The results of the 1995 parliamentary vote were also surprising (the parliament elected in 1993 was an interim body whose term expired after two years, instead of the normal four as prescribed in the constitution). In the two-year interval between the first and second Duma elections, Zhirinovsky's star had waned. Taking advantage of Zhirinovsky's demise was the Communist Party of the Russian Federation (CPRF), which reemerged as the leading force of the anti-Yeltsin coalition. The CPRF made impressive gains, winning almost a quarter of the popular vote and reclaiming its role as the leader of the opposition. Buoyed by party identification on the ballot, CPRF candidates also dominated the single-mandate races. Zhirinovsky won less than half his 1993 total, but still came second, and Prime Minister Viktor Chernomyrdin's Our Home is

Table 4.1 *Elections to the Russian State Duma, 1993–2003*

	1993				1995				1999				2003			
	List %	*List seats*	*SMC seats*	*Total seats*	*List %*	*List seats*	*SMC seats*	*Total seats*	*List %*	*List seats*	*SMC seats*	*Total seats*	*List %*	*List seats*	*SMC seats*	*Total seats*
LDPR	22.9	59	5	64	11.2	50	1	51	6.0	17	0	17	11.5	36	0	36
RC	15.5	40	27	67	3.9	0	9	9	–	–	–	–	–	–	–	–
CPRF	12.4	32	16	48	22.3	99	58	157	24.3	67	46	113	12.6	40	12	52
WR	8.1	21	2	23	4.6	0	3	3	2.0	0	0	0	–	–	–	–
AP	8.0	21	11	33	3.8	0	20	20	–	–	–	–	3.6	0	2	2
Yabloko	7.9	20	6	26	6.9	31	14	45	5.9	16	4	20	4.3	0	4	4
PRUC	6.7	18	1	19	0.4	0	1	1	–	–	–	–	–	–	–	–
DPR	5.5	14	1	15	–	–	–	–	–	–	–	–	0.2	0	0	0
OHR	–	–	–	–	10.1	45	10	55	1.2	0	7	7	–	–	–	–
Unity	–	–	–	–	–	–	–	–	23.3	64	9	73	–	–	–	–
FAR	–	–	–	–	–	–	–	–	13.3	37	31	68	–	–	–	–
URF	–	–	–	–	–	–	–	–	8.5	24	5	29	4.0	0	3	3
UR	–	–	–	–	–	–	–	–	–	–	–	–	37.6	120	105	225
Rodina	–	–	–	–	–	–	–	–	–	–	–	–	9.0	29	8	37
Others	8.7	0	–	–	34.0	0	32	32	12.2	0	9	9	17.2	0	33	33
Indepts	–	–	8	8	–	–	77	77	–	–	105	105	–	–	69	69
Agst all	4.2	–	141	141	2.8	–	–	–	3.3	–	–	–	4.7	–	–	–

Source: Based on Central Electoral Commission.

Party abbreviations are: LDPR: Liberal Democratic Party of Russia (competing, in 1999, as the Zhirinovsky Bloc); RC: Russia's Choice (in 1995, Russia's Democratic Choice); CPRF: Communist Party of the Russian Federation; WR: Women of Russia; AP: Agrarian Party; PRUC: Party of Russian Unity and Concord; DPR: Democratic Party of Russia; OHR: Our Home is Russia; FAR: Fatherland-All Russia; UR: United Russia; URF: Union of Right Forces.

Russia (OHIR) was the only reformist party to break through to double digits. Grigorii Yavlinsky's Yabloko, the self-proclaimed leader of Russia's democratic opposition, dropped almost a full percentage point, and former acting prime minister Yegor Gaidar and his Democratic Choice of Russia (a modified reincarnation of Russia's Choice from 1993) suffered the greatest setback, winning less than a third of its 1993 total. The Kremlin did not orchestrate this election result. On the contrary, Yeltsin aides created, generously funded, and provided massive media coverage to the Our Home is Russia, yet the pro-Kremlin bloc placed a distant third, while outright opponents of those in power scored major gains.

Coming just six months after the Communist comeback in the December 1995 parliamentary elections, the 1996 presidential election also exhibited great uncertainty, especially in the early months of the campaign. President Yeltsin began the New Year with a single-digit approval rating. Support for his policies, such as the Chechnya war, hovered in the low double digits. Russia seemed poised to follow the electoral trajectories in other post-communist countries in which first generation reformers lost their second election to left-of-centre parties.

Yeltsin, however, still enjoyed several advantages over his opponents that eventually helped him win a second term. Perhaps most importantly, Yeltsin was offered the opportunity to campaign yet again against an old-style Communist, CPRF leader Gennadii Zyuganov. The reemergence of the Communist Party as the main opposition force allowed those in power to frame the 1996 election as a referendum between communism and the past versus anti-communism and the future. With the contest framed in this way, Yeltsin could assert that he was the only reform candidate capable of defeating the communist challenge (McFaul 1997).

Yeltsin enjoyed the additional advantage of controlling Russia's two major television stations, ORT and RTR. Both channels broadcast relentlessly pro-Yeltsin and anti-Zyuganov ads, news, talk shows, and 'documentaries'. Russia's third national channel at the time, NTV, was a private company, but its owner, Vladimir Gusinsky, backed Yeltsin, as did all the other business tycoons – the so-called oligarchs – who had made their fortunes during the Yeltsin era. Yeltsin also employed the more traditional tactics of distributing government pork to obtain support from regional heads of administration (Triesman 1998). During the campaign, Yeltsin raised pensions and increased the salaries of government employees. For the first time since 1989, the administrative resources of the state were playing an instrumental role in deciding the outcome of a national election.

In a field of a dozen candidates, Yeltsin barely managed to win more votes than his communist opponent: in the first round he took 35 per cent of the vote, while Zyuganov captured 32 per cent. However, when the vote became a binary choice between the 'communist' and the 'reformer', the vast majority of Russians still favoured moving forward, not backward. In the second round, Yeltsin's entire campaign message painted him as the lesser of two evils. Yeltsin won easily in the second round, winning 54 per cent of the popular vote compared with Zyuganov's 40 per cent. In contrast with electoral trends in many parts of post-communist Europe, Russian voters opted to retain their first democratically elected leader for a second term.

The 1999 Duma elections continued to exhibit the same mix of certainty about the procedures, but uncertainty about the results. In fact, the December 1999 parliamentary election may have been Russia's most competitive in the 1990s, since the ruling elite was openly divided. In the prelude to the 1999 campaign, the combination of the August 1998 financial crash, the subsequent instability in the government, and Yeltsin's declining health created the appearance of weakness and disarray in the Kremlin. Those in power looked vulnerable. Just a year before the presidential election, they had not produced a candidate to replace Yeltsin. The Kremlin's lack of a game plan for staying in power eventually triggered the defection of many considered to be part of the ruling party of power. Moscow mayor Yuri Luzhkov planned to participate in the next electoral cycle as an opposition candidate. Former Prime Minister Yevgenii Primakov joined Luzhkov's coalition, Fatherland-All Russia (OVR), as a step toward winning the 2000 presidential election. At the beginning of the 1999 campaign, Primakov was ahead of all other presidential contenders by a large margin. For the first time in its post-communist history, Russia appeared poised to hand over presidential power from one political group to another through the ballot box.

Those close to Yeltsin in the Kremlin were not going to vacate their fortress without a fight. Because Primakov decided to compete in the 1999 parliamentary vote as a way to build momentum for 2000, his enemies in and close to the Kremlin decided to join the battle against the former prime minister in the parliamentary election as well. As a result, the 1999 election was the first time the federal government became actively involved in a parliamentary contest.

As in the 1996 presidential contest, the state played a tremendous role in shaping the outcome. Working closely with figures in the presidential administration, Russian tycoon Boris Berezovsky helped to invent a new pro-presidential electoral bloc, Unity. State resources contributed to this new electoral bloc, often referred to in the Russian press at the time as a 'virtual' party. Berezovsky hired the best electoral consultants money could buy and then deployed the full force of his ORT television station to promote Unity and destroy OVR. To a lesser degree, RTR assumed a similar mission. ORT newscasters and commentators unleashed the most vicious personal attacks of any Russian campaign against OVR leaders (White, Oates and McAllister 2005).

Indirectly, another arm of the state – the armed forces – contributed to the rise of Unity and the eventual presidential winner, Putin. Russian armed forces responded to an attack by Chechen rebel forces against Dagestan and alleged terrorist attacks against Russian civilians in Moscow and elsewhere by sending forces into Chechnya in September 1999. At the time, Prime Minister Putin had a negligible approval rating; however, the war effort – especially as portrayed on ORT and RTR – was popular, and soon catapulted Putin's popularity into double digits and above all other presidential contenders. Putin in turn endorsed Unity. The blessing of the popular prime minister helped the virtual electoral bloc win nearly a quarter of the popular vote.

The results of the 1999 parliamentary vote radically altered the balance of power within the Duma and determined the winner of the 2000 presidential race. As in 1995, the CPRF won the largest percentage of any party, 24 per cent, an outcome that ensured Zyuganov a second-place finish yet again in the presidential contest the next year. Unity came second with 23 per cent, followed by OVR in a distant third place with a vote that was so disappointing that Primakov decided not to run in the 2000 presidential election. The newly revamped liberal coalition, the Union of Right Forces (SPS), surprised many by winning more than 8 per cent of the popular vote, almost double the total of its chief liberal rival, Yabloko. Zhirinovsky's Liberal Democratic Party of Russia continued to fade, winning only 6 per cent of the party list vote and just barely crossing the 5 per cent threshold.

When the distribution of seats from single-mandate races was added into the equation, the balance of power within the parliament had moved in a decisively pro-Putin direction. The Communist Party still controlled a solid minority of seats, but it could not construct opposition majorities to Kremlin initiatives. The combination of a loyal Unity, a divided and weakened Communist Party, a sometimes supportive SPS, and strong backing from independents and other smaller factions produced a parliament supportive of Putin on major issues – an outcome that few would have predicted just a year earlier.

The Putin era: the rise of one man and one party dominance

The results of the 1999 parliamentary election made clear that Putin was going to win the 2000 presidential election. Upon naming Putin prime minister in August 1999, Yeltsin had hinted that he hoped Putin would replace him as president the following year. Yeltsin gave his heir one last boost by resigning as president on 31 December 1999, an act that moved the date of the presidential election from June to March. As Putin's popularity peaked in January and slowly declined until election day in March, Yeltsin's decision to resign was critical in helping Putin win the 2000 presidential election in the first round.

During the abbreviated campaign period in 2000, Putin continued to enjoy the unequivocal support of ORT and RTR. Though Putin did not run an official campaign, which he considered demeaning for a sitting president, these television stations continued to document his every move in glowing terms. His opponents, by contrast, received no attention at all from these Kremlin-friendly media outlets. Most oligarchs and regional heads of administration also stumbled over each other in trying to show their support for Putin, since everyone knew he was going to win. And they were right to jump on board since Putin won in a landslide, winning more than half of the popular vote in the first ballot, compared to 24 per cent for the runner up, Communist candidate Zyuganov.

Unity's surge in 1999 and then Putin's victory in 2000 marked the beginning of the Kremlin's dominance over national electoral politics in Russia. Throughout the 1990s, electoral support for Yeltsin and his allies always seemed precarious. Yeltsin orchestrated a dramatic comeback to win reelection in 1996, but parliamentary votes both before and after 1996 demonstrated that support for Yeltsin's policies was soft. The volatility in voter preferences in 1999, expressed in opinion polls during the campaign, suggested that the traditional cleavage among voters between 'democrats' and 'communists' had faded as the central driver of Russian electoral politics. Beginning in the 1999–2000 electoral cycle, Putin offered a different reason to support his party and his candidacy – stability. After a decade of chaotic revolutionary change, Russian citizens yearned for it. With the exception of the ongoing war in Chechnya, Putin delivered it. The Russian economy grew more in each year of Putin's first term in office than in all of the previous decade. Voters did not care whether this growth was due to Putin's economic reforms, which were substantial, or to the combination of high oil prices and low international interest rates. Putin got the credit regardless. More generally, Putin's positive rating as a leader hovered well above 70 per cent for his entire first term. In contrast to Yeltsin, Putin appeared to be a young and able leader who showed up for work every day and made Russians proud again of their president and their country.

It was not surprising, therefore, that Putin and his allies won again in the 2003 parliamentary elections and the 2004 presidential elections. In December 2003, his party – United Russia (the latest incarnation of Unity from 1999) – won a major victory, capturing more than a third of the popular vote on the party list and winning more than a hundred of the single-mandate contests. Two other parties close to the Kremlin also performed well beyond expectations: Zhirinovsky's LDPR doubled its total from the 1999 parliamentary election, winning 11.5 per cent of the popular vote. The other Kremlin-friendly party to cross the threshold on the party list, with 9.2 per cent of the popular vote, was *Rodina* (Motherland), a loose coalition of nationalist and left-of-centre politicians that the Kremlin helped to organise and then advertise over the course of the campaign. After the vote and after independents lined up behind different factions in the Duma, United Russia and its allies controlled the two-thirds majority needed to pass amendments to the constitution.

While the pro-Kremlin parties surged in 2003, the main opposition parties on both the left and right faltered. On the left, the CPRF lost half of its party-list vote from 1999, and managed only eleven victories in single-member districts. As a result, the CPRF faction in the Duma shrank by 61 seats, falling from 113 in 1999 to 52 in 2003. Liberal opponents of the Kremlin fared even worse than their comrades on the left. Both Yabloko and the Union of Right Forces (SPS) failed to cross the 5 per cent threshold. In the single-mandate contests, Yabloko won only four seats, while candidates affiliated with SPS won three seats. For the first time since competitive elections began in 1990, the liberals had no faction in the parliament. To varying degrees, all three parliamentary parties that increased their share of the popular vote since the 1999 election supported Putin and enjoyed support from the state. All three parties that criticised Putin (and hence did not enjoy state support) fared worse in 2003 than they had in 1999. By 2007, Yabloko and SPS would be effectively eliminated from the Duma.

The overwhelming victory of United Russia in the Duma elections made it clear that Putin would win the presidential ballot without any difficulty. Indeed, Putin's reelection was so certain that none of the party leaders who competed in the December parliamentary vote ran as presidential candidates in March. Zhirinovsky, Communist Gennadii Zyuganov, Yabloko leader Grigorii Yavlinsky, and SPS leader Boris Nemtsov all stepped aside, and let other lesser-known figures in their parties run in vain against Putin. In March, Putin won on the first ballot, capturing more than 71 per cent of the popular vote. The Communist Party candidate Nikolai Kharitonov came a distant second with 13.7 per cent. Former Motherland leader Sergei Glaz'ev came in third with 4.1 per cent; Irina Khakamada of the SPS garnered only 3.8 per cent; the LDPR candidate, Zhirinovsky bodyguard Oleg Malyshkin, managed just 2.0 per cent; and Putin backer and Russian Party of Life candidate Sergei

Mironov trailed the field with 0.7 per cent, well behind 'against all', the choice of 3.4 per cent of those who went to the polls.

By December 2007, and the most recent elections to the Duma, Russian voters had clearly lost the meaningful right to choose their leaders. In 2007, the Russian Duma was elected according to party list votes alone with an increased threshold, now 7 per cent. This effectively eliminated smaller, liberal parties like Yabloko and SPS, which had done better in single mandate than list voting, where they had barely cleared the previously required 5 per cent barrier for representation, from parliament. Further, the changes to campaign laws in late 2006 included restrictions of political parties on using airtime on television to campaign against other candidates and parties. The law also eliminated the minimum voter turnout requirement for elections at both national, local, and regional levels, such that even elections with a turnout of, for example 10 per cent or less, will be counted as valid.

The effect of these changes and some tougher party, candidate and voter registration requirements was another stunning victory for United Russia, which garnered more than 64 per cent of the popular vote, translating into 315 seats of the 450 seat Duma (see Table 4.2). For the first time, Vladimir Putin's name appeared on the United Party list – indeed, it was the only name on the list, and given his high personal popularity rating as president, this undoubtedly help fuel United Russia's big win. The CPRF received a respectable, although relatively meagre 11.6 per cent of the popular vote, which translated into 57 seats. LDPR followed

Table 4.2   *The Russian Duma election of 2 December 2007*

Name	Vote	Share of vote (%)	Seats
United Russia	44,714,241	64.30	315
Communist Party of the Russian Federation	8,046,886	11.57	57
Liberal-Democratic Party of Russia	5,660,823	8.14	40
Fair Russia: <u>Rodina</u>/Pensioners/Life	5,383,639	7.74	38
[7 per cent threshold]			
Agrarian Party of Russia	1,600,234	2.30	
Yabloko	1,108,985	1.59	
Civic Force	733,604	1.05	
Union of Right Forces	669,444	0.96	
Patriots of Russia	615,417	0.89	
Party of Social Justice	154,083	0.22	
Democratic Party of Russia	89,780	0.13	
Invalid votes	759,929	1.09	

Source: Based on Central Electoral Commission communiqué in *Vestnik Tsentral'noi izbiratel'noi komissii*, No. 19(222), 2007, pp. 5–22. The registered electorate was 109,145,517, or whom 69,537,065 cast a valid or invalid ballot (63.71 per cent).

with 8.1 per cent of the vote, giving Zhirinovsky's party 40 seats in the Duma, while Just (or Fair) Russia, a new party created shortly before the elections and strongly backed by the Kremlin as the second half of what was then envisioned as two party system (with United Russia), received 7.7 per cent of the vote or 38 seats. These were the only four parties to gain representation in the Duma, since single mandate seats had been eliminated and also the phenomenon of independents gaining representation in the Duma (in the previous election approximately 100 Duma seats had been occupied by independents). Moreover, the unsurpassed dominance of United Russia, along with the election in March 2008 of his protégé Dmitri Medvedev, truly cemented Putin's control of both the legislative and executive branches of government.

A political transition that did not bring about any change

Dmitri Medvedev was elected in March 2008 in the most highly managed political event in Russia's post-communist history. He was nominated to the position in December 2007, days after Unity's overwhelming victory in the Duma elections. Sure enough, upon accepting the nomination, Medvedev immediately announced his intention to run for the presidency only if Putin, his long time political mentor, would serve as his prime minister should he win. Putin consented to do so, and this afforded him the opportunity of staying in control of government without having to amend the Russian constitution to allow him to have a third term as President.

Even with Putin's personal seal of approval, no measure was spared in ensuring Medvedev's resounding victory in the presidential elections on 2 March 2008 (see Table 4.3). He faced no real opposition, his image flooded Russian television, and news of his and Putin's travels around the country dominated the largely now state-controlled Russian print media. Huge billboards picturing Putin and Medvedev walking shoulder to shoulder into Russia's evidently glorious future loomed over city squares – the largest of all on Manezh Square, just outside the Kremlin in Moscow. In case voters didn't get the message: Medvedev would continue the good times and good policies of his mentor, Vladimir Putin. Russian citizens were exhorted to vote at every turn – receiving reminders by text message and even on the back of Moscow metro tickets – since poor voter turnout might delegitimise what was correctly expected to be an overwhelming mandate for Medvedev – remarkable for someone running for elective office for the first time in his life – and Putin, by extension. Medvedev won convincingly with more than 70 per cent of the vote (just one per cent less

Table 4.3   *The Russian presidential election of 2 March 2008*

Name	Nominated by	Vote	%
Dmitri Medvedev	United Russia	52,530,712	70.28
Gennadii Zyuganov	Communist Party of the Russian Federation	13,243,550	17.72
Vladimir Zhirinovsky	Liberal-Democratic Party of Russia	6,988,510	9.35
Andrei Bogdanov	Independent	968,344	1.30
Invalid votes		1,105,533	1.36

Source: Based on Central Electoral Commission communiqué in *Rossiiskaya gazeta*, 8 March 2008, p. 1. The registered electorate was 107,222,016, of whom 74,746,649 (69.71 per cent) cast a valid or invalid ballot.

than Putin had won in 2004). The resurrected Communist leader, Gennadii Zyuganov, was second, followed by perennial presidential candidate and leader of the LDPR, Vladimir Zhirinovsky, and Andrei Bogdanov, a lightweight character thought to have been financed and parachuted into the election by the Kremlin to make the race look more competitive.

State limits on the electoral playing field

Given the president's popularity, it is hard to imagine how Putin and his surrogates could have lost free and fair elections from 2003 onward. We can only speculate about the results of free and fair elections, however, because the actual elections have taken place in a context that did not offer a level playing field. Instead, Putin's regime limited opportunities for political challengers while at the same it provided Putin, and then Medvedev, and their preferred party, United Russia, with virtually unlimited 'administrative resources' to wield during the campaign. To be sure, Putin did not inherit a consolidated democracy from Boris Yeltsin. At the end of Yeltsin's rule, Russia's democratic institutions were still weak (McFaul 2001). Nonetheless, Putin did little to strengthen democratic institutions and much to weaken them (McFaul, Petrov and Ryabov 2004; McFaul and Stoner-Weiss 2008).

First, Putin and his government initiated a series of successful campaigns against independent media outlets. When Putin came to power, only three television networks had the national reach to really count in politics – ORT, RTR, and NTV. By running billionaire Boris Berezovsky out of the country with a politically motivated criminal prosecution, Putin effectively acquired control of ORT, the channel with the biggest national audience. RTR was always fully state-owned, and so it was even easier to tame. Controlling the third channel, NTV, proved more difficult since its owner, Vladimir Gusinsky, decided to fight. But in the end, he too lost not only NTV but also the daily newspaper *Segodnya* and the weekly *Itogi* when prosecutors pressed charges. When the parliamentary campaign started, the Kremlin *de facto* controlled all television networks with a national reach. This continued through the 2007 and 2008 electoral cycles.

At the same time, the independence of electronic media eroded on the regional level. Heads of local state-owned television stations continue to follow political signals from regional executives, and most regional heads of administration stood firmly behind Putin in the last electoral cycle. Private and cable stations steer clear of political analysis altogether. Dozens of newspapers and web portals have remained independent and offer a platform for political figures of all persuasions, but none of these platforms enjoys mass audiences. Moreover, Putin changed the atmosphere for doing journalistic work. When journalists criticised his policies, such as the war in Chechnya or his handling the sinking of the submarine *Kursk* in 2000, he called them traitors. Similarly, during the August war with Georgia over South Ossetia and Abkhazia, critics of the Russian side were hard to find in the Russian press. As we note in Chapter 7, media independence eroded so significantly during Putin's first term that Freedom House downgraded Russia's media from Partly Free to Not Free, and it has maintained that rating every year since 2005. Reporters without Borders, which published their first worldwide press-freedom index in 2002, ranked Russia 121st out of 139 countries assessed (just one ranking above Iran), making it one of the worst performers in the post-communist world. The Committee to Protect Journalists accorded Russia the dubious distinction of being one of the ten worst places in the world to be a journalist.

Given these changes, the media has come to play a very different role in elections than they had in the 1990s. During the campaign for the 1999 parliamentary elections, Russian elites supported different electoral blocs: OVR or Unity. Russia's national media outlets lined up on both sides of this divide. ORT and RTR backed Unity, while Gusinsky's NTV as well as Luzhkov's Moscow television station TV–Tsentr and several other regional stations backed OVR. The playing field was not equal, but opposing points of view were represented in the national electronic media. In the 2003 and 2007 parliamentary votes and 2004 and 2008 presidential elections, by contrast, the Kremlin controlled all the major national television stations, and because most regional elites were now united behind Putin and then Putin and Medvedev, the vast majority of regional stations (including Moscow's TV–Centre) also sided with pro-Kremlin candidates.

A second important political change carried out on Putin's watch was 'regional reforms' and these have remained in place since he moved from the presidency to the prime minister's office. Almost immediately after becoming president in 2000, Putin made reining in Russia's regional barons a top priority. As we discuss more fully in Chapters 9 and 10, he began his campaign to reassert Moscow's authority by establishing seven supra-regional districts headed primarily by former generals and KGB officers. These new super-governors were assigned the task of taking control of all federal agencies in their jurisdictions, many of which had developed affinities if not loyalties to regional governments during the Yeltsin era. These seven representatives of federal executive authority also investigated governors and presidents of republics as a way of undermining their autonomy and threatening them into subjugation. As already discussed, Putin also emasculated the Federation Council, and regional leaders who resisted his authority found elections rigged against them.

These reforms regarding the distribution of power between Moscow and the regions had important consequences for national elections in 2003 and 2004 and 2007 and 2008 beyond that. Wielding carrots and sticks, the Kremlin eliminated the serious divisions among regional elites that had created the main drama of the 1999 parliamentary elections. By late 2003, almost all regional leaders were supporting Putin and United Russia. These regional executives also deployed their local resources to support United Russia candidates in the single-mandate district races. By 2007, there was no effective opposition to United Russia in the provinces, and governors were encouraged to deliver votes for the party and then for Medvedev in the presidential elections of 2008.

A third context-changing initiative by the Putin regime was a crackdown on the oligarchs. Very early in his first term, Putin made clear that the oligarchs could no longer treat the state as simply another tool to be used for their personal enrichment. Instead, Putin implied that the oligarchs had to get out of politics altogether. Eventually, he arrested or chased into exile three major oligarchs – Boris Berezovsky, Vladimir Gusinsky, and Russia's richest man, Mikhail Khodorkovsky, head of the oil conglomerate Yukos. All three had previously played significant roles in funding and supporting political parties and individuals not deemed loyal to the Kremlin. The marginalisation of these three sent a chilling message to other tycoons. In the 2003 parliamentary campaign, oligarchs continued to contribute significant resources to political campaigns, but only as sanctioned by the Kremlin. Compared to the previous electoral cycle, big business in 2003 was relatively united in backing United Russia and other pro-Kremlin candidates. In 2004, everyone backed Putin and in

2008, the best way to demonstrate continued support for Putin was to back Medvedev.

The absence of independence or internal divisions within media, regional elite, and oligarchic ranks reduced the freedom to manoeuvre for opposition political parties and candidates in elections since 2003. At the same time, the state's larger role in this electoral cycle gave incumbents enormous advantages, be it positive, continuous, and free national television coverage, massive logistical and administrative support from regional executives, or enormous financial resources from companies like Gazprom and Lukoil. Before the legislative balloting, the Organisation for Security and Cooperation in Europe (OSCE) issued its first-ever critical preliminary report on a Russian election, ruling that the State Duma elections had failed to meet many OSCE and Council of Europe commitments for democratic elections. In 2007, the OSCE refused to send a delegation to observe the Russian elections for parliament because representatives of the Office for Democratic Institutions and Human Rights (ODIHR) maintained that they were issued an invitation to observe so close to the elections that they could not field a meaningful mission of electoral observers. The OSCE also did not field a monitoring team for the 2008 presidential elections, asserting that the Russian government was insisting on too many restrictions on the monitoring team that observers would not be able to do an effective job. Although none of Russia's previous elections was wholly free and fair, the most recent ones have been the least free and fair of all.

Conclusion: do elections still matter?

In the last years of the Soviet Union and the first years of independent Russia, elections helped to weaken or remove communist incumbents and open political opportunities for non-communist challengers. In the context of social, political, and economic upheaval, elections in the USSR and then Russia often were convoked to serve an immediate political purpose. They were not simply ways to choose leaders, but were used and manipulated in the heat of battle over such major issues as the fate of the Soviet Union or the course of economic reform.

Since 1993, national elections were more regular and anticipated events conducted in the context of a widely accepted constitutional system. However, stability in the electoral calendar and electoral procedures have been paralleled by increasing stability in the outcomes of elections. The most powerful office in the country – the presidency – has not seen a true turnover of power: Medvedev has clearly governed in the shadow of his prime minister, mentor, and sometime boss, former

President Putin. The landslide victory of the party of power in the 2003 and 2007 parliamentary elections and the 2004 and 2008 presidential elections marked a new milestone in demonstrating how elections could be easily manipulated to maintain and strengthen the group of elites already in power.

In democracies all over the world, incumbents enjoy tremendous electoral advantages. For instance, in the 2002 elections for the US House of Representatives, incumbents seeking reelection won 98 per cent of the time. Before the election, fewer than 30 of the 435 races were even considered competitive. Parties of power have remained in power for decades in countries widely regarded as liberal democracies.

Nonetheless, the way in which Russian elites have begun to deploy state resources to stay in power represents a greater challenge to the democratic process than some of these other examples of incumbent entrenchment in liberal democracies. The imbalance in resources of the state compared to resources controlled by society give those already in power a tremendous and unfair advantage. The state's growing role in determining who gets on the ballot and who does not is an especially disturbing trend. The trajectory over the last fifteen or so years in Russia has been clear – a growing role for the state in determining electoral outcomes.

At the same time, the elimination of elections is unlikely, since too many actors are interested in preserving the process. The political elite need elections in their present form to legitimise their rule. International norms also place pressure on the Russian elite to continue the formal practice of elections. Moreover, polls indicate that very solid majorities of Russian citizens believe that their leaders should be elected (Colton and McFaul 2003).

Consequently, elections are likely to perform a quasi-democratic function in Russia for the foreseeable future. Elections in which several parties and multiple candidates participate (but don't exactly compete) will continue to occur, though the party of power – currently called United Russia – is likely to win these contests thanks to monopoly control over national television, and solid backing from most regional elites. In close elections they also are likely to benefit from the control of those state institutions that have demonstrated a capacity to falsify elections.

Elections of limited consequence, however, are perhaps still better than no elections at all. And as dictators in Kenya and Serbia recently learned, elections can unexpectedly change from a charade into a much more meaningful procedure during periods of crises. In Russia today, elections have less meaning than they did several years ago. In a time of crisis, they might acquire meaning again.

Chapter 5

Russia's Political Parties and their Substitutes

HENRY E. HALE

Many observers expected Russia to develop a competitive party system rapidly after the USSR broke apart in late 1991. Russia was democratising, the argument went, and the experience of Western countries had given experts little reason to question Max Weber's classic aphorism that democracy was 'unimaginable' without parties (Weber 1990). Russian developments quickly challenged this view, however. A plethora of parties did spring up during the 1990s, with as many as 43 appearing on the parliamentary ballot in 1995 alone, but by the end of that decade their growth had stalled. Independent politicians continued to dominate the country's most important posts. For example, only 3 per cent of Russia's regional leaders, when running for re-election, chose to do so as party nominees between 1995 and 2000. Likewise, President Boris Yeltsin himself consistently declined to join any party after leaving the Communist Party of the Soviet Union (CPSU) in 1990.

In the 2000s, Russia's party system did finally begin to take shape, but with a major twist. Putin instituted a series of reforms that weakened the most important pre-existing parties and corralled a majority of the most influential independent politicians into a new pro-Putin organisation called United Russia. Almost all governors are currently affiliated with United Russia, and by 2008 that party commanded majorities in the national parliament and nearly all regional legislatures. Despite this, United Russia's growth has never quite reached the point of complete dominance, even in the government. Thus while Dmitri Medvedev became the first party nominee ever to win the Russian presidency, he refused actually to become a member of the party. Former President and current Prime Minister Vladimir Putin similarly agreed to become 'chairman' of United Russia in 2008, but declared that even this did not mean he would actually be a party 'member'. Some have asked, how strong can a party be if its own top patrons will not fully commit themselves to it? Moreover, there is evidence that the Kremlin (that is, Russia's president and his close associates) continues to keep a stable of other parties 'in reserve' that can be used either to attack true opposition parties or perhaps one day replace United Russia if something goes wrong.

How did this situation come about, and what does the answer tell us about how politics works in Russia? This is the subject of the pages that follow.

The building blocks of Russian parties

Why would any politician ever bother joining a party in the first place? One short answer is: a politician will join a party when that party gives the candidate a greater chance of getting elected than he or she would have as an independent. Parties in Russia, and arguably everywhere, generally offer candidates at least two kinds of advantages. First, they can provide a candidate with money, organisation, connections, and other *resources* that can be used to campaign or otherwise win office. Second, they can connect a candidate with a set of ideas that the party has a *reputation* for pursuing, helping a candidate reach out to people who may support the party's ideas but who may not know anything about the candidate. Politicians who are rich in either resources or reputation, therefore, tend to be particularly successful party builders because they have something that other ambitious politicians want. These things, resources and reputation, are thus the building blocks of parties.

What building blocks were available to would-be party builders in Russia upon the USSR's demise? The only pre-existing party with any claim to have stood the test of time was the CPSU, but in the wake of the August 1991 coup attempt it was banned along with its Russian branch. Even in its heyday, it was mostly an instrument of control rather than a party geared for actually competing in free elections. Moreover, by 1991, its central Marxist ideas were widely discredited and it had been losing members since CPSU leader Mikhail Gorbachev started seriously reforming the Soviet system. Nevertheless, the party did leave behind some significant networks of true believers and people who had forged important personal connections that could eventually be reactivated for organising a party.

Once Gorbachev began reforming the Soviet political system in earnest, and even before parties other than the CPSU were formally legalised in early 1990, a huge number of 'informal' organisations sprang up to promote various political causes. Flush with the opportunity to publicly pursue almost any political agenda openly, these associations were extremely diverse and generally small, often focusing on the pet issues of all and sundry politicians. Some of these grassroots groupings did begin to coalesce into larger associations, with the most prominent being Democratic Russia. During the late *perestroika* period, Democratic Russia looked like it could successfully rival the Russian branch of the declining CPSU and was able to mobilise hundreds of thousands of people in some of Moscow's largest street rallies ever. But this was an extraordinarily motley movement, united almost solely by a common desire to end communist rule. Once the USSR broke apart, it splintered and left little in the way of reputation and resources for future party builders to utilise.

By far the most important source of building blocks for Russia's first party system was the Soviet state itself. In fact, almost every non-communist politician who has built a truly successful Russian party gained his or her primary fame or other party-building resource through some connection with the state structures of the USSR or the Russian Federation. Upon reflection, this is not surprising: the Soviet state penetrated nearly all aspects of life in some way and explicitly sought to own or at least control all the means by which someone could accumulate political influence, including mass media, social organisations, and, as Marxist ideology dictated, economic resources (including all enterprises and banking institutions). Even after political liberalisation removed most controls over political activity, the state remained overwhelmingly the greatest source of money, organisation, and media attention, which are among the most valuable building blocks for parties. Even after Yeltsin's governments privatised the bulk of Russia's economy in the 1990s, business (including the media it controlled) still remained highly dependent on aspects of the state for its profitability. All this meant that people within or connected to the state had major advantages in building the first non-communist parties. It also meant that people within the state continued to have tremendous resources that could be used against party-building projects that they did not like or to support parties that served their purposes.

The next two sections show how this particular array of building blocks translated into the party system that characterises Russia today.

The veteran parties: those first emerging in the early 1990s

Researchers have found that the outcome of a country's first multiparty elections, often called 'founding elections', can have a disproportionate long-run impact on how its party system develops (O'Donnell and Schmitter 1986: 61–2). This is because the parties that win gain the visibility, opportunities to impact policy, and access to resources that political office brings. These gains, in turn, can be ploughed back into the party-building project, giving the initial winners a great advantage in future rounds. Winners also gain an advantage just for being seen as winners: voters and potential donors generally do not want to risk wasting votes or money on parties that will not be able to 'pay a return' on the investment by holding office (Cox 1997).

The specialists who initially authored Russia's current Constitution in 1993, empowered after Yeltsin unilaterally abrogated the old Constitution and called early elections late that year, were well aware of research on the importance of founding elections. They were also aware of other research indicating that the results of such elections would depend heavily on the election rules that they themselves chose. They thus chose the rules strategically in order to pursue certain concrete goals. One of these goals was to buttress the power of Yeltsin and his allies while another was explicitly to promote the development of a multiparty system. A complex set of compromises ultimately produced a system that was expected to have mixed effects on the party system (Colton and Hough 1998; McFaul 2001). It was to be dominated by a strong president, and here no special advantage was given to candidates who wished to run as party nominees.

The constitutional drafters did, however, plan for the parliament to spur party-system development. While an upper chamber (the Federation Council) was to represent regions on a largely non-party basis, half of the lower chamber (the State Duma) was to be elected through a competition between nationwide party lists with a 5 per cent threshold. This effectively reserved at least half of the Duma's seats for parties capable of winning this proportion of the nationwide vote. The other half of the Duma was to be chosen in 225 districts, with one deputy elected per seat. While parties could compete for these seats too, in fact independents frequently won them. Regional authorities were left the freedom to determine their own rules for local elections. This basic setup remained in place until the 2007 elections.

Since the first presidential election to take place under the new Constitution did not occur until 1996, observers at the time saw the 1993 Duma elections as potentially being a founding election for Russia's post-Soviet party system. The passage of time reveals that these elections did have something of a 'founding' effect, but only in a specific sense: parties that failed to clear the 5 per cent threshold in the Duma race proved unable ever afterward to make it into parliament. The only parties capable of breaking into the Duma for the first time after 1993 have been those with the unusually strong backing of incumbent state authorities. There were only two of these 'upstarts' in the parliament by 2009: United Russia and A Just Russia. At the same time, success in 1993 proved no guarantee of long-term success. In effect, subsequent Duma elections served as what might be called 'weeding elections', successively winnowing down the field until by 2009 only two veteran parties remained in the parliament: the Communist Party of the Russian Federation (CPRF) and the Liberal Democratic Party of Russia (LDPR). The following paragraphs tell the story of the veteran parties, those first gaining traction in the founding elections of 1993. After that, we turn to the upstart parties. Readers are directed to Table 5.1 for summary information on Russia's most important parties from 1993 to 2009.

One-hit wonders

Among the eight parties to win official delegations ('factions') in the party-list Duma elections of 1993, four were never able to repeat the feat on their own: the Agrarian Party of Russia (APR), the Women of Russia bloc, the Democratic Party of Russia (DPR, an early breakaway from Democratic Russia), and the pro-Yeltsin Party of Russian Unity and Accord (PRES). All of them have since disappeared from Russia's political scene, though Kremlin supporters temporarily resurrected the APR and DPR 'brands' for various purposes. These purposes are said by some to include providing at least the superficial appearance of a 'democratic' candidate in the 2008 presidential election (where little-known DPR leader Andrei Bogdanov garnered about 1 per cent of the ballot) or dividing the leftist vote to weaken the Communists (as some say was the Agrarians' role in the 2007 Duma election). By late 2008 the APR had dissolved itself into United Russia and the DPR had merged with two other parties to found the pro-Kremlin 'Right Cause' party (more on this below).

The Communist Party of the Russian Federation

It is a common mistake to regard the CPRF as the direct continuation of the CPSU in Russia. In fact, Yeltsin banned the Russian branch of the CPSU in 1991 and confiscated its property. Even when the Constitutional Court effectively reinstated it at the end of November 1992, there was no longer any organisation in place to reclaim its mantle. Instead, there was a wide variety of small Communist organisations that were led by little-known former officials that had formed after the ban, all now competing for at least a share of the inheritance. Moreover, it was a decidedly non-communist idea (at least, according to Karl Marx) that enabled a little-known former CPSU official, Gennadii Zyuganov, to wind up as the heir. This idea was nationalism. During 1991 and 1992, he crafted a distinct ideology of nationalist socialism that helped cement a broad alliance of former communists and hardline non-communist Russian nationalists that proved able to mobilise tens of thousands in street protests. Such

Table 5.1 *Post-Soviet Russia's main parties*

Party	Main leaders	Years in Duma[1]	Main policy stands	Attitude to Kremlin	% loyalists in population 2008[2]	Party status 2009
United Russia[3]	Vladimir Putin, Boris Gryzlov	1999 –	Anticommunism, presidentialism, moderate pro-Westernism	Pro-Kremlin	30	Duma supermajority, Prime Ministership
CPRF	Gennadii Zyuganov	1993 –	Socialism, nationalism	Anti-Kremlin	8	Duma minority
LDPR	Vladimir Zhirinovsky	1993 –	Nationalism, law and order	Loyal opposition	4	Duma minority
A Just Russia	Sergei Mironov	2003 –	Moderate leftism	Loyal opposition	2	Duma minority
Yabloko	Sergei Mitrokhin, Grigorii Yavlinsky	1993–2003	Democracy, social market, pro-Westernism	Anti-Kremlin	< 2	Delegations in some regional legislatures
Right Cause[4]	Leonid Gozman, Georgii Bovt, Boris Titov, Anatolii Chubais	1993–5, 1999–2003	Liberal economy, pro-Westernism, democracy	Pro-Kremlin 1993–2007, anti-Kremlin 2007–8, pro-Kremlin 2008–9	< 2	Delegations in some regional legislatures
OHR	Viktor Chernomyrdin	1995–9	Anti-communism, moderate pro-Westernism	Pro-Kremlin	–	Merged into UR
FAR	Yuri Luzhkov, Yevgenii Primakov	1999–2003[5]	Moderate leftism, moderate nationalism	Anti-Kremlin	–	Merged into UR

[1] Official delegation earned in party-list competition. First year includes year of election.
[2] According to Colton-Hale-McFaul survey conducted after the March 2008 presidential elections, using Colton's (2000) measure of 'transitional partisanship'.
[3] Or its predecessor, Unity Bloc.
[4] Or its predecessors Russia's Choice, Russia's Democratic Choice, and SPS.
[5] Even after FAR merged with UR in 2002, the official FAR fraction remained registered until the next Duma was seated.

impressive displays of support, combined with fears that communism alone might not be potent enough to win many votes after the USSR's break-up, led key former CPSU leaders to hitch their wagons to Zyuganov's locomotive. This, then, was the origin of the Communist Party of the Russian Federation, which officially emerged in early 1993 after the Constitutional Court had ruled it would be legal. Once the CPRF gained a surprisingly high 12 per cent in the snap 1993 Duma election, the only leftist party to clear the 5 per cent barrier, it consolidated its position as the primary heir to the CPSU legacy and quickly reintegrated many of the CPSU networks that had fallen apart in 1991.

The party reached the pinnacle of its influence in 1996, when Zyuganov took Yeltsin to a second round in the presidential contest of that year and failed only after Yeltsin's allies resorted to media manipulation and other methods of machine politics to achieve their victory. The party also captured a large share of governorships and controlled many regional legislatures, especially in the 'red belt' of Russia's southwest. Then as now, the party was no longer calling for a return to full-blown communism, accepting a significant role for private enterprise and making democracy a central element of its platform. Rather ironically, the CPRF had actually become the primary source of political competition in Russia by the 2007–8 election cycle. Despite having its support nearly halved by a negative media campaign in 2003, it remained the only party with a large and independent following that had a hope of standing up to United Russia. While in the 1990s it drew significant financing from big business, which hoped to minimise its losses should the CPRF happen to win, by 2007–8 it had come to rely mostly on some modest state funding now allocated by law to large parties and on donations of time and money from its still-large pool of dedicated (if aging) members.

The divided liberals: Right Cause and Yabloko

Yeltsin's supporters repeatedly urged him to personally lead a party that could withstand the revival of the communists, but Yeltsin consistently refused, fearing that leading a party would alienate other voters and limit his room for political manoeuvre. That did not stop him from backing efforts by his key loyalists to build parties to support him, his market-oriented reforms, and his relatively pro-Western foreign policy orientation. In 1993 the new Russia's Choice party became the first 'party of power', led by Yeltsin's economic reform architect Yegor Gaidar and backed by the administrative resources of the Russian presidency. Initially expected to win a large majority in the glow of Yeltsin's 1993 victory over 'hardliners' in the shelled Congress, its party list netted a shockingly low 16 per cent due to dissatisfaction with the ongoing economic collapse and

Yeltsin's violent suppression of the parliament. Yeltsin effectively cut the party loose and it splintered, dropping out of the Duma altogether in 1995. It returned in 1999 by combining with a few fresher faces under the label Union of Right Forces (SPS) and by openly supporting the highly popular Putin for the presidency. The SPS ultimately flew too close to Putin's sun, however. Once Putin had adopted many of the market reforms the party had been pushing and the economy started actually to grow, it was the most clearly Putinite party, United Russia, that claimed and won the credit in voters' eyes. In 2007, the SPS sought to distinguish itself from United Russia by blasting Putin's authoritarian turn, but this rang hollow to many in light of its recent support for Putin and its backing of the not-very-democratic Yeltsin. After Kremlin-controlled media trained a blistering negative campaign on the SPS in late 2007, the party became widely seen as on the verge of collapse. Corporate conglomerates, which were often creations of Yeltsin-era privatisation and a key source of party financing, virtually halted donations for fear of drawing Kremlin ire upon their businesses. Hardly anyone by 2008 considered themselves an SPS loyalist. Thus few complained when the Kremlin made SPS an 'offer it could not refuse'. SPS accepted, shedding its most outspoken opposition-oriented leaders and merging with two other parties (Civic Force and the DPR) to form the pro-Kremlin Right Cause party in late 2008.

The Yabloko party followed a similar trajectory between 1993 and 2009, though clung to its independence. The party was founded by economist Grigorii Yavlinsky, who gained fame as a market reformer in the Yeltsin government just before the USSR's break-up. After Yeltsin abandoned Yavlinsky's reform plan for Gaidar's, Yavlinsky united pro-market, pro-Western, and pro-democracy politicians who thought that Yeltsin had actually undermined these ideals by his methods, with the 1990s economic collapse being important evidence. These stands and Yavlinsky's personal appeal to highly educated voters helped earn Yabloko (an acronym for the party's founders that literally means 'apple') representation in every Duma between 1993 and 2003, winning 5–8 per cent on each occasion. Its undoing was its complicated relationship with the oligarchs, the Kremlin, and the SPS. Opposing the Kremlin, it softened its critique to avoid banishment. Opposing the oligarchs, it had to take money from some of them (including Yukos chairman Mikhail Khodorkovsky) to finance a viable campaign. Opposing Yeltsin's reforms and hence the SPS, the SPS responded by simultaneously attacking it and calling Yabloko the main obstacle to integration of the 'democratic' camp in Russia. Khodorkovsky's dramatic arrest on the eve of the 2003 election not only exposed Yabloko's relationship to this controversial figure, but also eliminated its main source of funding. The party has not recovered and can claim only a handful of loyalists as of 2009.

The Liberal Democratic Party of Russia (LDPR) of Vladimir Zhirinovsky

Vladimir Zhirinovsky first burst onto the national political scene in June 1991, during presidential elections for the Russian Republic of the not-yet-disintegrated USSR. The fact that someone could win 8 per cent of the vote and come in third place with his radical nationalist rants, calls for territorial expansion, and authoritarian tirades shocked observers both inside and outside Russia. These observers found themselves even more shocked when Zhirinovsky's party, the famously misnamed Liberal Democratic Party of Russia, actually won the party-list Duma elections of 1993, scoring 23 per cent of the vote and humiliating the second-place Russia's Choice.

While the LDPR might seem to be an example of a party rising up independently of state resources due to a charismatic leader, some research suggests that the party (the first non-communist formation to officially register in the USSR) was actually the product of a KGB attempt to use Zhirinovsky to discredit the whole idea of democracy and electoral politics (Wilson 2005: 23–6). Remarkably, in the Duma itself, the LDPR frequently votes with the Russian government despite its seemingly radical opposition rhetoric, leading to widespread speculation that it gets financial help from the Kremlin along with the dues and corporate donations it publicly acknowledges. This has not prevented the party from winning roughly 10 per cent of the party-list vote in every Duma election after its 1993 victory except 1999, when it still got 6 per cent. Its organisation and brand are almost entirely centred on the personality of Zhirinovsky himself, whose over-the-top antics (from tossing a glassful of orange juice onto his reformist opponent during a televised debate to tugging on a female deputy's hair in parliament) are designed to entertain and grab attention more than to persuade. Disavowing both communism and liberalism in the process, he has proven consistently able to mobilise the support of both nationalists and people (especially poor males in small towns) who just want a way to register their dissatisfaction with the state of affairs in Russia.

Party substitutes

The building blocks available to party-builders were also available to people who had no intention of actually building parties, but still wanted to influence political outcomes in Russia. Thus alongside the 1993-vintage parties there quickly appeared what might be called 'party substitutes' (Hale 2006). These were types of political organisations whose bosses generally wanted to avoid the strings that would come attached to party membership (such as the need to adhere to an ideology or party rules that could limit one's room for manoeuvre), but who still wanted to get 'their people' elected to key state posts.

One key type of party substitute was the regional political machines run by powerful governors. Russia's reform process gave regional authorities a great deal of latitude to design their own provincial state institutions and to influence the way local firms were privatised, if they were privatised at all. Many of the original 'governors', as they are widely called, used this opportunity to make sure that their bureaucracies or their cronies gained ownership of former Soviet enterprises during the 1990s reforms. These governors also set up extensive licensing and inspection procedures for firms not owned by their close associates, and very often also established effective control over local police, courts, election commissions, and other state bodies. The result was a series of regional political machines that had great power to get candidates that it favoured elected, by hook or by crook. While such governors during the 1990s would frequently pay lip service to political parties supported by the Yeltsin administration in order to secure subsidies, the vast majority of them acted very independently, almost always running for office themselves as non-party candidates. To win an election in Russia in the latter half of the 1990s, in fact, a candidate was usually better off gaining the support of a regional political machine than a party, though parties did win many battles.

Another important sort of party substitute was a set of mega-rich and politically connected corporate conglomerates, led by figures popularly known as 'oligarchs' due to their influence on affairs of state. Corporations in virtually all countries engage in politics, usually by lobbying government or contributing to candidate campaigns. What made these politicised financial–industrial groups (PFIGs) special was that they often went straight to the electorate, recruiting their own candidates for office and supplying these candidates with their primary campaign organisation and resources. This was profitable for PFIGs because the candidate once elected could be counted upon to vote for the corporate interest when needed, and this was most reliable when the candidate was not beholden to any party that might impose other claims on his or her loyalty. Thus major Russian firms like Gazprom and the Alfa Group, not to mention corporate groups with less than national scope, also provided ways for ambitious politicians to win office without having to bother joining a party.

One might even interpret the Kremlin itself as being 'the ultimate party substitute' in Russia. Much like regional political machines could powerfully influence local politics, so could the Russian President and his administration have a major impact on national politics. In part, it could do so by putting pressure on regional political machines and PFIGs to support candidates backed by the president. For example, many PFIGs depended for their wealth on comfortable deals with the government, and the President also had a great deal of control over budgetary and non-budgetary financial flows that could be directed toward or away from particular regional political machines. Moreover, the Russian state continued to own or otherwise control the two most-watched television networks during the latter 1990s, which meant it could influence how campaigns were covered. This effect was greatest during presidential elections, when no individual PFIG or regional machine was big enough alone to guarantee a candidate's victory and when the Kremlin was likely to be most aggressive in mobilising its resources. Yeltsin's presidential victory as an independent over the CPRF's Zyuganov in 1996 was a pivotal moment in the development of the Kremlin as a party substitute. The Kremlin could also directly intervene in regional-level elections to significant effect, though it was often unsuccessful when working against the vital interests of the local political machine. What this has meant is that incumbent presidents generally do not need parties to win re-election and thus prefer to maintain maximum flexibility by remaining independent. No Russian president has ever sought to be an actual party member while in office.

One upshot of all of this is that Russia's parties failed to dominate the political system in the 1990s not so much because they were objectively 'weak', but because they in fact faced very strong competition from extremely powerful independents backed by regional political machines, PFIGs, and the Kremlin itself.

Parties originating in the Putin era: United Russia and A Just Russia

The most important party to appear in the Putin era, United Russia, might be thought of as a conglomeration of these party substitutes, increasingly tightly harnessed during the 2000s to Putin and the broad programme he has advocated. This 'administrative' path to party development is not as abnormal as one might think, even in democracies. American Senator Martin Van Buren founded the Democratic Party in the United States, for example, largely by cobbling together a coalition of state political machines and recruiting Andrew Jackson to lead it and win the presidency in 1828 (Aldrich 1995).

In Russia, events took a different twist. Its Van Buren was Moscow Mayor Yuri Luzhkov, who recruited the highly popular former Prime

Minister Yevgenii Primakov and successfully organised many of Russia's strongest regional political machines and corporate representatives under the label Fatherland-All Russia (FAR) in August 1999. But Luzhkov, unlike the original Van Buren, lost his struggle to capture the presidency for his team and himself personally. The battle in 1999–2000 was all the same so hard fought and so close that it had the effect of terrifying Kremlin insiders who feared losing power.

One lesson Kremlin insiders learned is that they ultimately needed a party of their own in order to defeat challenges from coalitions of party substitutes like FAR. In 1999–2000, the party they needed was the Unity bloc, the precursor to United Russia that was formed less than three months before the December 1999 Duma election in a last-ditch effort to prevent what initially looked like a sure FAR victory. Contrary to a common perception, Unity was not initially created to be a true party of power. The first party of power, Russia's Choice, was seen as a failure, as was the second, the Our Home is Russia (OHR) party formed by Prime Minister Viktor Chernomyrdin after Yeltsin abandoned Russia's Choice. OHR won only 10 per cent of the vote in 1995 and lost almost all of its support after Chernomyrdin was sacked as prime minister in 1998. Kremlin insiders thus did not at the time expect a new party of power to have much chance of success, especially since Yeltsin was as unpopular as ever and the newly appointed Prime Minister Putin's ratings were still in single digits as of the late summer of 1999.

Instead, as the Kremlin official most directly responsible for overseeing the Unity project later admitted openly, Unity had only one purpose at its creation, an extraordinarily narrow purpose that was limited to a single election: to counter the campaign of FAR (Shabdurasulov 2008). It was mainly to be a diversion, a 'decoy party' designed to muddy the electoral waters, to make governors and oligarchs think twice before joining forces with FAR, and to provide an alternative framework in which governors left out of FAR (or leaving it) could publicly express this in return for Kremlin favours. While positioning itself as slightly to the right-of-centre ideologically, it mimicked FAR's emphasis on competence and pragmatism and included the well-respected Emergencies Minister Sergei Shoigu atop its party list. Its platform was strikingly similar to that of FAR, one of whose representatives called it the 'purest plagiarism' (*Segodnya*, 4 October 1999). The governors who nominally supported Unity tended to come from regions that were the least successful and most dependent on the central government, and even they generally delegated only mid-level associates to appear on its party list (Hale 2004a).

Imagine Unity's creators' surprise when the party not only cleared the 5 per cent hurdle, but also got far more votes than FAR and came within one percentage point of the first-place CPRF! The party's informal

Kremlin curator, Igor Shabdurasulov, could not contain his glee, calling Unity's performance a 'colossal breakthrough' and even a 'revolution' (*The Moscow Times*, 21 December 1999). Between its last-minute creation in early October and the December balloting, Putin's popularity had soared after decisively sending troops into the rebellious Chechnya republic in retaliation for a series of terrorist bombings in Moscow and other cities, and state-controlled television had outcompeted pro-FAR television and done severe damage to the reputations of Luzhkov and Primakov, tarred as corrupt and old. Both Luzhkov and Primakov then dropped out of the presidential race as it became obvious that Putin would win handily even in a completely fair contest.

Almost immediately after the December 1999 elections, state officials began encouraging the transformation of Unity from a one-off campaign tactic into a full-fledged party of power. A first step was to develop the party's formal organisation and reputation. This began with the formation of Unity's official Duma delegation, which soon joined forces with a large number of independent deputies (and even some from other parties) who had been elected in the Duma's districts contests. Interestingly, FAR's representatives, elected primarily as pragmatists who had planned on benefiting from a close association with those in power, were quick to do an about-face and join the new Unity-led coalition in the Duma. Indeed, Putin and his top Kremlin aides (especially deputy presidential administration chief Vladislav Surkov, emerging as the party's main strategist) were happy to extend this offer even to Luzhkov personally (who accepted) since FAR governors controlled some of the most powerful political machines in Russia. In early 2002, the merger between FAR and Unity was formally consummated under the new name of the United Russia Party, with Interior Minister Boris Gryzlov the new party leader.

As part of the same process, the Kremlin went about corralling Russia's party substitutes into the new party of power structure and reducing their ability and incentive to ever again organise a collective challenge to the incumbent authorities. Putin first stripped governors of most of their political autonomy through a variety of reforms (see Chapter 9), ultimately replacing gubernatorial elections with a system whereby the Russian president nominates a candidate who then must be confirmed by the local legislature, usually dominated by United Russia. Putin also moved decisively against oligarchs to end their days as more or less autonomous political actors. His prosecutors initially targeted two of the most prominent ones, Boris Berezovsky and Vladimir Gusinsky, effectively forcing them to leave the country and give up their influence over key television networks to corporate owners more tightly under Kremlin control. Even more important was the demonstrative arrest in October 2003 of Khodorkovsky, owner of the Yukos oil company and Russia's richest man, who reportedly had designs on the presidency himself and had been launching a large hidden slate of Yukos candidates to run as independents in the 2003 Duma election. That arrest capped a major campaign to co-ordinate the political activities of both big businesses and regional political machines, directing their efforts to support United Russia candidates rather than to act as party substitutes.

Putin and his supporters also made a series of changes in law that have given United Russia a tremendous advantage over its rivals. Only organisations that are officially categorised and registered as national 'political parties' are allowed to nominate candidates in Duma and party-list regional legislative elections. A special registration agency inspects whether parties meet myriad requirements, from having (as of early 2009) at least 50,000 members spread out fairly evenly across Russia's regions to having approved a party charter according to very specific organisational procedures. The membership requirement is particularly onerous, since unlike in many Western countries, joining a party requires people to fill out an application and be formally accepted by party organs. The authorities can then verify whether people are 'really' members according to the formal requirements of the law. Campaigning also takes place according to a highly specific set of guidelines. All this, if one considers Russia's problems with the rule of law, makes opposition parties vulnerable to selective prosecution. United Russia, of course, has had no trouble with this, and by May 2008 it had already registered over 2 million members (*Polit.ru*, 27 May 2008).

Other rules are explicitly intended to weed out smaller parties. Parties can no longer run together in coalitions for the Duma, and instead must appear separately on the ballot or not at all, and parties receive state funding in proportion to their election performance. The length of time that televised election campaigning is permissible is quite limited, less than a month for parliamentary elections, which tends to benefit parties that are already in government because their activities are covered by media as 'news'. This also aids parties whose backers control the mass media, which tend to give highly positive coverage to United Russia and its supporters.

Putin has also adopted several institutional changes that have helped United Russia, including replacing the mixed system of Duma elections with a party-list-only system (which increased the power of central party authorities relative to regional ones and eliminated the opportunity for party substitutes to compete directly in elections) and raising the threshold for winning seats in that competition from 5 per cent to 7 per cent as from the 2007 election. The Kremlin also pushed through a measure that reserved a significant portion of regional legislative seats for national parties, which now compete for these mandates in party-list competitions. The latter reform has led to United Russia's dominance in most regional legislatures.

It would be a mistake, however, to dismiss United Russia as being solely an administrative product that represents no ideas and has no genuine popular support. Independent surveys show that as many as 26 per cent of the population could be considered loyal to the party in 2004 and that this figure had grown to 30 per cent in 2008. Thus while there is strong evidence of at least some ballot box fraud – for example, an improbably high number of precincts reporting turnout figures corresponding to round numbers in 2007 – this is not the main story of its rise (RFE/RL *Newsline*, 29 February 2008). Its popularity derives first and foremost from its close association with Vladimir Putin. The Unity and then United Russia fractions in the Duma have always characterised themselves as wholly supportive of Putin's agenda, and this was clearly a winning strategy since Putin retained 60 to 80 per cent approval ratings throughout his eight years in the presidency. Survey results also provide strong evidence that Russian citizens tend to credit United Russia (as well as Putin) for improvements in the economy. But the party does also stand out in voter minds for certain kinds of positions on important issues. It has been associated with a market economic orientation, opposition to communism, a moderately pro-Western foreign policy, and a tough stance on rebellious minority regions like Chechnya. Voters who support such positions, the survey evidence suggests (Hale 2008), have been significantly more likely to vote for United Russia than for other parties. It remains to be determined exactly how much of United Russia's success has been due to the coercive power of Russian authorities and how much has been due to the same kinds of things that make parties popular everywhere, including association with a successful leader, a growing economy, and widely supported policy positions. While Russia's shift to a more authoritarian system in the 2000s has clearly worked to United Russia's advantage, one could also argue that people would not have tolerated this authoritarian shift had there not been genuine popular support for Putin and his favourite party.

The Kremlin has also helped ensure United Russia's rise by manipulating the set of available alternatives. Partly, this has been through pressuring or spreading damaging information about the party's true opposition. One example is the negative state-controlled news reporting that portrayed the CPRF as hypocritical for accepting money from several 'dollar millionaires' during the 2003 Duma campaign. The authorities have also used less conventional means, including the support of what Andrew Wilson (2005) has called 'virtual parties', which the Kremlin intends to play the role of a 'loyal opposition' that will take votes from real opposition parties while not actually acting against the interests of the incumbent administration. Some virtual parties formally bear the brands of older real parties, such as the aforementioned Democratic Party during 2007–8. Others were actually created as virtual parties under Yeltsin, such as (reputedly) the Pensioners' Party, which first ran for the Duma in 1999 and is thought to have targeted the CPRF's base of elderly loyalists. As hinted above, the LDPR may in fact be Russia's oldest virtual party.

The most prominent virtual party appearing in the Putin era is A Just Russia, currently one of the four parties in the Duma. It has its roots in the Motherland bloc that was formed in 2003 through an alliance between the Kremlin and disgruntled CPRF allies who hoped to use the authorities' support for their own political gain at the Communists' expense. At the same time state media was depicting the CPRF as losing touch with true socialist values by accepting corporate money, as described above, these same media broadcast relatively positive portrayals of Motherland as a truer heir to communist ideals. Thus not only were CPRF voters given reason to doubt their old party, they were given an alternative that did contain some credible leaders, including the popular leftist economist Sergei Glaz'ev and the nationalist Duma deputy Dmitri Rogozin. The results were dramatic: during the final week of the campaign, the CPRF's ratings plummeted and Motherland's soared, surprising even its Kremlin supporters by reaching 9 per cent of the Duma vote. Once in the Duma, both Rogozin and Glaz'ev proved less than loyal to the Kremlin and were pushed out of Motherland's leadership. The new leaders then merged the party with the Pensioners' Party and a minor party founded by a close Putin associate, Federation Council Speaker Sergei Mironov. Mironov, not known for either leftist or nationalist views, then assumed the leadership of the new 'A Just Russia' party and tallied 8 per cent of the officially counted votes in the 2007 Duma election. Some speculate that it is part of a Kremlin plan to eventually engineer a two-party system in Russia, with A Just Russia potentially waiting in the wings to capture leftist votes should United Russia's popularity decline.

Of course, the true opposition's difficulties should not all be blamed on Kremlin manipulation. Some of their woes are surely due to the fact that, throughout Putin's presidency, the economy was improving and the incumbent president popular. Such trends normally weaken opposition parties even without repression (Erikson, MacKuen, and Stimson 2002). Russia's opposition parties have also made some serious strategic mistakes, as when Yabloko and the SPS seemed to spend more effort attacking each other than Putin in the 2003 Duma campaign in bids to become Russia's dominant liberal party (Hale 2004b). This made it much easier for United Russia to win away some of their liberal voters on the strength of market reforms under Putin.

All this made possible another United Russia step toward dominance in 2007–8: for the first time it began to play an official role in presidential politics. Initially, outgoing President Putin agreed to head the party's list in the 2007 Duma campaign, an unprecedented move in Russian politics, ensuring that it won a huge majority of over two-thirds of the seats. Putin declined his Duma seat after the election. Second, Putin's anointed successor, First Deputy Prime Minister Dmitri Medvedev, then ran for president as a party nominee, something neither Putin nor Yeltsin had ever done. Third, immediately after Medvedev succeeded Putin in office, Putin acceded to the post of United Russia chairman as well as Prime Minister. But despite all these moves, neither Putin nor Medvedev has yet proven willing to fully affiliate themselves with and thus fully lend their authority to United Russia by becoming members. They may yet do so, but their hesitancy indicates both that United Russia is not yet close to having the status of the old CPSU and that Kremlin insiders themselves see risks to their own power in taking this final step. They want, it appears, to make sure that the party remains an instrument of their personal leadership rather than an institution with its own interests and authority that could one day part ways with theirs.

Conclusion

Russia has come a long way in forming a party system since the USSR disintegrated in 1991, but its development was not what observers initially expected. While a set of parties did emerge and grow during the 1990s based largely on political resources and reputation gained through connections to the state, their growth was stunted as Yeltsin-style privatisation and overly strong executive authority led to the rise of party substitutes that often managed to outcompete parties for both candidates and votes. After Kremlin authorities nearly lost power to the Fatherland-All Russia coalition of party substitutes in 1999–2000, the newly elected President Putin began to transform Russia's party system by both reducing the power of party substitutes and organising them around one increasingly dominant party, United Russia. As these efforts were all linked with a growing economy and a popular president, and as state-controlled television could ensure that voters made this link, United Russia reached a point of near-dominance in the political system.

At the same time, Putin and his successor as president, Dmitri Medvedev, have remained reluctant to tie their personal authority too closely to any party (even United Russia) since their mighty Kremlin power base has given them great room for political manoeuvre that they have worried a strong party might limit. Thus Russia's political system is not yet fully a party system, even a fully 'dominant party system'. There is even speculation that the authorities are trying to engineer a two-party system, pairing United Russia with a 'very loyal opposition' like A Just Russia. Russia's party system thus remains in flux and could take on quite different directions in the years ahead.

Chapter 6

Russian Society and the State

ALFRED B. EVANS, JR

There is general agreement that in the history of Russia, from Tsarist times through the Soviet period to the present, the state usually has been the dominant partner in its relationship with society. Nevertheless, the Russian people have never failed to exhibit an impressive capacity for resourcefulness and adaptation. Thus Western scholars often have wondered whether the growth of a civil society might be detected in Russia. In the West the dominant conception of civil society refers to the sphere of organisations that are formed primarily by the independent initiative of citizens who devote their efforts to co-operative endeavours aimed at achieving common goals. Civil society is seen as distinct from the state, which exercises authority, and businesses, which seek to make profits. Civil society also may be seen as an intermediate level of social organisation that operates between families and the state. Most Western scholars believe that a vigorous civil society exercises a positive influence in a number of ways, by providing means for citizens to solve pressing problems, representing the interests of social groups in the political arena, and potentially restraining the state from the abuse of citizens' rights and interests.

It is the consensus of both Russian and Western historians that during the last several decades of existence of the Tsarist regime the number of voluntary associations in Russia was growing steadily and that those organisations provided a wide range of services. Mary Schaeffer Conroy (2006: 24) argues: 'Though the tsarist state was far from democratic, it allowed space for many independent initiatives by citizens, and in many cases even encouraged nonstate organisations as a means of gaining assistance in serving national interests.' She concludes that by the early decades of the twentieth century civil society was burgeoning in Russia. If that trend had continued it might eventually have led to a revision of the image of dual Russia. The Bolshevik revolution brought a fundamental change that ruled out that possibility, however. Though in the aftermath of that revolution there was a burst of social energy resulting in the creation of many new clubs and societies, it is apparent that the main tendency within the Communist leadership sought the replacement of existing social associations with a network of new organisations that would be controlled by the ruling Communist Party (Il'ina 2000; Evans 2006). By the middle of the 1930s that vision had been translated into reality. In the Soviet system all legally sanctioned *obshchestvennye* ('social' or 'public') organisations primarily carried out the function of assisting the political regime in attempting to achieve its goals, though each of those organisations also delivered some services to its members. The widespread awareness that the meetings and elections of an organisation were managed in detail by Communist Party officials presumably reinforced the sense of powerlessness in relation to political authority that was inherent in the image of dual Russia.

Civil society in post-communist Russia

Though there was a slight loosening of control of most social organisations in the Soviet Union in the post-Stalin years and the authorities tacitly tolerated the growth of some unofficial groups of citizens, the essential character of the relationship between the political regime and social associations did not change until Mikhail Gorbachev became the head of the Communist Party in 1985. Soon it became apparent that his programme for the radical restructuring (*perestroika*) of the Soviet system permitted 'informal' groups to form openly without being incorporated into the network of organisations controlled by the Communist Party. A wide variety of such groups sprang up rapidly in the period of *perestroika*, so that as many as 60,000 were said to exist by 1989. The proliferation of the 'informal' groups was associated with a radical increase in the frankness of discussion of political issues that could not have been mentioned in public a few years earlier. Those changes implied a shift in the relationship between the state and society of such fundamental significance that the most optimistic Western scholars predicted that a full-blown civil society would soon flourish in the Soviet Union.

In reality, however, the boom of social organisations in the Russian republic of the USSR in the late 1980s was followed by a period of many difficulties for such groups in the Russian Federation in the 1990s (Evans 2002). It was true that many organisations still survived at the end of that decade, and they benefited from the end of Communist Party rule and the increase in pluralism in the mass media. Nevertheless, associations formed by citizens were in a marginal position in Russian society by the end of the 1990s in terms of their base of support, their political influence, and their capacity to address social problems and fulfil citizens' needs. Non-governmental organisations (NGOs) in Russia suffered from a series of handicaps. First, the cultural legacy of the Soviet system included a low level of confidence in social organisations, and more broadly a pervasive distrust of the public sphere as a realm where self-seeking, amoral behaviour is to be expected. The collapse of the hopes for political reforms that had been aroused by Gorbachev intensified alienation from public activism. Second, the deep decline in the Russian economy in the 1990s forced most citizens to concentrate on a struggle for survival, making participation in civic or charitable groups seem to be a luxury that few could afford. Also, with most Russians in poverty or on the edge of it, the prospects for gathering substantial sums of money in the form of contributions were very poor for most NGOs. Third, the high degree of concentration of power in the hands of the main executive leader on each level in the political system created an incentive for cultivating relationships with key officials rather than building a broad base of membership support. As Fish (2001b: 22) puts it, such a concentration and personalisation of power 'tends to encourage the formation of small, closed, compact societal organisations that are adept at applying pressure on and currying favor with individuals in ministries and other executive-branch officials'. During the 1990s social organisations could form with relative freedom, but encountered conditions that discouraged them from seeking to expand their membership, raise funds from many potential contributors, recruit large numbers of volunteers to work in their projects, or draw widespread public attention to their goals and activities.

Vladimir Putin and civil society in Russia

Thus when Vladimir Putin took office as president of Russia in 2000 he was aware that civil society in Russia was relatively weak, as his statements confirmed. He has repeatedly emphasised the importance of civil society for the development of Russia into one of the great powers of the world, and this author agrees with the assessment by James Richter (2009) that Putin's statements in support of civil society 'are not mere posturing'. Richter notes that Putin's viewpoint does 'recognise a fairly large private sphere', where citizens should have space 'to pursue individual profits and interests without state interference, particularly in comparison with the extremely small private sphere recognised by the Soviet regime'. But for Putin civil society is in the public sphere, assumed to be narrower than the public realm as conceived by the Soviet Communists, but a space in which all who enter should subordinate their 'private interests to the collective interest of the nation as a whole, as embodied in the interests of the state'. In relation to the public realm Putin is extremely suspicious of disagreements over ideology or interests that would fragment the unity of the nation, so he has expressed a strong desire for a consensus on goals in Russian society. Though Putin counsels that a healthy civil society is needed to protect the state from stagnation, he believes that a strong state is a prerequisite for a healthy civil society (Evans 2008a: 19). He sees the relationship between the state and civil society not as one that is primarily adversarial (as many in the West would assume) but as a partnership in which social organisations work with the state in addressing social problems and providing needed services. In the view of Vladimir Putin and Dmitri Medvedev the institutions of civil society should also furnish channels of feedback to the state, giving information about the effectiveness of policies and offering criticism when the performance of bureaucratic officials is unsatisfactory.

Though Putin's general intentions for Russian society were probably clear by the time that he came to power, only after the beginning of his second term as president in 2004 did the regime turn its energies toward the proper structuring of civil society. Putin and his associates (including Vladislav Surkov, who then was a deputy head of the presidential administration) assumed that civil society in their country was weak and the state would have to take the initiative in strengthening it. Their plans for imparting more energy to the organisations within civil society also entailed efforts to integrate non-governmental organisations into the system of comprehensive support of the executive leadership of the state. On the one hand, the political regime directed the creation of a number of groups that were informally labelled 'government-organised non-governmental organisations', or GONGOs, and began to distribute grants to social organisations on a rapidly increasing scale. On the other hand, the regime tightened the legal requirements pertaining to social organisations. A bill bringing changes in the laws regulating NGOs was introduced in the Duma in November 2005 and was signed into law by Putin in January 2006 after it had been approved by both houses of the Federal Assembly.

Observers have disagreed sharply about the implications of that legislation, and its full consequences are not yet clear. There is no doubt that it requires NGOs that wish to be registered officially to spend much more time filling out forms (including annual reports), and even members of United Russia in the Duma have admitted that the legislation's requirements for registration and reporting should be eased significantly. One section of the current law also makes it possible for officials to ban any organisation that threatens 'Russia's sovereignty, independence, territorial integrity, national unity and originality, cultural heritage, and national interests', which potentially leaves wide discretion to the federal registration officials to decide on the life or death of any formally organised group. Apparently very few NGOs have actually been put out of business under that provision. The authorities contend that the organisations that have found it impossible to satisfy the requirements for renewing their registration (or have not attempted to do so, which appears to have been more common) largely consisted of those that had been inactive for some time and existed only on paper. Rather than using administrative means of closing a large number of contentious organisations, the main thrust of the political regime has been to marginalise such groups by making it more difficult for them to obtain funding or gain access to the mass media and decision makers. The leadership seems to assume that organisations that have few resources and little influence can for the most part be safely ignored, and will probably wither away in the long run. So the state's intervention is intended to stimulate greater vigour in the organisations in civil society in Russia and at the same time to ensure that organisations operate within the boundaries of a consensus of values.

The Public Chamber

In recent years Russia's political leadership also has created new institutions that are closely connected with the state but are officially considered as part of civil society. The most prominent of those is the Public or Social Chamber (*Obshchestvennaya Palata*) of the Russian Federation. In September 2004 Vladimir Putin proposed the creation of that body 'as a platform for extensive dialogue, where citizens' initiatives could be presented and discussed in detail' (Evans 2006: 151). The bill on the Public Chamber was approved by both houses of the parliament and was signed by the president in April 2005. Putin appointed the first third of the members of the chamber, who then selected an equal number; together those two groups chose the remaining third, with each member serving a term of two years. None of the members can be government officials or officers in political parties. The members of the Public Chamber, for which the selection process has now worked its way twice (in 2005 and 2007), are a strikingly varied collection of individuals, drawn from many different fields of endeavour, including business, science, art and culture, sports, and social services. Some of the members were widely known before they were selected for the chamber.

Putin's original conception of the Public Chamber emphasised the value of the expertise that its members would possess and envisioned it as evaluating proposed legislation and providing feedback to administrative agencies. Before the institution began to function some critics derided it as 'an attempt to create a dummy of civil society' or predicted that it would be 'the Kremlin's puppet theatre', sure to be completely lacking in independence from the top power holders. It must still be said that the Public Chamber is a work in progress and its character has not been fully formed. Yet even before it began to function it displayed a willingness to take on some state officials while serving as an advocate for the rights of various individuals and groups. As mentioned earlier in this chapter, proposed changes in legislation concerning the regulation of NGOs had been introduced into the Duma in November 2005. By early December all of those who by that time had been selected for the Public Chamber joined in appealing to the parliament to postpone voting on that bill until the chamber had begun to function and could give its evaluation of the proposed legislation. That request was ignored, and the bill was signed into law on January. When the Public Chamber met for its first session, in Georgievsky Hall in the Kremlin with Putin present, one of its members openly complained that the adoption of the legislation on NGOs without consultation of the chamber had been 'a gross political error' on the part of the Duma.

Almost immediately after that session the Public Chamber was plunged into the highly publicised controversy over the case of Private Andrei Sychev, a draftee in the army who had been subjected to extreme brutality by senior enlisted men in the Chelyabinsk Tank School at the end of December 2005, resulting in gangrene that forced doctors to amputate his legs and genitalia. The Public Chamber dispatched three of its members, headed by Anatolii Kucherena, a lawyer who headed a commission of the chamber, to investigate that tragic incident. Subsequently Kucherena's commission created a working group on the problem of extreme hazing of recruits in the military, which included representatives of the Public Chamber, the Duma, the Ministry of Defence, the president's council on human rights, and the Committee of Soldiers' Mothers. In June Kucherena and another member of the Public Chamber (Nikolai Svanidze, a well-known television broadcaster) played a conspicuous role in advocating protection for the rights of residents of South Butovo, a neighbourhood on the outskirts of Moscow, who were to be moved forcibly from their homes to clear the way for the construction of a large apartment complex. In the first few months after it was formed, the Public Chamber proved to be bolder than some people had expected in criticising problems created by government officials. The members of the chamber have not confronted the Kremlin leadership, however, which is not surprising, since the body derives its status from the authority of the Russian President.

In Putin's vision the Public Chamber would serve as the capstone institution of civil society in Russia, and also would present a model for the organisation and functioning of the whole society (Richter 2009). Thus the actions of the chamber not only show what criticism of government officials is acceptable, but also implicitly signal the limits of permitted conflict. The Public Chamber has assisted in the creation of public chambers in the regions of Russia and has seen the introduction of public councils (*obshchestvennye sovety*) that are supposed to advise the ministries in the national government. So far little is known about the operation of those organs. It is likely, however, that they will emulate the national Public Chamber, whose head, the renowned physicist Yevgenii Velikhov, has stressed the importance of co-operation with the state: 'The motto of the chamber's work should be, not confrontation of the authorities but active work with them, in order to make Russian citizens more interested in the country's destiny' (Evans 2008b: 347–48). The national chamber now offers advice in virtually every area of policy making, but some of its members have complained that the committees of the Federal Assembly do not pay much attention to that advice. The Public Chamber has no legislative or executive authority, and its impact on the shaping of major policies appears to have been marginal so far, but the members of the chamber do enjoy a degree of access to decision makers and the mass media that they would not have if they were not part of that chamber. The role of the Public Chamber is fundamentally similar to that of the office of the state's ombudsman for human rights (Vladimir Lukin) and the President's Commission on Human Rights and the Development of Civil Society (until recently headed by Ella Pamfilova), in the sense that the ombudsman and the members of that commission were chosen by officers of the state, but are supposed to represent society in its dealings with the state. On occasion Lukin and Pamfilova have been aligned with the Public Chamber and some independent-minded NGOs in directing criticism toward aspects of legislation or actions of state officials.

Types of non-governmental organisations in contemporary Russia

As we have noted, by the end of the 1990s most organisations in civil society in Russia were marginal in terms of their base of support, their influence on those in authority, and their impact on society. The NGOs that were most independent of the state and most attuned to the Western notion of civil society consisted, as Richter (2009) has put it, of 'a relatively small network of small, often professional advocacy organisations that usually received some support from outside assistance agencies'. Funding from Western governments and foundations was directed primarily to those Russian organisations that engaged in activities that seemed appropriate to those who provided the funding. Groups emphasising human rights issues, women's rights, and environmental protection were among those receiving the most outside funding. While contacts with like-minded Western activists and money from Western sources did raise the level of professionalism of the leaders of a few Russian NGOs, it has been well documented that organisations that relied primarily on financial support from the West tended not to build a domestic base of support by focusing on issues that could be presented within a framework compatible with the values of the majority of the local population (Sperling 1999; Henderson 2003). The leaders of such organisations typically became well integrated into international support networks but were isolated from the potential support groups in their own society.

A far larger segment of society in post-communist Russia, in terms of the scale of membership, consists of social organisations that have survived from the Soviet period. We should recall that in the Soviet system, while such organisations did perform some services for their members, they also were subject to control by the Communist Party and the state, and existed primarily to help realise the goals of the political regime. Some of those organisations disappeared with the end of Communist patronage, while others survived after the downfall of the old regime, in some cases adopting new names. Scholarly researchers have devoted little attention to such organisations, with some notable exceptions (particularly the labour unions, which have been the subject of a number of scholarly writings). Since the Russian people were well aware of the lack of independence of those organisations during earlier decades, we have reason to suppose that most of them are not highly respected.

Yet if the officers of an organisation work diligently to carry out tasks that are helpful to its members in everyday life (as anecdotal information about some groups suggests), the organisation might be regarded as important to those who depend on its services. The funding for such organisations was reduced dramatically after the abandonment of the Soviet system, but assistance from one level of government (national, regional, or local) was necessary for their continued existence. Since the early 1990s most of those organisations have received meagre funding from government, but many of them have been allowed to use government-owned office space and equipment, giving them a crucial advantage over other organisations that do not receive such support. It is widely reported that the organisations that depend on the state for support that is essential for their existence accept the necessity of a fundamentally co-operative relationship with government officials, particularly seeking the favour of the chief executive at their own level. In recent years the national government has discouraged NGOs in Russia from seeking financial assistance from abroad if any political goals might be involved, while the state has awarded grants to Russian social organisations on an increasing scale.

Business organisations

The relationship between business and the state that developed in Russia during the 1990s was quite different from that between government and the holdover social organisations. The circumstances of the massive privatisation of formerly state-owned enterprises under the Yeltsin leadership made it possible for some people who were very skilful in using good connections and seizing opportunities to accumulate large amounts of wealth with startling rapidity. By the middle of the decade observers referred to the richest men as the 'oligarchs', and some scholars spoke of the 'capture' of the Russian state by the titans of business. Those tycoons became a key source of support for Boris Yeltsin, and they were rewarded with great influence over economic policy. It has been alleged by some who served in high offices in the Yeltsin administration that some oligarchs even controlled appointments to positions at the level of ministers and deputy ministers (Stack 2008). Because of the weakness of the state and political parties, 'power shifted from formal political institutions to informal networks of influence among individuals who had political connections or economic resources at their disposal' (Rutland 2006: 76). Personal ties and insider dealing by powerful individuals overshadowed the feeble efforts of organised interests representing large groups of people. Though the oligarchs were riding high in the 1990s, they left themselves potentially vulnerable by failing to unify in a strong organisation dedicated to the collective goals of the large businesses. 'They devoted most of their energies to competing with one another for favours from the state and rarely worked together to protect or advance their common interests, or even to discuss what those common interests might be' (Rutland 2006: 79). After he came to power Vladimir Putin moved deftly to take advantage of that vulnerability, and the treatment of Gusinsky, Berezovsky, and Khodorkovsky showed that, by 2004, the relationship between the state and the oligarchs had changed.

Under Putin the national political leadership encouraged the growth of more formal, institutionalised means of representing the interests of business owners. Andrei Yakovlev (2006: 1043) has reported that after 2000 the federal authorities decreased the emphasis on 'direct informal contacts with business tycoons' and 'started to build a system of "collective representation" of all strata of business'. In a study of business associations (BAs) in Russia, Stanislav Markus (2007: 287) concludes, 'the evidence thus indicates successful interest aggregation within formal BAs as well as the ongoing formalization of the state–business dialogue in which BAs (as compared with individuals or single firms) come to play an increasingly important role'. There is a large number of business associations in Russia, and according to one well-informed Russian source interviewed by

William Pyle (2006: 498), as many as 5,000 may be officially registered. Membership in those associations has increased substantially since 2000 (ibid.: 503). Perhaps the most prestigious of those groups is the Russian Union of Industrialists and Entrepreneurs (RSPP), with about 130 members (Obshchestvennaya Palata 2007: 51), consisting of the largest companies in the country. After Putin established limits on the political power of the oligarchs, those who remained in business joined the RSPP and shared in its efforts to influence issues of economic policy. Delovaya Rossiya (Business Russia) is the main organisation of large companies outside the sphere of oligarchic capital, claiming around 1,200 members, with 72 regional divisions and 38 branches in various sectors of the economy. OPORA of Russia has enlisted small and medium-sized businesses in its ranks, and says that it has over 330,000 members in 78 regions of Russia. The Chamber of Commerce and Industry (TPP) has 155 regional and municipal centres and 14 foreign offices, which represent 20,000 companies and associations. Markus (2007: 287) reports that 'the Chamber assumed a much greater lobbying role after Yeltsin's departure', assisted by the leadership of Yevgenii Primakov (a former foreign minister and prime minister) since December 2001. We should emphasise that policymakers at the highest level *invited* business owners to strengthen their organised representation and to engage in regular consultation with the top leadership in order to decrease the autonomy of the state bureaucracy and overcome resistance to the implementation of reforms (Markus 2007: 292–4).

The increase in the importance of business associations, enhancing formal, collective means of representation of business interests, must be considered one of the most important trends in Russian society of the last several years. Of course, the rise of more formal, institutionalised means of lobbying has not prevented individual business owners from continuing to rely on informal means of lobbying government officials to seek benefits for their companies. It is likely that business actors choose various combinations of strategies to try to get what they want from government, and that many use both personal connections and collective representation to serve their interests. Also, there are multiple levels of political authority in Russia, and with tighter constraints on the manipulation of officials in the national government under Putin, many companies have concentrated on exercising influence over regional and local governments that have a direct impact on their operations (Yakovlev 2006: 1052–3). It is often more feasible for a company to gain useful access at a lower level of government, and a large company may build a close alliance with a regional leader. At the national level, however, the Yukos case gave a clear signal that the type of influence the oligarchs had possessed in the 1990s had been ruled out. Since the 1990s, in the words of William Pyle (2006: 520) 'business associations have become economic actors of consequence in post-communist Russia', and according to Pyle those associations usually lobby for policies that are designed to facilitate the more effective working of market mechanisms.

Labour unions

Labour unions in Russia have not shown the same upsurge in energy that has infused business associations in the current decade, which is troubling in light of the fact that the union movement played a major part in the growth of civil society and democracy in Western countries. In the Soviet Union almost all employed persons belonged to unions, and all union organisations belonged to a single federation that was called the All-Union Central Council of Trade Unions (VTsSPS). After the dissolution of the Soviet Union, Russia's component of the VTsSPS was renamed as the Federation of Independent Trade Unions of Russia (FNPR), with most of the officers of the old federation remaining in their leadership positions. The FNPR inherited impressive resources from the old order, which in fact have provided the main basis of its survival. After the dismantling of the Soviet system the FNPR owned property worth billions of dollars, which supplied most of its income (Davis 2006: 202). That property gave the union federation an incentive to avoid being confrontational toward the state, especially in the conditions of insecurity created by the privatisation of industry. The wealth inherited by the union federation and the perquisites for its officers that carried over from the old system also made it unnecessary for its leaders to be greatly concerned with winning support from workers. Initially after the end of the old order, membership in a union was virtually automatic for all workers in most enterprises. As a result, in 1992 the FNPR claimed to have 66 million members, or 92 per cent of the work force (Davis 2006: 203), though those numbers have declined since that time. Surveys have consistently indicated that labour unions are among the least trusted institutions in Russia and that most workers have little confidence in the capacity of their union to represent them if their interests are threatened.

A number of independent unions were formed during the late Soviet period and soon after, and some of them are more likely to push management for concessions, but only about 1 per cent of the labour force belongs to those unions. On the whole unions have had little influence on determining wages in industrial firms, or even on the suspension of wages that was common in many sectors of the economy during the 1990s (Crowley 2002: 241). The incidence of strikes has been low in Russia in the post-communist period in comparison with levels in West European countries. When a local union does carry out a strike or a protest, it usually does so on behalf of demands that are endorsed by both managers and employees, consistent with the FNPR's strategy of focusing its branches' efforts 'not on battling employers for improved work conditions, but on appealing in tandem with employers to the state for greater concessions and side payments to their industry and enterprise' (Crowley 2002: 235). The strikes and protests that erupted spontaneously during the late 1980s and the 1990s, such as those carried out by coal miners, were opposed by the traditional unions, and should be remembered mainly as setting an example that has been followed by other protestors in recent years.

On the whole labour unions are among the weakest social organisations in contemporary Russia. The FNPR in particular has paid a price for placing primary emphasis on ensuring the survival of its organisational structures and material assets, and continuing to act 'as if it were an administrative and managerial entity instead of a representative of the workers' (Davis 2006: 203). Recently, however, some journalists have reported an increase in strikes in Russia, apparently signalling bolder demands from the workers in some enterprises. It remains to be seen whether that trend is a reaction to economic expansion, in which some firms have become more prosperous, easing the fear that they might close down and leave all their employees without jobs. Foreign-owned firms seem to have been the target of more aggressive demands and a disproportionate number of strikes (Bush 2007: 35). It is possible that Russian unions may not prove impervious to change in the future, but it is too early to speculate on the possible character of their adaptation in the years to come.

Women's organisations

Women's organisations in Russia have not experienced such a rapid expansion in membership and growth in influence in the post-communist years; most of them have not been able to move beyond the margin of the society, even though their potential constituents are a majority in that society. The background to the attitudes that create obstacles for efforts to defend the rights of women in Russia must be found in the history of the Soviet system. The Bolsheviks promised that women would achieve equality if they subordinated their distinctive goals to the struggle for the victory of socialism. When the Soviet state brought socialism into being the Communist Party told the people of the USSR that women had achieved equality with men. Despite undeniable gains for women in terms of education and mobilisation in the paid labour force, 'equality' as defined by the Communists was not completely satisfactory for women (partly because it preserved aspects of inequality), so an appeal to that term has negative connotations for most women in Russia today. The cataclysmic changes in the economy of Russia in the 1990s added to the stress on most women, because they were more likely than men to be unemployed and women disproportionately felt the impact of cutbacks in social services by the state and privatised enterprises. In the new circumstances in the economy there was widespread discrimination against women in hiring and blatant sexual harassment in places of work. Job advertisements by employers frequently listed the sex, age, and even physical description of preferred candidates, and women who themselves advertised that they were seeking work sometimes found it necessary to specify that they wanted jobs 'without intimate relations' (McIntosh Sundstrom 2006a: 86).

A few highly educated women in Russia had become familiar with Western feminist writings during the 1960s and 1970s, and by the late 1980s independent women's organisations were forming and developing contacts with Western women's rights activists. During the 1990s Western governments and foundations provided grant funding to some Russian women's organisations. While that financial support enhanced the professional skills of the leaders of the organisations that received such funding and integrated them into transnational networks of activists, it did not lead them to expand their base of support among Russian women. The organisations that received grants from Western sources characteristically couched their rhetoric in terms that appealed to those who approved the grants but failed to evoke a positive response from the women they claimed to represent. In other words, the gulf between a few women's organisations and the majority of Russian women widened. A basic problem that such organisations face is that, because of the prevailing disillusionment with the promise of equality that had been made by the Soviet regime, 'Russian women tend to view feminist organisations as espousing an alien Western ideology unsuited to their conditions' (McIntosh Sundstrom 2006a: 90). Efforts to define employment discrimination and sexual harassment as violations of the principle of equality for all people, regardless of their sex, have not met with a positive response from most women in post-communist Russia. Rather than looking to women's organisations to improve the conditions of their work and life, in recent years most women in Russia have pursued individual strategies to try to achieve personal advancement or at least economic survival.

Scholarly research has found that two types of organisations formed by women have been successful in gaining substantial support from the public. The committees of soldiers' mothers have grown from one group that met in Moscow in 1989 to a network of hundreds of committees that have taken shape in almost all regions of Russia. Public opinion polls have shown that most Russians know about the soldiers' rights organisations and have a positive view of their activities (McIntosh Sundstrom 2006a: 70). Activists of those organisations have appeared frequently on television and generally have received favourable coverage. Those NGOs have achieved some victories in their attempts to influence government policies, though they have not been successful in persuading the state to eliminate conscription and institute an all-volunteer army. Lisa McIntosh Sundstrom has argued persuasively (2006a: 73) that the soldiers' mothers have gained broad popular support because they appeal to the norm against physical harm to individuals, which has particular resonance in Russia with respect to those inducted in the military, since it is widely known that the hazing of junior recruits (*dedovshchina*) sometimes assumes extreme forms and is thought to have caused the deaths of thousands of soldiers. The activity of the committees of soldiers' mothers also evokes the image of mothers as protectors of their sons (McIntosh Sundstrom 2006a: 186), presenting a role for women that is consistent with deeply rooted national traditions and therefore widely accepted. The committees of soldiers' mothers have taken an approach emphasising cooperation with agencies of the state, though a certain tension between those committees and the military is inherent in their relationship.

The movement to address Russia's serious problem of domestic violence, primarily focusing on the physical abuse of women, also has a record of considerable success, although so far it has not been able to gain changes in the national criminal code that would facilitate the prevention and prosecution of domestic abuse. The main achievement of that movement has been the establishment of women's crisis centres that offer services such as telephone hotlines, counselling, and legal and medical assistance. The first of those centres opened in Moscow and St Petersburg in 1993, and by 2002 about 40 of those centres were operating in Russia, with about 120 organisations responding to the problem of violence against women (Johnson 2006: 268). Financial assistance from foreign governments and foundations helped to make that expansion possible. As McIntosh Sundstrom has noted (2006a: 96–7), while most of the international funding organisations (and a few Russian leaders of the movement) see domestic violence in a feminist perspective as part of a larger problem of inequality between men and women, most of the leaders of the crisis centres frame the issue as one of protecting individuals from bodily harm, which is more acceptable to the majority of Russians. The expansion of the network of crisis centres has led some regional political leaders to try to co-opt the movement by establishing their own crisis centres as appendages of their governments, sometimes separating them from the influence of those who have worked to spread awareness of the problem of domestic violence.

Environmental organisations

The environmental movement in Russia began to grow quietly in the early 1960s in the biology and geography departments of Soviet universities, giving rise to the Student Nature Protection Corps. In the early 1980s the movement widened, as new groups seeking the protection of nature emerged from the Student Nature Protection Corps and the media began to pay attention to environmental issues. Between 1987 and 1991 the movement expanded still more and became more radical as the number of groups increased rapidly and mass campaigns protested against government plans for projects such as the construction of new nuclear power plants and the diversion of rivers. After 1991, however, the environmental movement declined, and many of those groups disappeared, as the attention of the public 'shifted away from environmental problems to more pressing concerns of personal survival' (Henry 2006b: 105). Many of those who had led the environmental protection movement a few years earlier moved into more secure positions in government or returned to their former professional careers. Under Yeltsin and Putin the state placed an overriding priority on the transition to a market economy and the revival of production, and was not interested in enacting new environmental legislation or even enforcing laws on that subject that had already been adopted. The political leadership's unfavourable attitude toward environmental activists had not changed significantly by the time that Medvedev became president.

Nevertheless, one expert has said that 'thousands of green groups' were in operation in Russia by the middle of the current decade (Henry 2006a: 211). The organisations that continue the tradition of the Soviet nature protection movement are led by members of the scientific intelligentsia (most often biologists), most of whom have advanced degrees. Those groups have often received grants from foreign donors and their leaders are embedded in the international network of environmentalists. Such organisations are more likely than other environmentalist groups to have an adversarial relationship with their own government, as they often oppose current policies and criticise a lack of enforcement of existing legislation. Such groups typically prefer to keep their distance from the general public, preserving their character as an elite movement of specialists with a high level of professional expertise. On the other hand, some organisations oriented toward the protection of nature in Russia mainly conduct environmental education programmes for children and carry out other projects such as cleaning up litter in local areas. Such groups are usually led by educators, the largest number of whom are teachers in elementary schools. They are largely apolitical and almost entirely non-confrontational in relation to government officials. Such organisations are more likely than the elite groups to recruit community members to take part in their activities, drawing on networks of family members, friends, colleagues, or parents of the children who are enrolled in their schools. All groups seeking more effective protection for the natural environment are aware that if they do not seek support from foreign donors, the only other potential source of substantial funding is government on one level or another within Russia. They also understand that organisations which accept assistance from government must accept limits on their advocacy and commit themselves to assisting the state rather than challenging it.

Still a dual Russia?

As the president of Russia, Vladimir Putin often emphasised the importance of a vigorous civil society for the development of his country, and Dmitri Medvedev has spoken in a similar vein. It should be apparent, however, that civil society as defined by Russia's current political leaders will not be autonomous from the state, nor will it be an adversary of political authority. In their view the Russian version of civil society should support the state and co-operate with it. Civil society should provide channels of feedback to the political regime and assist the agencies of the state in providing services to citizens. It is necessary that the institutions of civil society communicate suggestions to policy makers and criticise shortcomings in the operation of administrative agencies, but the expression of ideas and interests by social organisations will be legitimate only if it takes place within the boundaries of consensus, and implicitly recognises that common, national values must be of primary importance, while diverse, particular interests will be regarded as secondary. Recently the Russian state has created new structures that are intended both to assist in the institutionalisation of civil society and to establish the limits that organisations in the public space should respect.

The need for effective channels of feedback from society to the political leadership has been underlined in recent years by the phenomenon of public protests, which implicitly has drawn on the example of the strikes and other direct action tactics of coal miners and other workers in the late 1980s and 1990s. Large-scale protests by citizens in a number of cities, with elderly people as the majority of participants, erupted in early 2005 in response to problems in the shift to cash payments to replace certain types of services that had been free for people in some categories. Those protests caused obvious embarrassment for the government, resulted in backtracking by the parliament, and set a precedent that citizens would not forget. Since 2005 there have been protests of various sizes that have focused on a variety of issues, but all of which have expressed the indignation of ordinary citizens concerning behaviour by those in political authority that is seen as abusive and creates discomfort that people feel in their daily lives. From the point of view of the highest political leadership there might be a potential for instability if ambitious opposition figures took advantage of such mass dissatisfaction. Thus the leadership has taken the initiative in introducing institutions such as the office of the human rights ombudsman, the president's commission on human rights and civil society, the national Public Chamber, regional public chambers, and the public councils attached to government ministries. As we have seen, sometimes those who have been appointed to an institution created by the state can form an alliance with NGOs on a particular issue, in some instances even associating themselves with the position that relatively independent groups, which often take an adversarial stance toward the government, have adopted on a specific issue. At the same time some other groups are subjected to low-level harassment by state officials and a few are simply closed down, demonstrating the penalty for what the leadership sees as disloyalty to the interests of the nation and the state.

We may put the developments of recent years in a broader perspective by noting a conception with deep roots in Russian history that could be traced in the writings of Russian intellectuals such as Vasilii Klyuchevsky and Pavel Milyukov, which was identified by Robert C. Tucker (1971: 122) as 'the image of dual Russia'. Tucker described the traditional conception of the Russian state and society as distinct and separate entities, one represented by *'vlast'* or *gosudarstvo*, the centralised autocratic state power', the other consisting of 'the population at large, the society, nation, or people (*obshchestvo*, *narod*)'. The assumption implicit in that image is that the autocratic state has been perceived by the people as an alien force, which exerts power with a degree of arbitrariness and is always beyond the control of the society. In that view the state 'is the active party, the organising and energising force in the drama of dual Russia, whereas the population at large is the passive and subordinate party, the tool and victim of the state's designs'. Like Klyuchevsky, Tucker saw that image as fundamentally derived from the manner of the expansion of the Muscovite state into the vast Russian empire, but Tucker argued that the dualism was intensified by the transformations launched by Peter the Great, who set the precedent for reforms that transformed Russian society from the top down. It would be difficult to disagree with Tucker's argument that the use of an authoritarian state by the Communists to carry out even more radical transformation after 1917 firmly reinforced the image of a dominant political regime and a submissive society.

Has the image of dual Russia, with the state viewed as an alien force imposing its dominance over a society whose members must either submit to political authority or evade its reach, persisted into the present time? Surveys of the attitudes of contemporary Russians indicate that most of them share a sense of 'the pervasiveness of imposed power with a strong division between organs of power and society' (Clément 2008: 69), corresponding closely to the traditional image of dual Russia. Most Russians see the state, or 'power' (*vlast'*), as something that cannot be controlled or contested openly, so the prudent strategy is to show the appearance of subordination and loyalty, while either trying to obtain advantages by building connections with some people in positions of power or retreating from the public sphere into the security of 'your private micro-group' (ibid.: 70). The disjunction between the micro-networks that provide reciprocal help to their members and organisations that strive for collective representation of group interests reflects the separation between the public realm and private life. A very recent development that is important in the light of that condition of separation has been the rise of new grassroots movements that have taken shape in protests during the last few years (ibid.: 73). The informal groups that have emerged from the protests of pensioners, home owners, the drivers of automobiles, and others have been motivated by the desire to defend concrete interests that are felt on a practical level. The participants in such protests share a common sense of having been treated unfairly that drives them to unify against some people in authority, but they do not seek to overthrow the political regime. They focus on demands for specific changes in policies and the actions of administrative officials.

We may ask how initiatives from the bottom up that create self-organising groups demanding fairness will interact with the efforts of political leaders to organise civil society from the top down in order to improve the functioning of the state and prevent instability. The possible responses of those in political authority range from repression through co-optation (and manipulation) to recognition of the movements with genuine popular support and limited objectives. Overt repression of such movements seems unlikely in view of the fact that the current leadership of Russia has tried to avoid that option even when it had to make policy concessions to placate protesters. The recognition of such movements would imply acceptance of a degree of autonomy for them and the use of institutions that have been created by the state to grant representation to each group with a broad base and promise partial satisfaction of the interests of such groups. That strategy would be an extension of the efforts of Russia's top leadership in recent years to introduce new structures at the highest level of civil society, but it would be a step into the unknown that might seem too risky to leaders as cautious as Putin and Medvedev. It is possible to give good reasons both for and against expecting such a development. Whether grassroots movements can produce stable organisations, and whether initiatives from below can eventually mesh with structures created by the political leadership, are questions of crucial importance for the relationship between society and the state in Russia, and those questions remain unresolved.

Chapter 7

The Media and Political Communication

SARAH OATES and GILLIAN McCORMACK

From a distance, Russia provides a communications paradox in that there is so much information and so little democracy. The economic stability of the Russian media, in particular television, increased steadily as the economy improved under Putin in the first years of the twenty-first century. Yet, despite the actual growth in media companies, and their establishment as successful businesses, the last decade has seen a distinct decline in media pluralism and diversity of opinion in Russia. In some ways it would appear that the contemporary Russian media have more to do with the Soviet media than any Western model. While information sources have diversified and become technically more professional, the idea of the media as 'objective' or 'balanced' has never been widely accepted. All segments of Russian society, from politicians to the public to the journalists themselves, perceive the mass media as political actors themselves rather than watchdogs that can provide a check on political power. Thus, while there is no overt system of top-down state censorship in Russia today, the media are not free to contribute to the democratic process. This is due to an intertwined set of societal factors. These elements include a lack of professional acceptance of the concept of journalistic balance or objectivity; the use of the media as political pawns by leaders; and the public's acceptance of the media as a voice of authority rather than the purveyor of information.

While it might be tempting to dismiss these factors as an echo of the Soviet state or particular features of authoritarianism, the forces that drive the Russian media system are more subtle and complicated. Within the façade of social and political unity behind the Kremlin elite, there are sources of alternative information available to a large sector of the population. In particular, the global rise of the internet and its more limited reach in Russia could potentially challenge the Kremlin's dominant voice in the information sphere. However, there is still little evidence that the availability of information can have significant political or social effects.

118

This chapter will introduce readers to the media landscape in Russia, as well as to significant factors such as election and conflict coverage that have shaped the media and its message.

The Russian media landscape

Media outlets

What do Russians see, hear and read in their media? Currently, the Russian media sphere offers a wide range of broadcast and print alternatives. Unsurprisingly, television remains both the most favoured and the most influential medium, as it does in almost every country. Russia has a mix of state and commercial ownership across all of the print and broadcast industries. For wealthier citizens in urban areas, media diversity would appear to parallel that of European citizens. Russians have access to central state-run channels as well as some commercial television without paying for a subscription or a direct state television tax. For those who can afford it there are myriad satellite offerings, as in Western Europe. Radio stations, although mostly broadcasting music, also deliver some news (particularly the independent 'Echo of Moscow' station). There are periodicals across a huge range of political and economic spectrums, from world-class financial newspapers to hard-line communist propaganda to the popular local papers filled with classified ads. A range of magazines caters to every taste, from pets to pornography.

Despite all of this, there are two elements not present in Russia in the media sphere that are evident in Western Europe. First, there is no central television station that serves the public interest. State-run Channel 1 offers relatively high-quality news and other programming, but is markedly biased toward the political views of the Kremlin. In addition, the online sphere of the internet remains relatively underdeveloped in Russia, offering little serious alternative in political news or discussion. This is in contrast to some other post-Soviet countries, notably Ukraine, in which online information and mobilisation has played a political role (Krasnoboka and Semetko 2006).

A report by Internews Russia for the European Audiovisual Observatory in 2006 showed that the Russian television audience has a relatively wide and growing selection of broadcast offerings (Kachkaeva, Kiriya and Libergal 2006). Two state-run channels consistently attract the largest audience: Channel 1 (also known as The First Channel), which is 51 per cent owned by the Russian state, and the 100 per cent state-owned *Rossiya (Russia)* channel (see Table 7.1). Both channels have a prime-time news show, entertainment and analytical programmes, although they

Table 7.1   *Ratings of top Russian TV channels (2005)*

Channel	Ownership	Content	2005 rating (%)
First Channel	51% directly owned by state, rest is owned by entities including state enterprises	News and entertainment	22.9
Rossiya (Russia)	State	News and entertainment	22.6
A person's local TV company	Commercial and state	Varied	12.3
NTV	Commercial	News and entertainment	11.2
STS	Commercial	Entertainment	10.3
TNT	Commercial	Entertainment	6.7
REN TV	Commercial	Entertainment and news	5.0
TV-Centre	Moscow administration	News and entertainment	2.6
Kul'tura (Culture)	State	Cultural programming	2.5
Sport	Commercial	Sports only	1.8
DVT Viasat	Commercial	Entertainment, sports	1.5
MTV	Commercial	Music television	1.1
Muz TV	Commercial	Music television	1.0
Domashnyi (Home)	Commercial	Home shows	1.0

Source: Adapted from Kachkaeva *et al*. 2006.

have become progressively narrower in political diversity over time (Oates 2006b). For example, the Sunday night analysis shows on both central state channels used to feature some diverse information, but now critics of the Kremlin or serious political commentary on issues such as the Chechen War are not featured. In Moscow, TV-Centre is owned and run by the city administration. Commercial television, especially the national NTV network, is also relatively popular, while the state-owned 'Culture' channel for arts and historic programming has little market share.

It is interesting to note that regional television is relatively popular in Russia, coming third in the study conducted by Internews Russia in 2006. While analysis of regional television in Russia is relatively rare, work by Fossato (2007) suggests that regional television provides important information on key domestic social issues such as the spread of HIV and AIDS among the young, the abolition of subsidies as well as children's problems. These issues are virtually ignored on national television. Regional television and its audience started to gain more attention in 2005 after the

Moscow advertising market had grown to the point of saturation. The expansion into regional broadcast advertising led to more market research, and a study by TSN Gallup in 2005 showed that the regional public often disregards information on Russia's central, federal television channels and networks (such as The First Channel and *Rossiya*). Instead, as a report by TSN Gallup Media highlighted in an Internews-Russia media industry conference in Moscow in September 2005 (cited by Fossato 2007), regional audiences rely mainly on news and analytical programmes provided by regional broadcasters. Some live talk shows on regional television take in discussion on local attitudes that include sensitive topics such as the Chechen War, rising nationalism, xenophobia and corruption.

In interviews, Fossato (ibid.) found that local journalists do not have the 'luxury' of ignoring local concerns and complaints in the communities in which they live and work. However, she also highlights three elements that limit the ability of the regional media to create a consolidated alternative to the images projected by central Russian television. First, apart from responding to some local complaints, regional journalists generally do not adhere to the notion of disinterested service to the general public. In addition, there has been little coverage of international issues in the regional media. For instance, federal coverage of key international events, such as developments in Ukraine and Georgia after the revolutions of 2004, has not been balanced by local coverage that regional audiences would trust. Finally, the attention of the central authorities to the influence of regional television is growing, along with signs that relatively independent regional television companies will be challenged by centralised networks. Between January 2005 and late 2006, the St Petersburg broadcasting company *Pyatyi Kanal* (Fifth Channel) was awarded an unprecedented 73 regional broadcasting frequencies. In addition, a news-only channel called *Vesti-24* (Events-24) was launched by the state-owned broadcasting company VGTRK, which also runs the *Rossiya* channel. *Vesti-24* uses the frequencies of its regional subsidiaries. Both of these actions show that the state has helped to create unitary regional broadcasters that can be controlled by central authorities.

The most popular newspaper in Russia is the weekly *Argumenty i fakty* (Arguments and Facts), with a registered circulation of 2.9 million as of late 2008. The circulation audit service lists the following as the other top ten newspapers in Russia: *Weekly Life* (1.9 million), *TV Guide* (1.2 million), *Perm' Region Izvestiya* (1 million), *Komsomol'skaya pravda* (726,000), *Antenna* (654,000), *Metro-74* (551,000, a Chelyabinsk newspaper), *Our Newspaper for Television Programmes* (415,000, in Yekaterinburg) and *Ads of the South* (365,000 in Rostov-on-Don). The figures do not include all newspapers in Russia, as some are not registered with the non-profit circulation auditor. However, it is significant to note that four of the ten largest newspapers (as measured by circulation) are not based in Moscow. At the same time, there are some newspapers with more modest circulation that have more impact, such as the leading business broadsheet *Kommersant*. The National Circulation Service reports that this Moscow-based paper has a circulation of 70,625, but it would certainly include a relatively large number of important decision-makers amongst its readers.

The Russian media audience

While some Russians are wealthy by world standards, large segments of the population are relatively poor. As such, the media audience is very much divided between the information haves and have-nots. Paid television subscription with its many offerings and international programming remains relatively low at just 11 per cent of the population subscribed in 2005 (Kachkaeva *et al.* 2006: 76). Internet growth has been very rapid, but Russia still lags behind other developed countries in in-depth use (Cooper 2008). Cooper cites data from the Russian International Telecommunications Union suggesting that 2,500 out of every 10,000 Russians were online by 2007. President Dmitri Medvedev announced a goal of raising that rate to 4,000 out of every 10,000 Russians online by the end of 2008 (although how realistic this may be is debatable). Using economic indicators, Cooper has calculated that internet usage in Russia is actually surprising low for its level of development, although relatively high for the post-Soviet region. In addition, in some studies of the Russian internet it is not clear how often people go online, the quality of their connection or the availability of the connection (it may be a shared connection at work, school or in an internet café rather than a home connection). As studies of the internet emphasise (see Chadwick 2006), the accessibility and quality of connections are key to encouraging its regular and intensive use.

There are two significant trends in Russian media content, one linked to market forces and the other to political pressures. First, much like tabloid newspapers around the world, the Russian media often seek readership through sensationalist reporting. For example, some of the most popular newspapers in the country rely on tabloid-style reporting. In an appeal to populist tastes, more in-depth issues are often ignored or reported in superficial ways. Some of the most successful Russian tabloids use formats that would be familiar to British readers, particularly in the way that the Russian *Zhizn'* (Life) resembles the British *Sun*. Although it is tempting to dismiss tabloids as trivial or sensationalist, they popularise newspaper readership by publishing news that is short, sharp, often funny and provocative. The tone is opinionated, but informal – very different from the didactic and somewhat 'preachy' tone taken by many writers in the traditional Russian broadsheets. By the same token, newspapers are providing an important public service if they print information that readers find useful, interesting or engaging – ranging from classified ads to announcements about local government appointments. To suggest a parallel to the broadcast medium, game shows, soap operas, true-crime drama and other entertainment programmes may be deprecated as lacking in cultural or educational value, but they attract and entertain a large audience. While Russians often complain about how market forces have made media content more trivial, less cultural and more violent, they nonetheless watch these types of shows in fairly large numbers.

Media freedom

It is important to understand the gap that exists in Russia between media diversity and media freedom. While freedom of speech is guaranteed by the 1993 Russian Constitution, this has not served as the foundation for media laws that would support the ability of the mass media to serve as a force for democracy or even political plurality. Rather, the law has tended to work against the interests of free speech (Oates 2006b: 21–9). For example, there is no contemporary law on broadcasting, the key media sector in the country. In addition, as highlighted elsewhere in this volume, there is a general lack of rule of law in Russia. As such, the government can apply the law selectively in order to limit political opposition. This lack of transparency is particularly apparent in the media sector, in which the Putin administration used financial laws to force a change in ownership of a relatively outspoken media group (Media-Most) in 2001. In addition to problems with central government, media outlets face significant constraints at the local level. Not only can the 80-odd regions of Russia use their own laws to threaten outspoken media, local bureaucrats and officials can bring considerable pressure to bear on local media outlets by threatening to take away state premises, impose fines or taxes or even organise quite selective 'tax inspections' to confiscate material. In 2002, a law that bans 'extremism' in media coverage was passed as part of a package of anti-terrorism legislation. While many societies are concerned about the role of the media in radicalisation, this law in Russia also means that officials can interpret a wide range of government opposition as 'extreme'. Article 19, a non-governmental organisation that monitors censorship worldwide, points out that this Russian law was amended in 2007 and provides even more scope for controlling the media by defining extremism as 'defamation of public officials, relating to accusations of the commitment of a serious crime' and actions 'impeding the legal activities' of federal authorities 'linked to violence or threat of violence'. As even an ordinary political rally by the opposition could now be construed as a 'threat' of violence by Russian authorities, it is clear that the amended law gives the Russian government sweeping rights to interpret a wide range of political coverage as 'extreme' (*Article 19*, July 2006).

The law aside, there are other factors that seriously constrain the ability of journalists to pursue a broad range of creative and politically significant work. It is impossible to ignore the aura of threat and violence that – coupled with the essentially random nature of the legal system – makes it very difficult for individuals to engage in meaningful political communication. Put more simply, becoming a journalist who chooses to challenge the government can be a very dangerous profession in Russia. Russia is one of the deadliest countries in the world for journalists, as measured by international groups such as Reporters Without Borders. Part of this is due to the war in Chechnya as both Russian and foreign reporters are at risk of being detained or shot by Chechen *and* Russian forces. Although some journalists died in the violence of the first Chechen war, there was respect for the international norm of safe passage for war correspondents (to a degree) from both forces between 1994 and 1996. In the second war, from 1999 onwards, both sides showed little interest in preserving the life or liberty of journalists. The Committee to Protect Journalists reported that seven journalists were shot in Chechnya from 1999 to 2005 (including in crossfire and by targeted killings blamed on Chechen forces) and armed groups kidnapped five during the same time period (Lupis with Kishkovsky 2005: 26). The Center for Journalism in Extreme Situations believes the death toll of journalists in Russia will fall as media freedom decreases and fewer journalists are willing to risk reporting objectively, particularly on corruption, crime and Chechnya (Center for Journalists in Extreme Situations and the Russian Union of Journalists 2001).

Away from the war zone, violence against Russian journalists and even their murders have been well documented. The most high-profile case in recent years was the 2006 assassination of Anna Politkovskaya, who wrote in depth on the Chechen war for the liberal *Novaya gazeta* newspaper in Moscow. Politkovskaya was shot dead in the elevator of her apartment building in Moscow as she returned home from shopping. Her killers have never been tried. Although her death caused worldwide comment and outrage, then-president Putin was fairly dismissive of her work, saying she had little influence on political life in Russia. This sort of example is chilling for all journalists. The lack of uproar over Politkovskaya's death in Russia is not surprising, in that the Committee to Protect Journalists has estimated that 29 journalists were killed in a decade in post-Soviet Russia.

Aside from the international media attention to the murder of Politkovskaya, how are the Russian media perceived on the world stage? The simple response to this would be 'not well'. Despite the diversity and range of media outlets, it is clear that the Russian media are failing to provide objective or balanced information to the citizenry. Rather, the Russian media are mostly outlets for political interests, particularly those of the Kremlin. According to Freedom House, Russia tied with Azerbaijan for 166th place in the 2007 Freedom of the Press World Rankings. The US-based organisation lists several reasons for this low ranking, which is close to the bottom of the table of 195 country listings (Finland is first and North Korea is last: see www.freedomhouse.org for a full listing). The Freedom House report on Russia highlights changes in 2007 to the Law on Fighting Extremist Activity. The amendments expanded the definition of extremism to include media criticism of officials and authorised up to three years' imprisonment for journalists as well as the suspension or closure of their publications if they were convicted (Freedom House 2008). In addition, the 2007 report highlighted that journalists still faced criminal libel charges for printing or broadcasting statements that were unfavourable to public officials. According to the report, several journalists were sentenced on charges of 'inciting racial hatred' for publicising events in Chechnya. The report identified at least four journalists (apart from Politkovskaya) who were murdered. The report summarised the menacing environment for journalists: 'Journalists remained unable to cover the news freely, particularly with regard to contentious topics like Chechnya or the environment, and were subject to physical attacks, arrests, detentions, random searches, threats, and self-censorship.'

Development of media control in Russia

The problems reported by Freedom House and others raise the question of why the Russian media have largely failed as a democratic institution. The answer lies partly in the Soviet legacy, but also in the way in which Russia developed after the collapse of the Communist system. This section of the chapter will consider both of these problems, considering whether the Russian media are best understood as a 'neo-Soviet' institution or as more reflective of problems found in authoritarian states around the globe. The development of the media from the Soviet to the Russian period is both a lesson in how democratic institutions can fail as well as an interesting case study of the role of the media in the political sphere in general.

The Soviet media legacy

In the Soviet era, the media in the Soviet Union had a clear model. Their function was to educate the public in the central tenets of the ruling Communist Party and inculcate support for communist ideals. The country was run by the Communist Party (which did not tolerate any other political forces) technically in the name of the working class, but actually the utopian state of worker self-rule never emerged. Rather, the country was an authoritarian regime that punished dissent with imprisonment or death. Although the severity of repression varied under different Soviet leaders, no opposition to the regime or legitimate free media was tolerated. At the same time, the Soviets worked hard to develop a robust mass media system, convinced that it was necessary to instil the values of communism into Soviet citizens. By the end of the Soviet period in 1991, television could reach up to 98 per cent of the vast territory of the country, which covers 11 time zones. At the same time, only 32 per cent of Soviet homes had telephones, according to official statistics (Goskomstat 1996: 616). The ability to spread propaganda was clearly a priority. It was this vast propaganda machine that accelerated the collapse of the Soviet regime in 1991. In 1985, the new Soviet leader Mikhail Gorbachev introduced the policy of *glasnost'* or 'transparency' in the media. Gorbachev believed that this greater transparency would help people to understand and correct some of the problems of Soviet society. Yet, this new freedom to criticise minor problems soon led to vocal and public challenges to Soviet power itself. Once public opinion was unleashed, it turned against the Soviet leaders and the Soviet regime ended after a reactionary coup collapsed in 1991.

The Soviet past is key to understanding the current Russian media situation because journalistic norms appear to have changed relatively little from those times. From the time of *glasnost'* throughout the creation of the new Russian state, there was enormous variation, discussion and innovation in the mass media. However, the norms present in democratic systems did not emerge. For example, commercial media owners perceived their media outlets as tools for shaping public opinion for their own causes. State-run media outlets were clearly instruments to garner support for leaders such as first Russian president Boris Yeltsin and his successor Vladimir Putin. In both the US and British models, media outlets typically support the general principles and values of the state. Yet, in both systems there is a substantial attempt to find objectivity (in the US) or balance (on British television) on the part of journalists. There are many examples of how media in the West fail, but it is generally accepted that the media should serve as political observers or watchdogs in the service of citizens and/or consumers. In Russia, the media are perceived as political players. As a result, they are in the service of their political or commercial masters. While this is a condition that Russian media, politicians and the public accept as normal, it makes the growth of civil society enormously difficult. The Russian journalist has much in common with the Soviet journalist: he or she understands that the media are there to serve rather than to challenge. At the same time, the Russian audience has much in common with the Soviet audience, in that they understand and accept (to a large degree) that the media present a façade of order (Oates 2006b: 44–65).

One key way in which the Russian media have failed as a democratic institution is in their coverage of the elections held since the Soviet collapse. After the passage of the new Russian constitution in 1993, elections have been held regularly for parliament and the presidency in Russia (as well as for many regional and local leaders). It was expected that regular elections would aid in the development of democratic institutions, particularly political parties, and show the Russian public the value of free choice. What happened was rather different, in that from the very first elections for parliament in 1993, the government gave an unfair advantage to parties friendly to the Kremlin's agenda. Although the electoral law technically provides for free and equal time for all parties on state-run television – as well as fair news coverage – political influence has meant unequal treatment for parties that challenge the Kremlin's hegemony. This has been clear from content analysis of news coverage, free time and paid political advertising over several parliamentary and presidential elections (see European Institute for the Media 1994, February 1996, September 1996, March 2000, August 2000; Oates 2006b; Oates and Helvey 1997; Oates and Roselle 2000; Organisation for Security and Co-operation in Europe/Office for Democratic Institutions and Human Right, June 2004, January 2004; Center for Journalists in Extreme Situations 2008; White, Oates and McAllister 2005).

The media audience

Given the problems and deficiencies in the Russian mass media discussed above, it would seem likely that the public would be at best uninterested in and – at worst – very hostile to their domestic media outlets. In fact, there is compelling evidence that the opposite is true. Russian citizens appear to value, trust and pay close attention to their domestic media, according to many surveys and focus groups (Oates 2006b: 44–65). They are particularly fond of television: in a 2007 survey of 2,000 people from across Russia, 74 per cent reported using national television on a 'routine' basis, with another 19 per cent claiming to use it sometimes (see Table 7.2). While 59 per cent of the respondents also said they watched local

Table 7.2   *Media use in Russia, 2008*

Media	Use (rounded percentages)			
	Routinely	*Sometimes*	*Seldom*	*Never*
National newspapers	18	38	30	13
Local newspapers	27	40	26	9
National television	74	19	5	1
Local television	59	27	9	3
Internet	12	12	12	61

Source: Based on a national survey of 2,000 people in the Russian Federation in February 2008 directed by Stephen White with the support of the UK Economic and Social Research Council under grant RES-000-22-2532.

television routinely, only 27 per cent read local newspapers, 18 per cent read national newspapers and 12 per cent reported using the internet routinely. Meanwhile, 13 per cent reported *never* reading national newspapers, while only 1 per cent claimed to never watch television. The influence of television is underlined by the fact that 80 per cent of the respondents reported hearing about politics on television either daily or at least several times a week. This compares with 43 per cent who said they heard about politics on the radio or 35 per cent who read about politics in newspapers with the same frequency. State television news remains particularly popular, with 73 per cent of the respondents reporting themselves to be regular viewers of the flagship *Vremya* news programme on Channel 1. Sixty-one per cent of the respondents reported watching the *Vesti* news programme on Channel 2, with rather fewer (45 per cent) claiming to be regular viewers of the *Segodnya* news programme on the commercial station NTV. The Russian 'news junkie' habit is obvious here, as the figures make clear that people routinely watch more than one news programme.

It is not just consistent use that suggests the Russians are pleased with their news. In other research, Russians have reported a high level of trust in their media (Oates 2006b). In a 2001 survey of 2,000 people across Russia, two-thirds picked national state television as one of the 'most unbiased and reliable sources of information', far more than those who selected local newspapers (20 per cent), national newspapers (18 per cent), Russian radio stations (16 per cent), commercial television (13 per cent) or even relatives and friends (14 per cent). In addition, they rated television in general as one of their most trusted institutions, with 57 per cent of the respondents reporting that they had full or considerable confidence in state television, compared with 52 per cent for radio, 50 per cent for the armed forces, 48 per cent for the church, 47 per cent for the print media, 38 per cent for commercial television, 30 per cent for the government, 16 per cent for the parliament and only 11 per cent for political parties. When quizzed about these attitudes in more depth in focus groups in 2000 and 2004, Russians showed an interesting duality (Oates 2006b). They were aware that much of the news reporting on state television is selective, unbalanced or biased, but many of them viewed that as appropriate. Having lived through the economic and political chaos of the 1990s, they placed little value on wide-ranging political discussion. They viewed public debate as often leading to poor policy and economic chaos. Many of the respondents made clear that they believed the role of state-run television was to provide central authority and order in troubled times. This explains what might seem a paradox: Russians citizens appear to know that state-run television essentially functions as a propaganda machine for the authorities, but they often approve of this as they value order over democracy.

While understandable, this lack of interest in balance or objectivity has meant little public support for alternative media. The most high-profile case of this is the commercial media organisation Media-Most, which founded and ran the national commercial television network NTV. Up to the late 1990s, NTV proved an important success story in the commercial broadcast media in Russia, providing news, analysis and entertainment programming that showed more depth and diversity than state-run broadcast channels. By 2001, the network reached approximately 75 per cent of the Russian population and analysis showed that those who watched the NTV news tended to be more sceptical and questioning of the state-run news programmes (Oates 2006b: 89–111). In 2001, Russian authorities wrested control of Media-Most and its media empire from its owner, Vladimir Gusinsky, charging him with fraud and tax evasion.

While the financial underpinnings of Media-Most were complex, it was clearly a case of using the law selectively to remove an influential media owner who could not always be relied on to promote the Kremlin parties. Many prominent journalists immediately left NTV and the editorial line that was sometimes challenging of the Kremlin (and providing some news about the second Chechen war) shifted to a noticeably more pro-Kremlin stance. An analysis by the author of the NTV 2003 election coverage found that while the station's flagship evening news programme *Segodnya (Today)* remained somewhat more ironic and detached from the government, the show had dropped any serious or direct criticism of Putin's regime. The NTV editorial team was eventually shunted even further away from a public voice, when the television station to which they moved (TV6) was changed to an all-sports outlet.

From one perspective, the story of NTV is about the failure of one channel, which had some shaky financial backing. However, more importantly it represents the failure of commercial media to provide a balance to state-run media outlets in Russia. In a broader analysis of the Russian media that included five television channels, the OSCE/ODIHR found significant bias across the media spectrum during the 2003 election campaign, with most channels supportive of the pro-Kremlin parties and providing a disproportionate amount of negative coverage of the Communists. Although it was a parliamentary election, President Putin dominated the news throughout the campaign (OSCE/ODIHR January 2004). This pattern was repeated in 2007, according to a study of five state and commercial television broadcasters carried out by the Center for Journalists in Extreme Situations. After monitoring seven weeks of television coverage before the December 2007 Duma elections, this Moscow-based group found 'disturbing problems in news coverage of the contestants and other political subjects in majority of the monitored media outlets' making it 'very difficult for Russians to get accurate and unbiased coverage of political parties, candidates and other issues' (CJES 2008). The group found that the majority of the monitored media showed a clear bias in favour of President Putin and the ruling party United Russia. Out of the five monitored TV channels, four gave the ruling powers more than 75 per cent of their news coverage. Unsurprisingly, President Putin received coverage that was overwhelmingly positive or – at worst – neutral in tone.

The monitored media, at the same time, failed to offer the opposition any significant airtime and opportunities to challenge the political opinions of the ruling powers. The report remarked that that it was particularly disappointing that state-run media had failed so spectacularly to provide voters with adequate information to make informed vote choices (CJES 2008). Despite their love of television and TV news, Russians are understandably unenthusiastic about following rather non-competitive elections in the media. In the 2007 survey cited above, only 20 per cent said that the media attracted their attention to the Duma elections. In addition only 20 per cent found that the media clarified the election process, while 8 per cent felt that the media election coverage had been a source of confusion, and a miniscule 3 per cent reported that media coverage had helped to sway their vote choice. Most – 32 per cent – said that the media coverage of the elections had no effect at all.

At least in earlier Russian elections there had been a broader range of information and debate. In the 1995 parliamentary elections, NTV provided key coverage of the first Chechen war that challenged the sanitised and inaccurate portrayal of the conflict on state-run Russian television (Oates 2006b; EIM 2006). This coverage of the war was important in keeping the public aware of the conflict and contributed to the decision by the Yeltsin administration to broker a shaky ceasefire in 1996.

However, NTV soon lost much hard-won credibility by overtly siding with President Yeltsin in his bid to win re-election against a strong Communist Party challenger (Mickiewicz 1999). NTV officials have justified this decision as necessary to fend off the threat of renewed communism, but the lack of transparency in commercial television only confirmed suspicions on the part of the Russian audience that commercial media – like state-run media – have particular political agendas. The history of NTV would suggest that is true – NTV provided an alternative voice, but that voice also lacked balance and objectivity to a certain degree.

In its 2007 report, Freedom House highlighted concerns about media ownership in general. In many ways, Russian media outlets endure the worst of both worlds of state and commercial ownership. The state directly owns a significant share of the national media, including all of the *Rossiya* television channel and 51 per cent of Channel 1. In addition, these are clearly 'state' as opposed to 'public' media outlets. While public broadcasting such as PBS in the United States or the BBC in the United Kingdom are at least designed to fend off government interference, the state media outlets in Russia are in fact intended to broadcast the views of the rulers. In addition, the Russian state (through state enterprises such as Gazprom, the huge energy concern) owns or controls significant stakes in Russia's three main national television outlets, Channel 1, *Rossiya* and NTV (Freedom House 2007). There is a relatively broad range of opinions in the national press, but as Freedom House reports, 'ownership of regional print media is less diverse and often concentrated in the hands of local authorities'.

There is little coverage of Chechnya at the time of writing, with the exception of some websites and individual critical newspapers such as *Novaya gazeta*. In terms of overall attention, there is evidence from Russian focus groups and interviews with journalists themselves that there are two compelling reasons that keep the ongoing conflict out of the news (Oates 2006b: 37–40). First, it is a difficult and dangerous story for journalists to cover, both in terms of trying to get information on the ground and the fact that the government is known to be intolerant of any coverage that could be deemed sympathetic to the Chechen cause. This attitude has continued to harden over time, particularly with the horrific slaughter at the Beslan school by Chechen terrorists in 2004. The second factor is related to the audience, in that there is a weariness of Chechen coverage, and even a growing distaste for any coverage of the conflict that smacks of a lack of Russian patriotism. In this way, Russians are like their US counterparts after 9/11, with little tolerance for deeper explanations or analysis about the events (Oates 2006a). Journalists are aware of this attitude on the part of both the government and the audience – and both are factors that contribute to the dearth of coverage of Chechnya in the Russia mainstream media.

While the case for avoiding coverage of Chechnya is linked to perceived audience preferences to a degree, journalists routinely practise self-censorship across a range of subjects in Russia (European Institute for the Media March 2000, August 2000; Oates 2006b). This is an area in which there is a strong legacy from the Soviet era, when journalists were obliged to adhere to strong central censorship. The key question about Russian journalists is whether they have fundamentally changed from the Soviet era. It would be understandable if older journalists who acquired their training and professional experience during the Soviet period had trouble shifting to different attitudes toward reporting.

Worryingly, though, there is evidence that the post-Soviet generation of journalists fail to perceive themselves as political watchdogs or even conduits of a range of political information to the public (Voltmer 2000; Pasti 2005). In both commercial and state-funded media outlets, journalists are expected to adhere to the editorial line, which in turn is limited by government pressure and interference. With the lack of an independent court system, there is little legal recourse for media outlets selectively targeted by financial or libel lawsuits. While the unsettled political and economic situation in the early 1990s allowed for a fairly wide variation of opinions, no major sector of the media developed an attempt to provide balanced information of use to citizens. Rather, it was a cacophony of opinionated news that has quieted as political opinions have themselves been reduced. It is a spiralling phenomenon – the narrower the political elite, the smaller the range of media outlets. This demonstrates the importance of media that serve the public rather than cater to political masters.

The Russian internet: beacon of democracy or tool for repression?

As there is a lack of media freedom in Russia, could the unique features of the internet as a mass medium fill this gap? The internet's potential for democratisation can be summarised as a very low-cost ability to distribute information to a potentially limitless global audience; relative freedom from editorial filters and controls; relative independence from national media control and an ability to build an international audience; and an interactive environment in which people can easily cross from being news consumers to news producers (Oates 2008). The evidence from the Russian online sphere – including internet content, control, usage and audience – suggests that the Russian internet can do little to counter the Russian media's more general failure as a Fourth Estate. Part of this is due to the relatively low penetration of the internet, as noted above. However, other factors are important as well, although the Russian internet is not controlled as heavily as in countries like China (Open Net Initiative 2005).

While there are well-known, professional websites that address Russian news and politics, many of them reflect the limited spread of news found in the mainstream media. This is not surprising, in that the Web is dominated by mainstream media sites in various countries, including the United States and the United Kingdom. A 2007 project by the Reuters Institute for the Study of Journalism at Oxford University examined three of the most popular blogs with political content in Russia in an attempt to understand the nature of the Russian Web. The researchers found a disturbing echo of the dynamics of the Russian traditional media and political elites. In the Reuters Institute project, researchers examined both the general state of the internet in Russia as well as the Russian blogosphere. The researchers noted that Western expectations about the internet's ability to deploy 'democratisation mechanisms' were not shared by local analysts of the Russian online sphere. Notably, Russian analysts felt that Russian political norms would be more likely to be replicated rather than challenged online, such as by being used by elites to discuss politics within a relatively closed circle. It would seem that Russia is *shaping* the internet, rather than Russian society being *shaped by* the internet. This is a particularly clear and compelling image of how the internet is constrained by domestic, rather than international, political communication norms.

Conclusions

It is clear that the main aim of most of the media in Russia is not unbiased or even balanced reporting; rather, the media seek to maintain the current elites in power. As a result, the news is remarkably unbalanced when covering domestic politics, using every opportunity to showcase current leaders while marginalising those seeking to contest that power. Focus-group discussions and survey research suggest that the Russian audience is comfortable with trading fairness and balance for the notion of a strong, stable state offered in much of their media. While alternative critical voices still exist in the Russian media sphere, for example in the liberal Moscow-based newspaper *Novaya gazeta*, they have little impact on public opinion and wider political forces in Russia. The voices challenging the Kremlin's authority are there – it is just that very few people are listening. For example, there is little discussion and debate about the war in Chechnya, even though Russian citizens (on both sides of the conflict) continue to die in the war. If any media outlet is perceived to threaten the state, it risks closure.

Does this mean that the Russian media echo the Soviet media, a docile chorus of approval in the service of the state? There are worrying similarities between the Soviet and Russian media spheres, in particular in terms of widespread self-censorship on the part of journalists. The range of political patrons appears to be broader than in Soviet times, yet there is little serious opposition to the ruling elites in Moscow. On the other hand, the post-Soviet world has introduced a new lawlessness and violence against journalists, controlling the information sphere by discouraging investigative journalists with violence and even death from unknown assailants. Russian journalists and media outlets are caught in a virtually impossible situation, squeezed between market and state forces that are hostile to the tenets of journalism in the service of the public good. The result is a limited range of information across a wide number of outlets, an appearance of media diversity that actually masks the dearth of adequate information to support a civil society. Nor can global communication forces such as the internet defy the Russian media logic. As a result, there is little chance that the Russian media can advance democratisation or even resist the country's increasing authoritarianism.

Chapter 8

Legal Reform and the Dilemma of Rule of Law

GORDON B. SMITH

In the more than fifteen years since the enactment of the new Constitution of the Russian Federation, substantial progress has been made in establishing a workable and independent judiciary and legal system. Many new laws have been enacted and important legal reforms have been undertaken. At the same time, the enforcement of laws has been uneven and at times politicised, which erodes public support and belief in the courts and other law enforcement bodies.

In order for law to function in a modern society, three ingredients are necessary. First is the enactment of new laws and legislation. The second element necessary for a functioning legal system is the creation of institutions, such as courts, bailiffs, police, and other agencies to implement and enforce laws. These institutions must have sufficient authority and independence to ensure fair and uniform enforcement of laws. They also require sufficient funds, equipment, personnel and other resources in order to function effectively. But new laws and enforcement mechanisms alone are not sufficient for legal systems to function in a civil society. The third necessary ingredient is citizen compliance with and reliance on both the laws and the enforcement institutions to secure their rights and interests. For true rule of law to exist, citizens and law enforcement authorities alike must internalise the values of the supremacy of law, due process, justice, impartiality, and equality before the law.

This chapter will survey recent trends in legal reform in Russia beginning with major revisions in the written laws. Then we will turn to examine the institutions – courts, police, prosecutors and other agencies – whose job it is to enforce the laws. After that, we will assess the quality of implementation of laws and realisation of the principles of justice and due process, noting areas of progress and areas where abuses may threaten the future development of rule of law in Russia. Finally, we will explore the degree to which the values of rule of law appear to be taking root in Russian society today.

Reforming Russia's laws

Russian conceptions of law derive from a complex amalgam of legal traditions, including Russian centuries-old customary law, elements of codified civil law introduced from Europe in the eighteenth and nineteenth centuries, Marxist and Soviet notions of social engineering through law, and extensive borrowing of Western models after the collapse of the USSR. The result is a legal culture that stresses the prerogatives of the state and has historically placed less emphasis on private property rights and civil liberties.

With the collapse of the USSR in 1991 whole new codes of law had to be drafted and ratified and thousands of former Soviet laws that remained in force out of necessity had to be drastically revised and updated to reflect Russia's aspirations of becoming a democratic and capitalist nation. This legal drafting was a massive undertaking requiring assembling teams of experts to draft new and revise codes of criminal law, criminal procedure, civil law, civil procedure, labour law, land law, tax law, environmental protection law, bankruptcy law, housing law, administrative law, family law, inheritance law, health and safety law, maritime law, and laws governing joint stock companies, banks, media, utilities, public corporations, just to name a few. New laws were also promulgated to spell out the legal jurisdiction, structure and function of the courts, police, prosecutors, court bailiffs, and other law enforcement agencies. In 1994 and 1995 alone more than 185 major pieces of new legislation were passed by the Duma and signed by the president. The process of drafting of new laws and codes was hampered prior to December 1993 by the absence of a new constitution. In continental legal systems, the constitution provides the foundation upon which all other codes and bodies of law are based. Consequently, it was difficult or impossible for Russian legal reformers to enact major new pieces of legislation until the constitution was in place.

The quality of legal drafting was also uneven. Russia's newly elected deputies to the Duma lacked both prior experience with legislative drafting and adequate staffs of trained lawyers to assist them. Not surprisingly, many of the laws initially enacted during the 1990s proved to be inadequate or unworkable and had to be revised.

The Criminal Procedure Code

Among the most notable changes and additions to Russian law in recent years was the new Criminal Procedure Code. Russian lawyers and their Soviet predecessors had long lobbied for major revisions to Russian criminal parocedure to bring Russia into closer alignment with legal systems in Europe and North America. After considerable debate and consultation with legal experts in Russia and abroad, a new Code of Criminal Procedure was passed by the Duma in 2001 and went into effect in mid-2002.

Among the key features of the new code are a formal statement of presumption of innocence (Article 14); the obligatory participation of defence counsel in all criminal cases; the right of suspects to meet with a lawyer in private before being interrogated by police (Article 56); a prohibition on repeated interrogations of suspects (Article 173); the exclusion of testimony or other evidence given during an interrogation without a defence lawyer being present in order to reduce potential for torture or overly aggressive interrogation techniques (Article 75); a restriction on detaining persons suspected of committing criminal offenses to no more than 48 hours without the consent of the court; the assigning to the court of sole authority to approve detentions, arrests, or prolong terms of detention or imprisonment of persons; the requirement that the court authorise all search warrants, wiretaps, and the seizure of property, records, or other material evidence; a prohibition on the court returning cases to the prosecutor for further investigation; a provision for plea bargains (Chapter 40); the prohibition of double jeopardy (Article 405); and expansion of jury trials in especially serious cases throughout the federation.

These changes were not popular with Russia's law enforcement community and conservative members of the Duma, and the new code only passed thanks to President Putin's personal lobbying. The new Criminal Procedure Code was hailed in the Western press for making bold and decisive strides forward toward rule of law. Kristina Pencheva of the Council of Europe notes, '[The new code] is a positive development since it brings Russia more into line with the standards of the European Convention on Human Rights' (Balmforth 2002). The overall effect of the new code has been to instil a more adversarial dimension into criminal proceedings, in which the prosecution and defence present their evidence and the court remains the neutral arbiter of cases. But how is the new Criminal Procedure Code working in practice?

While the Criminal Procedure Code contains a formal statement of presumption of innocence in criminal trials, the very nature of the investigatory process favours the prosecution. In Russia, as in most continental European legal systems, a person is only formally charged with a criminal offence after an extensive preliminary investigation. The prosecutor then submits a 'summary of accusations' to the trial judge for review. If serious deficiencies exist in the prosecution's case, the matter will not be recommended to go forward to trial. Thus, any case that comes to trial carries an unofficial, yet powerful presumptive bias against the accused.

During criminal proceedings the accused is normally confined to a barred cage-like dock. It is also common practice to give very short haircuts to all male suspects being held in pre-trial detention. Consequently, when the accused stands trial he often appears in the courtroom as a convict behind bars, which can seriously prejudice a jury and undermine the concept of a presumption of innocence.

The new Criminal Procedure Code also mandates that jury trials, which were first introduced in 1993 on an experimental basis in nine regions, be expanded to the entire country (with the exception of Chechnya). The jury is composed of twelve Russian citizens (and two alternates) between the ages of 25 and 70. Jurors decide questions of guilt or innocence, while judges decide questions of law. The jury reaches its decision based on a majority vote, with a vote of at least seven to five necessary for conviction. It is up to the judge, guided by the Criminal Code, to set punishment; however, the jury may if it chooses, recommend leniency in a case.

Compensation or payment for jurors is very modest. Consequently, many people do not want to miss work to serve on a jury. One Russian trial attorney characterises jurors as mostly 'elderly, conservative people who will do whatever the judge wants them to do' (Rogotsev 2008). However, it is notable that jury trials have a higher acquittal rate – approximately 18 per cent, compared to only one or two per cent of bench trials with one judge and two lay assessors (US Department of State 2007: 8). On the other hand, almost one-third of the not guilty verdicts in jury trials have been appealed by prosecutors and reversed by the Supreme Court (ibid.: 8). Sergei Nasonov, a professor of criminal law at Moscow State Law Academy, observes, 'Nobody thought so many verdicts would be overturned. The reasons for overturning jury verdicts were supposed to be very limited, but the Supreme Court has interpreted the law very broadly. A jury verdict is hardly ever the final word' (Finn 2005: A12).

According to several criminal defence lawyers and legal scholars in Russia, provisions in the new code on interrogations are generally working. Police investigators take care to have a defence attorney present for all interrogations. However, accused persons who cannot afford their own counsel have to rely on court-appointed public defenders. Some public defenders are known to be 'in the pockets' of the police. Nevertheless, the Association of Advocates takes disciplinary action against defence attorneys who violate ethnical or professional norms, and advocates with disciplinary actions taken against them or who are under investigation are barred from serving as legal counsel. The threat of professional sanctions has helped to ensure that defence attorneys protect the rights of suspects and accused.

The provision in the new code requiring that judges approve all search warrants has had a similar mixed pattern of implementation. Although search warrants can no longer be written by police or criminal investigators on the scene, they are easy to obtain from judges and can even be obtained after the fact in cases of an 'emergency' or other extenuating circumstance. Violations of provisions of the new criminal procedure code relating to searches and interrogations have in a few cases resulted in acquittals, charges being dropped, or reduction of charges, but it is not common. Most Russian lawyers specialising in criminal law acknowledge that the practices of the police and criminal investigators have not changed much over time (Central and East European Law Initiative 2008).

New laws regulating commerce and the economy

A second area of rapidly evolving legislation in Russia relates to business practices and the economy. The Russian economy has experienced rapid growth and development since 1999, fuelled in large part by exploitation of the nation's massive oil and gas reserves. During the past decade Russia has become increasing integrated into the global economy and is now in the process of joining the World Trade Organisation. The influence of this globalisation has helped to bring about several new laws or revisions to previous laws governing various aspects of the Russian economy and business practice. For example, amendments have been made to the Law on Joint Stock Companies to protect against the dilution of minority shareholders' influence through issuance of additional shares and 'closed subscriptions' – the sale of shares to a particular class of individuals or entities. The revised law also mandates that when a company goes through reorganisation, dividing the company or creating new spin-off companies, shareholders must receive *pro rata* portions of shares of all new or reorganised companies. The revised Law on Joint Stock Companies also grants greater access to shareholder lists and enhances corporate transparency by opening accounting records. Finally, it establishes the right of shareholders to nominate candidates to boards and management positions and makes it easier to force the removal of poorly performing chief executive officers and directors.

A new Code of Labour Law was enacted in 2003. Among other things, it allows private firms to hire and dismiss workers, guarantees workers' rights, including a minimum wage, a 40-hour work week, and the right to be represented by a single union chosen by the majority of workers. The new legislation also requires employers to pay wage arrears with interest.

The privatisation of industrial and commercial property as part of Yeltsin's 'shock therapy' programme in the 1990s was widely seen by the

Russian public as fraudulent and corrupt, benefiting a few at the expense of the masses. Consequently, when discussions began on private ownership of land in 2002, it sparked a public outcry. Nevertheless, President Putin and his economic advisers recognised that allowing for private ownership of land was necessary if Russia was to attract Western investment and if Russia's chronic agricultural stagnation was to be addressed. As with the Criminal Procedure Code, Putin lobbied a reluctant Duma, which eventually enacted major revisions to the land law in 2003 allowing for the sale of farmland to private companies and to Russian citizens.

The notoriously convoluted and ineffective tax laws in Russia have been replaced by a simplified code featuring a 13 per cent flat tax on personal income and 24 per cent tax on corporate profits. As a result of the simplification of the tax system and increased enforcement, the tax collection rate has increased dramatically in recent years. The revised tax laws also prohibit the seizure of property by tax authorities unless such an action is ordered by a court.

Creating a 'unified legal space'

During the chaos of transition and the ineffectual leadership of President Boris Yeltsin and his team, the power of federal authorities diminished markedly. Power flowed to regional and local levels, or to non-governmental actors, including enterprises and some 10,000 organised crime syndicates. In 2000 President Putin inherited a government unable to enforce its own laws, collect taxes or defend its borders, much less guarantee the safety and security of its citizens. Terrorism, which was largely unknown in the Soviet Union and Russia prior to the 1994 Russian invasion of Chechnya, thrived in the increasingly weakened state of Russia, culminating in the downing of two civilian airliners and the Beslan school hostage tragedy in 2004.

Putin's earlier experience in dealings with officials in Russia's regions convinced him that many were corrupt and some were actively co-operating with organised crime groups engaged in trafficking in illegal arms, narcotics, and human beings. Because the governors of the regions held seats in the upper house of the Russian parliament, the Council of Federation, they enjoyed immunity from criminal prosecution. Under the slogan of creating a 'unified legal space' in Russia, Putin mounted a campaign to scrutinise local and regional laws and other normative acts to ensure that they are consistent with the Constitution and other laws of the Russian Federation. In a televised address to the nation Putin observed: 'Russia currently has more than one thousand federal laws and several thousand laws of the republics, territories, regions and autonomous areas. Not all of them correspond to the above criterion [of constitutionality]' (Putin 1999). He called for prosecutors to review the legality of normative acts of various executive and legislative bodies at all levels. In response, 60 constitutions and charters of regional governments and tens of thousands of locally and regionally enacted laws and rules were brought into line with the Constitution and federal legislation. 'It is simply incredible that we can continue to exist in such conditions', Putin remarked (Bessarabov and Rybchinsky 2001). In several cases, regional authorities challenged the federal government's nullification of their laws and rules in court, and without exception, courts have sided with federal authorities (Hahn 2003). The very fact that such disputes are being decided in appellate-level courts has also elevated the status of the courts and enhanced their legitimacy.

Not only have hundreds of new laws been drafted and existing laws revised in the past few years, the quality of the legal drafting has improved markedly. The Duma, the Presidential Administration, most executive agencies and regional governments have established legal staffs to assist in drafting laws. The Ministry of Justice holds periodic conferences to discuss pending legislation and issues instructions to courts, law enforcement agencies, and regional governments to improve the quality of rule-making and enforcement. The results have been notable. For example, in the area of intellectual property law new legislation designed to curb pirating, especially of music and computer software, appears to be greatly improved. A leading American lawyer specialising in intellectual property issues asserts: 'Russian law on copyright provides a more than adequate legal framework for protecting intellectual property rights ... the development of this area of the law is clearly important to Russia ... and has created an atmosphere of legal predictability' (Preston 2008: 4). Russia's new copyright laws have been successfully applied in courts in the United States and Europe, and foreign copyright laws have also been successfully applied in Russian courts. Of eight reported appellate cases involving Microsoft Corporation seeking to enforce its rights in Russian courts, Microsoft won in six cases and lost in only two (ibid.).

Reforming the courts and law enforcement agencies

In recent years we have witnessed not only the enactment of new laws and efforts to bring laws and rules enacted by regional governments into conformity with the Constitution and federal legislation, we have also observed progress toward improving the functioning of the judiciary and enhancing its independence.

The Ministry of Justice administers all of the courts and is responsible for drafting legislation on the courts, judges, and substantive law codes. In addition, the Ministry provides training of judicial personnel, supervises the appointment and review of judges and other personnel and undertakes research on trends in law enforcement.

At the bottom of the judicial hierarchy are the courts of general jurisdiction that exist throughout Russia at the local level. With the exception of the commercial courts (*arbitrazh*) and military courts martial, the courts of general jurisdiction handle all legal matters, whether they are criminal, civil, administrative or related to family law, inheritance, adoption or other issues. The courts of general jurisdiction are organised into two separate chambers, one for criminal trials and one for civil and other types of cases. In most cases, trials are heard by panels of one professional judge and two lay judges. Lay judges are ordinary citizens, 25 years old or older, elected for terms of two years. Lay judges have the full powers of a judge, including the right to review all investigatory documents, call and question witnesses, examine evidence, set punishment and award damages. Judicial decisions are made in private by a vote of the judge and the two lay judges. However, in most cases, lay judges defer to the professional training and experience of the judge.

Technically reporting to the courts of general jurisdiction are justice of the peace courts, which were authorised at the end of 1998 but were delayed in being established due to budgetary constraints and the absence of implementing legislation. By 2003 there were some 5,000 justice of the peace courts in Russia and there are plans to double their number in the next few years (Solomon 2003: 387–8). Justice of the peace courts consider minor civil and criminal cases, reducing the caseload and improving the quality of judicial consideration of more complicated and serious cases in the courts of general jurisdiction.

Courts in the constituent republics, regions and territories of the Russian Federation, as well as the cities and Moscow and St Petersburg, hear cases on appeal from lower courts and also serve as the courts of first instance in major cases. At the top of the judicial hierarchy is the Supreme Court, which hears cases on appeal from inferior courts and in a limited number of cases of 'exceptional importance', the court has original jurisdiction. The Supreme Court is composed of twenty justices and is divided into three chambers or collegia for civil cases, criminal cases, and military cases. In all three chambers cases are heard by panels of three judges and in cases of original jurisdiction, one judge and two lay judges.

In 1995 a separate system of commercial (*arbitrazh*) courts was established to resolve commercial disputes, including disputes involving foreign companies. The jurisdiction of the commercial courts extends to a wide array of issues, including disputes associated with privatisation, taxes, bankruptcy, reorganisation and mergers. Above the commercial courts in each of Russia's (as of 2008) 83 constituent regions are ten federal commercial courts that function as appeals courts. The Higher Commercial Court of the Russian Federation oversees the commercial courts and hears cases on appeal.

The nationwide system of commercial courts has experienced a significant increase in cases in recent years – 1.2 million in 2004 and rising at a rate of 15–20 per cent every year (Trochev 2005: 17). The largest share of cases before the commercial courts concern the imposition of taxes and fines, non-payment for goods, and the non-delivery of goods purchased (Hendley 2004: 340). Two-thirds of the cases in the commercial courts involve commercial enterprises filing complaints against government bodies or officials (Trochev 2005: 18). Often such cases relate to the imposition of fines, taxes or duties. Tax cases alone numbered 188,162 in 2001 and taxpayers prevailed in 70 per cent of them (Solomon 2004: 556; Hendley 2002: 122). It is often alleged that powerful political figures attempt to influence judicial decisions. However, contrary to general perceptions, courts of general jurisdiction and commercial courts rule against the government in approximately 80 per cent of cases (Solomon 2004: 562).

Separate from the hierarchy of regular and commercial courts is the Constitutional Court of the Russian Federation. The Constitutional Court was modelled on similar courts in Western Europe, especially the German Federal Constitutional Court. The Constitutional Court is the only court empowered to review constitutional questions and access to the court is relatively unrestricted; most cases require no previous hearing. Decisions of the court are final and not subject to appeal. There are 19 justices on the Court, the Court has a large staff organised into departments reflecting major branches of law (constitutional law, criminal law, international law, administrative law, land law, etc.) and hears approximately between 120 and 150 cases each year.

Stopping telephone justice?

For more than two decades Russian lawyers and judges have striven to establish the independence of the courts, insulating them from political pressures, whether from powerful political figures or business interests. Unfortunately, the legal system in the USSR left a legacy of political meddling in the work of the courts. Communist party officials, mayors, and even directors of commercial enterprises would routinely telephone judges to 'advise' them on cases pending before them. This practice, known as 'telephone justice', was widespread and persists today, despite efforts to guarantee the independence of the courts.

Changes have been enacted to the process for selecting and evaluating judges. The President now appoints all judges from a list of candidates who have been screened by a judicial qualifications committees. After an initial three-year appointment, judges serve for life, but there is mandatory retirement at age 65 for most judges and 70 years for judges in the highest courts. In 2006 judges' salaries were increased by 40 per cent and improvements were made in staff support, facilities and equipment in order to enhance their independence, effectiveness and prestige (US Department of State 2007: 7). According to Sergei Kazantsev, a justice on the Constitutional Court of the Russian Federation, raising the salaries and living standards of judges has helped considerably in enhancing judicial independence and reducing corruption (Kazantsev 2008). The judicial qualifications committees were also expanded to include more lay people and given responsibility not only for nominating candidates to judicial positions, but also responsibility for dismissing judges. These changes, while increasing judicial independence from external influences, may have made judges even more exposed to political pressures from the presidential administration.

Authorities note that judicial independence has improved in the past few years. Today (at the time of writing) the most common infringement of judicial independence comes from powerful economic interests or high-ranking government officials. According to one Constitutional Court justice, problems of judicial independence are more pronounced in the commercial courts, where powerful enterprises with close ties to the government expect favourable treatment (Kazantsev 2008). A Russian lawyer who routinely tries cases in the commercial courts observes: 'Big firms, such as Gazprom, don't have to overtly exert pressure on the court since they are so well connected and have their own powerful legal staffs' (Rogotsev 2008).

Although judicial corruption has diminished and experts acknowledge that it is only a small minority of judges who accept bribes, the problem persists. In the first six months of 2006 the Ministry of Justice reported that 39 judges were dismissed and 151 given warnings (US Department of State 2007: 7–8). However, the Ministry of Justice does not report the causes for dismissal or warnings. It is likely that many of these judges committed other violations, rather than accepting bribes. President Dmitri Medvedev has made eradicating corruption among judges a top priority. Shortly after his inauguration, Medvedev convened a special conference of judges and law enforcement officials. In his opening remarks Medvedev said: 'The main objective is to achieve judicial independence.' He added, 'As we all know, when justice fails it often does so because of pressure of various kinds, such as surreptitious telephone calls and money – there is no point beating around the bush about it' (Medvedev 2008).

Putin's shake-up of law enforcement agencies

It is not just the courts that have experienced problems: other law enforcement agencies have also been accused of bribe-taking and have been reorganised in recent years. In early 2003 law enforcement agencies came under intense scrutiny for corruption, bribe-taking, and harassing businesses. President Putin met with the heads of all law enforcement agencies on 11 March 2003 and singled out the Tax Police, the Ministry of Internal Affairs (which governs the police), the Customs Service, and several regulatory agencies for the harshest criticisms – accusing them of demanding bribes, special favours, and other attempts to abuse their positions of authority to 'terrorise' private citizens and businesses. The next day the Tax Police was disbanded and the police and Customs Service reorganised to ensure compliance with the law. The only agencies to escape criticism were the Federal Security Service (FSB) and the Procuracy (Shvaryov 2003: 1–2). The Ministry of Internal Affairs, the Ministry of Emergency Situations, the State Construction Committee and the Ministry of Labour were all stripped of their powers to close commercial enterprises for various unsubstantiated violations of trade, tax, fire safety or employment regulations. The threat of closure had been frequently employed by these agencies in an effort to extort money or other benefits from commercial enterprises. The closure of private businesses can now be approved only by a court.

In his 2005 'State of the Nation' address, Putin again criticised tax and customs offices for 'terrorising' private businesses and advocated several measures designed to benefit struggling businesses, including reducing the statute of limitation from ten to three years for prosecution for various illegal commercial transactions and more lenient terms for businesses to pay tax arrears (Putin 2005b). The concern with protecting private business and stabilising the legal system in order to attract foreign investment was a recurring theme of the Putin administration. He repeatedly emphasised the need to protect private property and the rights of entrepreneurs, noting that the development of the Russian economy depends on effective laws and law enforcement institutions (Zakatnova 2001: 3). In his annual speech to prosecutors in 2005, Putin urged them to devote more effort to protecting businesses from pressures from criminal groups and corrupt government officials (Putin 2005a: 1, 4).

It appeared that the Procuracy and the Federal Security Service had avoided criticism and restructuring. However, in June 2007 Putin signed legislation creating a separate Investigations Committee to undertake all criminal investigations. This action, which was strongly opposed by prosecutors, strips the Procuracy of responsibility for overseeing criminal investigations and transfers some 18,000 federal investigators to the

Committee. The official reason cited for the move was the desire to separate criminal investigations from the prosecution of cases in court, a division that occurs in most Western legal systems and had long been advocated by Western consultants and the Council of Europe. However, others speculated that the Committee on Investigations was created to counterbalance an increasingly powerful and politicised Prosecutor-General's Office. Still others linked the Procuracy and the new director of the Committee on Investigations to competing political 'clans' that were jockeying for power in the last days of Putin's presidency (Blank 2008: 24). Not surprisingly, the transfer of authority has experienced problems. More than 60,000 pending cases had to be transferred to the Committee and in many instances case materials disappeared (Central and East European Law Initiative 2008). Prosecutors also worry that violations of suspects' due process rights during criminal investigations will result in problems for them during trials (ibid.).

Challenges confronting the Russian legal system

Despite the progress in both drafting new and better laws and reorganising various law enforcement agencies to enhance their performance and independence, several challenges continue to plague the realisation of rule of law in Russia today. Among the most chronic and persistent problems are a culture of corruption, politicisation and selective enforcement of the law, and non-implementation of judicial decisions.

A culture of corruption

The legacy of corruption from the Soviet system is deeply ingrained in Russia. Although much attention has focused on the courts, in reality the problem is much more extensive in the private sector and among petty bureaucratic officials. The Prosecutor-General's Office estimates corruption in the Russian Federation at $240 billion per year, approximately equal to the annual federal budget (Central and East European Law Initiative 2008). President Medvedev reported that in 2007 more than 10,500 corruption cases were investigated but added that this represented 'just the tip of the iceberg' (Medvedev 2008).

Obtaining licenses for businesses, construction permits, or even registration and inspection for an automobile often requires paying a bribe or an 'unofficial fee'. A Russian lawyer working in commercial law reports that companies often hire people to 'expedite' the registration paperwork for new joint stock companies. The going rate is 10,000 roubles (approximately $400). He concludes: 'The bribe culture runs deep in Russia; it is just part of the cost of doing business here' (Rogotsev 2008). There have also been reported cases of enterprises paying law enforcement officials to harass their competitors. According to one report, getting police to open a criminal investigation against a rival costs $20,000 to $50,000, an office raid is as much as $30,000, and a favourable court ruling runs anywhere from $10,000 to $200,000 (Bush 2008).

In an attempt to break the culture of corruption, President Medvedev is heading up a new federal council to fight graft and corruption. He instructed law enforcement officials to develop a national plan to deal with the issue. Proposed solutions to official corruption by judges and law enforcement officials include raising salaries and benefits to reduce the incentives to accept bribes; strict annual reporting of income, gifts, automobiles, apartments, and other property for all law enforcement officials and their families; and passage of new legislation that better defines corrupt practices. Foreign countries and various international bodies have identified 15 specific types of corruption, while current Russian law only recognises two: bribes and fraud (Panfilov 2008).

Opinions vary on the prospects of eradicating corruption among judges and law enforcement officials. Pavel Astakhov, a prominent lawyer and member of the Public Chamber, estimates that an independent judiciary requires the education of a new generation of judges and that will take seven to ten years (Krainova 2008: 1). Astakhov also suggested that reforms need to be made in the process for appointing judges. 'Over the past five years not a single lawyer (*advokat*) has been appointed a judge; judges are mostly former employees of law enforcement agencies,' he has observed (ibid.). But all seem to recognise that reducing corruption in Russia's judiciary is essential to restoring citizens' confidence in the courts.

Politicisation and selective enforcement of the law

Selective enforcement of the law is problematic in all societies, but has been especially pronounced in Russia's highly politicised legal culture. Highly visible cases, such as the prosecution and conviction of former chief executive of Yukos oil company, Mikhail Khodorkovsky, and the subsequent nationalisation of the assets of the company have been initiated at the request of the presidential administration.

Administrative regulations were often used by the Putin administration in a blatant fashion against their opponents. Protestors or opposition political candidates seeking parade permits to hold public rallies were turned down or were granted permits only in obscure locations, and rival political candidates were excluded from the ballot because of minor infractions of campaign laws. Human rights organisations and other

NGOs, including organisations such as Amnesty International, were initially denied the right to operate in Russia and only obtained permission after a lengthy registration process that included turning over a mountain of documentation on the organisations' missions, sources of financing, and background checks on their directors and staff.

The pattern of selective enforcement and politicisation is often repeated at regional and local levels, where mayors and other powerful figures manipulate administrative regulations such as those that relate to the issuing of business licenses, construction permits, or order health and fire inspections, or even initiate criminal investigations in order to punish their rivals. Eventually, practices of this kind undermine public support for the courts and law enforcement.

Non-implementation of judicial decisions

Judicial decisions in any country are seldom self-enforcing; courts must generally rely either on the voluntary compliance of the parties to the dispute or on enforcement measures by other agencies, such as bailiffs or marshals. The enforcement of rulings of the commercial courts in Russia has generally not been a problem in contract disputes between private parties. The commercial court can freeze the assets of the losing party and simply transfer them to the winning party. Problems only arise when the losing party has no assets.

A system of marshals was established in 1997. There are approximately 20,000 marshals, armed officers of the Ministry of Justice, who are charged with enforcing court rulings. Marshals, most of whom have a law school education, are empowered to confiscate and sell property, gain access to and attach bank accounts and other assets, gather evidence of non-compliance, and detain parties and bring them before the court with a recommendation for a finding of contempt of court. According to lawyers working closely with the commercial courts, the marshals are working well. They report that when confronted by marshals, most firms 'simply pay up rather than hassle appealing the judicial ruling' (Rogotsev 2008).

Enforcing judgements against the state is another matter. Thousands of Russian citizens have brought lawsuits against governmental entities seeking unpaid pensions, tax and insurance claims, improperly imposed fines, evictions, disability claims, damage claims against the armed forces resulting from the war in Chechnya, and any number of other issues.

As a member of the Council of Europe, Russia recognises the jurisdiction of the European Court of Human Rights. In recent years the court in Strasbourg has been flooded with complaints from Russian citizens concerning the failure of Russian authorities to enforce court rulings

(Bigg 2007). More cases before the European Court originate from Russia than from any other of the 47 member nations; 12,000 in 2006 alone. The European Court often sides with the Russian plaintiff against the Russian government, which has caused 'extreme displeasure in the Kremlin', according to Yuri Shmidt, a prominent Russian lawyer (ibid.).

To some extent the failure to implement court judgements is seen as a bureaucratic problem since no one agency feels responsible. Even if an agency does accept responsibility, it has no dedicated budget line for paying settlements or claims. For example, if a soldier is injured as a result of hazing during basic training, the Ministry of Defence will deny responsibility, blaming the supervising officers for misconduct. If the Russian court awards damages to the injured recruit, both the Ministry of Defence and the Ministry of Finance will refuse to pay, citing the absence of funds allocated specifically for such a purpose. In recent years thousands of cases from Russia have been taken to the European Court seeking enforcement, but each year Russia's budget for settling claims has been quickly exhausted. As a result, in 2008 the European Court was still trying to wrap up claims from cases they heard in 2002 and 2003 (Central and East European Law Initiative 2008). The Russian Government has been severely embarrassed by repeated rebukes from the Strasbourg court and is considering measures to handle enforcement of court judgements more efficiently.

Signs of progress

Despite the flurry of press articles on corruption, there are also signs of progress in the development of rule of law in Russia. Courts in Russia, both courts of general jurisdiction and commercial courts, handle an estimated 6 million cases each year (Hendley 2007: 110). Whereas a decade ago many commercial disputes were often resolved by rival mafia organisations in shootouts or contract killings, today the courts have become the recognised medium for resolution of disputes. Russian enterprises and firms are increasingly likely to take their disputes to the commercial courts and in the vast majority of cases, the court's judgement is successfully enforced (Hendley 2006: 366–7).

Similarly, every year thousands of civil cases in the courts of general jurisdiction and the justice of the peace courts involving divorce, adoption, inheritance, work-related disputes, minor damage claims or many other issues are handled routinely and with an increasing degree of professionalism. As we noted earlier, in surprising number of cases – 80 per cent of the total – citizens have successfully challenged governmental bodies or officials and won (Solomon 2004: 556; Hendley 2002: 122). And in most of these cases the court's decision has been implemented.

Corruption is widespread in Russia, but judges, bailiffs and marshals are much less prone to accepting bribes than in the past. Similarly, the number of instances in which outside parties attempt to exert improper influence on judges appears to be relatively small. In 2007 the Ministry of Justice reported 10,500 corruption investigations, however, this represents only a fifth of one per cent of all cases – one case in 500. This is not to say that corruption is no longer a problem. However, it may be less extensive than the public believes. Nevertheless, public opinion matters.

Public opinion: the dilemma of rule of law

Since the collapse of the USSR, the courts and other state institutions have not enjoyed high levels of trust among citizens. In 2008 a poll found that only 28 per cent of Russians generally have a positive view of the courts and judges, while 39 per cent have a negative view (Public Opinion Foundation 2008). A similar poll conducted in 2004 reported 26 per cent with positive views and 46 per cent negative (ibid.).

Negative assessments of the functioning of Russian institutions – both governmental and non-governmental – have been a consistent feature of the post-Soviet period. To some extent, public opinion polling may reflect lack of awareness of Russian citizens about the actual performance of the courts and other law enforcement institutions. It may also reflect cultural norms, where pessimism is much more the norm than optimism. One of the leading American scholars of Russian commercial litigation reports that in her own research she has encountered directors of commercial enterprises who insist that taking disputes to the commercial courts is a waste of time only to discover in discussions with the enterprises' legal staff that they are actually making regular and productive use of them (Hendley 2006: 347). A study by another scholar, Marina Kurkchiyan, concludes that 'the negative myth of the rule of law is dominant' in Russia, and that it is self-perpetuating (2003: 25, 30).

Given this propensity toward negativism, it is significant that today just over half of Russian citizens (51 per cent) see legal action as a reasonable way to protect their rights, up from 42 per cent in 2003 (Public Opinion Foundation 2007). Attitudes toward the legal system also vary depending on age: 68 per cent of young respondents consider taking legal action a feasible way to protect their rights, while only 29 per cent of senior citizens do (ibid.). All of these trends provide room for hope that trust in and support for legal institutions in Russia is gaining important ground.

In an effort to expand public awareness of the courts, television channels in Russia have started broadcasting televised court programmes. These have proved exceptionally popular with the Russian public; more than three-quarters of all Russian adults are familiar with the shows and half of the public regularly watches at least one of them (ibid.). Televised court programmes are particularly popular with rural residents; and 59 per cent say they 'help increase people's legal awareness' (ibid.).

The middle class in Russia has increased substantially in the past decade; estimates now range between 30 and 60 per cent of the population. The increasing size of the population with vested interests needing protection and an awareness of legal rights provide a necessary ingredient for the expansion of rule of law. Many of the entrepreneurs who have become very wealthy are now among the biggest proponents of rule of law because they want legal protection for their interests and properties and, above all they value predictability. These are the very values upon which the development of rule of law is founded in most societies.

It is often pointed out that in Russia we see rule *by* law, rather than rule *of* law. Law is conceived as a creation of the state and used to protect the interests of the state. Such a view is not unusual in transitional legal systems, especially those not part of the common law tradition. However, with the rapid accumulation of wealth we have witnessed in Russia and increasing awareness of legal rights and the means to use legal instrumentalities to protect one' rights and interests, commercial enterprises and even individual citizens have begun to challenge the state's supremacy over the law. The rule of law in Russia, including laws that are equally binding on the state as well as on the private citizen, appears finally to be taking root.

Chapter 9

Reforming the Federation

CAMERON ROSS

Article 1 of the December 1993 Constitution declares that the Russian Federation is 'a democratic federative rule-of-law state with a republican form of government'. However, as discussed below, during the Yeltsin era a 'federation' was formed although the guiding principles of 'federalism' were never fully implemented. Instead, a highly asymmetrical and 'negotiated' form of federalism was developed, central–local relations became highly politicised and personalised, and the rule of law and constitutionalism were seriously undermined. Moreover, after the inauguration of Vladimir Putin as President in 2000, we witnessed an outright attack by the President on the principles and practices of federalism and a recentralisation of power in the Kremlin. Under the Putin presidency (2000–8) the Russian Federation was transformed into a quasi-unitary state that pays only lip service to the guiding principles of federalism, as defined below. In May 2008 Dmitri Medvedev took over the reins of power as President and Putin was appointed Prime Minister. As discussed below, there is now a power struggle at the centre of the Russian polity over who should have the dominant control in the regions.

Defining federalism

As Watts rightly argues, *federations* 'are descriptive terms applying to particular forms of political organisation ... in which, by contrast to the single central source of authority in unitary systems, there are two (or more) levels of government thus combining elements of *shared rule* through common institutions and *regional self-rule* for the governments of the constituent units' (Watts 1999: 6–7). *Federalism,* on the other hand, is 'a normative term and refers to the advocacy of multi-tiered government combining elements of shared-rule and regional self-rule. It is based on the presumed value and validity of combining unity and diversity and of accommodating, preserving and promoting distinct identities within a larger political union' (ibid.: 6). Watts lists the key features of federations as follows:

- two orders of government each acting directly on their citizens;
- a formal constitutional distribution of legislative and executive authority and allocation of revenue resources between the two orders of government ensuring some areas of genuine autonomy for each order;
- provision for the designated representation of distinct regional views within the federal policy-making institutions, usually provided by the particular form of the federal second chamber;
- a supreme written constitution not unilaterally amendable and requiring the consent of a significant proportion of the constituent units;
- an umpire (in the form of courts or provision for referendums) to rule on disputes between governments; and
- processes and institutions to facilitate intergovernmental collaboration for those areas where governmental responsibilities are shared or inevitably overlap. (Ibid.: 7)

Problems of developing Russian federalism

The 1993 Constitution may have provided Russia with all of the major institutional prerequisites necessary for a federation. However, as Elazar stresses, 'True federal systems manifest their federalism in culture as well as constitutional and structural ways' and 'the viability of federal systems is directly related to the degree to which federalism has been internalised culturally within a particular civil society' (1987: 78). In other words, federalism can only be fully implemented in democratic polities with strong civil societies and legal cultures. But the Russian state that emerged after the collapse of the USSR at the end of 1991 inherited a highly authoritarian political culture and a weak civil society. Moreover, the Yeltsin leadership had no tradition of federalism to fall back on to guide it through its post-communist transition. Although the 1977 Soviet Constitution declared that the USSR was a 'unified, federal, multinational state formed on the principle of socialist federalism' and granted its fifteen republics rights of sovereignty (Article 76) and secession (Article 72), in practice these were only paper rights. Federalism in the USSR was a sham. In practice, party and state bodies operated on the basis of 'democratic centralism', whereby each administrative level was subordinate to the level above it, and centralised control from Moscow. Likewise, under Putin, as Heinemann-Grüder concludes, 'the official conception of federalism ... to some extent returned to the Soviet fig leaf type of federalism ... [whereby] regions are treated as merely parts of an inter-governmental, administrative-territorial division of labour ... [and]

normative regulations governing the work of the state apparatus, in force since 1999, speak of a uniform and undivided hierarchical administrative system' (2009: 58).

A multinational federation

With a population of 142 million citizens made up of 182 nationalities and covering an area of 170 million square kilometres, Russia is one of the largest and most ethnically diverse multinational federations in the world. According to the Russian Constitution of December 1993, the Russian Federation comprised 89 federal subjects: 32 *ethnically* defined subjects (21 republics, 10 autonomous *okrugs* (districts) and 1 autonomous *oblast'* (region)), and 57 *territorially* based subjects (49 oblasts, 6 krais (territories), and two federal cities: Moscow and St Petersburg; see the map on pp. 156–7). Over the period 2005–8 there has been a process of regional mergers, and thus, the number of federal subjects had fallen by the end of 2008 to 83 (see below).

An asymmetrical federation

The federal subjects vary widely in the size of their territories and populations, their socio-economic status, and their ethnic makeup. Thus, for example, the territory of the Republic of Sakha-Yakutiya is 388 times greater in size than that of the Republic of North Osetiya-Alaniya. The population of Moscow is 474 times greater than that of the sparsely populated Evenk autonomous district. There are also vast differences in the socio-economic status of the federal subjects. For example, income per capita in the oil rich Yamalo-Nenets autonomous district in 2003 was 178 times greater than in the Republic of Ingushetia. In 2008, 'the gross regional product (average gross added value) per capita in Russia was 156,500 roubles. However, in Moscow it comprised 493,200 roubles, while in Ivanovo region it was just 48,000 roubles, the same level as Adygeya, Dagestan and Kabardino-Balkaria' (*Kommersant*, 14 April 2008).

Constitutional asymmetry

Although the Russian Constitution declares that all subjects are constitutionally equal (Article 5), in practice the twenty-one ethnic republics have far greater powers than the other territorially defined subjects of the federation. The foundations of Russia's constitutional asymmetry go back to the early period of the 1990s when there was a fierce struggle for power between the Russian presidency and parliament. Taking advantage of this period of political turmoil a number of republics ratified radical 'confederalist' constitutions.

In order to bring a halt to regional demands for ever greater levels of political and economic autonomy, the Yeltsin regime reluctantly signed a Federation Treaty in March 1992 that ceded major powers to the ethnic republics. In fact, there were three separate treaties, with separate agreements for the ethnic republics, the ethnic autonomies, and the territorially based oblasts or regions. Each of these three types of federal subject was awarded a different set of legal powers and status: 'national–state status (sovereign republics), administrative–territorial status (*krais* (territories), *oblasts* (regions), cities of Moscow and St Petersburg), and national–territorial status (an autonomous oblast and autonomous *okrugs* (districts))' (Stoliarov 2001: 86–7). According to the Federation Treaty of 1992 the republics were recognised as sovereign states and they were also granted independent powers over taxation and ownership of their land and natural resources. In addition, the republics were to have their own 'constitutions, legislation, elected legislative bodies (parliaments), supreme courts, and presidents' (ibid.: 87). In contrast the territorially based regions were given none of the above rights and their chief executives (governors) were to be directly appointed by the President.

Tatarstan and Chechnya both refused to sign the Federal Treaty and in November 1992 Tatarstan adopted its own rival constitution which declared that it was a sovereign state and a subject of international law, 'associated' with the Russian Federation on the basis of a treaty and the mutual delegation of powers. Chechnya, which had declared its independence as early as November 1991, proclaimed that it was an independent sovereign state and a full and equal member of the world community of states (see Ross 2002a).

The December 1993 constitution

In the aftermath of Yeltsin's victory over the parliamentarians in October 1993 the President now sought to win back many of the powers he had ceded to the ethnic republic in the Federation Treaty. The new Constitution that was ratified in December 1993 declared (in Article 5) that all federal subjects were equal, and reasserted the sovereignty of the federal government over the republics. Thus, for example, Article 4.1 proclaims that 'the sovereignty of the Russian Federation extends to the whole of its territory'. Moreover, Article 15.1 declares that 'the Constitution has supreme legal force, is directly applicable and applies throughout the territory of the Federation. Laws and other legal enactments adopted in the Federation must not contradict the Constitution'.

The Constitution also ratified the creation of two other important

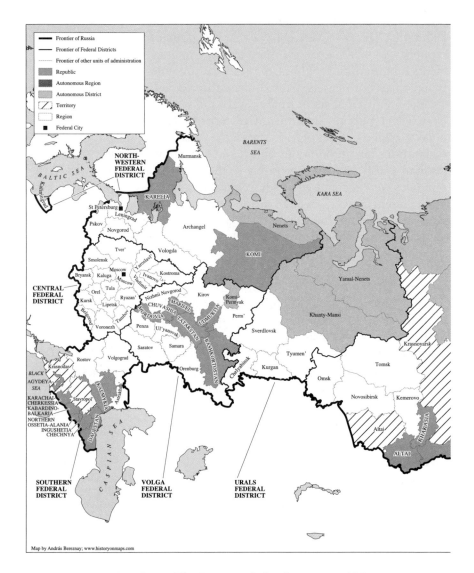

Map 9.1 *The Russian federal system, 1993*

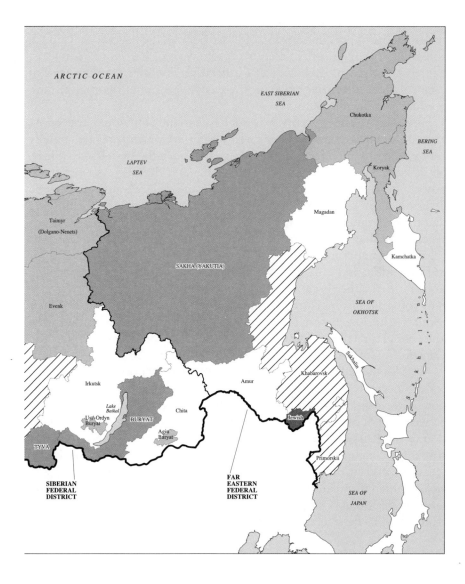

federal bodies: a Constitutional Court and a new upper chamber of the Russian Parliament, the Federation Council. Members of the Constitutional Court are appointed by the President subject to the approval of the Federation Council. From 1995 up to Putin's radical reform of the upper chamber in 2000 (see below), the Federation Council consisted of two ex-officio members from each of Russia's 89 subjects, namely the chair of each subject's legislative assembly and the head of each subject's executive body, known as governors in the regions and presidents in the republics.

However, Yeltsin's victory was not as clear-cut as it would appear. As argued elsewhere, many of the provisions of the Constitution are actually very vague or ambiguous, while others are contradictory (Ross 2002a). For a start, Article 11 of the Constitution states that the distribution of powers between the federal government and federal subjects is to be determined by both the Constitution and the Federal Treaty, implying that the Federation Treaty is still operative. Second, there has been much speculation that turnout for the 'national vote' on the Constitution was below the mandatory 50 per cent of the electorate that was required for its ratification, and in 42 of the 89 federal subjects the Constitution failed to be ratified either because turnout was too low or the majority of citizens voted against it. Third, a number of republics that had ratified their own constitutions before the December 1993 Federal Constitution were able to claim that their constitutions took precedence over the Constitution of the Federation as a whole.

By 1996 the federal government reported that 19 of the 21 republican constitutions were in breach of the federal constitution. Those constitutions (Chuvashia, Sakha-Yakutia, Chechnya, Tatarstan and Tuva) ratified between the signing of the Federal Treaty in March 1992 and the ratification of the Russian Constitution on 12 December 1993 were the most confederal, including as they did declarations of sovereignty, rights of secession, and citizenship. As noted above, Tatarstan declared that it was an *associated* member of the Russian Federation. Only Chechnya went so far as to declare its complete secession, and in 1994 and 1999, Russian troops had to be sent into the republic to (attempt to) restore federal control.

The distribution of powers: federal, regional, and local

The distribution of powers in the Constitution is set out in articles 71 to 73. Article 71 grants the federal government exclusive powers over a broad range of national policies (including the national economy, federal budget, federal taxes and duties, foreign and defence affairs), and Article 72 lists a number of powers which are to be shared between the federal authorities and the federal subjects. Whilst there are no specific powers set down for federal subjects, Article 73 concedes that any powers not covered by Articles 71 and 72 rest with the federal subjects. Not surprisingly there has been much debate and discussion over the provisions of article 72, which deals with the thorny area of 'shared powers'. As Leksin observes:

> Over 60 per cent of federal laws regulating relations in such areas as the economy, natural resource management, and social development require co-ordination of actions of federal and regional governments to deal with concrete issues. And every twentieth federal law specifies instances when consultations must also be held with local governments. (2004: 70)

Remarkable as it may seem, there were virtually no legal procedures to regulate such co-operation. In order to address these issues, a special commission was set up by President Putin in 2001 that was charged with clarifying the powers of federal, regional and local governments (see below).

Bilateral treaties

An important article in the Constitution is Article 78, which allows the centre to transfer 'the implementation of some of its powers' to the federal subjects and vice versa. This article was used by the Yeltsin regime to promote the development of 'contract federalism'. Over the period 1994–8 forty-six bilateral treaties were signed between the federal government and subjects of the federation which granted the local signatories a whole host of political and economic privileges. Thus, for example, Tatarstan's treaty, which was signed in February 1994, legitimised Tatarstan's radical confederalist constitution and reaffirmed the republic's sovereignty over its economic and political affairs, including foreign trade and foreign policy. By 'early 2000, about 65 per cent of the region's wealth was under the control of the governing political elite' (Kusznir 2007: 2).

The vast majority of the treaties (42 of the 46) also contained provisions that violated the Russian Constitution. Special and often secret agreements attached to the bilateral treaties granted the republics the right to appoint federal officials in their territories, conduct their own independent relations with foreign states, set up their own national banks, and create their own political and administrative organs (see Ross 2002a). As Stoner-Weiss observes, 'North Osetiya-Alaniya, Voronezh, Samara, Arkhangel'sk, Irkutsk, Tyumen', and Omsk all passed legislation restructuring their judiciaries, a right exclusively reserved to the federal government by article 71 of the constitution' (2006: 57). The treaties also widened the number of areas coming under joint jurisdiction as stipulated in article 72. In other cases the treaties called for powers that were exclusively reserved for the federal government to be transferred to the sole jurisdiction of federal subjects. In June 1999 the Russian Parliament adopted a law to regulate the treaties, which reiterated that all new treaties had to conform to the federal constitution. However, no new treaties were concluded after the bilateral treaty that was signed with Moscow region in June 1998.

The fears of ethnic secessionism

During the period 1991–3, or what is now known as the time of the 'parade of sovereignties', there were real fears the Russian Federation would follow the fate of the USSR and fall apart. However, there are a number of ethnic, geographical and economic factors which make it highly unlikely that the Russian Federation will fragment in this way. As Turovsky demonstrates, an examination of the ethnic composition of Russia's 89 federal subjects in 2004 (before the recent round of regional mergers discussed below) showed that Russians comprised an absolute majority in 74 of them (2006a: 217). Moreover, in 31 regions they made up over 90 per cent of the population, and in 25 they comprised 80–90 per cent. In a further five federal subjects no single ethnic group had a majority (ibid.). In only ten regions did the titular nationality comprise a majority of the population: Agin-Buryat autonomous *okrug* (AO) or district, Chechnya, Chuvashia, Ingushetia, Kabardino-Balkaria, Kalmykia, Komi-Permyak AO, North Osetia-Alania, Tatarstan, and Tuva. The three ethnic republics with the smallest percentage of Russians were Ingushetia (1.2 per cent), Chechnya (3.7 per cent), and Dagestan (4.7 per cent). In Dagestan there is a multitude of tiny ethnic groups and no single group comprises a majority of the population. In Chechnya over 90 per cent of the population was made up of non-Russians.

Moreover, the second largest ethnic group (after the Russians), the Tatars make up only 3.8 per cent of the Russian population. In fact, as Turovsky notes (ibid.), there are currently only three ethnic groups that number over one million in their own territory – Tatars in Tatarstan (just over 2 million), Bashkirs in Bashkortostan (1.2 million), and Chechens in Chechnya (just over 1 million). If we assume that viable demands for secession can only come from those subjects whose territories border foreign states and where a majority of the population is indigenous, then this leaves us with just seven republics which meet these criteria: Chechnya, Dagestan, Ingushetia, Kabardino-Balkaria, Kalmykia, North Osetia-Alania, and Tuva.

Another factor that must be taken into consideration is the economic status of these republics. All seven are highly dependent on subsidies from the federal budget for their economic survival. Thus, for example, financial subsidies comprised nearly 88 per cent of Ingushetia's budget revenues in 2002, and more than 82 per cent in 2003. In the republics of Dagestan and Tuva federal transfers comprised 80 per cent of budget revenues in 2003, and they made up between 70 and 80 per cent of the revenues of the republics of Kabardino-Balkaria and North Osetia-Alania (Turovsky 2006a: 555–6). Thus, it is not surprising that only Chechnya has gone so far as to declare its outright secession.

Putin's radical assault on the principles of federalism

By the end of the Yeltsin era, constitutional federalism had been replaced by a highly politicised form of 'contract' federalism. According to the Russian Ministry of Justice, of the 44,000 regional acts adopted over the period 1995–6 almost half were in violation of the Russian Constitution and federal legislation (*Izvestiya*, 4 March 1997: 4). As Sakwa notes, 'By the end of Yeltsin's term in office Russia was beginning to become not only a multinational state, but also a multi-state state, with numerous proto-state formations making sovereignty claims *vis-à-vis* Moscow' (2008a: 281).

On coming to power in 2000 Putin quickly adopted a number of radical federal reforms whose primary aims were to reassert the powers of the Kremlin and to rein in the power of the regional governors; to create a uniform legal space throughout the federation; and to bring an end to the 'negotiated federalism' of the Yeltsin era. There are eight major strands to Putin's federal reforms which were implemented over the period 2000–8: (i) The creation of seven new federal super-districts, (ii) reform of the Federation Council, (iii) the creation of a State Council and a Council of Legislators, (iv) new rights of presidential appointment and dismissal and changes to party and electoral legislation, (v) a campaign to bring regional charters and republican constitutions into line with the Russian Constitution, (vi) the adoption of new laws aimed at clarifying the powers of federal, regional, and local bodies of power, (vii) fiscal centralism and federal intervention, and (viii) the merger of federal subjects. Each of these will be examined in turn.

The creation of seven federal districts

In 2000 Putin divided the country into seven super-districts, each of which contained a dozen or more federal subjects, and appointed an envoy ('plenipotentiary representative' or *polpred* for short) to each district. The high status of the envoys was reflected in their membership of the Russian Security Council, and their right to attend meetings of the federal government. The key tasks of the *polpredy* were: (i) to monitor the regions' compliance with the Russian Constitution, federal laws and presidential decrees, (ii) to oversee the selection and placement of personnel in the regional branches of the federal bureaucracy, (iii) to protect the national security interests of the regions, and (iv) to set up and co-ordinate within their districts interregional economic programmes (see Sakwa 2002; Teague 2002). In addition to the above formal powers, Petrov and Slider note the following 'unstated functions' of the *polpredy*: '(i) Bringing military, police and security organs out from under the control of the centre ... (ii) Overseeing and controlling the process of gathering compromising material (*kompromat*) on regional leaders ... [and] (iii) removing from the political stage the heads of a number of regions' (Petrov and Slider 2007: 85).

Reform of the Federation Council

In 2000 Putin ratified a new law that robbed the governors and chairs of regional assemblies of their *ex officio* right to sit in the upper chamber of the parliament. These were to be replaced (from January 2002) by 'delegates', chosen by the regional assemblies and chief executives. The new body would now meet on a full-time basis, and not as in the past just for a few days a month. The new members, it was thought, would have far greater opportunities to scrutinise legislation coming from the Duma and presidency.

However, many of the regions chose high-ranking entrepreneurs and politicians from Moscow and St Petersburg to represent them in the upper chamber rather than residents of their own regions. Moreover, now that (since 2005) the Russian President has the power to make nominations to these positions, he has been able to gain considerable control over who gains entry to the Council, thereby seriously compromising its independence. As a result of these reforms we now have a much more compliant and passive upper chamber that is dominated by élites from Russia's two capital cities (Moscow and St Petersburg), and representatives of United Russia. Such developments have also undermined one of the key principles of federalism, namely the direct representation of federal subjects in federal policy making.

The State Council and the Council of Legislators

In order to compensate regional governors and the chairs of regional assemblies for their exclusion from the Federation Council, two new advisory bodies were set up by the President – a State Council and a Council of Legislators. The State Council meets once every three months and is chaired by the President. All of the regional governors are members. There is also an inner Presidium made up of seven governors (one from each of the federal districts), whose membership rotates each six months. Members of the Presidium meet with the President once every month. The State Council has no formal law-making powers and is primarily an advisory body for the President. At best the Council has served as a direct channel for the governors to the President and has provided them with some limited input into policymaking.

In similar vein the Council of Legislators, which is meant to provide a forum where the chairs of regional assemblies can participate in federal policymaking, is in reality nothing more than a 'talking shop'. It has no formal law-making or decision-making powers. Regional assemblies have the right of legislative initiative, and therefore, a key function of the Council is the co-ordination of regional and federal legislation. However, a recent study of 444 regional laws considered by the State Duma in 2006 shows that only 32 were adopted as federal laws, largely because they failed to comply with existing federal legislation and norms (Russian Federation Council Report 2006: 132).

Presidential appointments and dismissals, and changes to party and electoral legislation

Another major reform initiated in 2000 was a law giving Putin powers to dismiss popularly elected governors and to dissolve regional assemblies. Although, as Gel'man notes, this power was never used in practice, 'the very threat of its use had a serious deterrent effect and reinforced the subordination of regional elites to the Centre' (Gel'man 2009: 10). This was followed up in the aftermath of the Beslan school hostage crisis of September 2004, in which over 300 schoolchildren held hostage by Chechen terrorists were killed during a botched rescue operation by Russian security forces, with even more radical legislation that gives the President the power to directly nominate regional governors and republican presidents. According to new legislation adopted by the Duma on 11 December 2004, regional assemblies were charged with the task of giving approval to the President's nominees. If a legislature twice declines to confirm the President's nominee, the President has the right to disband the assembly and to appoint an acting regional head to serve until a new legislature is elected. The President also has the right to dismiss any regional head for failure to fulfil his/her duties or if they lose the President's confidence (Coalson 2004: 1).

Putin argued that these reforms were necessary to preserve the unity of the country. Critics of the reform argued that it would destroy the country's federal system and replace it with a unitary state. Thus, for example, former member of the Duma, Vladimir Ryzhkov, argued that the new law granting Putin the right to appoint the heads of federal subjects violated ten articles of the Russian Constitution. According to Ryzhkov, the President violated three constitutional principles: 'the principle of democracy, by depriving citizens of their right to elect their own leaders; the principle of federalism, since appointment from above has nothing to do with the principles of a federation; and the principle of a law-based state, since the President is proposing that we ignore the Constitution, the laws, and the decisions of the Constitutional Court' (ibid.: 2).

In utilising his new powers, Putin tended to reappoint incumbent governors. Thus for example, of the 53 regions that had passed through the new appointment system by April 2007, Putin reappointed 36 incumbents and there were just 17 newcomers (Ivanenko 2007: 11). Many of those who have been reappointed have already been in power for over a decade. Thus, for example, 'Konstantin Titov the Governor of Samara Oblast, the President of Tatarstan, Mintimer Shaimiev, and the governors of Khanty-Mansiskii AO, and the Jewish Autonomous Oblast, Alexander Filipenko and Nikolai Volkov' have held office since 1991. On completion of their new terms, these governors will have served for 18 or 19 years (Chebankova 2007a: 294). Nor has Putin been averse to reappointing unpopular or autocratic leaders. Thus, for example, he reappointed Murtaza Rakhimov, the President of Bashkortostan, who has been accused of human rights violations, corruption and electoral fraud.

In 2001 the Duma ratified a new federal law, 'On Political Parties', which prohibits regional parties from competing in elections and further amendments were made to party and electoral legislation over the period 2004–6 that have strengthened the powers of the centre over the regions. The ban on regional parties is clearly designed to prevent regional governors and republican presidents using local political machines to capture control of their regional legislatures. Moreover, from 2003, as Gel'man notes:

> The Centre required the regions to introduce for elections to regional legislatures the mixed electoral system which had been used for State Duma elections in 1993–2003: no less than 50 per cent of seats must be reserved for federal party lists. These measures were introduced to increase the influence of parties in general and the 'party of power', United Russia in particular, over the regional political process and regional administration. (Gel'man 2009: 12)

Party control over regional assemblies is especially important since it is the regional legislatures that are charged with approving the President's nominees for regional governors. Moreover, in a further amendment to legislation governing the Presidential appointment of governors, which was adopted in July 2005, the party that wins the most party-list seats in a regional legislature now has the right to nominate a candidate for the post of governor. 'It [was] perhaps no coincidence that these new rulings coincide[d] with United Russia's newly acquired electoral success in the regions. Over the period December 2003–March 2006 elections took place in 52 regions. United Russia gained the largest number of seats in 47 regional assemblies (with an absolute majority in 12) and they took second place in five regions' (Ross 2009b: 286).

Direct appointment of mayors

Putin has also called for governors to be given the right to directly appoint the mayors of their capital cities. However, such a development would require major changes to the Russian Constitution. Article 32.2 of the Russian Constitution states that 'Citizens of the Russian Federation shall have the right to be elected to bodies of state governance and organs of local self-government.' Furthermore, Article 130.2 declares that 'local-self government shall be exercised by the citizens through referendums, elections, and forms of expression of their will, through elected and other bodies of local self-government', and Article 131.1 states that 'the structure of bodies of local self-government shall be determined by the population independently' (Ross 2009a: 22). If implemented, this policy would extend the Kremlin's 'power vertical' down to the cities.

Bringing regional charters and republican constitutions into line with the Russian Constitution

Putin also launched a major campaign to bring regional legislation into line with the federal constitution and, as noted above, he created a special commission headed by Dmitrii Kozak, the deputy head of his presidential administration, to oversee this work. As Leksin points out, 'From July 2000, when the campaign started to 2003, local procurators disputed about 10,000 illegal acts, of which over 8,000 were harmonised with federal legislation' (2004: 57). Putin also called for the bilateral treaties to be rescinded. By the summer of 2004 only eight of the original treaties were still operative, the most important with Moscow, Tatarstan and Sverdlovsk, and by the summer of 2005 all of the treaties had been revoked.

Nonetheless, despite these achievements many republics have continued to adopt legislation which violates federal laws. The Tatarstan leadership, in particular, has steadfastly refused to renounce the republic's sovereignty. Article 1 of the Republic's revised Constitution, adopted in April 2002, continues to uphold the 1994 bilateral treaty with Moscow, even though it contradicts both the federal and republican constitutions in several places. Moreover, in July 2007 Tatarstan ratified a new bilateral treaty with Moscow that grants it considerable autonomous powers, many of which continue to contradict the Russian Constitution. Thus, for example, 'The agreement gives authorities in Tatarstan a greater say in decisions on economic, cultural, and environmental issues, and calls for joint management of the region's oil fields by federal and local authorities' (Arnold 2007b: 1).

Chechnya's new Constitution, by contrast, is a much more conservative document. Ratified in a referendum that was held on 23 March 2003, it declares that: 'the territory of the Chechen Republic is an inextricable part of the territory of the Russian Federation. The only source of power in the republic is its multinational people. If the laws of the constitution of the republic contradict those of the federation, the laws of the federation override those of the Republic' (Makinen 2008: 173). Following the ratification of the Constitution there was speculation that Chechnya's autonomy would be bolstered with a new bilateral treaty. However, President Ramzan Kadyrov, a Moscow client who came to power in 2007, has now poured scorn on the idea of such a treaty (Sakwa 2008a: 274).

Clarifying the powers of federal, regional, and local bodies of power

The Kozak Commission was also charged with drawing up new proposals on the distribution of powers between federal, regional and local bodies of power. Two key laws were produced as a result of the Commission's work: the July 2003 Law, 'On Amending the Federal Law "On the Fundamental Principles of the Organisation of Legislative (Representative) and Executive Bodies of State Power of the Subjects of the Russian Federation"', and the October 2003 Law 'On the General Principles of Organising Local-Self Government in the Russian Federation'. As Leksin observes, the adoption of these laws 'necessitated a revision of the basic provisions of 155 previously adopted federal laws (including the Budget and Tax Codes of the Russian Federation) and termination of 42 federal laws' (2005: 39). Moreover, 'the provisions of several thousand laws passed by subjects of the Russian Federation had to be amended' (ibid).

According to Heinemann-Grüder, the Kozak reforms have led to a more 'unified', 'systematized' but also 'centralized' system of intergovernmental relations. Whereas the federal government was granted approximately '700 areas of responsibility', the regions retained just 50

(2009: 59). Moreover, according to a 2006 Report of the Federation Council, as a result of the Kozak reforms:

> a significant cut was made to the competences of constituent entities of the Russian Federation on issues of joint authority. Many of the most important groups of public policy were completely transferred to the competence of federal bodies of state power, and mechanisms for joint execution by federal and regional bodies of the most important tasks that require joint implementation were eliminated. (Russian Federation Council Report 2006: 111)

Previously, at a meeting of the State Council in July 2005, Putin had promised that 114 powers of the federal government would be given back to the federal subjects, in the areas of forestry, water resources, environmental protection, veterinary services, licensing, protection of historical and cultural monuments, education, science, land use and housing legislation, including the governors' rights to supervise the heads of the power ministries, Ministry of Interior, Emergencies, and Justice (although not security bodies or the procuracy) in their respective regions (Belin 2005: 1). Many commentators hailed these moves as an indication that Putin was reversing his centralising policies in favour of a new programme of devolution. However, such developments should more rightly be viewed as a process of deconcentration of duties rather than a decentralisation of powers. Now that Putin appoints the regional and republican heads of government he is quite happy to return administrative control over these policy areas to the regional administrations (Ross 2009a). Moreover, according to the 2006 Federation Council Report:

> a delineation of authorities within a federal system is being substituted by the administrative delegation 'from the top down'. As a result, federal relations between the Russian Federation and its constituent entities are being replaced by administrative relations between federal and regional bodies of state power that concern the performance of delegated federal authorities. Federal units are turning into administrative-territorial ones, which threatens to reform a federal state into an administrative and unitary one. (Russian Federation Council Report 2006: 112)

Fiscal centralisation and federal intervention

There has also been a centralisation of finances in the federal budget and a reduction in the share of budget funds allocated to the regions. Thus, for example in 1996 regional tax revenues comprised nearly 58 per cent of the total revenues in the Consolidated Budget of the Russian Federation, but by 2005 this had fallen to less than 32 per cent (Likova 2008: 108). Moreover, the federal government has also been given new rights of intervention. Thus, for example, regions with budget deficits exceeding 30 per cent of their income are subject to direct administrative control by the federal government. Whilst, intervention may be justified in cases of administrative malpractice, there is always the worry that federal bodies will use these new rights to penalise politically disobedient regions.

The merger of federal subjects

In December 2001 the Federal Law 'On Procedures Related to Admission to the Russian Federation of a New Subject of the Russian Federation and the Creation within the Federation of a New Subject of the Russian Federation' was adopted. According to the law, all changes to existing administrative boundaries must be voluntary, and requests must come from both the regions in question. Before a merger process can begin the citizens of both regions must give their approval in a referendum. Legislation is then drawn up that requires the support of two-thirds of the members of the Duma and three-quarters of the members of the Federation Council.

By March 2008 five mergers had been completed (involving six federal subjects) reducing the number of federal subjects from 89 to 83. All of the mergers to date have involved the unification of autonomous *okrugs* (which are situated inside other federal subjects) with their 'mother regions': (i) the unification of Perm' region with the Komi-Permyak autonomous *okrug* to create Perm' *krai* on 1 December 2005, (ii) the unification of Krasnoyarsk *krai* with the Taimyr and Evenk autonomous *okrugs* to create Krasnoyarsk *krai* on 1 January 2007; (iii) the unification of Kamchatka *oblast'* with the Koryak autonomous *okrug* to create Kamchatka *krai* on 1 July 2007, (iv) the unification of Irkutsk Region with the Ust-Ordyn Buryat autonomous *okrug* to create Irkutsk region on 1 January 2008, and (v) the unification of Chita *oblast'* with the Aginskii-Buryatskii autonomous *okrug* to create the Zabaikalskii *krai* on 1 March 2008 (Kusznir 2008: 10–11).

In addition, according to Kusznir, 'Kemerovo Governor Aman Tuleev would like to merge his region with the neighbouring Altai Republic and Altai Territory; Moscow Mayor Yuri Luzhkov suggested merging Moscow City and Moscow region. St Petersburg Governor Valentina Matvienko strongly supports merging her city with Leningrad region to form a Baltic Territory', and there have even been proposals 'by representatives of the Chechen Republic to merge with Stavropol' Territory' to create a new Republic (ibid.: 10).

At a press conference held in 2007 Putin stressed the fact that 'any territorial changes, whether mergers or separations, can only go ahead if this is the will of the citizens' (2007a: 2). However, as Chebankova observes, a number of the mergers have been 'imposed by the federal centre top-down often against the background of ethnic resistance, and mostly in accordance with the interests of ruling elites' (2007a: 442). Thus, although there was consensus over the merger of Komi-Permyak autonomous *okrug* with Perm' *oblast'* and the merger of Taimyr and Evenk autonomous *okrugs* with Krasnoyarsk *krai*, there was much more opposition from ethnic Adygeis to the unification of their republic with Krasnodar *krai* (Goble 205: 1). 'The refusal of governors Alexii Barinov and Vladimir Loginov of Yamalo-Nenetsk and Koryak autonomous *okrugs*, respectively, to support the merger of their regions with neighbouring territories led ... to their dismissal' (Chebankova 2007a: 444). In addition we also have one instance when the Kremlin stepped in to prevent a merger taking place. As Gel'man notes, 'the Centre blocked the proposal by a number of financial–industrial groups to merge Tyumen *oblast'* and the Khanty-Mansiskii and Yamalo-Nenetskii autonomous *okrugs*; the economic potential of such a "super-region" would have been too great' (Gel'man 2009: 12–13).

Moreover, as Yasmann observes, 'there are many signs that political considerations are behind the merger efforts, and that the Kremlin's goal is effectively to dissolve the troublesome ethnic republics in the North Caucasus and Volga regions' (2006: 1). According to a plan drawn up in 2006 by the influential Council for the Study of Productive Resources, a think-tank that has close connections with the Russian Government, all the ethnic republics are to be merged with the territorial subjects, and the number of regions reduced to just 28. This radical plan for revamping the federation provides a revealing insight into the policy options currently under consideration by federal officials. However, there is a great deal of regional opposition to such a radical redrawing of the contours of the federation and it is unlikely that such a plan will be implemented in the near future and particularly during the period of dual leadership.

The dual leadership

As Petrov stresses, 'whoever controls the regions controls the county' (2008: 1). With the election of Dmitri Medvedev as President in March 2008 and the appointment of Vladimir Putin to the post of Prime Minister in May 2008, a new battle has emerged between the presidency and government over which of these offices should have the dominant voice in the regions. An interesting development in this regard is the proposal made by Dmitri Kozak, the Minister of Regional Development, to create then ten macro-regions whose heads would be appointed by the Ministry subject to the approval of the Prime Minister. Such a development would undoubtedly bolster Putin's control over the regions and weaken the power of the presidential representatives.

According to a recent report it is the Prime Minister and not the President who is to be in charge of 'developing and approving a list of indicators' to assess the effectiveness of regional governors. Putin signed a degree to this effect in April 2008, just before he left office (RFE/RL *Newsline*, 30 April 2008: 1). According to this decree, governors will have to report on their progress in meeting federal targets to both the President and Prime Minister. In addition, according to the Deputy Director of the Institute for Social Systems, Dmitri Badovsky, the government may in future take over the responsibility of nominating candidates for the posts of regional governors (RFE/RL *Newsline*, 1 April 2008: 1).

The end of federalism in Russia?

In his Address to the Federal Assembly in April 2007, Putin (2007b) declared that 'greater powers for regional and local authorities constitute one of the main criteria for measuring a society's degree of political culture and development. Decentralisation of state power in Russia is now at a higher point today than at any other time in our country's history'. However, far from promoting decentralisation, as Petrov and Slider observe, 'Putin has aggressively pursued an antifederal policy designed to take away or circumscribe most powers exercised by regional leaders' (2007: 76). In federations, according to Watts, (i) neither the federal nor the constituent units of government are constitutionally subordinate to the other, i.e., each has sovereign powers derived from the constitution rather than another level of government, (ii) each is empowered to deal directly with its citizens in the exercise of legislative, executive and taxing powers, and (iii) each is directly elected by its citizens (1999: 99). Moreover, in federations, in contrast to unitary states, regional autonomy is not only devolved but also constitutionally guaranteed. But in Russia, Putin's reforms have led to the reinstitution of Soviet-style principles of hierarchy and centralised administrative control from Moscow. Russia is now a unitary state masquerading as a federation. It is too early to speculate on future developments in the regions under the dual leadership of Medvedev and Putin but early indications are not promising for the revival of the federal principles that were so central to the politics of the Russian 1990s.

Chapter 10

Politics in the Regions

DARRELL SLIDER

In this chapter the focus is on how Putin's policies to centralise control have played out in the regions. What impact has this had on the politics of Russian regions? And how has it affected the agenda for change in Russian politics?

As we saw in Chapter 9, Russia's diversity makes it unique among nations. The socio-economic variation among regions is perhaps the most striking. At one end of the spectrum is the city of Moscow, which is in a category of its own. Moscow's role could be compared to the role played in the United States by multiple cities: Washington DC (national government offices), New York (financial and cultural hub), Las Vegas (entertainment and gambling centre), Hollywood (film-making), Chicago (commodity trade and industry), and Boston (higher education, science and advanced technology). Moscow attracts the young and ambitious from all over the country in search of higher earnings and career advancement, and its standard of living is among the highest in Russia. At the other extreme are regions such as Tuva or Ingushetia, where an overwhelmingly rural population faces high rates of unemployment, poverty, and few prospects for improvement. The United Nations Development Programme developed the Human Development Index to provide a composite indicator of factors such as health, longevity, and education that reflect the potential of 'human capital' in a region. The index for Russia as a whole puts the country just above Brazil and below Malaysia. Regional data for 2004 place Moscow at about the level of the Czech Republic or Kuwait. The oil-rich region of Tyumen' compares with Poland or Argentina, while Russia's second largest city, St Petersburg, and Tatarstan rank lower – near Bulgaria or Mexico. The poorest regions of the country, the republics of Tuva and Ingushetia, were at the level of Guatemala or South Africa (UNDP 2007a: 112).

It would be strange if regional economic, social and ethnic variation did not express itself in political diversity. One way of looking at the Putin agenda is that he sought to prevent regional differences from prevailing in the political realm. His first acts as president were directed against the main separatist threat faced by Russia, and he used brute force to subdue Chechnya. Nothing so dramatic occurred in subsequent years, but Putin always paid close attention to political developments in the regions and sought leverage to influence those developments. Ironically, the increased centralisation did nothing to reduce regional inequalities – in fact, socio-economic differences among them actually increased in the Putin era.

Two measures Putin introduced in his second term (2004–8) strongly affected regional politics. One was the decision in late 2004 to end the direct election of regional leaders. In the mid-1990s Yeltsin allowed the post of governor to be popularly elected; prior to this he had appointed the chief executives in each region. Earlier, from 1991 mayors were elected in Moscow and St Petersburg, and in the republics there were elections to select republic presidents. Events in Beslan, North Ossetias in September 2004, when a poorly co-ordinated attempt to rescue hostages held in a school ended with hundreds dead, shocked Russia and its leadership. Putin responded with a decision to end the popular election of governors. He argued that regional elections undermined the unity of the country and reduced his ability as president to govern. The shortcomings of regional elections were also used to justify the change. Voters at the regional level (though apparently not at the national level) were too easily manipulated and misled, resulting sometimes in the election of incompetent governors or governors with ties to criminals. The second change introduced by Putin after 2004 was not announced with the same fanfare, but was just as important. The Kremlin began systematically facilitating the creation of what was in essence a one-party system in virtually all regions of Russia. This affected above all governors and regional legislatures, but extended to lower administrative levels as well.

Political power in the regions

Who are the major political players in a region? The Russian journal *Ekspert* published the results of a survey of prominent journalists, officials, and scholars in thirty-two regions in 2007. They were asked to estimate the degree of influence exerted in their region by various officials or other persons. A list of the posts experts rated as the most influential at the regional level is presented in Table 10.1. Another part of the survey asked experts to rank the ten most influential figures in their region, and it provides additional insights into regional politics.

In every region, the governor or republic president was ranked as the most powerful, sometimes by a large margin. The political system at the regional level largely mirrored that at the national level, with executive power dominant. Governors received by far the most attention in the

Table 10.1   *Regional officials' relative influence in their region, overall and in particular areas (ranked on a 10-point scale)*

	Overall influence	Policy making	Media influence	Law enforcement
Governor	8.5	8.6	7.9	7.5
Region Legislature Chair	6.2	6.0	5.3	4.7
Mayor of Capital	6.1	5.8	6.0	4.5
Religious Leader	5.2	na	4.6	na
FSB Head	4.9	na	na	7.1
Chief Federal Inspector	4.9	4.5	na	5.0
City Council Head	4.6	4.6	4.4	na
Prosecutor	4.6	na	na	6.6
MVD Head	4.4	na	na	6.7
Head of Regional Court	4.2	na	na	5.3

Source: Adapted from survey of 670 experts in 32 regions, *Ekspert*, 26 March 2007.

media, and the resources at their disposal exceeded those of any other actor. One could argue that this was not in contradiction with centralisation, since now governors were part of a central hierarchy with Putin at the top. Governors' powers, though, as discussed below, are often independent of the support they receive from the Kremlin. If anything, the results shown in Table 10.1 understate the importance of the governor and his administration in a typical region. When one examines the ranking assigned within each region to the top ten most powerful figures, in 15 of 32 the second most influential turned out to be a member of the governor's administration such as a prime minister or deputy governor. Overall, of the 320 top officials ranked in these regions, 131, or almost 41 per cent, were in the executive branch of the regional government. The governor and his top aides have a hand in virtually everything that takes place in their regions. These officials oversee the region's bureaucrats who make decisions that determine not just government spending and institutions funded by the state, but also regulations governing business, property, taxation, housing, and everyday life.

With Putin's recentralisation, one would expect a much greater role for federal officials and Moscow-based ministries. Yet in only three regions did federal appointees such as the presidential representative or chief federal inspector hold second place in the regional rankings. The chief federal inspectors in a region are part of the new control system created by Putin in 2000; they are directly subordinate to the presidential representative in one of the seven federal *okrugs* and can play an important role in regional politics. They serve not just as the 'ears and eyes' of the Kremlin, but can be important in co-ordinating the work of federal agencies in a region and can establish an independent role in regional politics. In 14 of the 32 regions federal inspectors (this includes the presidential representatives themselves in three regions which had the headquarters of the federal *okrug* on their territory) were ranked among the ten most powerful officials.

Other appointees named by central government from outside the region are among the most influential officials in a region. Regional *siloviki* (officials with a military or security background) have grown in significance under Putin, just as they did at the national level. Overall, 22 *siloviki* at the regional level were named among the top ten officials in the 32 regions surveyed. These are the officials connected with law enforcement: the head of the regional branch of the Ministry of Internal Affairs (the top police official), the head of the FSB office, the chief prosecutor in a region, and the top judicial official. All are appointed by the corresponding federal agency or ministry, sometimes with direct input from the Kremlin. This is not to say that the governor is unable to influence the selection process for these officials, however. Governors, particularly those who have held office for a long time, often are given a veto – even if technically the offices are under the control of federal ministries or agencies. According to Dmitri Kozak, the federal Minister for Regional Development, in the last years of the Putin presidency governors were given *de facto* veto power even over the choice of the top police officials in their region.

In two of the regions surveyed, the director of a major factory in the region was rated as the second only to the governor in importance. Both happened to be directors of major steel companies, Severstal' headquartered in Vologda and Lipetsk's NLMK. The role of major businesses in the political life of a region can be considerable. In 23 of the 32 of the regions in the survey, businessmen were among the top ten most powerful persons. As a rule these were the directors of oil or gas companies, major industrial factories, or electrical companies. In some cases, the region's entire economy is dominated by one enterprise or sector, and that translates into a direct political role. In any region, though, there is a mutual dependency between economic power and the state. Governors often rely on off-budget funds that are 'voluntarily' contributed by major enterprises in a region; in return, local enterprises receive preferential treatment in other areas.

A surprising finding is the importance regional experts attached to local religious leaders' influence. Table 10.1 puts them in fourth place in overall influence. As at the national level, the degree of attention paid to religion and the church increased dramatically with the end of communism. Russian Orthodoxy, in particular, became intertwined with Russian nationalism, and even leaders of the Communist Party sought to demonstrate their faith and support for the church. Islam, Buddhism, Catholicism, and other religions are at a disadvantage, however, since they are linked to hierarchies and religious leaders based outside of Russia. Overall, the survey data in Table 10.1 appear to overstate the influence of religious leaders. When the top 10 figures in the 32 regions are examined, only in two regions, Belgorod and Khabarovsk, did a local religious leader make the list. Both were heads of the local Russian Orthodox Church.

Of officials in the regions, mayors and representatives in the regional or city legislatures are the only ones who are directly elected. In a quarter of the regions surveyed the second most influential was the head of the legislature, while mayors of the largest city held that rating in only four of the regions. Overall, 47 regional legislative figures and 42 mayors or city council chairs were among the 320 top officials. Other potential influences on political life in the regions are conspicuous by their absence. Leaders of regional branches of political parties were rarely mentioned – only in two regions was the regional leader of the ruling party, United Russia, included in the list of the powerful. The head of regional television channels, newspaper editors, leading journalists are not listed in any region as among the top ten influential actors. Mass media in the regions have little independence and are often under the control of either the governor or the mayor. Civil society is absent too. No trade union leaders were considered major players, nor were prominent figures in education or the arts. In the regions, just as at the national level, the weakness of civil society was given as a justification for creating 'public chambers' or councils that were supposed to represent influential people in a region from human rights organisations, lawyers, doctors, educators, and cultural figures. As of July 2008 such bodies were listed on the website of the Russian public chamber for 77 regions. Some of these organs predated the national public chamber and were hand-picked by governors. Few had any significant impact on the political life of their region, and none of their chairmen was listed among the most important figures in a region.

Contours of executive power

The end of gubernatorial elections from 2005 onwards significantly changed the nature of regional politics. The nature of the game changed dramatically, since the voter was no longer the audience that mattered to a sitting governor. Now a governor's status and his future depended almost totally on the strength of his relationship with the Russian president. Prior to this change, governors who had a troubled relationship with the federal centre were able to stay in power by manipulating the electoral process. So-called 'administrative resources' were the key. This term refers to instruments available to regional executives to influence the political and economic playing-field that go far beyond what in other political systems are called the 'advantages of incumbency'. Presidential appointment did not eliminate the administrative resources of governors; nor was this their purpose. Powerful governors, even if they have some independence, are needed by the Kremlin so long as they are loyal at critical moments. At the time of national elections, for example, governors are called on by the Kremlin to demonstrate their fealty by meeting turnout targets and mobilising voters in favour of the president and his political party.

For regional leaders several complicating factors were introduced by Putin's recentralisation. Changes in centre–region budget processes meant that more of what they needed for their regions now passed through federal ministries and were earmarked for specific purposes. This meant in practice that regional officials had to spend more time working the corridors of power in Moscow to get needed resources. The unsystematic nature of this process – in other words, he or she who lobbies best gets the most – is part of the explanation for the worsening inequality between regions. Centralisation of government functions also created at the regional level a boom in the number of federal officials who were at least not formally subordinate to the governor and his administration. Putin also increased legal pressure on governors, especially those with whom he had a poor relationship. In the period before the end of popular elections, Putin attempted to show governors that they were not immune to prosecution. Federal indictments on criminal charges were brought against many elected governors starting in 2002. Charges were filed against governors in Tver', Kamchatka, Kursk, Saratov, Smolensk, Altai Republic, Ryazan', Yaroslavl', Ivanovo and elsewhere. Usually the charges related to the improper use of federal funds. It was very easy to launch criminal cases of this nature, and not only because of rampant corruption among regional elites. Inadequate federal funding often forced governors to redirect funds from their original purpose to another, more pressing need and it was easy to violate rules on expenditures. Conviction would have resulted, not only in removal from office, but a lengthy prison term. What actually happened in most of the cases, though, was that the charges were later dropped. Apparently the purpose was to send a message to governors that they were not 'untouchable'. One case that actually produced a conviction and imprisonment was that of Nenets autonomous region governor Aleksei Barinov. Barinov was the last to be popularly elected, in February 2005, and his candidacy had been opposed by the Kremlin. The criminal case allowed Putin to remove Barinov as governor in 2006.

The political power of regional executives has many components. In the political sphere, many government institutions are dependent on the governor for funding or other critical resources. The media are usually kept in line through multiple mechanisms of economic, political, and legal pressure. Election commissions are dominated, as a rule, by the regional executive. In the economic sphere, governors are usually closely linked to regional economic elites. 'Outsiders' are kept outside the critical sectors of the regional economy or are quickly co-opted. Governors have used their power to take control over key enterprises in many regions. A bankruptcy law adopted in 1998 allowed even small debts to be used as a justification for 'restructuring' enterprises, after which co-operative police and courts allowed a new manager to be installed. Governors, through the long-standing method of 'telephone justice', were often able to dictate the outcome of court cases, which can be important in staking out other executive powers. Control over the courts can ensure that complaints and suits filed over elections, business activities, ownership, or anything thing else uphold the decision favoured by the regional leadership. It can also be used more directly by governors, as for example, lawsuits claiming slander when journalists accuse a governor of corruption. To summarise, even after Putin's changes it was still 'good to be governor'. It was also good to be the spouse or offspring of a governor, and there are many cases demonstrating the profitability of such family ties.

Perhaps the best example of how a regional leader can consolidate power and achieve some autonomy from the centre is, paradoxically, in the centre itself: Moscow's mayor Yuri Luzhkov. Mayor since 1992, Luzhkov through the city government maintains tight control over the Moscow economy, which is heavily regulated and taxed. The city tax base is far greater than Moscow's share in the Russian economy, simply because taxes are collected based on where the corporate headquarters are based, not where business is conducted. Generous benefits provided out of city coffers have helped Luzhkov to enjoy a high level of popularity throughout his tenure in office, and he has developed a reputation as a 'Yuri the Builder' for his efforts to remake the city, sometimes at the expense of its historic buildings. His political power is unmatched among regional leaders, even though in 1999 he had been a rival of Putin for the presidency. Luzhkov has been one of the top leaders of United Russia since its foundation. He successfully lobbied for special status for Moscow in federal legislation. He is one of the few mayors in the world with his own foreign policy and foreign aid budget, and has been active in supporting Russians in Ukraine as well as breakaway regions in Georgia and Moldova.

Most surprising to an outside observer is that Luzhkov's political reputation has remained untarnished in spite of very high levels of corruption in the Moscow city government. The construction projects for which Luzhkov is famous are reportedly rife with abuses of this kind. According to official declarations made in order to get on the ballot at election time, Luzhkov lives very modestly and has not benefited from his position. Yet in 2004, when the Russian edition of *Forbes* magazine first presented its list of the hundred richest businessmen, the only woman on the list was Yelena Baturina – Luzhkov's wife. She heads Inteko, a construction empire that got its start with city contracts and then expanded to control a large percentage of Russia's cement output. *Forbes* estimated her personal wealth in 2008 at $4.2 billion. Although Moscow has many independent news media, critical reporting or commentary on the mayor and his administration are rare. Luzhkov and his wife frequently sue national and local publications that allege malfeasance, and they always win – in Moscow courts. A corruption scandal at the Moscow arbitration court in 2008 fuelled speculation about how court decisions are influenced. It was discovered that the mayor's office helped a judge exchange one apartment for two, at a rate far less than the market value. She later sold one of the apartments for a huge windfall profit. What the mayor may have received in exchange is unclear, but the arbitration court constantly rules on cases involving city business. In February 2009 the judge was forced off the bench after the scandal was examined by the court's ethnical review committee.

Despite predictions to the contrary, the new powers taken by Putin to appoint governors did not result in a massive, rapid turnover in the governor corps. One could argue, in fact, that the new system was designed to allow Putin to retain key governors and republic presidents who had served for many years in their posts. Forced retirement was nearing as a result of term limits legislated in the Yeltsin era for such regional leaders as Moscow's Yuri Luzhkov and Tatarstan's Mintimer Shaimiev. Leaders who had already served two or three terms in office were less likely to be replaced by Putin than less experienced governors. In some regions, however, Putin sought to break the dominance of established elites by bringing in a complete outsider from another region to serve as governor. These 'carpetbaggers' (called *varyagi* in Russian, a word that has its origins in the name Russians gave to Viking invaders) were sometimes transferred from a national-level post or from another region. In 2005 three former deputies to Moscow's Yuri Luzhkov became governors of Ivanovo (Mikhail Men'), Kaliningrad (Georgii Boos), and Nizhnii Novgorod (Valerii Shantsev) regions respectively.

There were a few patterns in Putin's appointments of new governors or republic presidents. There was no change in the gender of Russia's governors. Both elected and appointed governors were almost exclusively male:

only one woman was head of a region, Valentina Matvienko, governor of St Petersburg. Putin at the beginning of his term favoured several candidates for governor who had a background in the military or FSB; by the time he began appointing governors none was from the ranks of the *siloviki*. There was an unwritten rule that leaders of ethnically based republics should continue to be drawn from that ethnic group. As of early 2009, no republic president in a region with a non-Russian majority had been replaced by an ethnic Russian. How candidates for replacing governors are chosen by the Kremlin remains a mystery. At a meeting with his regional representatives in mid-2008, President Medvedev complained that there was no functioning system in place for such personnel questions, and that 'every time we rack our brains trying to find appropriate candidates for filling the highest posts' in the regions. In a thinly veiled criticism of the personnel policies of his predecessor, Medvedev (himself a longtime friend and associate of Putin) denounced appointments made 'on the basis of personal ties, on the principle of personal loyalty' as well as the selling of government posts (Medvedev 2008c) in the regions. Medvedev indicated that he planned to institute new procedures and policies, creating a 'presidential quota' of potential candidates for governor and other top posts. Leaders of United Russia also talked of creating a similar 'cadre reserve' for the same posts under the auspices of the party, which has now been established. Both proposals were very reminiscent of the Soviet-era *nomenklatura* system that was used by the Communist Party to maintain control at all levels of the society and economy.

A major change under Putin took place in governors' party allegiances. In national elections held in the Yeltsin years, regional political differences were expressed in the vote percentage won by the Communist Party of the Russian Federation. Voters in the 'red belt', consisting largely of southern, mostly agrarian regions and republics, tended to support communist candidates. When the post of governor became an elected one, the result was a number of 'red governors'. Under Putin the category of 'red governors' virtually disappeared. Instead, between 2003 and 2007 almost all governors were persuaded to become members of the United Russia party. In the months preceding the 2003 Duma elections 28 governors were asked to head the regional lists of United Russia in a practice called the *parovoz* (meaning locomotive). At approximately the same time, many of the regional organisations of UR came under the control of governors. In the 2007 Duma elections the number of governors heading the party's regional lists grew to 65. None ever intended to leave their posts to enter the Duma, of course, but their visible support for the party helped it to win a majority in the parliament in both elections. It also directly tied their reputation with the Kremlin to the vote totals UR received, and the Kremlin expected regional leaders to use their administrative resources to help the party. United Russia's national organisation and even its regional organisations typically had little role in controlling or overseeing the actions of governors. United Russia usually did not play a major role in personnel decisions at the regional level either. One apparent exception to the pattern was in Ul'yanovsk, where in 2006 the governor introduced the requirement that all members of his government should be members of United Russia. In 2008, the notion of a party-approved cabinet was introduced in the region – all candidates for posts in the regional government were submitted to United Russia for approval. This is mostly a procedural difference, however; as in other regions, the governor controls both his ministers (whom he orders to join the party) and the UR party organisation.

Finally, another effect of Putin's policies was that governors largely ceased to be major figures in national level politics. Public opinion polls conducted in July 2008 found that only six regional leaders had a reputation outside their own and neighbouring regions. These were, in the order that they were cited by respondents, Moscow's Luzhkov, Kemerovo governor Aman Tuleev, St Peterburg's Matvienko, Chukotka's Roman Abramovich (Russia's richest man at the time and owner of the Chelsea football team in England; he resigned in July 2008), Krasnodar's Alexander Tkachev (who was in the news frequently because of preparations for the 2014 winter Olympics in Sochi), and Tatarstan's Shaimiev. Luzhkov and Tuleev had by far the most positive image among respondents, with Luzhkov most often cited as the regional leader who had done more to address the everyday problems of residents, law and order, and economic development in his region (VTsIOM poll, 24 July 2008, consulted at www.wciom.ru).

Legislatures in the regions: uniformity despite diversity

When Putin eliminated gubernatorial elections, he chose not to make the post simply an appointed one. Regional legislators had to approve his choice, and this had the potential to increase the role of elected assemblies in the political process. In practice, however, regional legislatures almost never objected to the choice put before them and never voted against the president's candidate once he was officially nominated. In part, this was because the law provided for the dissolution of a parliament if it rejected the president's candidate twice. Any potentially democratic opening from this procedural change was negated by another Putin policy: helping United Russia become the dominant political party in virtually all regional assemblies.

This result came about not because of overwhelming popular support for United Russia. Rather it was the outcome of a number of changes in the electoral and party system, combined with the application of administrative resources. Some of the first United Russia majorities in legislatures were produced by a regional leader instructing 'his' legislators to join the party. A 2002 change in the election system required at least half of the deputies to regional legislatures to be chosen by party-list voting. In some regions the entire assembly is chosen by this system rather than through the single-member districts that were used almost exclusively in the past. In regions that still had single-member districts, established parties were given advantages in registering candidates for these seats as well. The result of this change and changes to the law governing political parties was to reduce the number of political parties able to participate in regional elections. By the regional election cycle of December 2007 and March 2008, only the four parties in the Duma (the Communists, the Liberal Democrats, A Just Russia and United Russia) participated in all elections to regional assemblies. A contributing factor was a systematic rise in the costs associated with participating in elections. The amounts that parties were permitted to spend in regional elections were raised dramatically, as was the cost of participation by non-Duma parties. For example, in Irkutsk *oblast'* in 2004 the maximum expenditure allowed by law was 5.5 million roubles for a political party. For the October 2008 elections the limit was increased to 60 million. This benefits above all United Russia, since it can raise money from regional enterprises who seek influence in regional legislatures, influence that is wielded by the UR majority (who were of course the ones who had increased the election limit). Would-be backers of opposition parties, on the other hand, are actively dissuaded by regional authorities. The required monetary deposit for getting on the ballot for parties that are not in the Duma is also correspondingly higher, since regional election laws set it at between 10–15 per cent of the spending limit.

The same political device used in national parliamentary elections, the *parovoz*, also gave substantial advantages to United Russia in the regions. Governors again were used at the top of party lists in order to attract votes. This shifted voters' attention from who would actually be serving in the legislature and turned the election into a referendum on the governor. This provides an enormous incentive for governors to step up the application of the 'administrative resources' described earlier. A common tactic adopted by governors in regional legislative elections was to target opposition parties of any type. Courts and election commissions can disqualify parties and candidates and have them removed from the ballot. The only serious opposition party that could get on the ballot without difficulty was the Communist Party, since it was a party in the Duma.

Even they complained that regional leaders systematically interfered with their candidates, campaigns, and fund-raising efforts.

In 2006 a development that could have undermined the emerging dominance of United Russia in the regions was the creation of a second pro-government party, A Just Russia (*Spravedlivaya Rossiya*, or SR). This created an opening, at least temporarily, for some political pluralism at the regional level. SR was headed by Sergei Mironov, speaker of the upper chamber of the Russian parliament, the Federation Council. The SR party almost immediately attracted political forces in regions who had been in opposition to the dominant, governor-led élite that usually controlled the regional branch of United Russia. One of the Kremlin strategists' motives was to position SR to take votes from the CPRF, in effect creating a loyal social-democratic party. It apparently came as a shock to the Kremlin that bitter disputes soon followed as UR and SR fought for power in the regions. In Tuva there was a split between the UR-backed president and the opposition, which joined SR. The republic election commission, loyal to Sherig-ool Oorzhak, the long-serving Tuvan president and UR member, refused to certify the victory of five SR candidates in the October 2006 election, thus depriving the party of its hard-won majority. For over six months, an SR boycott of the assembly deprived the assembly of a quorum, and the Tuvan legislature was unable to convene. The Kremlin finally intervened and resolved the dispute by a compromise that replaced Oorzhak with a more acceptable candidate from United Russia and then installed a SR leader as speaker of the parliament.

In March 2007 elections to the Stavropol' parliament the mayor of Stavropol', Dmitri Kuz'min, headed the SR list for the regional assembly and ran against the UR list headed by governor Alexander Chernogorov. Like Oorzhak, Chernogorov's popularity had ebbed, and the SR candidates won a majority in the assembly. By 2008 the Kremlin resolved the ongoing conflict by removing Chernogorov as governor. It also orchestrated an end to the SR majority, with police jailing the SR ex-speaker of the assembly and prosecutors issuing an arrest warrant for Kuz'min on corruption charges. Deputies who had run under the SR label were persuaded to shift allegiances to UR, thus giving the latter a majority in the legislature. In the light of this experience, the Kremlin ultimately decided that even this very limited regional political pluralism was too much; it threatened the 'stability' that the new electoral system and United Russia were supposed to achieve. As a result, United Russia was allowed to unleash on SR the same tactics it used against other parties. In late 2007 elections SR was removed from the ballot for regional assemblies in several regions, while in Smolensk, in an unprecedented case, the votes cast for SR were nullified and the seats it had won were given to United Russia. By mid-2008 it was reported that the SR was finding it

difficult to raise funds from private or corporate sponsors and was closing some of its regional offices as a result. Pressure on would-be donors
from United Russia was said to be an important factor.

Local politics: cities and municipalities

A new law on local self-management, the 'third level' of administration in
Russia, was passed in 2003. The result of an intense drafting process that
favoured governors over mayors, the law attempted to specify and regu-
larise relations between the centre, regions and local government. It was
scheduled to take effect in 2006, but full implementation of some provisions has been repeatedly delayed. An important element of the new
framework is a massive redrawing of administrative boundaries, which
was to be carried out by officials under the control of governors. The old
system of local government relied on Soviet-era administrative–territorial
divisions, and many entities had no local government bodies. Henceforth,
there would be a comprehensive and uniform scheme of 'municipal
formations', resulting in a larger number of entities (over 24,000). One
complication is that the increased number of municipal entities has
created a shortage of qualified personnel to fill the newly created posts.

Under Yeltsin the principle of 'local self-management' became the basis
for local government, and mayors were usually popularly elected. What
political pluralism exists in Russian regions is often the result of the
competing and conflicting interests of city and regional government. The
result has been inevitable conflict between mayors and governors in many
regions. In part this also reflects the different sets of business interests that
stand behind them. City politics, as regional politics, are dominated by
the head of the local executive who, along with his administration, works
in close co-operation with heads of agencies and bodies that are technically outside his control – the head of the city police, the prosecutor, and
the courts. From this it should be apparent that mayors also have 'administrative resources' that they can use in their struggle with governors. The
logic of Putin's establishment of a hierarchy with non-elected governors
portended trouble for Russia's mayors and local government. Putin's
centralist policies had limits, and he gave repeated assurances that the
self-management of municipalities would continue. Meanwhile, governors lobbied for increased power over local officials, and many sought the
same power that Putin had over them: appointment of mayors with
formal approval by city councils. The erosion of popularly elected mayors
has been facilitated by a change brought by the law that permits an alternative to the popularly elected mayors – election by the city council or
appointment of a 'city manager' who would be hired to take over most of

the mayor's powers. Though there has been no official policy announced, it is clear that Putin's Kremlin was siding with governors and was unhappy with the political independence of mayors. In an operation that mirrors the policy toward governors several years earlier, starting in 2006 criminal cases were opened against a large number of mayors, usually for misuse of funds or corruption. A partial list of cities whose mayors were arrested or charged with criminal activity includes Arkhangel'sk, Baltiisk, Elista, Kislovodsk, Volgograd, Vladivostok, Tomsk, Tol'yatti, Ryazan', Samara, Orel, Pyatigorsk, and Pskov. A number of the investigations were handled directly by the FSB in order to circumvent allies of the mayor among local *siloviki*. In early 2009 the Duma passed a measure that would allow city councils or governors to initiate the dismissal of an elected mayor by a two-thirds vote by the council.

The new law on local government not only did not eliminate local elections, it created a large number of new elected assemblies at every level. In cities, the most important local elected bodies, the equivalent of regional assemblies, were city councils. One controversial aspect of the new law is that it was left to regional authorities to determine how city and municipal councils would be elected. In 2008, as new laws were being formulated, governors most often favoured introducing party-list voting for at least half of seats in local councils. This set the stage for extending the reach of United Russia into city government just as it had in regional government, only here it would be an instrument for control by governors. Another provision in the law, one that was under attack in mid-2008, would prevent local governments from sponsoring their own newspapers. The law allowed only for a publication that would print the text of laws and decisions made by local government agencies. In effect this would deprive mayors of the opportunity to compete with governors on a level playing field, and would further reduce pluralism of views in the media.

One critical set of issues that has delayed implementation of the local government law concerns money and resources. How would the productive assets in a region and tax revenues be distributed? Budgetary finances do not go directly to cities, but pass through federal ministries and regional officials. Part of the change in inter-budgetary policy was designed to define clearly who was responsible for what: for example, the federal centre would finance universities, regions – secondary and technical schools, and municipalities – primary schools. Once that were clarified, then budgetary decisions could be calibrated to anticipated expenditures. At the same time, most of the taxes in a region are usually collected in the cities. Mayors of big cities suspected that the outcome of the reform would deprive them of key revenue sources. It has always been the case that Russian cities were underfunded relative to the functions that municipal officials were responsible for performing. Given the rapid deterioration of Russia's infrastructure (such as roads, airports, train stations, hospitals, water and sewerage pipes, and centralised heating systems) mayors were placed in an untenable situation. In the Putin years a number of prominent mayors resigned their posts in protest at the lack of funding (something that governors have not done).

United Russia's leaders have actively pushed mayors to join the party, recognising that their power is incomplete if major urban areas are under the control of opposition or independent forces. Still, United Russia remains a party that is dominated by governors. As long as there are conflicts between mayors and governors, co-operation in the framework of one political party appears unlikely. The SR party began to position itself overtly as the 'party of mayors' after it became obvious that this was an important base of recruitment for the party. This was a way for the party to tap into the administrative resources that remained under the control of mayors; as was shown above in the case of Stavropol', allying with a popular mayor against an unpopular governor can win regional elections – even if only temporarily. United Russia has fought back by trying to appear more 'mayor-friendly'; in December 2006 it formed a 'mayor's club' to attract new members and show that it was attuned to the interests of cities. Negative tactics have also been applied; in some cases United Russia has blatantly threatened to reduce budget financing to cities whose mayors refuse to join the party.

Regional democracy and prospects for the future

Any balance sheet of regional performance on political indicators would form a troubling picture. The dominant role of regional executives at the expense of other institutions means that there are few checks and balances that would facilitate democratisation or other political reforms. Legislatures, local government, civil society, and even federal agencies are most often dependent on the will of governors who are in turn dependent on the will of the president. This has led to growing authoritarianism, one-party dominance, unfree media, and deepening corruption.

The freedom of the media is critical to any effort to change the status quo, just as *glasnost'* was critical to beginning Gorbachev's reforms. Newspapers and television both nationally and in the regions need to be able to investigate and criticise, but this is viewed with great suspicion by regional leaders, and they have worked hard to minimise such irritants. Press freedoms in Russian regions, just as at the national level, peaked in the early 1990s and declined dramatically in the Putin years. The Russian NGO, the Glasnost Defence Foundation (GDF; its website is www.gdf.ru), conducts annual studies of media freedom in the regions on the basis of events monitoring and polls of experts for the given time period. Among the factors considered are the number of privately owned media, the nature of the distribution and licensing system, access by the opposition to the media, attacks on or harassment of journalists, evidence of censorship and self-censorship, and access of journalists to information. Rarely is a region rated as having 'free' media. In its 2007–8 survey the GDF found that, of 81 regions surveyed, none was 'free' but that nineteen regions had 'relatively free' media. The regions that fell into this category were quite diverse: St Petersburg, Karelia, Dagestan, Altai (both *krai* and republic), Kamchatka, Kirov, Sverdlovsk, Nizhnii Novgorod, Novosibirsk, Krasnoyarsk, Stavropol', Ul'yanovsk, Tyumen', Chelyabinsk, Murmansk, Tver', Tomsk, and Yaroslavl'. The largest group, of forty-five regions, was designated as 'relatively unfree'; among these were regions that are often viewed as relatively liberal, such as Moscow, Novgorod, and Perm'. The remaining seventeen regions, designated 'unfree', included many of the non-Russian republics (Bashkortostan, Ingushetia, Kalmykia, Karachai-Cherkessia, Mari El, Mordovia, Tatarstan, and Chechnya) as well as Khabarovsk, Amur, Kaluga, Kemerovo, Magadan, Orel, Penza, Chita, and the Jewish autonomous *oblast'*.

In this setting, corruption at the regional level is pervasive. Putin never made a serious effort to reduce it; if he thought about it at all, it was viewed as a problem that should be dealt with in the distant future. His main concern seems to have been that by attacking corruption the Russian government would be undermining its own power base, both at the national level and in the regions. Putin reappointed many of the governors who were most directly linked to crime and regional networks of corruption – among these Primor'e governor Sergei Dar'kin, Moscow's Yuri Luzhkov, Bashkortostan's Rakhimov, and others. As Yelena Panfilova, the director of the Russian branch of Transparency International put it in July 2008, 'All of this system, all of our vertical which was erected in the last few years, both politically and economically is held up by a corruption vertical which, in turn, is cemented by mutual *kompromat* [compromising material] … you keep quiet and they will keep quiet about you' (quoted on *Polit.ru*, 21 July 2008). Just as on every other indicator, there is wide regional variation in corruption – though the phenomenon is extremely difficult to measure. Surveys of perceptions of corruption have been conducted, but there are problems with interpreting the results. Controls on the press, for example, often lead to a reduced perception of corruption in a region that may actually have a very high incidence. One study of Russian regional corruption (Dininio and Orttung 2005) found a significant correlation between the overall number of bureaucrats in a region and levels of corruption, and that increased numbers mean that bureaucrats have less reason to be concerned that someone may be monitoring their behaviour.

One of Dmitri Medvedev's first priorities as president was to emphasise the importance of the struggle against corruption. This has important implications for the politics of the regions. Rather than strengthening hierarchical control by the centre, a serious anti-corruption effort would target many of the key parts of that hierarchy – particularly governors and republic presidents. If Medvedev were to make significant changes in the governor corps, this would be an important sign of a new era in regional politics. Medvedev shocked many observers in January 2009 when he appointed the radical opposition leader Nikita Belykh to be governor of the Kirov region. Belykh, who had headed the Union of Right Forces party list in the 2007 Duma election, was an outspoken critic of Putin. Belykh viewed his appointment as a chance to demonstrate that market-based reforms and an anti-corruption agenda could produce major improvements in a relatively backward region. In February 2009 Medvedev replaced another four governors, including Yegor Stroev, who had controlled Orel since communist times. The new governors were more conventional candidates than Belykh, but the mere fact that long-serving governors were being forced out helps to undermine entrenched corruption in the regions.

Systemic causes of corruption are hard to deal with, but were also a focus of Medvedev's early efforts. Successful prosecution of corrupt officials would require wholesale changes in the courts. Medvedev talked extensively about the need for court reforms that would increase (or more accurately, bring about) the independence of judges. Concurrent political reform would demand the dismantling of administrative resources controlled illicitly by governors and remove the accumulated and unfair advantages that have accrued to United Russia at all levels. In a real sense, a serious anti-corruption campaign would require a dismantling of much that Putin had constructed. While this is unlikely with Putin serving as a powerful prime minister and with several of Putin's top strategists still in the Kremlin, the fact that Medvedev has even raised these issues is surprising. In the most optimistic scenario, a wholesale anti-corruption effort could become a stalking horse for democratisation of Russian politics both in the centre and in the regions.

Chapter 11

Managing the Economy

PHILIP HANSON

Putin's two terms as president, observed the Russian economist Yevsei Gurvich, were like two different political regimes: 'The authorities went from building a market economy to building a business' (Gurvich 2008). The implication was that they had turned to building a business empire of their own. This was the comment, not of an outsider, but of the head of the Economic Expert Group, a think-tank that advises the Russian Ministry of Finance. One might hazard a guess that Aleksei Kudrin, the Minister of Finance himself, would not necessarily disagree.

The making of economic policy in Russia, in other words, is the work of a more diverse and less consensual cast of characters than is the case even in Britain or the United States. In this chapter I will review approaches and outcomes in different domains of economic policy and then offer an interpretation of the politics of Russian economic policy from the late Putin years to the start of the Medvedev presidency. The interpretation is no more than a plausible conjecture. The central argument is that two influences came together around 2003–4 to alter the course of Russian policy making: rising oil prices, and a challenge to the political monopoly of the Putin inner circle. In responding to these developments, that small group of leaders stumbled across ways of becoming rich as well as powerful, and proceeded accordingly. At the same time, some liberal policies remained intact and some liberal policy makers remained in place.

An overview of recent economic policy

Background: the Russian economy under Yeltsin

It has been part of Putin's public relations policy to paint the 1990s as a decade of disorder and failure for Russia – disorder and failure to which Western states contributed. It was indeed a time of disorder, with highly visible and widespread crime, falling economic activity and rising inequality. But it was also the period in which the foundations of a market, capitalist economy began to be laid.

The transformation from an overwhelmingly state-owned and centrally planned economy to a market economy had by 1998 produced a population of privately owned, profit-seeking firms. In that year, the rouble was devalued some four-fold; this new population of firms responded in a normal, market-economy way. Imports were suddenly rendered vastly more expensive than before, and domestic producers seized their opportunity and increased supply. That was the beginning of the recovery from which, politically, Putin benefited.

Most of the new market institutions were in place, albeit often in a primitive or embryonic form. There were real firms, with finance and marketing divisions; there were banks, even if most of them were doing much less deposit-taking and lending than was needed; most prices were no longer controlled, and reflected – roughly – supply and demand; many investment decisions had become commercial rather than political, even if they often led to placing assets offshore; money had become a store of value and a means of exchange, even if people were inclined to prefer dollars to roubles. Growth, in other words, began while Yeltsin was still in place. After the devaluation, the rise in oil prices in 1999 kept the recovery going.

For all that can be said about the fundamental nature of reforms in the 1990s, economic policy under Yeltsin was a mess. The president and his appointed governments, on the one hand, and parliament, on the other, were at loggerheads over privatisation and – more damagingly – over macro-economic stabilisation. Gaidar, Chubais and the other 'young reformers' were deeply unpopular, had no direct democratic mandate of their own, and were not consistently supported by the President. Compromises and fudges allowed the appearance of macro-economic control to be presented to Russia's then-paymasters, the World Bank and the International Monetary Fund (IMF), without the substance. The growth of the money supply was brought under control but this anti-inflationary measure was not carried through to its logical conclusion: most large enterprises were not forced by monetary tightening to restructure or close down; they were allowed to carry on as before, often producing for inventory, with no customers, by resorting to barter and promissory notes (for the whole story see Gaddy and Ickes 2002). The pain of unemployment was mitigated but the gain of restructuring was largely missed.

Nonetheless, the economy had begun to recover before Vladimir Putin was installed as President.

Economic policy in Putin's first presidential term

The improvement in economic conditions was reinforced by confidence in the new leader. Putin was relatively young and energetic, and rode into office on a wave of Chechnya-based popularity. The lower house of parliament, the Duma, was more compliant than any parliament that Yeltsin had dealt with. Against this background, Putin initially pursued two lines of economic policy that augured well for Russia's future.

First, he and his government team sought macro-economic stability. Public spending was constrained while export earnings from oil and gas boosted budget revenue through export duties and natural resource extraction taxes on hydrocarbons. A surplus was maintained in the federal budget. It was maintained through Putin's second term as well, as Table 11.1 illustrates.

Russia's record of fiscal conservatism consists so far of eight successive years of fiscal surpluses. No contemporary Western country can match that. But is the comparison fair? With a flood of petro-dollars coming into Russia, it might be argued, running a budget surplus is easy. This is not necessarily the case, however; pressures to spend that inflow on any number of worthy causes have been intense. The important point about Russia policy is that those pressures have been resisted.

Overall state revenue and expenditure also comprised off-budget funds and sub-national (regional and local) budgets. These were brought under stronger central control during Putin's first term; now regions receive substantial transfers from the federal budget but have near-zero borrowing

Table 11.1   *Federal budget revenue and expenditure, 2000–7 (as % of GDP); inflation (end-year, year-on-year increase in consumer prices, %) and broad money supply growth (M2 end-year, year-on-year growth, %)*

	2000	2001	2002[a]	2003[b]	2004	2005	2006	2007
Revenue	15.4	17.6	20.3	20	20.5	23.7	23.5	23.6
Spending	13.2	14.6	18.4	17	16.1	16.2	16.0	18.2
Balance	2.2	3.0	1.9	3	4.4	7.4	7.5	5.4
CPI change	20.2	18.6	15.1	12.0	11.7	12.5	9.8	11.9
M2 change	62.4	40.1	32.3	52	35.8	39.0	48.8	47.5

Notes: a. Social and pension funds included in both revenue and expenditure from 2002, so not precisely comparable with earlier figures.
b. Annual total missing from source, so interpolated; approximate.

Sources: Adapted from Economic Expert Group (attached to the Ministry of Finance), www.eeg.ru/pages/39?PHPSESSID=40061151cBfa39bd523ae903349elcc5, last accessed 20 April 2008, for 2000–5 budgets; *BOFIT Weekly*, 20 March 2008: 1 for 2006–7 budgets; M2 and CPI from Troika Dialog.

powers, and the overall government balance is usually close to the federal budget balance. This is one aspect of Putin's reduction of regional autonomy that has some undoubted benefits: it has assisted macro-economic stabilisation (Hanson 2006).

The second area of policy might be called micro-economics or structural reform. Here there is a sharp contrast between roughly the first and second terms of Putin's presidency. In the first term free-market reforms were pursued, and tax rates were cut. This included a shift to a flat-rate personal income tax. Several 'debureaucratisation' measures were passed that were designed to reduce the barriers to creating and expanding small firms by reducing regulatory requirements for registration, licensing and the like. A large part of the rationale of this last policy was to reduce the scope for bribe-taking by official regulatory bodies. Monitoring through surveys of small firms has continued to show some resulting reduction of barriers (see, for instance, Cefir 2007). Legislation facilitating the development of a land market was passed. The labour code was amended to make legal strikes almost impossible – on the face of it, an extremely business-friendly approach. It has not, however, prevented a surge of strikes in 2007–8 as the economy began to overheat (Teague 2008).

It was evident even before 2003 that Russia had a weak rule of law, extensive corruption and an intertwining of politics and the economy that was not helpful to long-run development. But changes, it could reasonably be argued, were under way. Businessmen who had made fortunes in often dubious financial and trading operations were beginning to invest in industry, and therefore evidently feeling able to take a longer view of Russian economic prospects; they no longer feared at every moment that the state might snatch their assets away. The rapid growth of the oil industry in 1999–2004 was driven precisely by companies run by sharp young men who had moved across from the banking sector. Growth in the industry was very largely the work of such companies: Yukos, Sibneft and TNK (OECD 2004: 43–4). It could be conjectured that the growing business class would increasingly demand independent courts and impartial legal treatment – for themselves, but with a spin-off for others.

The most obvious point at which authoritarian management of the polity began to damage economic policy was the arrest in summer 2003 of Platon Lebedev, a stake-holder in the Yukos oil company. Later the same year, having apparently rejected an implicit invitation to flee the country, the main owner of Yukos, Mikhail Khodorkovsky, was also arrested. Thus began the state's attack on Yukos. With it came a change in economic policy and the business environment.

The continuation of prudent macro-management

The first point to note is that something important did not change. As Table 11.1 reminds us, macro-economic policy remained prudent. More precisely, it remained prudent until the 2007–8 electoral cycle loomed on the horizon. In 2007 budget spending was revised upwards. That contributed, along with worldwide food-price rises and perhaps some overheating inside Russia, to a re-acceleration of inflation. And the 2008 federal budget was drafted to break even – in other words, to produce neither a surplus nor a deficit – at $60 for a barrel of Urals oil; previous budgets had been more conservatively designed, with a $30 break-even point (Sutela 2008). The 2007 budget showed a surplus and so did the 2008 budget. But the direction of change was one that helped to reignite Russian inflation, as the penultimate row of Table 11.1 indicates.

Therefore Russian economic policy under Putin has not only changed dramatically over time; it also has continued to differ radically across policy domains: largely orthodox in a Western sense in macro-economic management; completely at odds with Western orthodoxy over micro-economics. This prudent macro-economic management is usually credited to the long-serving finance minister, Aleksei Kudrin. This is fair: he has been the immediate author of fiscal policies and a dogged champion of fiscal prudence. But if the weight of feeling in the Kremlin had been against fiscal restraint, that restraint, and probably Kudrin himself, would have gone.

This policy stance may not have been quite as hard to maintain as might at first be thought. It may be that a political leadership that tries to reduce inflation in contemporary Russia is acting with the grain of popular opinion. The Russian people learnt in the 1990s how damaging high inflation could be. The pressure for more public spending, superficially a popular cause, has probably come mainly from particular groups within the élite with their own schemes for getting rich on the back of various state spending programmes; evidence of a great deal of popular support for these schemes is not clear. Russian opinion polls show high approval of Putin but very low expectations of politicians in general. At all events, it took the near approach of elections to loosen the Putin–Kudrin spending restraints. Russia entered the global economic crisis in 2008 with strong reserves. After July 2008, with the oil price falling steeply and the rouble, soon after, following suit, the entire economic situation changed for the worse. But Kudrin was still in post, battling to control the budget deficit that – for reasons beyond the reach of Russian policy-makers – was looming in 2009 (*Vedomosti*, 10 February 2009).

The turn to statism from 2003

The policy change occurred in micro-economic policy. In retrospect, the attack on Yukos looks to have been the turning point. It has been described in detail elsewhere (see especially Sakwa 2009). The attack was initially directed above all against an individual – the Yukos chief executive Mikhail Khodorkovsky – who was charged with personal tax evasion and fraud in connection with his holding company's acquisition of a mineral fertiliser works, Apatit, in 1994. Then in 2004 tax claims were brought against the Yukos itself. At one point President Putin said that nobody was planning to bankrupt the company. But eventually, through the courts' freezing of Yukos assets, the company was in fact made bankrupt. Its assets were acquired in uncontested or otherwise oddly conducted auctions, for the most part by the state oil company, Rosneft.

Since the start of the Yukos affair, there have been three main elements in the increase in state intervention in the economy:

- There has been an increase in state ownership in the hydrocarbons sector.
- There have been some other increases in state ownership in other sectors, mainly in engineering.
- And there has been legislation restricting the participation of foreign companies in a list of 'strategic' industries.

These changes do not amount to anything resembling general renationalisation of the economy. They have however been accompanied by a new submissiveness to central authority on the part of big business and a more obvious involvement of senior members of the presidential administration and the government in the direct control of assets. In addition, much (not all) of this extension of state economic power has been accomplished by blatant manipulation of available administrative weapons and with an absence of due process.

The common instruments are claims for back taxes, claims of infringement of the conditions of natural resource exploitation licences, and claims of breaches of environmental regulations. It has constantly appeared as though the courts were, in these cases, following instructions from the executive branch. In May 2008, remarkably, a judge, appearing as a witness, testified on the record to an instance of such direction of the court by an official of the presidential administration (Pleshanova 2008).

The hydrocarbons sector

One component of the turn to statism, accordingly, was the partial rena-tionalisation of the oil industry. In 2004 state-controlled companies accounted for 11 per cent of Russian oil production. In 2007 the share had risen to 39 per cent (Milov 2008). This was the result partly of the Yukos takeover, but also of Gazprom's purchase of Sibneft. In addition, Gazprom used administrative pressure to acquire control of the Sakhalin-2 offshore project from Shell, Mitsui and Mitsubishi and of the Kovykta gas-field from TNK-BP, a 50–50 Russian-British joint venture, to the accompaniment of FSB raids on BP's representative office in Moscow.

The situation in the gas industry was not much altered. Gazprom had been, and remained, the producer of 80 to 90 per cent of all Russian natural gas. It continued to have a monopoly of gas export pipelines and of gas storage. The controlled domestic gas prices to industrial users (including a large part of electricity generation) were kept low: in late 2007 they were about a third of the 'European' price (the Russian-border price of exported gas net of export duty and transport cost). The policy changes in the gas industry amounted to having Gazprom's export monopoly legally entrenched and securing Gazprom control of Sakhalin-2; negotiations over the disposal of gas from the ExxonMobil-led Sakhalin-1 project continued. In short, Gazprom's monopoly was already strong in 2003 and has since been somewhat strengthened.

It is not clear that policy makers intend to nationalise much more of the hydrocarbons sector, and there is no sign at all of plans to assert direct state control over the natural resources sector as a whole, including coal, timber and metals. It could be argued that Russia, indeed, is unlike most major oil-exporting countries in not subordinating its oil industry to a state-owned national oil company.

The stance of the Russian leadership on the management of natural resources in general is more difficult to identify. Plans to merge the two major state hydrocarbons companies Gazprom and Rosneft, endorsed in 2004 by President Putin, were never implemented. Many Russian observers put this down to rivalry between Igor Sechin, then a deputy head of the presidential administration (PA), as well as chairman of the board of Rosneft, and Dmitri Medvedev, then also a senior member of the PA and chairman of the board of Gazprom. Legislation to clarify the terms on which foreign firms might take a stake in major natural resource deposits was promised by President Putin for late 2005 and delivered, with many questions not clearly answered, in spring 2008 (see *Perechen'* 2005; PBN 2007, 2008).

One thing that is clear is that businessmen in the oil industry who for some reason are not *personae gratae* to the political leadership are likely to have their companies taken away from them, not necessarily to be acquired by the state but perhaps to be handed over to a more trustworthy tycoon. That was the conclusion drawn by several Russian commentators in the case of tycoon Mikhail Gutseriev's loss of control of the Rosneft oil company in 2007 (see *Vedomosti*, 30 and 31 July, 10, 15 and 29 August 2007).

I will come back to the interpretation of these policies after considering the other two components of the turn to statism.

Other sectors

The main development outside hydrocarbons has been the creation of a network of state-holding companies to manage enterprises and research institutes in shipbuilding, aerospace, civil nuclear energy, nanotechnology and an assortment of mostly military-related assets that now come under the Rostekhnologii holding company. The last of these holding companies incorporates a concern whose core business is arms exports – Rosoboroneksport – but which also has stakes in car-making and metals, as well as in the production of weapons.

Some analysts have suggested a more general drift towards state control. In its 2006 survey of Russia the Organisation for Economic Cooperation and Development (OECD) listed 22 examples of state acquisitions made in 2005–6 (OECD 2006: 33–4). They included media businesses and banks. That list has continued to grow. The core, however, of the acquisitions is in oil and more-or-less defence-related engineering. In at least some of these cases, as in the hydrocarbons sector, administrative pressure was used to force reluctant private owners to sell assets (for an account of the state acquisition of the world's largest titanium producer, VSMPO-Avisma, from private owners, see Finn 2006).

It is common enough for governments to own at least some arms producers. The unusual feature of the new Russian holding companies is that they extend far back from the making of weapons systems into metals and civil ships and aircraft. As with Rosneft and Gazprom, moreover, members or close associates of the Putin circle have been placed in oversight positions in these companies, typically as chairmen of the board.

Keeping out the foreigners?

In spring 2005 Putin told a business audience that what the state did and did not consider a strategic asset would soon be clarified. In May he ordered Prime Minister Fradkov to ensure that such legislation was drafted by November of that year (*Perechen'* 2005, point 5). Two pieces of legislation seemed to be involved: a revision of the law 'On the Subsoil' and a new law on strategic industries. In the event, struggles over the drafts of both were prolonged and tortuous – and mostly hidden from public view.

On 2 April 2008 the Duma passed on third reading the law 'On Procedures for Making Foreign Investments in Russian Commercial Entities of Strategic Importance for the National Security of the Russian Federation'. It was signed into law by Putin on 5 May 2008 (the details are given in PBN 2007, 2008). The law sets normal, or default, ceilings on foreign ownership stakes in 39 quite narrowly defined activities (such as 'Launch and control of space vehicles') plus major TV and radio broadcasting companies, major telecoms companies and major printers and publishers, and hydrocarbons and mineral deposits. For all but the natural-resource assets the default ceiling is 50 per cent (25 per cent if the foreign investor is state controlled). In the natural-resource sector the default ceiling is 10 per cent (5 per cent for state-owned foreign investors), for major deposits. Those deposits are defined as more than 70 million tons of oil, 50 billion cubic metres of natural gas, 50 tons of gold, 50,000 tons of copper and zero (in other words, normally no foreign access at all) to a further list including diamonds, uranium, cobalt, nickel and platinum (for more details on the natural resource provisions see Ivanitskaya and Mazneva 2008). The ceilings in the legislation are default limits in the sense that a foreign company may seek permission from the government for the acquisition of a larger stake on a case-by-case basis.

The passing of such a law is a step towards clarification of the rules of the game. Uncertainty remains, however, over how the exemptions would work and which agency would advise the Russian government over decisions. If it were the Federal Anti-Monopoly Service (FAS), the Russian economy would become a good deal more open than if it were the Federal Security Service (FSB). The FAS is, along with the Ministry of Finance, one of the few free-market outposts in a predominantly illiberal state machine.

The law's provisions for the natural-resource sector look, on paper, highly restrictive. Ten per cent is well below the so-called 'blocking stake' (*blokpaket*) of 25 per cent + one share (of voting stock). Sub-*blokpaket* minority shareholders cannot veto major corporate decisions. The drafting of the default limits on foreign stakes, together with the relatively low size of oil and gas fields above which the restrictions apply, suggests a belief that foreign control is to be minimised. The framers of the law either rate Russian control above strong foreign inputs of technology, finance and management or they believe foreigners will provide those inputs even if they have little control over their use. It remains to be seen how applications for exceptions will be received. Obviously, a practice of granting numerous exceptions would alter the picture.

What does it all mean?

Several interpretations of this policy shift are, at first sight, possible. First, it could be a strategy chosen by people who believed it would work better for Russians in general than the liberal orthodoxy that was – however shakily – pursued in the 1990s. A Russian leadership, with its confidence restored by petro-dollars, no longer needed to please Western sponsors. It could instead become a 'developmental state', part of the 'world without the West', with a faith in state-led growth.

Second, it could be a set of actions aimed primarily at keeping a monopoly of political control for the small group around Putin. Vladislav Surkov, the deputy head of the PA who might at a stretch be called the ideologist of Putinism, has distinguished between nationally-minded tycoons and 'offshore aristocrats'. The latter were to be discouraged. The political élite reportedly also distinguish between 'trusted' (*doverennye*) tycoons and 'cosmopolitans' (*kosmopolity* (for sources see Hanson 2007: 881); incidentally, knowledgeable Russians whom I have asked whether 'cosmopolitan' carries the anti-Semitic connotation it did in Stalin's time are divided in their answers).

In other words, the move for control of parts of the economy – both by direct state ownership and by ensuring that politically compliant businessmen are running things – would on this view be a move to ensure that no significant base of independent social and political power exists. On this interpretation, the attack on Yukos was not – or not necessarily – the start of a general renationalisation of the oil industry. Rather, it was a message to big business in general: don't forget who's the boss.

The third view is that the turn to statism is above all propelled by greed on the part of the politically powerful. They were able to get control of assets yielding very large revenues, so they did; end of story. This view is widely held in Russia.

The first interpretation fits the evidence least well. When the policy changed, it was not supported by the ministers of finance or economic development. The official economic policy makers, in other words, were not on board. Documents setting out long-run strategy and published as late as 2007 and 2008 do not endorse it, and that includes the major strategic document on energy strategy put out by the Ministry of Industry and Energy (Minpromenergo 2007), as well as by the more traditionally liberal Ministry of Economic Development and Trade (MERT: see MERT 2008). Both stress the importance of competition and neither sets out any programme for further increases in state control. The MERT document, in particular, stresses the need to strengthen property rights: precisely the opposite of the methods used to increase political control in the oil industry.

The shift in micro-economic policy came from the PA. The presidential administration has its economic advisers; the best known of them for a time was Andrei Illarionov. He described the Yukos affair as a 'negative development' (*Finansovye Izvestiya*, 28 December 2004) and state-company takeovers of private companies, financed by borrowing abroad, as 'the swindle of the year' (*Vedomosti*, 22 December 2005). He later resigned.

The questions, then, are why the shift of policy should come from the PA, why it should be implemented contrary to economic advice within the state machinery, and why it should come when it did. A combination of explanations two and three looks best able to answer these questions.

The PA is, or at any rate was under Putin, the pinnacle of political power in Russia. Senior PA members and other close associates of Putin took oversight positions as board chairmen of key state-controlled companies: Gazprom, Rosneft, Transneft (the oil pipeline monopoly), Rostekhnologii and others. In a state with a high level of corruption, chairing the board of a state company may be a source of private wealth over and above the official emoluments of the post. That might perhaps be sufficient to account for the turn to statism.

The timing tends to support this interpretation. Urals oil prices, having fallen as low as $10/barrel in 1998, rose to the mid-20s in 2000, dipped in 2001, and began a spectacular climb in 2003. Gurvich (2008) has calculated that of the $500 bn of petro-dollar (export) earnings of Russia during Putin's presidency (he is probably referring to the calendar years 2000–7 inclusive), $450 bn came in Putin's second term. And this is when the PA acted to raise state control of the oil industry.

Strikingly, action against the Yukos oil company came in the year following the arrests of Lebedev and Khodorkovsky – in 2004, not 2003. Yukos shares rose to a record high in April 2004, six months after Khodorkovsky's arrest, and fell only then, when the tax cases against the company began (private communication from Chris Weafer of Uralsib). In other words, the market reacted to an attack on the company rather than to the earlier attack on its owner. Investors, Russian and foreign, did not read the arrests of Lebedev and Khodorkovsky as signs of the impending death of the company. The idea that stock-markets price in all available information may be a simplification – at times a gross and misleading simplification – but the behaviour of the Yukos share price in 2003–4 suggests that either there was initially no intention in the PA of bankrupting and nationalising the company or that there was such a plan but it was kept secret from investors for six to nine months. The former is more likely.

Hence it is suggested here that what started as an attack on a man perceived to be challenging the Kremlin's monopoly of power evolved, as oil prices rose, into an attack on Russia's leading oil company, with a view to taking it over. So far no comparable extension of state ownership has taken place in metals, where pure asset-grabbing might seem almost equally attractive. Nor indeed has there been a move by the state against the remaining major Russian private oil company, Lukoil. That tends to support the notion of an almost accidental slide into asset-grabbing that started merely as the slapping-down of a troublesome tycoon.

A different logic may apply to the development of state-holding companies in shipbuilding, aerospace, defence production, atomic energy and nanotechnology. These, after all, are hardly honey-pots exuding giant natural-resource rents. Russia's arms exports were $7.5 bn in 2007 (*Oxford Analytica Daily Brief* (OADB) 2008), against oil, oil products and gas exports totalling $217 bn. Here the reassertion of state control may be motivated by the realisation that the state now has funds to put into these activities, plus a reluctance on the part of the PA to leave anything to do with national security – even an activity as loosely connected as shipbuilding – in private hands.

Also present in this policy shift is a keen suspicion of the intentions of foreigners. That is manifest in the legislation on foreign investment in strategic industries. It is hardly likely that suspicion of foreigners suddenly overwhelmed Kremlin thinking in 2003 – early 2004, ahead of the Orange Revolution in Kiev. It is more likely that the political leadership found at that time that it had the money to indulge its suspicions and seek a way forward that would be a little closer – though still not all that close – to going it alone.

Outcomes

I have devoted a great deal of this chapter to those parts of Russian economic policy that are most open to criticism from a conventional Western perspective. Russian citizens might well take the view that this is excessive: they, after all, have become a great deal better off since 1999. Many Western investors in Russia could say the same.

Household consumption is officially estimated to have risen at more than 10 per cent per annum from 1999 to 2007 (Rosstat data reported in Troika Dialog, *Russia Economic Monthly*, February 2008). Poverty has been reduced: 25 per cent of the population were estimated to be living below the official subsistence minimum in 2002, and only 14 per cent in 2007 (*BOFIT Weekly*, 22 February 2008).

The improvements are real and, in human terms, of great value. What is less clear is the relationship between the economic gains and the policies pursued. It is not unusual for countries, particularly middle-income countries such as Russia, to experience growth accelerations lasting for at least eight years; they may be attributable to a wide variety of developments that act as triggers for the improvement: one such development is a rise in the price of a key export commodity (Hausmann *et al.* 2004).

Macro-economic development

Russia has experienced strong growth, and that growth did not slow with the turn to statism. Inflation has been brought under control, though it showed some signs of breaking out again in 2007–8.

Russia's GDP growth from 1999 through 2007, however, at an average annual rate of 7 per cent, has not been especially impressive when compared with other CIS countries. For the eleven countries whose growth is illustrated in Figure 11.1, rising natural resource export prices have played a major role for three: Russia, Kazakhstan and Azerbaijan. Having a high ratio of natural-resource export earnings to GDP, as those three do, is evidently not necessary for rapid growth among CIS countries. The factor that is common to all of them is recovery from a large and prolonged fall in economic activity. Particularly high rates of growth in

Figure 11.1　*Russia and other CIS countries: average annual GDP growth, 1999–2007 (%)*

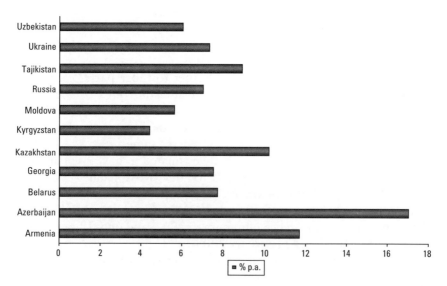

Note:　Meaningful data for Turkmenistan are not available.
Source:　Adapted from Mezhgosudarstvennyi statisticheskii komitet SNG.

Armenia, Azerbaijan, Georgia and Tajikistan reflect recovery from especially damaging output falls associated with military conflicts.

The clearest achievement of Russian economic policy has been the reduction of inflation between 1998 and 2006. This, and the weakening of policy in 2007–8, have already been discussed. The leading annual data are in Table 11.1 above. With due allowance for the influence of elections on public spending, even in a (soft) authoritarian state, macro-economic policy should, I think, be accounted a success. We shall return in the final section to a consideration of how macro policy may fare in the future.

Policies and institutional change

Even after the turn to statism in 2003–4, many market institutions continued to develop. Companies gained and lost market share, took other companies over or were taken over, and found they could borrow more readily from the banks (whose spread between deposit and lending rates continued to shrink); big Russian companies, chiefly in metals, invested abroad and began to function as multinationals; mortgage lending developed; the stock-market capitalisation of companies grew to exceed GDP and raising money on stock-markets at home and abroad became a widespread practice; new companies appeared in typically post-industrial lines of business, such as public relations and recruitment; as the economy began to overheat in 2007–8 and labour shortages became more acute, workers took to going, usually unofficially and semi-legally, on strike, and sometimes won the pay rises or improved conditions they wanted (Teague 2008).

This was bottom-up development, including the evolution of economic institutions, not driven by policy. It does not, however, make Russia a well-functioning market capitalist economy. Table 11.2 lists some well-researched rankings of Russia's public administrative capacity and economic environment. A continuation of market reforms after 2003 would have improved the 'ease of doing business' ranking, which is more closely connected to the conditions for future economic performance than the World Economic Forum's competitiveness index. Successful reform of public administration and the judiciary would have lifted the governance score, which is low for a country of Russia's development level.

Another, more narrowly focused consequence of recent policies has been a slow down, and latterly stagnation, of oil production. This has been reflected in a marked deceleration of the volume of oil exports, as Figure 11.2 illustrates. The rise in oil prices from 2004 has meant that Russia's oil revenues continued to grow fast, masking the drastic slow down in export volume. But it makes Russia's prospects of future export

Table 11.2 *Russia's governance and business environment: rankings by international organisations for 2006–8 (rank number or percentile ranking, with number of countries surveyed)*

	Russia	Out of (n countries)
WEF Global Competitiveness Index 2007–08	58	131
World Bank Ease of Doing Business 2008	106	178
World Bank Governance 2006 (percentile rank)		
Government effectiveness	37.9	212
Regulatory quality	33.7	212
Rule of law	19.0	212

Note: In the percentile rankings 1 = worst, 100 = best, so the rankings shown here put Russia, in descending order of the indicators shown here, near the top of the bottom-ranked two-fifths of countries; marginally above the bottom third; and in the bottom fifth, or of the order of 132nd, 141st and 172nd, respectively
Sources: adapted from Kaufmann *et al.* 2007; www.doingbusiness.org/ ExploreEconomies/?economyid=159, last accessed 21 March 2008; www.gcr. weforum.org/pages/analysis.aspx, last accessed 23 November 2007.

Figure 11.2 *Russia's governance and business environment: rankings by international organisations for 2006–8*

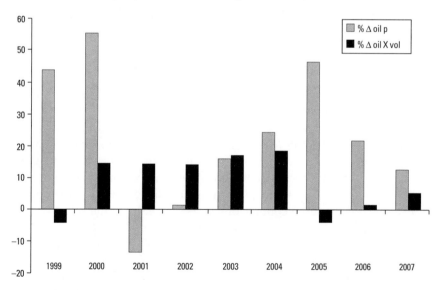

Sources: Adapted from Russian Customs Service (www.customs.ru) for tonnage figures; Troika Dialog for average annual price.

earnings less robust than they would otherwise be. (Gas prices follow oil prices; gas production volume growth has been very slow for decades, and gas in 2007 accounted for less than a quarter of all hydrocarbons export earnings, so it is oil that matters so far as foreign earnings are concerned.)

The sources of the slow down in production and exports include a lack of investment in developing new fields, and that in turn can be attributed to some combination of the following: the (justified) lack of confidence in their property rights on the part of private-sector oilmen; constraints on export volumes set by a sluggishly developed, state-controlled export pipeline system, and high taxation on the oil industry. In other words, state actions are a very large part of the problem.

The natural resource extraction tax was reduced in 2007–8 in recognition of the last of these problems, but the state, in the person of deputy prime minister Igor Sechin, continued to intervene, reportedly securing commitments from oil companies that funds saved as a result of the tax cut would be used only to invest in increasing output (Vesti TV, 28 May 2008). Given other components of policy, this may not be enough.

Conclusions and prospects

Russian economic policy since 2003–4 presents a curiously divided picture. Broadly, macro-economic policy has been sound and effective. Policies that affect the development of economic institutions have been damaging to the business environment. State actions, driven by the presidential administration, have included what can only be described as attacks on particular businesses, conducted without due process and tending to stall any development of a rule of law and confidence in property rights.

At the same time, these actions have been concentrated in certain sectors of the economy and may not be impeding, after some initial, general shock, development in sectors that are believed to be beneath the politicians' radar. Russian and foreign business people seem to believe that they now understand a new set of informal rules of the game and can operate within them – at least in most services, agriculture and part of manufacturing. Probably some lasting damage has nonetheless been done to the oil industry: the goose that lays the golden eggs has not been killed, but it has taken a beating.

The reasons for this post-2003 policy dispensation, I have suggested, may lie less in the considered pursuit of a new strategy than in a serendipitous chain of events. These events began with the Kremlin inflicting exemplary punishment on one over-mighty citizen who challenged their monopoly of power. This tipped over into state asset grabs in which very senior officials saw opportunities to control large and highly remunerative assets. But the search for political control and personal enrichment does not, apparently, entail an indefinite extension of state ownership. The Putin élite implicitly recognises the effectiveness of a mainly private-enterprise, market economy. Its members seek to ensure that their own material interests are served and that Russian tycoons can be relied upon to do what their political masters wish, as and when those political masters see a need to intervene.

Russian economic policy faces a number of possible difficulties over the coming decade. Some are new, or at any rate would be if they materialise:

- A large and sustained fall in the oil price cannot be ruled out.
- The working-age population, which had been rising even while the total population was falling, is likely to fall from 89.8 million in 2007 to 77.5 million in 2020 (MERT 2008: 31), or at a rate of about 0.9 per cent a year.
- The margin of under-utilised capacity that assisted output growth after 1998 has been used up.
- Bottlenecks are emerging in domestic gas and electricity supplies, which may or may not be eased by politically difficult increases in domestic prices for these sources of energy.
- The real (inflation-adjusted) exchange rate of the rouble against the dollar and the euro will probably continue to appreciate, hampering the competitiveness of Russian producers.
- Inflation has revived and may prove difficult to bring back under control.
- Ambitious plans to diversify the economy and make it a leading knowledge economy by 2020 (MERT 2008) rely heavily on top-down innovation managed through the state holding companies in aerospace and other industries, described above. This is not a promising approach. Research and development (R&D) spending in Russia is quite high for a medium-developed country (around 1.5 per cent of GDP) but it is very unproductive. According to the World Intellectual Property Organisation, in 2007 Russia accounted for 0.3 per cent of all international patent applications as compared with 3.5 per cent for China and 4.5 per cent for Korea (see www.wipo.int, last accessed 15 May 2008).

In addition, Russia has proved to be very far from immune to the global financial crisis. Production and investment growth had begun to slow a little in the second quarter of 2008, partly because of growing difficulties for business in getting credit, both from abroad and at home.

These problems multiplied from August onwards. The high level of business debt to the outside world began to be a problem. So did the rather peculiar nature of the Russian capital market. Many (not all) Russian big businesses are majority owned either by the state or by one particular tycoon or a partnership of tycoons. The characteristically modest free float of regularly traded shares is highly sensitive to foreign-investor sentiment. That turned sour, sending shares plummeting. As investors around the world became fearful, they tended to become especially fearful about the emerging markets, and in the case of Russia this was made worse by incidents such as Putin's public harassment of the boss of Mechel and the difficulties experienced by TNK-BP.

From its peak in May, the Russian stock-market had lost over 70 per cent of its value by late October. Russian magnates were in some cases having to surrender assets they had bought on credit, as their creditors called either for settlement or the surrender of collateral. It was estimated that the business sector was due to repay $160 bn of debt between September 2008 and end-2009. That was one of several reasons for a series of bail-out packages announced by the government. At 20 October 2008 these totalled R5.6 trillion, or about $228 billion (*Vedomosti*, 21 October 2008), equivalent to 13 per cent of GDP – a larger bailout-to-GDP ratio than in any other G8 country, at any rate at the time of writing. In short, Russia faces a severe slow down for reasons very broadly similar to those facing OECD countries, but with some particular, longer-term structural problems in the background. Moscow's policy makers could be lucky but the sort of state-led development they practise in Russia is not well adapted to tackling these looming difficulties.

Chapter 12

Social Policy

NICK MANNING

Social policy conventionally includes activities funded or regulated by governments such as social security (pensions, poverty alleviation and so on), health care, education, housing, and the social care of children and older people. This typically absorbs some 50 per cent of a government's budget. There are in addition social services purchased in the market, and those provided free by families and community members, and by voluntary or community agencies in civil society. Social policy has a number of functions in any society, but chiefly it is to meet citizens' social needs, and thereby sustain the productive capacity of labour, and ensure the reproduction of healthy and capable citizens. In principle this is achieved in a manner that helps to promote the legitimacy of the political system through mitigating social risks and creating a sense of security and solidarity for citizens.

In Soviet Russia, the state presented itself as the purveyor of such social goods for free, or at a very low price, as an expression of the beneficence of the state for its people. Much of this was organised through the place of work, including housing and food, or the trade unions (for social security), or in local communities (for education and health care). However the approach to social policy varied considerably over the course of the twentieth century. There was a broad policy cycle which moved between meeting social needs on the one hand, most vividly expressed by Nikita Khrushchev in the programme that was adopted in 1961 at the 22nd Party Congress, *The Road to Communism*, and meeting other priorities, such as labour market mobility (most clearly expressed in Stalin's strict labour code, whereby the meeting of social need was closely tied to labour discipline).

By the 1980s there was a growing gap between the state's claims to meet social needs, and the experiences of citizens in everyday life. Gorbachev's reaction to the years of drift under Brezhnev and his successors was to popularise these unmet social expectations by launching a series of social initiatives aimed at health (particularly reversing falling life expectancy by reducing alcohol consumption), poverty and

Table 12.1   *Official poverty levels in Russia, 1992–2006*
(% of population)

1992	1993	1994	1995	1996	1997	1998	1999	2000	2001	2002	2003	2004	2005	2006
33.5	31.5	22.4	24.8	22.1	20.8	23.4	29.9	29.0	27.5	24.6	20.3	17.6	15.8	14.3

Source: Data from *Russian Federal State Statistics Service,* accessed at www.gks.ru/wps/portal.

educational inequalities, and the availability of housing. To achieve this he allowed the growth of community and civil society initiatives and small market based enterprises. However, public expectations rose faster than any possibility of effectively dealing with these issues, and by the end of the 1980s these expectations engulfed the very state system itself in almost all communist states.

The new Russian government of the 1990s was no more able to meet social needs and expectations than its predecessor. Indeed with a massive reduction in industrial production, the state's capacity to deal with social issues was considerably reduced, and the only option was to reduce public expectations in line with the realities of post-Soviet life. This was achieved in an abrupt set of price reforms in the early 1990s, combined with the marketisation of many previously free or subsidised goods, such as housing and food. Public salaries, such as those for doctors and teachers fell in real terms, as did pensions and family allowances, while poverty and inequality grew rapidly (see Table 12.1).

Social policy in Russia has thus had several stages. From the beginning of the 1990s up to 1996–7 there was little real social reform as such but a basic reaction to chronic financial deficits. Only from the beginning of 1997 did the attitude to social reform gradually change. At the end of the 1990s it became clear that there was an urgent necessity for social reform. A serious demographic situation, weak institutions in the social policy area, and a disorganised labour market were obstacles to further economic growth. Politicians began to discuss seriously and more pragmatically new labour legislation, pension reform, the existing system of privileges and benefits and other social issues. There was a marked appetite for serious institutional change.

The Putin years

What was the situation Putin inherited when he received the presidential reins of government from Yeltsin? Russian society had paid a high price for the vacuum in social policy, which existed during the first decade of market reforms, and there was a public appetite for serious efforts to deal with concrete social problems such as poverty, public health, high mortality, chronic unemployment, and so on. However the shape of a desirable long-term model was not clear.

Since 2000 the context for social policy development has experienced major change. Putin's government was able to announce social reforms and set out to draft a ten-year plan mapping out a strategy for sweeping change under three headings: modernisation of the economy, social policy, and restructuring of government itself. Among the creators of this plan were German Gref and Aleksei Kudrin (economic and finance ministers in all of Putin's cabinets), with close ties to the former architect of the state privatisation programme, Anatolii Chubais, a relatively right-leaning liberal politician. Positive trends in economic development, stable finances and the market allowed the government to discuss forming a new model of social security for Russian citizens to ensure their constitutional rights. This new model was based on the social insurance principle, including retirement insurance, social insurance and obligatory medical insurance. The president again called in 2005 for a fulfilment of the above-mentioned large-scale strategic tasks the country faced to retain high levels of competitiveness in the world. These tasks were considered 'system-forming': 'We need an integral vision of the prospects of Russia's development, with very clear aims and with due account taken of the possibilities to attain them', he observed (RIA-Novosti, July 2005). Putin added that Russia was unable to solve its strategic tasks 'without freedom of economic activity and an effective social policy'.

The year as a whole was marked by the movement of social problems from the political periphery to the centre of the government's socio-economic programme and politics. In 2005 the new federal law 122 came into force, kick-starting the reform of social benefits. The task of poverty reduction came to be seen as equal in importance to the task of doubling GDP. The president proclaimed four high-priority national projects: health, education, affordable and comfortable housing, and development of the agricultural sector. In his 2006 annual message to the Federal Assembly he announced a follow-up, a large-scale programme of overcoming the demographic crisis and particularly of stimulating the birth rate. Thus 2005 could be seen as a crucial year for social policy in which Russia has entered a third stage of development since the fall of the USSR.

The economic background was favourable. Russia's GDP increased by nearly 35 per cent from 2000 to 2005. Official sources reported that over the first four years of Putin's government, real incomes increased by 40 per cent. By 2006 Russia's gross domestic product exceeded the level it was at when the Soviet Union collapsed in 1991. Russia's Stabilisation Fund, set up in 2004 to accumulate surplus revenue from high world oil prices, amounted to $55.7 billion in 2006 and reached $157 billion in

2008. The Central Bank reported that Russia's gold and foreign currency reserves stood at $480 billion as of January 2008, leaving the country with the world's third largest foreign currency reserves after China and Japan.

Putin insisted that he did not want to miss the opportunities emerging in the Russian economy, but stressed that the government could spend only as much as it earned. The 2006 budget was the first 'development budget' in several decades, it was officially reported. A 'development budget' implied primarily the implementation of national projects and the development of science-intensive technologies. Under it, spending on education and agriculture increased by more than 30 per cent, on health care by 60 per cent, and spending on housing quadrupled.

The president proposed setting up a council to implement these priority national projects that he intended to control personally, and underlined that it was extremely important that legal institutions supervised the proper use of funds. The Stabilisation Fund, where the government accumulated extra funds received from oil exports, had not been set up to solve social policy problems *per se* but to maintain Russia's macroeconomic stability. It was created to prevent price growth, to keep inflation in check, and deal with only the most pressing social issues. However in September 2006 the government initiated the creation of a new 'fund for future generations', which could use up to 10 per cent of the Stabilisation Fund. The money has been earmarked for education, health care and social security programmes.

The relative success in addressing social issues under Putin's administration is due to three critical advantages over his predecessor: a more co-operative legislature, a growing economy with rising real incomes, and greater state capacity. However, speaking at the 10th International Economic Forum in St Petersburg in June 2006, Putin admitted that high inflation, sectoral monopolisation, bureaucracy and corruption were the main problems holding back Russia's economy. The shadow economy still exceeded 40 per cent of GDP, and net capital flight from Russia reached $9 billion in 2005. The Fitch international rating agency has observed that despite increasing macro-economic stability, the high level of capital flight from Russia reflects a complex business climate and a lack of confidence in state institutions and observance of property rights.

Numerous surveys indicate that a majority of the public believes that the most needy (invalids, orphans, large families, pensioners, unemployed, single parents, low-paid workers, students) should receive free or subsidised support, particularly medical care, nursery and kindergartens, housing, professional training, and municipal transport. There is also a disturbing lack of faith in the future among many sectors of society and most particularly among the poorest sections of it. The prospect of coming social reforms has not yet altered this pessimism.

According to the Constitution, Russia is still a 'social state'. But the social state is no more than a declaration of intentions for an indefinite future. This inconsistency in modern Russian social policy is a result of its conceptualisation. The 'social state' is just a special case of the liberal project in Russia. The project is supported by the World Bank and implemented through the state budget. A welfare state aspires for all to enjoy good social standards in pensions, in health services, and in education. But a liberal society guarantees only minimal standards and consequently supports only the most vulnerable citizens. Russia has announced that it aspires to good social standards, but in fact the state provides only minimal guarantees for all. From here there is a basic contradiction: the ambitions are large, but the resources are not sufficient.

The state remains, in spite of everything, the main actor in social policy. There is a continued centralisation of power: strong authority of the president, practically a one-party (pro-president) State Duma, and the state dependency of local self-governance. The relations of state authorities and business have not achieved a state of easy and lawful dialogue. The institutions of civil society (such as non-governmental organisations, trade unions and associations of employers) because of their general weakness are not ready to form their own constructive alternatives in the sphere of social policy. These tendencies leave insufficient resources and space for self-organising communities and citizens, yet on the other hand state actors propose policy changes that would actually reduce the state's role, eliminate broad subsidies, and transfer much responsibility for social provision to local communities, individuals and markets.

The economic growth which has been achieved in Russia since the beginning of century has not been sufficient to reduce social inequalities and distortions, as Table 12.2 makes clear.

Private markets in housing, education and public health services co-exist alongside insufficient basic benefits, low living standards and a deterioration of health. Even though the beginning of the new century demonstrated an increasing concern with social problems in Russian society (and not only by the public, but also the government), the conception of 'social policy as such' is still not debated and determined. The borders of social policy resources and responsibility are not outlined, either in a public, political or academic sense. Two approaches and ways of understanding are still confused: practically any action in the economic sphere can have social consequences. At the same time there is an urgent need for a transformation of basic institutions in the social sphere, but these transformations in turn will be costly.

Economic growth itself has two consequences. First, the growth of

Table 12.2   *Inequality in Russia and other countries (Gini coefficient, mid-1990s)*

Brazil	1996	.571
Mexico	1995	.494
Russia	*1995*	*.447*
Argentina	1996	.442
US	1997	.372
Canada	1998	.305
Germany	1994	.261

Note: The Gini coefficient is a measure of inequality in income distribution, and varies between 1 (completely unequal) and 0 (completely equal).

Source: Adapted from T. Smeeding, 'Globalisation, Inequality and the Rich Countries of the G-20: Evidence from the Luxembourg Income Study (LIS)', Center for Policy Research Working Papers, No 48 (New York: Syracuse University, 2002).

incomes and salaries is concentrated in successful economic branches, in other words the growth is for the top 20 per cent of the Russian middle class. Second is the growth of state expenses and the increase of budget financing of social projects, indexation of pensions and budget-sector salaries. Maleva (2007) argues that only the top and lower layers of the population are gaining from current economic growth, but that the middle – the bulk of the population – are not. Economic growth figures remain something of an abstraction to many people. Consequently the problem for Russian social policy in the near future is to spread the positive results of economic growth to the rest of the population. The simultaneous problem of implementing different but very serious social reforms including housing, public health services, and education, is a heavy load even for more or less well-off Russians. The achievement of social goals is impossible without the right priorities, and Russia should include here the emerging Russian middle class.

The failures and successes of Russian social policy have co-existed at stages of the Russian reforms. For example, Russia avoided the social explosion that was assumed to be inevitable by many Western experts because of mass latent unemployment in the middle of the 1990s. The price of this success was poverty and low incomes for the population caused by the low salaries necessary to pay for the artificially high rate of employment. But Russia in the middle of the first decade of the new millennium is in a different place from the Russia of ten years ago. In relative terms, there is now a greater sense of political and social stability compared to the 1990s. The near future should tell whether we are witnessing a trend of growing state capacity and policy coherence in Russia, or not.

The situation in different social areas

Demographic situation

The government acknowledges that the demographic problem is one of the most serious problems Russia is currently facing. In his annual 2006 address to the Federal Assembly the president observed that the decline in Russia's population over the previous ten years had been 700,000 people a year. The United Nations has warned that Russia's population, which stood at roughly 145 million in the 2002 census and 142 million in 2006, could fall by as much as a third by 2050. The country's economic productivity and even state sovereignty could be threatened if the situation does not improve.

The population has been steadily shrinking in recent years as the death rate has greatly exceeded the birth rate. There is concern about the country's rapidly ageing population and the problem of alcoholism, which are responsible for some alarming demographic trends. Alcoholism is particularly corroding Russian provinces where the economy and infrastructure are poorly developed and there are few jobs for people. In addition to alcohol abuse, other causes of early deaths include cardiovascular diseases and unnatural external factors such as road accidents, and crimes.

Tackling Russia's demographic crisis is another significant project that is connected to the four priority national projects. Life expectancy for men, at 58 years, is ten years less than in China. From the official point of view the problem could be solved in three ways: by cutting the death rate from unnatural causes, by conducting a clear and effective migration policy, or by encouraging people to have more children (including an increase in child benefits as one way to ameliorate the situation, which is also affected by unhealthy lifestyles and poor living conditions). From 2007 the government has given women at least 250,000 roubles ($9,200) each as financial tax-free aid following the birth of a second child. The payouts will be revised annually to adjust for inflation, and can only be spent on education, invested in housing, or put to an individual pension account, and only after the child is three years old.

There is debate as to whether it is possible to solve the Russian demographic problem by allowances. The most disadvantaged and poorest part of the population will react first of all to the new programme. For middle class and well-off people higher salaries will reduce the effect of 'second-child' money. It is definitely a substantial aid, but it may fall short of making enough difference to a family's income to raise the fertility rate. The government may have to go further and create conditions for parents to earn adequate wages, and for this purpose it will be necessary to change labour legislation to provide women with easier opportunities to return to the labour market after the birth of a child. In other words, flexible forms of employment for women with children are required first of all.

The pension system

The accumulation of huge pension arrears since the mid-1990s shows that the Russian distributive pension system is in long-term crisis. The burden on working people is growing, especially as, in general, businesses operating in the shadow economy rarely deduct taxes. In addition, the ratio of payers to recipients is gradually falling: in 1991, employed people exceeded pensioners by a ratio of 2:1, but by 1997, only by 1.7:1 (Bureau of Economic Analysis 1998). People over 65 make up 14 per cent of the population at the present, and the prospect of a rapidly ageing Russian population, resulting from the marked fall in the birth rate, will aggravate this problem a great deal in the future.

This kind of social security issue is already a major talking point in many countries. Pensions are highlighted as a crucial problem for a country's financial system. But to achieve political consensus on the reform of pension provision has proved to be extraordinarily difficult in Russia, since pensioners are the most active section of the electorate. Fajth argues that as in the West, in Eastern Europe, and in Russia in particular, most public cash social expenditure went to the old age pension system which was based on social insurance ('pay-as-you-go' principle). 'Through linear earmarked taxes on wages (levied in most cases on both employers and employees) annual contributions fed current expenditures without any direct links between individual contributions and pensions. However in post-communist countries boundaries between the state budget and social security budget were symbolic and expenditure was not only exposed to day-to-day political decisions but these decisions lacked any public control and transparency' (Fajth 2000: 81).

The discussion of pension reform with an emphasis on the pay-as-you-go component started as far back as in 1995. The government proposed to reform the existing distributive system, gradually introducing elements of a compulsory funded pension financing. The foundation of this reform is a so-called 'mixed model', predicated on implementing three levels of provision that envisaged a combination of distributive and accrual principles when securing pensions, as well as an opportunity for citizens to acquire an additional optional pension through non-governmental pension funds. The three parts of the pension system include a basic fixed pension for all senior citizens (approximately no more than subsistence minimum), a state social insurance pension depending on tax contributions and work experience, and supplementary pension insurance through private individual pension accounts.

However the arrangements to carry out the reform were comparatively slow to materialise. Although approved by government, it was postponed because many of its operational mechanisms were vague. The real pension system reform became an event of note only in 2002. The government initiated the creation of individual pension accounts and the creation of non-state pension funds. In practice the traditional system was reinforced with two more systems with stronger viability, created due to the pension tax paid by employers to create insurance coverage, and pension savings invested into the stock market. Russia has chosen a compromise model, with changes spread over time, and does not envisage making the funded method of insurance the main component of the pension earned over a working lifetime.

As of 2008, the average monthly pension is about 26–27 per cent of the average wage, which means that retirement entails a considerable deterioration in living standards. Under International Labour Organisation standards, the figure should be 50 per cent. Moreover the Russian Pension Fund has been and remains a consistent opponent of raising the pension age because it would have only a modest effect economically and would be highly unpopular (the pensionable age in Russia at present is 55 for women and 60 for men).

Monetisation of benefits

This is the replacement of privileges with monetary grants. Was the monetisation of benefits necessary? Was it the right time for a radical reforming of the long-standing system of social protection for millions of Russians, whereby large segments of the population were granted special privileges in the form of reduced rates for energy, telephone service, housing, communal services, and transportation? Too low to cover costs, such rates not only generated losses for service providers and, in turn, put pressure on the budget but also encouraged over-consumption and misuse (Heller and Keller 2001). The benefits and privileges inherited from the Soviet past did not solve social problems in the way they worked. They never reduced poverty but prevented effective and real policy in relation to those groups, which really could not survive without the help of the state. For most politicians and experts the urgent necessity of reform measures is evident and clear. The system revealed itself as very excessive and expensive.

From the rational point of view the reform of benefits is not disputed since the majority of them actually bear no relation to the purpose of receiving them (for example, social support for the disabled people in

Russia often is not connected at all to real physical disability). Ovcharova (2005) in turn emphasises the way that benefits often justified an absence of actions towards socially disadvantaged groups. Shlapentokh (2006) argues that though the system changes were necessary, the reform itself is conservative. In Russia it is commonly held that in the West, in particular in the USA, people receive the majority of benefits in money terms. This is not the case. In America people who are entitled to benefits receive only 20 per cent of them in cash, partly to resist inflation, and also to direct consumption towards needs for which they are intended.

The consequences of benefit system monetisation, in the context of the general framework of social protection of the population, is hotly debated. According to the ILO (2005), argument and discussions both in government circles and among various categories of benefit recipients are centred on a key issue: what is more beneficial for various groups of federal and regional benefit recipients and to what extent?

Poverty

From the beginning of the Russian reforms, the issue of poverty revealed itself as very evident and severe, symbolising the social cost that the population paid in the transition from the Soviet model of welfare to the market. The economic reforms triggered a 50 per cent reduction in Russian GDP, the consequence of which was a corresponding fall in the population's incomes. Price liberalisation in the early 1990s not only provoked large price rises but also devalued the savings of most of the population – bringing about, in effect, a large-scale redistribution of wealth.

Over the final decade of the twentieth century, the worst years from the point of view of poverty were 1992–3 and 1999–2000. In 1992–3, the rise in the number of poor people was the consequence of price liberalisation and rampant inflation. In 1999, the high rate of poverty was the consequence of the 1998 financial crisis and the default on public and private debt. In recent years the rate of poverty in Russia has seen a steady downward trend. But despite the relatively satisfactory dynamic of the poverty situation presented by official statistics, there continues to be distinct divergence in the scale of Russian poverty. Poverty levels varied from 8–9 per cent to 70 per cent in some areas in 2004, and according to survey data, the real rates are higher than the official figures. Against the background of Russia's recent dramatic petroleum-led economic growth, an estimated 30 million Russians still live in poverty.

Monitoring of poverty conducted by the World Bank (2005) highlights the groups that are at particular risk of impoverishment. These are: the rural population (according to survey data from Russian Institute of

Sociology in March 2006. 30 per cent of them were poor, while the proportion of poor people in the urban population was 16 per cent); children (while the rate of poverty overall across the country was 20 per cent, among children under 16 it was 27 per cent); and the unemployed (one in three unemployed people was poor, while among the whole population capable of work one in five was poor). Finally, there are workers with a low standard of education (the probability of falling below the poverty line for people with only primary education was 50 per cent higher than in the population as a whole).

Among the countries of the CIS, Russia occupies first place for inequality in the distribution of incomes. The share of the best-off 10 per cent of the population was just under 30 per cent of the total volume of incomes, while the share of the poorest 10 per cent was 2 per cent in 2004 (Rosstat 2006). This situation differs from the position in other industrial societies, where the difference in incomes between the decile groups at the two extremes is far less. In Russia, the Gini coefficient is closer to that of the countries of the Third World (Manning 2007).

Further growth in inequality may essentially weaken the positive influence of economic growth on the reduction of poverty since, if the advantages of economic growth are not distributed evenly, then its influence on the poverty rate will be weakened. It is in this regard that most serious analysts emphasise that the goal set in 2004 to reduce poverty sharply is potentially achievable; however, it is extremely difficult.

Employment and wages

In starting to move towards a market economy, Russian reformers made allowances for social effects as these applied to employment issues, but in a very particular way (Manning 1998). On the macro-economic level, they consciously chose a strategy of supporting inefficient producers, with the aim of preventing mass redundancies and consequent unemployment. This also meant that the government's intentions to put bankruptcy measures into operation became purely rhetorical. This macro-economic choice expressed itself in the formation of high levels of hidden unemployment, whereby workers remained technically employed (their labour books were held by an employer), but on permanent leave. No other country with an economy in transformation has experienced this scale of hidden unemployment (20 per cent of the active population in the mid-1990s).

The Russian labour market comprises four segments: high levels of official employment, which nevertheless displays a trend toward decline; relatively low open unemployment, which is gradually becoming chronic; large-scale latent unemployment, which has also become chronic in certain regions and sectors of the economy; and informal employment, which extends to all groups of the economically active population, whether employed or formally unemployed. From 2000 to 2005 the number of the unemployed in Russia on the ILO survey based definition fell from 9.8 per cent to 7.1 per cent of the economically active population. The reduction of unemployment rate occurred during a period of economic growth and, as a consequence, the growth of employment was not connected with government measures. According to Russian official statistics, in July 2007 ILO-defined unemployment was 7.3 per cent of the economically active population.

Other problems of employment such as the deficit of qualified specialists, or high structural regional unemployment or inequality of wages were overshadowed in this discussion. In the 1990s wage differentials in various sectors of the economy, among regions and groups of workers, increased considerably in the context of a sharp decrease in real wages and widely spread non-payment of wages. No fewer than one-third of Russian workers received wages that did not satisfy their basic needs (ILO 1999). The ILO recommended that the government create favourable macro-economic conditions conducive to a significant increase in real wages, and Putin's first step in the employment sphere was to eliminate wages and pensions arrears, and at the end of 2001 a new Labour Code was adopted.

The role of the minimum wage is to fix the minimum level of remuneration for work, preserving workers' dignity. From the other side, the minimum wage is an instrument of social protection for the most vulnerable workers and a base for social benefits calculation. At the start of the reforms in 1991, the minimum wage was 1.5 times the subsistence minimum, but in the course of transition period this relationship had fundamentally changed (at the end of the 1990s, the gap was fivefold). Up to the present time the minimum wage remains well under subsistence level. According to estimates for 2007, an average Russian needs around 4,000 rubles ($155) a month to survive. Long debates resulted only in doubling the minimum wage from 1100 rubles ($42) to 2,300 rubles ($89) in September 2007. The government plans to gradually bring minimum monthly pay into line with subsistence level by 2011.

The Russian labour market has undergone sweeping changes during the period of reform. But the years 2009–11 could be crucial for Russia's economy and its global competitive capacities. The accession of Russia to the World Trade Organisation (WTO) may lead not only to the liberalisation of trade and attraction of investments but also to serious implications in the social sphere, which are common for every country facing the globalisation process. One of the main future problems may be the growth of unemployment in the industrial sector. In order to manage the consequences of globalisation it is necessary to improve the quality of professional training, which is one of the goals of current educational reform.

Education and health care

Reform of education and health care was inevitable, since they still relied in the 1990s on residual budget funding. But the question then arises as to whether the new system will be a state or a private one. Taking a purely market approach to health and education will simply put a sizeable section of the population outside the scope of access to this most important of public services. In most Western countries, the degree of privatisation of these social areas is currently not very large. This question stands high on the Russian cabinet's priority list. On the one hand it is acknowledged that post-Soviet Russia faced a dramatic deterioration in general physical, mental and social health. Self-reported levels of ill health in Russia are between 50 and 100 per cent higher than the West European average (Manning and Tikhonova 2009). Health has proved to be one more price that the Russian people are paying for the policy of reform (see Figure 12.1).

Figure 12.1   *Life expectancy by gender from birth, Russia, Finland and UK*

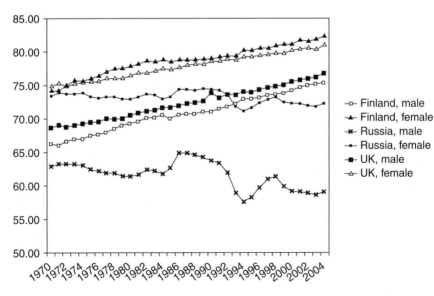

Source: Adapted from the European Health for All Database www.euro.who.int., last consulted 16 June 2009.

On the other hand, the country will have to sustain its competitive advantage in the field of education to compete within a global market. Public expenditure on healthcare and education has fallen considerably compared with the communist period and, as a percentage of GDP, is below levels in Western Europe. Since 2005 Russia has started to implement the national projects on health and education, which were the central signposts of current policy reform. In 2005 Russia's Education Minister said that for the first time in the history of modern Russia expenditure on education had exceeded the expenditure on defence (RIA-Novosti, 16 January 2005). Under the country's 2006 budget, spending on education and health care was increased by more than 30 per cent and 60 per cent respectively.

Some 60 per cent of the population is involved in the sphere of education, and about 80 per cent of Russians up to 35 years of age consider higher education their main goal. The results of the 2002 census indicated that the major positive shift is in higher education (the decade after the 1989 census was marked by a doubling of higher educational student enrolment). It is also the first time that the census has revealed more women with a university education in comparison with men. The president praised these trends and confirmed that the state should support its citizens in their desire to improve their level of education.

The modernisation of the education system in Russia includes two groups of measures: first, to ensure access to quality university education, and, second, to improve the quality of secondary and professional education. In September 2007 the law extending compulsory general education from nine to eleven years came into force. Authorities underline that the reform is also aimed at legalising informal practices in the education process. Since some people pay for getting enrolled at universities it may be better to let them pay the money legally. From the other side the reform presupposes that low-income families should also have the opportunity of getting high-quality education. According to the official position, the current education system in Russia should be flexible. The new concept presupposes that both higher and primary/secondary schools have the right to engage in independent economic activities, including market principles.

The success or failure of Russia's educational policy and the country as a whole depends to a large degree on whether it blends with the world economy. At the conference of European education ministers held in Berlin on September 2003 Russia joined the Bologna Convention, whose participants aspire to create by 2010 a unified European zone in the sphere of higher education. But the educational reform is proceeding slowly and with a lot of difficulties. According to a working group of the Council on Science, Technologies, and Education, 'the quality of basic secondary education in Russia is getting worse', and schools lack educational materials, equipment, and skilled teachers. A left-oriented coalition called 'Popular Government' claims that state spending on education has dropped and is still falling. Therefore, they insist on a further increase in spending on education, the development of infrastructure and on social guarantees for students and teachers, whose average salary was only 70 per cent of the national average.

The marked polarisation of the Russian population on the basis of income levels is slicing education into layers, with the gradual formation of a hierarchy of 'élite' and 'cheap' educational establishments. Consequently, the chance of receiving specialist or higher education varies dramatically for members of different social layers. The same situation can be easily traced in the health care sector. The poorest strata of the population showing the lowest levels of health find it hardest to obtain access to good-quality health care, since free medical services are being gradually phased out (Davidova 2007). In interviews, experts have called the present situation with medical service in Russia 'the triumph of paid health care' (as Table 12.3 shows). State guarantees are covering less free services than before, and the Ministry of Trade and Economic Development has suggested amending the Tax Code to stimulate voluntary medical insurance.

The new package of social reforms seems to place on the shoulders of the population a part of the responsibility for tackling a whole range of social and health problems. It hardly needs to be pointed out that this excludes a significant proportion of poorer Russians from access to healthcare.

Apart from this by the end of 2006 the Health and Social Development Ministry found itself under a cloud over a corruption scandal caused by a nationwide subsidised drug shortage. Officials of the compulsory health

Table 12.3   *Out-of-pocket payment on health as % of total health expenditure*

	Finland	Russia	UK
1998	19.4	23.6	10.9
1999	20.3	28.6	10.7
2000	20.4	31.2	10.5
2001	19.7	29.6	10.6
2002	19.4	28.7	10.8
2003	19.1	29.2	11
2004	18.4	29.7	12.6

Source: Adapted from HFA database/WHO.

insurance fund, which is subordinated to the ministry, were arrested on suspicion of receiving bribes from pharmaceutical and other companies. Subsequently it turned out that there are more corruption probes against officials subordinate to the ministry, including the Federal Health and Social Development Agency, the Pension Fund and Social Insurance Fund.

Trying to free themselves from dealing with mounting costs for health care and education, central government has decentralised public hospitals and schools, passing responsibility for them to local governments. The merits of decentralisation notwithstanding, local governments were not in a better fiscal position to support these facilities – hospitals with excess bed capacity, extensive spa and recreation services, redundant health practitioners, and schools with many teachers and small classes. Their task is complicated by demands for higher wages, as workers tried to cope with inflation, and by opposition to privatisation, which many workers feared would lead to large-scale layoffs. Resources were typically channelled toward curative care, leaving little for primary health and preventive services. Similarly, a large share of educational spending went to universities at the expense of primary and secondary education. Moreover, utility costs and wages absorbed most of the funds allocated to schools, while spending on teaching materials and maintenance of the educational infrastructure plummeted.

Housing

Housing was a major source of frustration under the Soviet system. Waiting lists were very long except for privileged groups such as senior military and party members. From 1991 government reform of housing and municipal services envisaged the transfer of housing either to private ownership, or to municipal control. At the end of 1997 citizens paid, on average, only 38 per cent of the cost of electricity, water, housing services and repairs. The rest was covered by local budgets. But since the end of the 1990s, utility rates have been gradually rising with the intention that they should be shouldered entirely by Russian citizens by 2003, a process that in fact is almost complete in 2007. The free privatisation of housing began swiftly in the early 1990s, and over 70 per cent of Russians were living in their own flats or homes by 2006.

A radical housing programme began in 2002, and its second stage, for 2006–10, aims to provide affordable and comfortable housing for people. Russia has inherited outdated housing and utility sectors from the Soviet Union and needs to increase construction volumes considerably in order to achieve this ambitious goal. The important elements of the project are the joint development of regional markets for affordable housing, including housing mortgage facilities, regional infrastructure formation and innovative capacity promotion. The second stage of the programme seeks to increase housing construction to up to 80 million square metres a year by 2010, better living conditions for 314,000 families entitled to budget subsidies, more mortgages, and a lower number of people on the waiting lists for free housing.

While a national priorities list is in itself a major step forward for socio-economic progress, so far the nationwide housing project has created more problems than it has helped solve. According to the Russian builders' association, the start of the housing project coincided with a failed public service reform, and this put the construction industry outside government control. This is catastrophic, since the construction industry is critical to the entire Russian economy. The 'affordable housing' package, passed by the State Duma at the end of 2004, was drafted in a hurry and secretively, without any regard for the opinion of the professional business community. The package was conceptually in line with Russia's main development trends, but it contained serious errors that led eventually to a situation where housing supply decreased, and prices rocketed. The biggest problem is that there is no balance in how the government plans to bolster supply. Funds are readily funnelled into 'targeted' support for various social groups, fuelling an already high and unmet demand for housing in Russia. Unmet demand for housing is estimated to be somewhere between 35 per cent and 50 per cent, and that drives real estate price rises.

The concept of a national housing project needs to be considerably reworked and supplemented in consultation with experts and the business community. Poor implementation of the housing project has created many problems. Local authorities have sharply criticised the housing project, saying that it has neither an ideology nor standards, and that most important of all, it provides no funding for the regions. St Petersburg Governor Matvienko has indeed stated that the national project to build affordable and comfortable housing for a great number of Russian households is unrealistic: 'Unless we learn how to make citizens, authorities and market professionals work together, I'm afraid there isn't much hope for the national housing initiative' (Interfax Agency, March 2006).

Conclusion: Russian social policy

A new, more realistic welfare model is arguably needed all over the world. A leading issue is that the minimisation of poverty and income insecurity is a pre-condition for an effective social investment strategy (Esping-Andersen 2002). Though the Soviet system combines features of universality and corporatism, characteristic of some Scandinavian models of social welfare (full employment, developed and universal social insurance, advanced system of social protection at the enterprises), it is in reality a 'non-welfare state' (Esping-Andersen 1996). State socialism was a strong and stable system, in which the state was the exclusive employer (Standing 1999). In post-Soviet Russia the centralisation of power and resources is still high, but the withdrawal of guaranteed employment and protected jobs from current policy priorities is notable (Manning, Shkaratan and Tikhonova 2000). The state retains the basic function of exclusive distributor of social benefits.

In contrast to the Scandinavian model, Russia is a country with contradictory ideas and structures that are in part historical, and which continue to function despite their poor performance. The downfall of the Soviet system caused not only serious changes in the legislative and executive institutions of social policy, but also the destabilisation of the public situation as a whole. In the period of crisis for the state and its population the decentralised system appeared to be unable to support social stability in the country or to render real support to citizens facing the difficult conditions of the period. The long period of solving social problems using only the 'state beneficence' system, combined with its sudden termination, has left many people feeling vulnerable. People used to receiving state support appear to have difficulty in accepting the social responsibility that became necessary in the new sociopolitical and economic circumstances.

In terms of welfare models the new Russian social policy comes nearer to those in which the social provision and services are goods in the background behind a marked stratification and an increased of role of the market. The main problem for current Russian social policy is the great gap between the framework of social policy or 'social projects with special national priorities' and its realisation through the existing systems of social insurance, social security, social service and social work. Russia will not raise the volume of social payments at the cost of increasing income tax, as for example in Scandinavia, despite increasing protests by employees.

In this respect the Russian state has much more common in common with Western countries of the combined 'state and market' type, and the interaction of these two systems of social welfare maintenance still appears to be tense. The costs of the non-provision of social services have played little if any role in the discussion of Russian social welfare reform. There has been no systematic attempt to calculate the actual direct costs and delayed indirect costs of radical cuts in social services and the parallel decline in public health, education, research and social welfare which have followed the implementation of neo-liberal models.

Nevertheless, changes in social policy have now become an object of study both at academic institutes and the new independent think-tanks.

According to IREX (International Research and Exchanges Board 2006), regardless of the nature of research centres (academic or independent), most studies contain a wealth of information that is relevant for practical and academic purposes. Their topics reflect the main areas of social policy, such as new tendencies in the labour market, problems of level and quality of life, accessibility and affordability of social services, social support to vulnerable groups, and so on. Russian researchers also work in partnership with foreign colleagues to identify positive social developments in Western countries. This experience is helping Russia to develop policy arguments and reshape the social order without the convulsions of the recent past.

Chapter 13

Russian Foreign Policy

MARGOT LIGHT

In the first few years after Russia became independent, its foreign policy tended to be incoherent. This reduced its effectiveness, limited its influence, and confused Russian citizens and their international partners. Incoherence is not uncommon in the foreign policies of new states and, in many ways, Russia was a new state. Moreover, the 1993 constitution was very different from the constitution in operation when the state became independent. Not surprisingly, therefore, the Russian Federation had the problems all new states have of setting up foreign policy institutions, establishing how they should relate to one another and deciding what goals the state should pursue in its relations with the outside world.

It is also not unusual for the foreign policy of a country that has lost an empire to be unpredictable. It was unclear that Russia *had* lost an empire, but there was general agreement within the country that Russia had lost its identity when the USSR disintegrated. There was also confusion about Russia's status in the international political system. Attempts to establish Russia's identity and status affected the coherence of foreign policy, and so did the numerous concepts and doctrines adopted by the government to define its foreign, military and security policies.

By 1996, although discordant voices could still be heard, the contours of a more predictable foreign policy had been established. In Vladimir Putin's first presidential term, predictability and pragmatism characterised Russia's foreign policy. However, in his second term, he embarked on a more forceful foreign policy, and assertiveness is even more evident at the beginning of Dmitri Medvedev's presidency. This chapter argues that the initial incoherence of Russian foreign policy can be explained by the domestic context – the structure and processes of decision making and the establishment of a new identity. The following two sections explore Russia's policy, first towards the other Soviet successor states (Russian policy makers initially referred to them as the 'near abroad'), and then towards the 'far abroad' (other foreign states). They illustrate how initial incoherence was replaced by a more stable and then a more assertive foreign policy. The chapter concludes with a brief consideration of how Russian foreign policy is likely to develop in the next coming years.

The domestic context of Russian foreign policy

The initial incoherence of Russian foreign policy was caused by the structural features and processes of decision making and exacerbated by confusion about Russia's identity and its role in the world.

Foreign policy decision making: structures and processes

Foreign policy coherence requires a well organised and widely accepted division of responsibility with clear channels of communication between institutions and individuals. In Russia immediately after the USSR disintegrated, the division of responsibility between government institutions was unclear and often contentious, and there were no established channels of communication.

The 1993 Constitution gave the president predominance in foreign policy. He is responsible for determining the framework of policy, representing Russia abroad, appointing diplomats and Security Council members, and conducting international negotiations. He heads the Security Council, which is responsible for assessing the challenges and threats Russia faces. The Ministry of Foreign Affairs (MFA) is responsible for the conduct of foreign relations. International treaties must be ratified by the Duma and the Federation Council, and the Duma has the right to scrutinise foreign policy, while the Federation Council has jurisdiction over the use of Russian troops abroad. However, the constitution does not clarify how authority is divided between the government and the president, and it encourages a proliferation of administrative structures serving the president. In 1995 there were legislative changes to make the power ministers, including the MFA and the Ministry of Defence (MoD), directly subordinate to the president.

The incoherence of Russian policy in the 1990s was exacerbated by the president's personality and his management style. President Yeltsin's aides and advisers often made statements on his behalf without co-ordinating them with the MFA, while he himself was prone to making impromptu policy announcements, taking his own staff and his interlocutors by surprise. Moreover, MFA and MoD statements sometimes contradicted official policy. Yeltsin frequently reprimanded his ministers, including the Foreign Minister, in public. This undermined the Foreign Minister's status, making him a less credible interlocutor with foreign governments, and it weakened the authority of the MFA. When Yevgeny Primakov

Table 13.1   *Russian foreign ministers, 1990–date*

Appointed by	Name	Dates of appointment
President Yeltsin	Andrei Kozyrev	June 1990 (as foreign minister of RSFSR) to January 1996
	Yevgenii Primakov	January 1996 to September 1998, when he was appointed Prime Minister
	Igor Ivanov	September 1998 to March 2004
President Putin	Sergei Lavrov	March 2004 to May 2008
President Medvedev		May 2008 – present

replaced Andrei Kozyrev as foreign minister in 1996, the status of the MFA rose (the entire succession of appointments, from 1990 onwards, is set out in Table 13.1). Moreover, the structural problems began to improve; the relationship between the various ministries with foreign policy interests was gradually sorted out, co-operation between the different branches of the state improved, and channels of communication became established and accepted. Nevertheless, complaints continued to be heard, including from those involved in decision making, that policy was poorly co-ordinated (Kosachev 2004: 31).

In the 1990s, the conflictual nature of politics in Russia aggravated the incoherence of its foreign policy. Foreign policy became an arena in which wider political struggles took place and parliamentary deputies frequently used foreign policy as an instrument in their conflict with the president, for example, by adopting resolutions that appeared to contradict Russia's official foreign policy, or by postponing ratifying treaties.

President Putin established a very different management and foreign policy style from that of Yeltsin. Although he was a more overt nationalist (he calls it patriotism) and was even more insistent about Russia's great power credentials, he recognised the relationship between the economy and international power. Moreover, he was aware that the inconsistencies in Russian foreign policy harmed Russia's national interests. Putin soon set about centralising power and reasserting the authority of the federal government. His centralising policies made the Duma more subservient to the presidency and the conflict between the legislature and the executive came to an end. By 2004 United Russia, a party loyal to the presidency, dominated the Duma and presided over the chairmanship of all its committees, including those that deal with foreign affairs. Although the Duma and its committees continue to be involved in the foreign policy-making process and so, to a lesser extent, does the Federation Council, both tend to support the president's policy. The MFA remains responsible for the conduct of Russia's foreign policy, but during

Putin's second presidential term particularly, it was the president and his apparatus who decided what the policy should be (for a full discussion see White 2006: 21–44). The 2008 Foreign Policy Concept sets out who is responsible for what aspect of foreign policy. It specifies that the Security Council assesses the challenges and threats Russia faces, the President directs foreign policy and represents Russia on the international stage, while the Federal Assembly provides legislative support, and the government implements Russia's foreign policy and is responsible for co-ordinating the foreign policy activities of other executive bodies (Ministry of Foreign Affairs 2008).

When Dmitri Medvedev became president, it became clear that Putin intended to retain a prominent foreign policy role in his new position of prime minister. At his first cabinet meeting, he reconstituted a 15-member presidium, including in it the Foreign Minister, the Minister of Internal Affairs and the Defence Minister, who are technically directly responsible to the president. He also appointed Yuri Ushakov, Russian Ambassador to the United States since 1999, as deputy chief-of-staff to the government, tasked with creating an independent foreign policy division to serve the cabinet and prime minister (*ITAR-TASS Daily*, 31 May 2008). Although as Commander-in-Chief, the president gave the military orders during the conflict with Georgia in August 2008, Putin played a significant role in making the decisions (a schematic outline of the decision-making process as of the start of the new presidential term is set out in Table 13.2).

Identity and concepts

In addition to the structural, personal and political factors that caused confusion, there was also uncertainty about Russia's identity. Most Russians found it difficult to accept that some areas of the USSR were no longer part of Russia. In part this was simply a question of nostalgia for past greatness, but there was also genuine confusion about Russia's role in the world. The establishment of new, independent states separating Russia from the rest of Europe revived an old debate: was Russia part of Europe, or had the loss of empire turned it into an Asian or Eurasian power?

There was also a question of Russia's status in the international system. Russia had inherited the Soviet Union's international treaty obligations, its seat on the United Nations Security Council and its diplomatic institutions and nuclear capabilities. In many respects, therefore, Russia inherited its international status. But it had few of the traditional attributes of power: its economy was close to collapse, it did not have an extensive sphere of influence, and although still vast, it was far smaller than the

Table 13.2   *The Russian foreign policy decision-making process*

President's Office	Government	Legislature
President	Prime Minister	State Duma Committee for International Affairs
President's Aide for Foreign Policy and International Relations	Ministry of Foreign Affairs	State Duma Committee for Defence
President's Aide for Issues of the Development of Relations with the European Union	Ministry of Defence	State Duma Committee for Security
Presidential Directorate on Foreign Policy	Ministry of Economics and Trade	State Duma Committee for CIS Affairs and relations with Compatriots
Security Council	Federal Security Service (FSB)	Federation Council Foreign Affairs Committee
Presidential Commission for Military Technology Cooperation of the Russian Federation with Foreign States	Foreign Intelligence Service	Federation Council Committee on Defence and Security
State Council	Various co-ordinating committees	Federation Council Committee on the Commonwealth of Independent States

USSR. Russia was clearly not a superpower; indeed, it was questionable whether it was a great power. Yet to ordinary people as well as politicians, it was unthinkable that Russia could be anything less than this. The insistence that Russia should be regarded as a great power became an important theme in foreign policy statements and discussions and it remains an important driver of foreign policy. In the 1990s, however, the mismatch between the self-perception of great power status and the reality of Russia's declining power contributed to the incoherence of foreign policy.

Many intellectuals believed that Russia's identity could be established by defining its foreign policy principles. They demanded that the government should provide a framework for its foreign policy. By April 1993 when the first Foreign Policy Concept was adopted, a broad consensus had been reached about Russia's status and its foreign policy priorities. The concept portrayed a far less benign view of Russia's external environment than the rather idealistic and uncritically pro-Western policy Russia was pursuing at that time. It asserted a prominent international role for Russia, particularly in the 'near abroad', and revealed considerable suspicion of Western intentions towards Russia. The first Military

Doctrine, adopted in October 1993, adopted a harsher stance about Russia's national interests than the foreign policy concept.

The view of Russia's place in the world expressed in these documents did not make Russian foreign policy more coherent. First, the disparate foreign policy statements made by various politicians and officials did not reflect the contents of either document. Second, there seemed to be little relationship between the priorities set out in the documents and the practice of Russian policy. A series of subsequent official doctrines and concepts compounded the confusion. A National Security Concept was adopted in December 1997, for example, only to be replaced by a new one in January 2000 which, in turn, was replaced in 2009. A new Military Doctrine and a new Foreign Policy Concept were adopted in June 2000 (replaced in July 2008 by the document to which reference has already been made). There are also Concepts for Scientific and Technical Cooperation (2000) and Border Cooperation (2001), a Maritime Doctrine (2004), and a Strategy for Policy towards members of the Commonwealth of Independent States (2005) (texts of the various concepts may be consulted at the Ministry of Foreign Affairs website www.mid.ru). The later documents were responses to perceived changes in Russia's internal and external environment, but what alarmed Russia's foreign partners was that they indicated a significant hardening of Russian foreign policy. The feature of the 2000 National Security Concept that aroused most anxiety outside Russia was that it envisaged looser conditions under which Russia might resort to nuclear weapons. For Russians themselves, the most important feature of the 2000 National Security Concept and Military Doctrines was that they envisaged the use of military force inside the country, retroactively legitimising army action in Chechnya.

Western policymakers were confused. They could understand the external factors that made Russians feel more vulnerable, although they disagreed that they represented a threat to Russian security. But what was striking was that the new documents defined domestic problems (such as the critical state of the economy, the criminalisation of Russian society and the absence of a rule-based state) as far more threatening to Russian security than external factors. These domestic threats had nothing to do with foreign countries, so Western policy makers could not understand why they required a more assertive foreign policy stance.

Ironically, by 2008 Russia was actively pursuing a more assertive foreign policy, yet the 2008 Foreign Policy Concept is more benign than its predecessors. It lists a series of general threats to world order, for example, but apart from mentioning the West's intention to 'contain' Russia, it does not specify particular threats. It also asserts that Russia has now become strong enough to resolve regional and international problems and to exert a substantial influence upon the development of a new architecture of international relations (*Rossiiskaya gazeta,* 16 July 2008).

The 2000 Foreign Policy Concept stated that Russian foreign policy was based on consistency and predictability and on mutually advantageous pragmatism. Pragmatism was indeed a recurring theme of the foreign policy statements of Putin and his government, particularly during Putin's first presidential term, but it was also often invoked during his second term. When Sergei Lavrov was appointed foreign minister in March 2004, for example, he announced that 'Russia will display flexibility and readiness to compromise in the work for its national interests' (*Itar-Tass,* 17 March 2004), while in his 2007 address to the Federal Assembly, Putin declared that Russia's foreign policy 'is based on the principles of pragmatism, predictability and the supremacy of international law' (Putin 2007b).

It was clear, however, that the considerable clout that Russia acquired from its vast energy resources as energy prices rose changed the definition of what was considered pragmatic (in the sense of achievable). The tone of official foreign policy statements sharpened and they were frequently perceived to be assertive rather than pragmatic. In a speech at a security conference in Munich in February 2007 that resonated throughout the West, for example, Putin insisted that Russia, 'a country with a history that spans more than a thousand years,' would pursue an independent foreign policy and he appeared to threaten that Russia might rearm itself with intermediate-range nuclear missiles (abolished by an historic Soviet-American Treaty in 1987) in response to US plans to deploy anti-ballistic missiles (*Rossiiskaya gazeta,* 12 February 2007). Similarly, although the 2008 Foreign Policy Concept reiterates the claim that 'Russia pursues an open, predictable and pragmatic foreign policy', many of Medvedev's foreign policy statements, particularly since the Georgian conflict of the late summer of 2008, have been forceful rather than pragmatic. Among the five principles that Medvedev claimed that he would observe in conducting Russian foreign policy at this time, for example, was the promise to protect the lives and dignity of Russian citizens '*wherever they [were]*', and the assertion that there were regions in which Russia had 'privileged interests' (Medvedev 2008).

Russian policy towards the 'near abroad'

The mismatch between what policymakers said and what they did has been particularly striking with regard to Russia's relations with its immediate neighbours. Strengthening relations with the countries of the Commonwealth of Independent States (CIS) has always been proclaimed a priority, 'the most important part of the Russian Federation's foreign policy' (*Rossiiskaya gazeta*, 27 April 2007). The 2008 Foreign Policy Concept, like its predecessors, emphasises the importance of 'regional and subregional integration' in the CIS. In practice, however, little multilateral integration has been achieved, and in the last few years, Russia's bilateral relations with its neighbours have frequently been tense, culminating in a war between Georgia and Russia in 2008.

Russia and multilateral relations in the CIS

By 1993, the CIS consisted of all the successor states except the Baltic republics. However, Ukraine has never ratified the agreement, while in 1995 Turkmenistan declared itself only an associate member and Georgia announced that it had left the organisation in August 2008. The CIS has an elaborate institutional structure which aims to further interstate cooperation and integration, as well to develop and strengthen 'relations of friendship, good neighbourliness, inter-ethnic accord, trust and mutual understanding and cooperation' between its members (Preamble, Charter of the Commonwealth of Independent States, in *Rossiiskaya gazeta*, 12 February 1993: 6). However, few of these aims have been realised.

One reason why the CIS has had limited success in integrating its members is that it does not have supranational powers. Not only does it operate on the basis of consensus; it also permits any member to opt out of a decision to which it objects. A second reason is that in size and in military and economic power, Russia is by far the largest member. Consequently, even the most enthusiastic participants fear Russian hegemony. A third reason is that the variable pace at which the successor states have reformed their economies makes integration very difficult. The main obstruction, however, has been Russian ambivalence. Although Russian policy makers frequently support integration verbally, they have done little to promote it.

A succession of vehicles for integration have been created, starting with an Economic Union in 1993 (Ukraine became an associate member in 1994), a Free Trade Area in 1994 (ratified by all members except Russia), a Belarus–Kazakhstan–Russia Customs Union in 1995, renamed the Free Trade Zone in 1996. It became the Eurasian Economic Community (EurAsEc) in 2000, with Belarus, Kazakhstan, Kyrgyzstan, Russia and Tajikistan as full members (Uzbekistan joined in 2005), with Moldova, Ukraine and Armenia obtaining observer status in 2002–3. None of these vehicles has resulted in a functioning free-trade regime or customs union, however, primarily because of Russia's insistence on a long list of exclusions and quotas.

Russia has been more enthusiastic about the collective defence of the

CIS. A Collective Security Treaty was signed in Tashkent in 1992 by Russia, Belarus, and Armenia (Moldova, Ukraine and Turkmenistan acceded in 1993, but effectively seceded when the Treaty was renewed in 1999). Five of the six signatories agreed to establish joint peace-keeping forces; in effect, however, CIS peace-keeping forces are primarily Russian, raising the suspicion in the CIS and more widely that Russia has neo-imperialist intentions. A treaty providing for the collective defence of the Commonwealth's external borders was concluded in May 1995, but Azerbaijan, Moldova, Turkmenistan, Ukraine and Uzbekistan did not accede to it, nor did they join the treaty establishing a common air defence system in February 1996 (by 1998, however, Turkmenistan, Ukraine and Uzbekistan had joined the latter).

The existence of a number of parallel multilateral regional organisations suggests that Russian policy makers are not alone in being ambivalent about the CIS. The Central Asian states, for example, are members of the Central Asian Co-operation Organisation (Russia joined in 2004; in 2005 the member states decided to merge CACO with EurAsEc), of the Economic Cooperation Organisation (Azerbaijan is also a member) and also, with the exception of Turkmenistan, of the Shanghai Cooperation Organisation (which includes Russia and the People's Republic of China). There is also the Organisation of the Black Sea Economic Co-operation, consisting of the littoral states, as well as Armenia and Azerbaijan. In 1997 the four countries that have been most resistant to closer CIS integration, Azerbaijan, Georgia, Moldova and Ukraine (joined between 1999 and 2005 by Uzbekistan), established GUAM as a counterweight to Russia's perceived hegemonic ambitions in the post-Soviet space.

President Putin somewhat reduced the gap between Russia's rhetoric about integration and its policy. On his initiative, for example, the six original Tashkent Treaty members formed a rapid reaction force in May 2001, primarily to deal with incursions into Central Asia by Islamic militants. The CIS (minus Turkmenistan) also established an Anti-Terrorist Centre in Bishkek in September that year. In 2001 Kyrgyzstan, Tajikistan and Uzbekistan granted the USA and its allies access to their bases for the 'war on terrorism' in Afghanistan (Uzbekistan cancelled the agreement in 2005), arousing the prospect that Russia would no longer exercise sole influence in Central Asia. However, in 2002 the Tashkent Treaty was upgraded to the Collective Security Treaty Organisation, and in November 2003 Russia opened an air force base in Kant in Kyrgyzstan, just a few kilometres from the Ganci air base (at Manas international airport) of the US-led coalition forces.

In September 2003, again in response to a Russian proposal, the presidents of Russia, Belarus, Ukraine and Kazakhstan agreed to form a single economic space, which was envisaged as progressing in three stages, from a free trade regime to a customs union, and finally to a single economic space in 2007 with freedom of movement for services, capital and work-force (*Russia Journal*, 19 September 2003). It took until 2007, however, for the first agreements to be signed on the creation of a Customs Union between Russia, Belarus and Kazakhstan by 2010 (*RIA Novosti*, 25 January 2005). Although Russian analysts predicted that 'operation CIS' would be a major objective of Putin's second term (Trenin, 2004), progress on CIS integration was not much faster than it had been in the previous decade. Moreover, the considerable overlap between the stated goals and geographic extent of these organisations (particularly the SCO, the CSTO and EurAsEc), rather than providing Russia with a 'belt and braces' to increase security and economic co-operation, runs the risk of encouraging them to compete, to the detriment of their efficacy (Safranchuk 2008: 161, 166–7).

Russia and internal and inter-state conflicts in the CIS

When the USSR disintegrated in 1991, three violent conflicts were already taking place in the South Caucasus, and two more soon erupted in Tajikistan and Moldova. Russia soon became involved both in peace keeping and in attempting to mediate between the conflicting parties, laying it open to accusations of using or instigating the conflicts to further its own neo-imperialist goals.

There was no controversy about the role of Russian border and army troops in Tajikistan. By 1997 the Russian government had helped to mediate a peace agreement. Following an Islamist insurgency in 1999 that initially targeted Kyrgyzstan (Uzbekistan was the ultimate goal), there was little pressure on Russia from the Central Asian governments to with-draw its troops.

Russia was directly involved in the conflict that erupted when the Moldovan region of Transdniestria declared its independence from Moldova in 1992. Soldiers from the Russian 14th Army stationed in the area were accused of fighting with the separatists. When a cease-fire was agreed in June 1992, Russian troops were entrusted with keeping the peace. Protracted negotiations have failed to resolve the issue of Transdniestria's future status. In 2004 the Organisation for Security and Cooperation in Europe (OSCE) proposed a federative solution, guaran-teed by Russia, Ukraine and the OSCE and monitored by OSCE peace-keepers. The Moldovan government appeared to be prepared to accept the proposal, but Transdniestria continued to insist on a confederation. A constant bone of contention between Russia and the West is the failure of Russia to fulfil an undertaking made to the OSCE in 1999 to withdraw its troops and military equipment from Transdniestria (Todua 2007).

The conflicts in the South Caucasus, over the right of minorities to self-determination, erupted when the central governments reduced the degree of autonomy the disputed areas had enjoyed under the Soviet constitution. In Nagorno-Karabakh, a predominantly Armenian enclave within Azerbaijan, the conflict escalated into a war between Armenia and Azerbaijan during which Armenia annexed the Azerbaijani territory that had previously separated Nagorno-Karabakh from Armenia itself. Although there has been a cease-fire since 1994, the conflict has not been resolved. A draft settlement proposed by the 'Minsk Group' of the OSCE (which includes Russia) provides for the autonomy of Nagorno-Karabakh, the return of occupied territory, and assured access from Karabakh to Armenia. However, Armenia, Azerbaijan and Nagorno-Karabakh have not been able to make the necessary compromises to finalise a settlement.

There were three separate conflicts in Georgia. The first, essentially a struggle for political power, began before the USSR disintegrated and ended when Eduard Shevardnadze, the former Soviet Minister of Foreign Affairs, returned to become President of Georgia in March 1992. The other two were secessionist conflicts between the central Georgian government and Abkhazia and South Ossetia. Under CIS auspices and with some UN co-operation, Russia intervened directly in the conflict between Georgia and the Autonomous Republic of Abkhazia, sending peacekeeping forces in September 1993 after Georgian troops (and the ethnic Georgian population of Abkhazia) had been evicted from Abkhazia and the Georgian state appeared on the brink of collapse. In South Ossetia, after two years of sporadic fighting, a cease-fire was agreed, policed by Georgian, Russian and South Ossetian troops. Attempts to mediate a resolution to the conflicts between Georgia and the two secessionist areas constantly failed because, as in Nagorno-Karabakh, a mutually acceptable compromise on the future status of the two areas could not be found.

Russia's bilateral relations with the successor states

Russia has been more active in advancing its bilateral relations in the near abroad than in promoting multilateral integration within the CIS. Given the dependence of many of the former Soviet states on Russian energy, achieving economic influence has proved a more cost-effective way of fulfilling Russia's economic and political aims than investing in multilateral integration. In the 1990s, Russia tended to use its energy resources as 'soft power', subsidising the price CIS states paid for their oil and gas (Hill 2006). During Putin's presidency, however, Russia has raised energy prices, often with little warning, and has turned off the taps when its customers have refused to agree to the new price or have failed to settle their energy debts. Although the Russians have insisted that decisions to raise prices are based entirely on commercial criteria (and, indeed, close allies such as Belarus and Armenia have also been charged higher prices), many in the CIS and the outside world accuse Russia of using energy as a coercive instrument of foreign policy.

Russia's closest relationship in the near abroad has been with Belarus. In 1996, the two presidents declared that Russia and Belarus would establish a Community of Sovereign Republics. A year later the Community was converted into a Union of Sovereign Republics and in 1999 a confederal Russian-Belarusian union state was proclaimed. However, the harmonisation of the two countries' legal and economic systems is a prerequisite of a confederal state and, since Belarus has adopted few economic and political reforms, there has been little real progress. In 2004 there was a dispute about the price Belarus pays for Russian oil and gas, which resulted in Russia temporarily shutting off supplies to Belarus (Bruce 2005). The dispute was settled fairly quickly, and relations improved, but President Putin showed little enthusiasm for the Russia–Belarus Union and, so far, nor has President Medvedev. Nevertheless, the 2008 Foreign Policy Concept pledges Russia to 'continue efforts to create favourable conditions for effective establishment of the Union State'.

Russia's most difficult bilateral relations have been with the Baltic states and, more recently, with Georgia and Ukraine. The status of the very large Russian minorities in Latvia (34 per cent) and Estonia (30 per cent) has been a cause of constant friction since the USSR disintegrated. The Russian government complains regularly about the infringement of the human rights of the Russian minorities in those countries. Since the accession of the former socialist states of Eastern Europe and the Baltic states to NATO and the EU, the Russian government has been convinced that they have turned the two organisations against Russia.

Russia's relations with Ukraine and Georgia have never been easy, but they have become far more difficult since the two states experienced 'colour revolutions' in 2003 and 2004. In the early years, the most contentious issue in the Russian-Ukrainian relationship was the division of the Black Sea fleet and the location and status of naval bases in Crimea for the Russian fleet. The problem was resolved in May 1997 when a 20-year lease was signed. Other difficulties remained, however, including heavy debts incurred by Ukraine to Russia for its energy supplies and the division of the Azov Sea. After the 2004 'Orange Revolution', President Viktor Yushchenko adopted a firmly pro-European foreign policy, aimed at early membership for Ukraine of both NATO and the EU. The Russian government is strongly opposed to any further NATO expansion into the territory of the former USSR and Ukraine's 'European choice' remains a bone of contention between the two states (and in Ukrainian domestic politics).

Georgia and Russia have been in intermittent dispute about the presence of Russian peacekeepers in Abkhazia and South Ossetia, the difficulty of returning Georgian refugees to Abkhazia, and Russia's delay in implementing an undertaking given at the OSCE Summit in 1999 that it would withdraw from its remaining military bases in Georgia. The Russian government also accuses Georgia of harbouring Chechen terrorists in the Pankisi Gorge region. In 2002 the US sent military advisers to train Georgian forces to conduct anti-terrorist operations, provoking the prospect in Moscow that in the South Caucasus, as in Central Asia, Russia no longer exercises uncontested influence.

In the absence of a political agreement, South Ossetia and Abkhazia operated as quasi-independent states. Russia gave them political and economic support, while officially supporting Georgia's territorial integrity. When Mikheil Saakashvili became president of Georgia in January 2004, he pledged that he would restore Georgia's territorial integrity. He also announced Georgia's intention of seeking NATO membership. Relations between Russia and Georgia deteriorated. In September 2006 four Russian military officers were arrested and accused of spying for Russia; Russia applied severe economic sanctions on Georgia in response. Throughout 2007 and 2008 there were mutual accusations of aggression and repeated clashes between peace keepers in Abkhazia and South Ossetia and Georgian troops. By June 2008 military clashes were occurring daily, particularly in South Ossetia, and each side declared that the other was about to launch a war. On 7 August Georgia launched an attack on South Ossetia which appeared initially to take Russia by surprise (neither Putin nor Medvedev was in Moscow). Within a few days, however, Russian troops had driven the Georgians out of South Ossetia, launched air attacks on targets in Georgia, sent troops and armour into Abkhazia and occupied a 'buffer zone' in the area between Georgia and the two separatist areas (Allison, 2008, pp. 1145–71). The EU brokered a ceasefire agreement on 16 August, but Russia almost immediately reneged on its terms. After a further agreement with the EU, Russia began to withdraw its troops from Georgia at the beginning of September in return for a Georgian pledge not to use force against Abkhazia. By that time, however, Russia had formally recognised the independence of South Ossetia and Abkhazia and Georgia had withdrawn from the CIS.

Russia's conflict with Georgia affected Russian-CIS relations, alarming those members that have large ethnic minorities and real or potential secessionist problems and once again renewing the fear of Russian hegemony in the post-Soviet space. It also had enormous repercussions on Russia's relations with the West.

Russian policy towards the 'far abroad'

In the 1990s, the contradiction between the insistence that Russia should be treated with the respect that its great power status warranted and Russia's need for economic assistance contributed to the incoherence in Russia's policy towards the 'far abroad', particularly towards the United States and Europe. After an initial euphorically pro-Western policy, Russian leaders, disappointed that their orientation to the West did not bring the expected benefits, began to revive relations with some former Soviet allies. At the same time, Western countries, having initially concentrated on Russia, turned their attention to the other successor states, arousing anxiety in Moscow that they would make inroads into an area which Russians regarded as their own sphere of influence. Although political and economic co-operation continued, a number of contentious issues created tension between Russia and the United States and Europe. These tensions became far more severe in Putin's second presidential term and, in the wake of the Georgian war, Russia's relations with the West are worse than they have been since the end of the Cold War.

Sources of tension: NATO expansion and arms control

The issue of NATO expansion has been a persistent irritant in Russian-Western relations. Expansion was perceived as a threat to Russian security. The establishment of a NATO–Russia Permanent Joint Council (PJC) in May 1997 did not alleviate Russian anxiety, particularly since NATO announced an 'open door' policy to membership at the same time as the Czech Republic, Hungary and Poland joined NATO in 1999. NATO also adopted a new strategic doctrine in 1999, which envisaged the Alliance undertaking military operations in non-NATO countries when it thought necessary. Since NATO had already launched an attack on Serbia, Russians perceived the doctrine as a direct threat to Russian security. They suspended co-operation in the PJC.

Following the terrorist attacks on the World Trade Centre and the Pentagon on 11 September 2001, Russian-NATO relations improved. In May 2002 Russia and the 19 NATO member countries established a NATO-Russia Council (NRC) to replace the PJC. Russia has an equal voice in the NRC on issues such as combating international terrorism, peacekeeping, civil emergency planning, defence modernisation and preventing the proliferation of weapons of mass destruction. However, Russian objections to further NATO enlargement did not abate. Despite Russian protests, the Baltic states, together with Slovakia, Slovenia, Bulgaria and Romania, were admitted to NATO in May 2004. At the same time, Ukraine and Georgia began to petition for membership. The

Russian leadership has constantly repeated that Georgian and Ukrainian membership of NATO is unacceptable. Foreign Minister Lavrov, for example, warned in 2008 that 'Ukraine's entry into NATO will entail a deep crisis in Russian-Ukrainian relations ... which will most adversely affect pan-European security' (Lavrov 2008).

Apart from the issue of NATO enlargement (blamed almost entirely on the US), arms control has also been a source of friction between Russia and the West. Russian-US relations began with a flourish, when the second Strategic Arms Reduction Treaty (START) was signed in January 1993. It envisaged each side reducing its nuclear arsenals to 3,500 warheads, as well as a 50 per cent reduction in US submarine-launched nuclear warheads and the elimination of all multiple warheads and of Russia's heavy land-based intercontinental missiles. However, the Duma postponed the ratification of START until April 2000. In December 2001, in response to President Bush announcement that the USA was unilaterally withdrawing from the 1972 Anti-Ballistic Missile (ABM) Treaty, President Putin announced that Russia was withdrawing from START. Nevertheless, a new US-Russian strategic arms limitation treaty was concluded in May 2002, limiting each side to a nuclear arsenal of 1,700–2,200 warheads.

The ABM treaty limited Russia and the United States to one anti-missile system each. The US wanted to modify or abrogate it so as to develop a national or ballistic missile defence (NMD or BMD) system. The Russian government, believing (as did many European governments) that the ABM treaty was the foundation of the strategic deterrence that had kept the world safe from nuclear war, was adamantly opposed to any modification. They also argued that the deployment of even a limited US NMD system would undermine Russian deterrent capabilities (Pikayev 2000). Russian protests did not deter the US president. Having abrogated the ABM treaty, the US continued to develop NMD and began negotiations to deploy elements of the system in Eastern Europe (a radar system in the Czech Republic and 10 interceptors in Poland). President Putin and other Russian officials have insisted that the deployments will threaten the security of the Russian Federation and have threatened that if it goes ahead, Russia will be forced 'to retarget [its] missiles against the sites that represent a threat' (Putin 2008).

The 1990 Conventional Forces in Europe (CFE) treaty, which marked the end of the Cold War, also fell victim to increasing tensions in Russian-Western relations. When the USSR disintegrated, the conventional forces permitted it by the CFE agreement had to be divided between the European successor states. By then, however, the Russian government believed that the forces it was permitted on its southern flank were inadequate to deal with the security threats arising from the conflicts on its periphery. After initial reluctance, NATO members agreed to renegotiate the treaty and a new CFE agreement was adopted at the OSCE Istanbul summit in November 1999. Russia ratified the treaty in 2000, but NATO members refused to ratify it until Russia had fulfilled a commitment made at the Istanbul summit to withdraw all its forces from bases in Georgia and Moldova. President Putin called this an 'invented pretext' and threatened that Russia would declare a moratorium on its observance of the treaty 'until such time as all NATO members without exception ratify it' (Putin 2007b). In July he put the moratorium into effect, and in December 2007, the MFA announced that Russia had suspended the treaty (*Itar-Tass*, 12 December 2007).

Political and economic relations

The decision to expand NATO and the abrogation of the ABM treaty convinced many Russians that the US wanted to undermine Russian security. The US was also blamed for the hardships Russia's economic reform produced (American advisors had played a prominent role in designing it) and the corruption that accompanied it. Other issues began to affect Russian-US relations, for example, US objections to Russian arms and civil nuclear sales, Russian opposition to US policy in the Balkans and towards Iraq. Russians became increasingly bitter about the 'unipolarity' that they believed the United States wanted to impose upon the international system.

Well before the US and its allies acquired bases in Central Asia for the 'war on terrorism', Caspian Sea energy resources and the route by which they reached world markets had become a contentious issue in Russian foreign policy. Russia controlled the pipelines through which the resources were exported and the Russian government was determined both to ensure that it had a major share of the resources and to retain the leverage controlling the pipelines gave it over the other former Soviet littoral states. The multinational oil companies involved in extracting the resources were equally determined to diversify transport routes. The other littoral states wanted to reduce Russia's leverage, while surrounding countries like Georgia were keen to provide lucrative transit facilities. A legal framework was agreed in 1999 for the construction of a pipeline from Baku, in Azerbaijan, via Tbilisi, in Georgia, to the Turkish Mediterranean terminal at Ceyhan. Since then, Russia has made a concerted effort to re-establish its dominance over energy transport by investing in pipelines such as Nord Stream, Blue Stream and South Stream to deliver gas to Europe and world markets.

Initially, Russians had far more benign perceptions of Europe than of the US, and Russian-European multilateral and bilateral relations were not affected by NATO expansion or the CFE difficulties. Like NATO, the European Union (EU) also planned to enlarge. It tried to ensure that Russia was not sidelined by enlargement, concluding a Partnership and Cooperation Agreement (PCA) with the Russian Federation in June 1994 which aimed to develop closer political links, foster trade and investment, and support economic and political reform. The EU was already a major aid donor to Russia and when the ten-year PCA came into force in December 1997, it created a dense network of institutions and political consultations between the EU and Russia, including regular six-monthly EU-Russia summits. In 2005 Russia and the EU agreed four 'road maps', setting out the steps that they would take to reach 'common spaces' in the fields of economics, Justice and Home Affairs, External Security, and research, education and culture (European Commission 2005). The EU is extremely important to Russian foreign trade: 40 per cent of Russia's exports go EU member countries and they provide 38 per cent of Russia's imports.

As enlargement approached, however, a number of difficulties arose in Russian-EU relations. Russians became increasingly apprehensive about the effects of the Schengen visa regime on cross-border movement between Russia and the accession countries and, particularly, between Kaliningrad, which would become an exclave in the EU, and the rest of the Russia. In 2006, as a result of a Ukrainian-Russian gas dispute, energy security suddenly became a problem. When the supply of Russian gas to Europe was disrupted during the dispute, EU members became alarmed by the EU's increasing dependence on Russian energy (by then, the EU imported more than a quarter of its energy from Russia) and called for a diversification of its energy supplies. By January 2009 little diversification had occurred and a second Ukrainian-Russian gas dispute left a dozen European countries with major gas shortages for a fortnight. A project to build a 1,200 km-long North European Gas Pipeline (Nord Stream) will increase the EU's dependence on Russian gas but supplies will no longer be subject to disputes between Russia and transit states.

A series of tensions in Russia's bilateral relations with the newer EU member states delayed the negotiation of a new agreement to replace the PCA when it expired at the end of 2007 and confirmed the Russian belief that the former socialist members of the EU have turned the organisations against Russia.

Russian policy makers developed good bilateral relations with individual European states (in particular, Germany, France and Italy) and they also began to revive relations with former Soviet partners such as Cuba, North Korea, Iraq and India. They established good relations with Iran. Border disputes with the People's Republic of China were settled, and Sino-Russian trade relations expanded. In 2007 Russia and China held joint military exercises for the first time and there have also been joint SCO military exercises (Lo 2008). More recently, Russia has established good relations with Venezuela. The 2008 Foreign Policy Concept policy refers to this diversification of relations as Russia's 'multi-vector policy' which responds to the emerging multipolarity of the international political system, and the diversification of risks and threats facing all countries.

President Putin's foreign policy certainly fulfilled one of his primary aims, which was to raise Russia's international stature. Having achieved a long-standing Russian ambition – Russian membership of the G7 (an annual meeting of the leaders of the major industrial democracies to deal with major economic and political issues), which turned it into the G8 – he served as chairman of the G8 in 2006. For him and for many Russians, this reflected international recognition of Russia's great power status. However, by the time his presidency had come to an end, Russia's increasingly assertive rhetoric, and the many disputes with the US, NATO and the EU, had caused analysts in both Russia and abroad to wonder whether a new Cold War had begun.

President Medvedev and the 'far abroad'

In the run-up to the presidential election in March 2008, there were predictions that President Medvedev would pursue a less confrontational policy than his predecessor. In fact, while his statements tended to be more polite than Putin's, he was equally firm, calling for a 'pause' in NATO expansion, in missile defence deployment and recognition of Kosovo's independence. He also proposed the creation of a new all-European security pact – an old proposal that has been mooted at regular intervals since the 1950s – although he can scarcely have expected that the West would agree to disband NATO in favour of a wider pact (*RIA Novosti*, 5 June 2008).

Beyond the level of rhetoric, Russian foreign policy appeared to harden, with increased pressure on Ukraine and Georgia to discourage them from proceeding with their NATO aspirations. On 7 August, before Medvedev had completed his first 100 days in office, the war with Georgia began. Although Putin seemed to be the main foreign policy actor at first, it was Medvedev who ordered the Russian army to respond and who negotiated the ceasefire terms. He has also been the main target of external criticism of Russia's conduct. There was little recognition in the West that Georgia had initiated the war. Russia was admonished for disproportionate use of force, failure to adhere to cease-fire terms to which they themselves had agreed and the decision to recognise the independence of South Ossetia and Abkhazia. Nevertheless, there was manifest Western confusion about how best to respond to a resurgent Russia. The confusion persists but it seems clear that the Russian-Georgian conflict will continue to have an adverse effect on Russia's foreign relations.

Conclusion: Medvedev's foreign policy

By 2008, many of the inconsistencies and discordant voices in Russian foreign policy had disappeared. Moreover, there was strong popular support for the policy that Putin had been pursuing across his two presidential terms. Medvedev is unlikely, therefore, to change Russia's foreign policy course, and there will almost certainly be a very large degree of continuity between the positions that were taken in Putin's second term and the positions that will be taken under his successor.

In a television interview after the Georgian war, Medvedev listed the five principles on which his foreign policy will be based. First, Russian foreign policy will be based on the fundamental principles of international law. Second, he insisted that Russia 'will not accept a world order in which one country makes all the decisions'; the international system must be multipolar. Third, he insisted that Russia wants neither isolation, nor confrontation; it wants friendly relations with other states. His fourth and fifth principles were rather more alarming for Russia's neighbours. Medvedev reiterated that one of Russia's priorities is the protection of the rights and legitimate interests of the Russian diaspora and he warned that future foreign policy decisions will be based on the need to protect Russians abroad. Finally, he claimed that there are 'regions in which Russia has privileged interests' and that he will pay particular attention to Russian policy in those regions (Medvedev 2008b).

Medvedev's third and fourth foreign policy principles are likely to affect Russia's relations with the CIS, and particularly with those countries that have large Russian minorities. As a result, although Russia appears to be less ambivalent about the costs of further CIS integration, it is doubtful that CIS institutions, with the exception, perhaps, of the CSTO, will become more effective in advancing integration.

Medvedev's third and fourth foreign policy principles will also affect Russia's relations with the West. Ukraine and Georgia are both within the region of Russia's 'privileged interests'. Russian opposition to their accession to NATO, therefore, is unlikely to subside. If NATO remains determined to incorporate the two countries, there is bound to be further friction between Russia and NATO. Similarly, if the US proceeds with NMD deployment in countries close to Russia's border, this will cause tension not only in Russian-US relations, but also in Russia's bilateral relations with Poland and the Czech Republic and, indirectly, in Russian-EU relations. On the other hand, Medvedev, like Putin, is a realist, and he recognises that there are some issues on which Russia needs to co-operate with the West. Moreover, the effect of the global financial crisis on the Russian economy will reduce the means Medvedev has for pursuing his foreign policy goals. If President Barak Obama really wants – in the words of his Vice-President Joe Biden – to 'push the reset button' and revisit areas where the United States and Russia can co-operate (Biden 2009), therefore, Medvedev is likely to respond. Although Russia's relations with the outside world are likely to continue to be troubled, it would suit nobody to return to the confrontational politics of the Cold War.

Chapter 14

The Military, Security and Politics

JENNIFER G. MATHERS

The security challenges facing Russia are formidable. Although the end of the Cold War means that Russia is less likely to be involved in a large-scale conflict than at any other time since 1945, Russia's leaders nevertheless face a wide range of security threats, including political instability in neighbouring countries and within the Russian Federation itself. In the period since Vladimir Putin first became president, Russia's political leaders have presented the country's security as being dependent upon Russia's ability to establish a strong state, and one of the main symbols of the strength of the Russian state is the armed forces. However, Russia is struggling to develop a military that is effective, affordable and acceptable to society, both as a symbol of the state and as an institution in which young people are willing to serve. These are challenges faced by every state, but they are complicated in Russia's case by the chaotic circumstances in which its armed forces were created. Uncertainties about the role which the army should play in politics, society and ensuring the security of the state were mirrored by doubts about Russia's identity and its role in the international community. Although the Putin presidency provided answers to some of these questions, as we saw in the previous chapter, the Russian armed forces continue to face serious problems and the course of defence and security policy under the new president is by no means clear.

The Russian military in the twenty-first century

The Russian armed forces have the task of defending Russia's territory, its state and society. But while the military enjoyed increased funding and a high profile during Vladimir Putin's presidency, its leaders have failed to tackle many of the problems that were inherited from its Soviet predecessor. In spite of many plans for reform (and announcements that reform has been successfully completed), Russia still has a military that is too large and unwieldy to provide an effective response to the security challenges posed by low-level conflicts and which too few of its young people are willing to join. If the limited improvements that were introduced during the Putin years are to become the start of a trend rather than another false start, his successor in the Kremlin will need to devote considerable attention and resources (political as well as economic) to the task of creating a military fit for the needs of the twenty-first century.

Size and structure

Russia has a large standing army and every intention of maintaining such a force in the foreseeable future. An estimated 1.03 million troops are under the control of the Ministry of Defence, including ground, navy and air forces equipped with both conventional and nuclear weapons and anti-aircraft and anti-missile defences. The Russian military is organised into the following commands: Ground Troops; Air Force; Navy; Strategic Deterrent Forces (including submarines, strategic missile forces, long-range aviation command and radar); Space Forces (responsible for missile defence and military spacecraft); and Airborne Forces. The heads of each of these commands report to the Minister of Defence, who in turn reports to the Russian president as Commander-in-Chief. The Minister of Defence has a number of deputy ministers, each with their own area of responsibility, such as armaments, logistics and accommodation. There are also two first deputy ministers, one of whom is the Chief of the General Staff, who oversees operational and administrative functions such as mobilisation, military intelligence and communications.

In addition to the armed forces under the command of the Ministry of Defence, which are the main focus of this chapter and which are generally regarded as 'the military', Russia has a number of other forces. These increase the number of personnel serving under arms by a further half a million: the Federal Border Guard Service (160,000 soldiers directly subordinate to the President); Interior Troops (170,000 soldiers controlled by the Ministry of the Interior or MVD); the Federal Security Service or FSB (4,000 troops); the Federal Protection Service (up to 30,000 troops including the Presidential Guard); and the Federal Communications and Information Agency (55,000 troops) (IISS 2008: 221). The forces of the security services tend to be better trained, better equipped and better paid than those of the Ministry of Defence. While each of these agencies has its own responsibilities, such as counter-intelligence against organised crime and terrorism (FSB) or dealing with violent disorder in the Russian Federation (MVD), the missions of the security services complement and sometimes overlap with the responsibilities of the Ministry of Defence. This can be seen in the case of the conflict in Chechnya, which was initially fought by Ministry of Defence troops but gradually augmented by forces controlled by the MVD, which was later given overall responsibility for the operation.

The Russian military has undergone a great deal of turmoil since it was created in the spring of 1992 in the aftermath of the collapse of the USSR and amid the withdrawal of Soviet troops from Central and Eastern Europe. The Russian Federation was slow to establish its own, separate military forces in comparison with many of the other newly independent states of the former Soviet Union, which regarded a national army as an essential symbol of their new statehood, along with a flag and national anthem. Russia, by contrast, sought the continued existence of a unified command over all of the armed forces of the former USSR and only followed the example of its neighbours when it was clear that the disintegration of the Soviet military was too far advanced to be reversed.

Although Russia was the largest of the Soviet successor states, it did not receive a commensurate share of the Soviet armed forces. Instead other newly independent states asserted their claims to virtually everything located within the borders of their territories in order to provide a basis for their own national armies. The Soviet practice of deploying troops, facilities and weapons systems near the periphery of the USSR meant that there was quite a bit for Russia's new neighbours to claim. Russia lost control of some key military installations, such as large radar stations in the Baltic states and Ukraine and the Baikonur missile and space complex in Kazhakstan, while inheriting many under-strength units located in remote parts of Russia. Eventually Russia and the other Soviet successor states agreed on a distribution of equipment that gave Russia approximately half of what had formely been owned by the Soviet Union (Miller 2004: 5–7), and the agreements that were reached on troop withdrawals and repatriations meant that Russia retained approximately 2 million of the estimated 3.4 million Soviet military personnel (IISS 1991: 36; IISS 1993: 99).

During the first decade after the formation of the Russian military, fierce debates about the best way forward effectively prevented any significant action from being taken. Russia's military and political leaders urgently needed to consider the optimum structure and composition of the country's armed forces in light of the changed nature of the threats that they would be facing, but instead discussions about the future of the military degenerated into bureaucratic in-fighting and personality clashes in the absence of leadership from President Boris Yeltsin. Many of the officers who supported radical reform were the first to leave the military. Most of those who remained occupied themselves with preparing for the last war, in this case the Cold War, and spent years attempting to recreate the Soviet armed forces on a slightly smaller scale (Barany 2007).

Putin recognised the need to improve the combat readiness of the armed forces from an early stage in his leadership, and during his two terms as president took steps to tackle some of the most pressing problems in the military, such as delays in the payment of wages and the failure of conscription to fill the ranks of even a reduced armed force. The frequency and amount of training increased significantly, especially for highly skilled specialists such as pilots, although the levels achieved still fall well below those that are regarded as standard in Western militaries. As will be discussed below, the amount of state funding for the armed forces and the defence industry increased, and a new generation of weapons systems began to enter service. Putin also demonstrated greater decisiveness than his predecessor in dealing with in-fighting within the Defence Ministry. He was responsible for removing the conservative Chief of the General Staff Anatolii Kvashnin, who had been a significant obstacle in the path of serious military reform (Herspring 2006: 523–4). In spite of these improvements to the overall condition of the armed forces, the Russian military has yet to undergo the sort of reform which would transform it into a force which is prepared to meet the diverse and rapidly changing challenges of the twenty-first century. The Ministry of Defence instead continues to cling to structures, weapons systems, staffing practices and a body of strategic thought which assume the need to prepare for large-scale nuclear and conventional warfare against major (Western) powers and alliances.

Recruitment, retention and morale

The Russian armed forces continue to suffer from a crisis in recruitment which began in the late 1980s. During the Gorbachev period, the system of conscription began to break down as large numbers of young men evaded compulsory military service. As a result of *glasnost'*, the Soviet media began to publicise serious problems in the armed forces which made many families reluctant to entrust their sons to its care. At the same time, the nationalist movements that swept through many of the Soviet republics made military service in the armed forces particularly unappealing for young men from these nations. By 1991 less than a quarter of the conscript quotas were being met in republics such as Lithuania, Armenia and Georgia (IISS 1991: 34).

Rather than encouraging their teenage sons to carry out their patriotic duty, increasing numbers of parents began to help their children to avoid conscription in any way possible. Many turned (and continue to turn) for help to their local Committee of Soldiers' Mothers (CSM), a network of civil society organisations which seek to protect the human rights of soldiers and to provide material and moral support for their families. In addition to high-profile actions taken at the national level, such as lobbying for changes in legislation on alternative forms of service for conscientious objectors and opposing Russia's war in Chechnya, CSM organisations provide practical advice on legal ways to avoid conscription (Bogoslovakaya *et al.* 2001). Such advice is widely sought-after and very effective. According to then-Minister of Defence Pavel Grachev, in 1992 some 75–80 per cent of the young men in Russia who were eligible for military service actually evaded conscription (Dawisha and Parrott 1994: 243). Very little had changed in this respect by Putin's second term as president, when the Ministry of Defence estimated that as few as 9 per cent of young men entered the armed forces (Barany 2007: 117). Although the targets for the spring and autumn call-ups were often met in the last years of Putin's presidency, this was due to reductions in those targets and lower standards rather than an increase in the number of healthy young men prepared to serve.

In the early 1990s a form of voluntary military service (known as contract service) was introduced to supplement conscription. In spite of the manifest failures of conscription, the decision to introduce even an element of voluntary service was, and continues to be, deeply controversial among many senior Russian officers. They believe that universal (male) military service is the best way to instil civic values into the nation's youth, as well as providing trained reserves that can be mobilised quickly in a national emergency. Support for the continuation of conscription is often linked to the argument that Russia needs a mass army rather than a smaller, professional force in order to meet current and future security threats. The arguments in favour of conscription have been strengthened by the fact that contract service has not solved the manpower shortages of the Russian military. The Ministry of Defence was slow to realise the need to offer competitive salaries, reasonable living conditions and an attractive career path in order to attract the calibre of recruits the armed forces both wants and needs. Instead it seemed to expect that some of the country's most intelligent, able and physically fit young men would volunteer to serve in an institution that they had already gone to great lengths to escape. Such young men have shown that they prefer to take up opportunities now open to them in the civilian economy. Those who do volunteer for military service tend to be the ones who struggle to find or keep a civilian job as well as young men from the countryside, for whom military service is seen as offering an opportunity for advancement, and few of them re-enlist after their original terms of service have ended. As a result, the military has little choice but to accept those who present themselves for service, whether as conscripts or volunteers. In 2007 the chief of the Russian Air Force Colonel General Vladimir Mikhailov estimated that as many as 30 per cent of those joining the Air Force (which is regarded as an elite service) suffered from some mental illness, 10 per cent were addicted to drugs or alcohol and 15 per cent were either ill or undernourished (Arnold 2007a).

A significant proportion of contract soldiers are women. Indeed almost 10 per cent of Russia's armed forces (approximately 90,000 soldiers) are now composed of women, all of whom serve as volunteers. Although millions of women served in the Soviet armed forces during the Second World War, many of them in combat conditions, after the war they were quickly demobilised. Since 1945 conscription has only been applied to men, and while women were allowed to volunteer even before the introduction of contract service, only a tiny number ever did so. But while contract service has brought women into the military in large numbers, the Ministry of Defence does not see this segment of the population as providing a solution to its recruitment problems. Women are only permitted to serve in a very narrow range of military positions, chiefly in areas such as administration and medicine, and few are able to advance very far up the career ladder due to restrictions on the length of time they can serve and on opportunities for advanced training. In addition, most of the women who volunteer for contract service do so for short-term, economic reasons. Many are the wives of officers who live in remote areas where there are few opportunities for paid employment. Contract service offers the chance of a second income for the family until the main breadwinner gets a promotion, a transfer or leaves the military altogether (Mathers 2006).

The persistence of poor living conditions for soldiers and officers is another reason for the continued crisis in recruitment. Throughout the 1990s , it was normal for soldiers to wait for months to receive their pay, and often by the time they were paid, the spending power of their wage packets had been diminished by rapid inflation. Under Vladimir Putin the problem of delayed wage payments was finally addressed. Officers' salaries also increased during Putin's presidency, but they nevertheless failed to keep pace with salaries in the civilian economy, while the reduction in 2005 of benefits in kind formerly enjoyed by officers proved to be deeply unpopular. Housing, especially for officers with families, continues to be difficult to obtain and inadequate even where available. Speaking in 2006, Putin identified the year 2010 as the target for solving the housing problem for officers, although in September 2008 President Medvedev indicated that the construction of military housing would need to continue until 2012. Living conditions for conscripted soldiers are not only uncomfortable but can also be life-threatening, as they are often subjected to abuse by officers and fellow soldiers alike. The failure of the Ministry of Defence to stamp out this practice, known as *dedovshchina,* is probably the chief reason for the continued crisis in recruitment.

Dedovshchina is translated into English as 'bullying', but that term does not fully convey the extent and horror of this systematic abuse of conscripts. *Dedovshchina* is derived from the Russian word *ded* or grandfather, and refers to the power that the most senior conscripts (or grandfathers) exercise over the newest group of soldiers to enter their unit. There are many well-documented cases of young conscripts suffering savage beatings, sometimes requiring hospitalisation, surgery and the amputation of limbs, and such cases continued to be reported throughout Vladimir Putin's second term as president (Arnold 2007). Soldiers have been beaten to death by their fellows as punishment for some transgression while others are willing literally to do anything to escape the relentless abuse and torture, including risking lengthy prison sentences by deserting their units or even committing suicide (Colin Lebedev 2006: 66–70; Webber and Zilberman 2006: 169–75).

The Ministry of Defence has been forced to acknowledge the existence of *dedovshchina* as a result of pressure from elements of the media and from the Committee of Soldiers' Mothers, although senior military figures continue to dispute the extent and significance of the phenomenon. There is debate among observers of the Russian armed forces about whether the Defence Ministry is unwilling or unable to address this serious problem. Some have argued that *dedovshchina* is tolerated and even encouraged in some units as a method of controlling the raw conscripts under the command of overstretched officers. Others suggest that it reflects a fundamental callousness towards the individual on the part of a large and impersonal bureaucracy, while still others see it as an indictment of the Russian military and its claims to effectiveness and combat readiness. If the Ministry of Defence cannot even control what happens to its own troops within its own barracks, what hope does it have of providing an effective fighting force to defend and protect Russia's territory and its citizens?

Defence budgets and military spending

After a brief period of relative openness during the late Gorbachev and early Yeltsin years, which coincided with a downturn in the fortunes of the military and the defence industry, secrecy in relation to the amount of state funding devoted to defence has been reinstated, and this trend shows no signs of being reversed. During Putin's second term as president, the number of items that were classified (not available to the public) increased and included procurement and research and development (IISS 2008: 209). Restrictions on the information that can be released about the state defence budget do more than make it difficult for outsiders to calculate how much Russia is spending: they place significant obstacles in the path of Russian citizens, journalists, civil society groups and even Duma deputies who wish to scrutinise policy decisions and to hold to account the Ministry of Defence and other beneficiaries of the state defence budget. Many Duma deputies are reportedly unwilling to undergo the security clearance required to gain access to the details of the defence budget because they fear it would impose onerous restrictions on their own actions, such as limits on meeting foreigners and travel abroad (Cooper 2006: 143). These rules have discouraged them from sitting on the Duma's Defence Committee, with the result that the Committee is dominated by former members of the armed forces. This in turn reduces the range of defence expertise in the Duma as well as limiting *de facto* civilian oversight of a key element of Russian policy.

Although the figures that are available for the Russian defence budget are estimates, it is possible nevertheless to discern the impact of changing economic conditions and policy decisions on defence spending. During the 1990s Russia allocated more than 5 per cent (and perhaps as much as 7–8 per cent) of its gross domestic product to defence. While this is a very high proportion of GDP for a country to devote to its military budget, it needs to be seen in the context of the condition of the Russian economy during that decade, which was characterised by slow growth rates and high inflation. The result was a sharp decline in defence spending, which dropped by an estimated 45 per cent in the first half of the 1990s (IISS 1996: 107). The presidency of Vladimir Putin, by contrast, coincided with a substantial rise in the growth of the Russian economy, fuelled by the export of Russian oil and gas at high international prices. The defence sector was one of the major beneficiaries of Russia's new prosperity, and although the proportion of GDP allocated to defence during Putin's presidency was lower than in the 1990s (approximately 2.5–2.8 per cent between 2000 and 2008), the rise in the gross domestic product, the slowing of inflation and the reduction in the size of the Russian armed forces (from 2 million in the early 1990s to just over 1 million in 2008) meant that there was significantly more money in the military budget to go around (IISS 2008: 210).

By the end of Putin's second term as president, the Russian armed forces were beginning to see the benefits of this investment. The long-awaited *Topol-M* intercontinental ballistic missiles began to enter service in 2006. The *Topol-M* is designed to carry up to 6 warheads and is intended to replace Russia's ageing, Soviet-built nuclear missile arsenal. The submarine-launched version of the missile, the *Bulava*, began testing in 2007, while new *Borei*-class submarines, intended to carry the *Bulava* missiles, are under development and expected to enter service in 2009. The development and deployment of a new radar, the *Voronezh-M*, means that Russian strategic defences can now operate independently of radar stations in other former Soviet states, thus reducing Russia's military and political dependence on its neighbours (IISS 2008: 206–7).

Russia's defence sector was given a further boost in June 2006, when a major arms procurement programme involving an estimated US$190 billion of additional investment was announced for the period 2007–15. This programme is intended to provide an across the board build-up of military equipment, including tanks and armoured vehicles, aircraft, ships (including nuclear submarines) and air defence complexes, although there are doubts about whether the Russian defence industry, with its aging facilities and workforce, will be able to achieve such ambitious targets (Bjelakovic 2008: 527–35).

But while the defence budget grew during Putin's presidency, corruption within the Ministry of Defence continues to be a serious problem. Corrupt practices are widespread in the armed forces and range from the actions of opportunistic individuals, such as senior officers making use of soldiers as unpaid labour, to organised fraud and embezzlement on a large scale. As a result, the amount of money which actually reaches the defence sector is significantly less than the sums which are authorised. For example, it has been reported that in 2004 almost no new funds reached Russian defence contractors, in spite of the substantial increases for the production of new weapons and equipment specified in the state budget for that year (Bukkvoll 2008: 260).

The military and politics

The military's relationship to politics in Russia is a complex one that has gone through a number of distinct stages. During the Soviet period the armed forces were co-opted supporters of the *status quo*. In the 1990s large numbers of officers entered electoral politics and became challengers of the regime, chiefly over the issue of defence spending, although the military proved to be unsuccessful as an interest group and had to wait for the election of a new president and a dramatic improvement in the country's economy to enjoy more generous funding. The reconciliation between the military and the state during Putin's presidency was accompanied by the appointment of the *siloviki* – those with a background in the armed forces or security services – to many important positions in Russian politics. This phenomenon prompted many observers to express concerns about the growing power of the military (see particularly Kryshtanovskaya and White 2003), although there are reasons to question the coherence of this group and whether they will prove to be effective at promoting any shared values or policy preferences.

The military as a political actor

A feature of Russian politics is the presence of former members of the 'force structures' (the military and security services), whether in elected or appointed positions. In some respects this is a contemporary version of an old phenomenon. It was common for representatives of the military and security forces to serve at senior levels in politics during the Soviet period, although this nearly always took place under carefully controlled conditions. Successive Soviet political leaderships sought to guard against any tendency towards 'Bonapartism' (the pursuit of political power by military officers) and to ensure the loyalty of the military by co-opting the officer corps into the political elite, providing the armed forces with generous resources and permitting them a certain degree of autonomy. Most officers were members of the Communist Party, while representatives of the armed forces were visible at the most senior levels of political life through their presence in such bodies as the USSR Supreme Soviet and the Communist Party's Central Committee.

The relationship between the military and civilian authority began to change from active partnership and mutual support to something more adversarial during the late Gorbachev period. As part of the processes of *glasnost'* and *perestroika*, military personnel were encouraged to use their compulsory political education sessions (previously devoted to ideological instruction) to debate current political issues. Groups of like-minded officers organised officers' assemblies to articulate and publicise their political views and some individuals sought elected office. Forty-four officers were elected to the Russian Congress of People's Deputies in 1990 (Barany 2008: 587), while two senior officers stood as Russian vice-presidential candidates in the 1991 elections. One of them, Major-General Alexander Rutskoi, served as Boris Yeltsin's vice-president until he was removed from office during the confrontations between parliament and the president in late 1993.

Throughout the 1990s, serving and former Russian military officers participated in politics in large numbers, standing for and in some cases being elected to political office at the national and regional levels. Although some of these candidates did seek to address wider social, economic and political problems facing Russia, many appeared to be motivated by the desire to create a lobby group at the upper reaches of politics on behalf of the Ministry of Defence. This was clearly related to the fact that the armed forces were relatively unsuccessful in the struggle for state funding during Boris Yeltsin's presidency. As indicated above, Russian defence spending was in sharp decline. There was a strong view among senior Russian military officials that the needs of the Defence Ministry were not being met by the politicians and that the only way to remedy this situation was for members of the armed forces to occupy positions of political power. This view was articulated most explicitly during the campaign for the 1995 Duma elections, in which the Minister of Defence himself called upon members of the armed forces to stand for election precisely in order to create this kind of military lobby. But while 123 officers were chosen as official Ministry of Defence candidates and another 40 stood as candidates for various political parties in 1995, only 22 'military candidates' were elected to the Duma, and only two of those had been put forward by the Defence Ministry (Thomas 1996: 536). There has not been a concerted attempted by the military to fill large numbers of elected positions since 1995, although a steady trickle of serving and retired officers has continued to enter the Duma and several prominent former officers have been elected as governors of Russian regions. Alexander Rutskoi, for example, was governor of Kursk region from 1996 to 2000. Alexander Lebed' (who stood as a candidate in the 1996 Russian presidential election) served as governor of Krasnoyarsk from 1998 until his death in a helicopter crash in 2002, while Boris Gromov was elected governor of Moscow region in 2000 and re-elected in 2003.

During the 1990s the armed forces also began to be viewed by candidates of all political persuasions as an important constituency. Political parties and their aspiring Duma deputies would go out of their way to court 'the military vote', and parties across the range of the political spectrum would place one or two high-profile officers near the top of their party lists. There is little evidence, however, to support the assumption that members of the armed forces did vote as a distinct bloc. On the contrary, the fact that so many different political parties were able to attract military officers as candidates demonstrates the failure of the military to organise around a single political position or party. The experience of the military's involvement in electoral politics in the 1990s instead illustrates the diversity of views within the armed forces as well as the open and chaotic nature of party politics at this time, which was characterised by the rapid formation and abandonment of parties and even more rapid shifts in political loyalties.

Several of the wider political trends of the Putin presidency have had a significant impact on the nature of the military's participation in politics since 2000. The consolidation of political parties, the greater degree of party discipline and the fact that most of the parties represented in the Duma now support rather than oppose the policies of the government, as well as reductions in the power and influence of the Duma itself, means that there are far fewer opportunities for individual military officers to enter parliament as challengers to the *status quo*. Changes in the way that regional governors are chosen following the hostage-taking in Beslan in

September 2004, from direct election to presidential nomination of candidates for approval by regional legislatures, has also reduced the potential for regional governors to oppose Moscow and its policies. These structural changes mean that electoral politics no longer provides an opportunity for disgruntled officers to build support for their own political positions.

Putin's presidency also marked a major shift in the relationship between the political leadership and the armed forces. From the very beginning of his campaign for president in 2000, Putin stressed the importance of the military to the future of Russia in his speeches and made high-profile gestures of support for the armed forces, such as visiting troops in Chechnya soon after he was appointed acting president at the end of 1999. These actions were not lost on the leaders of the armed forces, who were keenly aware of the contrast between Putin's active interventions on behalf of the military and the passivity of Boris Yeltsin in this area. As President, Putin continued to express his support for the military and to declare that attention must be paid to pressing defence and security issues, frequently speaking of Russia's return to its proper position in the international community as a great power and of the importance of building a strong Russia based on a strong military. Perhaps most importantly, though, Putin's pro-military rhetoric was matched by a substantial increase in spending which reassured them that at last Russia had a leader who could be trusted to look after the defence of the nation.

A feature of Putin's presidency which has gained a great deal of attention is the appointment of men with backgrounds in the security services to high-level positions. The rise of these *siloviki* (or men of the force structures) was noted early in Putin's first term, when they were chosen to lead five of the seven federal administrative districts created in 2000, but former officials of the security services and the armed forces have been appointed to other prominent positions including Minister of Defence and Interior Minister as well as aide to the president. It is far from certain, however, that the *siloviki* share common values and political priorities or that their presence at high levels of politics necessarily means that Russia is moving in a more authoritarian direction. Close investigation into their backgrounds and views reveals a surprising degree of diversity which may be attributed to their length of service and level of seniority in the security sector. Some members of the *siloviki* also have experience of working in other professions, such as journalism, academia or public relations, which may have influenced their values and priorities as much as or even more than their service in the security forces. In other words, there are good reasons to question whether the *siloviki* should be regarded as a coherent group (Renz 2006).

The military and the security forces clearly have a presence in Russian politics. They occupy a range of elected and appointed political positions, but they do not necessarily act together in support of common goals and in those cases where they do have shared political aims (such as increasing defence spending), the military have been remarkably unsuccessful in achieving them without the support of the president. Rather than viewing the military as a powerful institutional actor that exercises undue influence over the political leadership, the evidence of the military's involvement in Russian politics so far suggests that its fortunes are highly dependent on the goodwill and priorities of the political leadership.

Civilian control of the armed forces

Concerns about the extent of control which Russia's political leaders exercise over the armed forces tend to focus on extreme scenarios involving the complete or near-total loss of control. In the 1990s there was much speculation on when, rather than if, the military would attempt to seize political control of the country. But while conditions of economic, political and social turmoil have indeed been the catalyst for military takeovers in other countries, in Russia the armed forces proved to be incapable of uniting around any single political figure or programme. The only instance of direct military involvement in a political dispute took place during Boris Yeltsin's confrontation with parliamentary rebels in September/October 1993, but on that occasion the leadership of the armed forces supported the elected civilian leadership. During Vladimir Putin's presidency discussions about civilian control have focused on the rise of the *siloviki*, and the concern that they influence policy on a range of issues in order to serve the interests and priorities of Russia's security services and its leaders. This emphasis on such extreme possibilities has tended to distract attention from more subtle, although no less important, factors that determine the nature of the relationship between Russia's civilian and military authorities.

The most serious obstacle to effective civilian control of the military and security forces in Russia is the reliance on highly personalised relationships between the leaders of these organisations and the president. This has created a tendency to equate civilian control with the loyalty of the force structures to the president which in turn has its origins in the 1990s, when the presidency was given extensive powers in comparison with other political actors and institutions. This has led to the neglect of other forms of civilian control that would enable greater accountability of the military and security services to society. One such form of accountability relates to parliamentary and public scrutiny of the defence budget which, as discussed above, is very limited.

Another measure which could lead to greater institutionalisation of civilian control of the military is the introduction of civilians at senior levels of the Ministry of Defence. The presence of senior civilians in the institution could be a mechanism for challenging established ways of thinking and patterns of behaviour as well as providing agents for greater accountability and civilian oversight. Some steps have been taken in this direction, although the pace of change has been slow and the results uncertain. Former First Deputy Minister of Defence Andrei Kokoshin advised Gorbachev and helped to shape his radical approaches to security and defence issues. Kokoshin was first deputy minister from 1992 to 1997 and was responsible for liaising between the Ministry of Defence, the defence industry and the Duma, but his impact on the activities and the working culture of the Ministry was minimal. Kokoshin's responsibilities were, in effect, duplicated by other officials within the institution and he found himself having to function with reductions in both influence and staff (the latter an important indicator of the power and status of a senior official). Deputy Minister of Defence Lyubov' Kudelina was appointed by Vladimir Putin in September 2007 and given the responsibility for improving accounting and financial controls within the Ministry. But while Kudelina – a civilian and a woman – appeared at first to be a radical choice, she has demonstrated an enthusiasm for maintaining and extending the secrecy surrounding the military budget which exceeds even that of her uniformed colleagues. Far from increasing the level of external scrutiny and accountability of the Ministry of Defence, she has become one of the strongest supporters of the *status quo* (Betz 2004: 103–5).

The experiences of Kokoshin and Kudelina suggest that civilians, even when appointed to very senior positions, are not effective as agents of change within the Ministry of Defence and it is too soon to say whether the latest experiment in senior civilian appointments will be more successful. The presence or absence of a civilian Defence Minister is widely regarded as a test of the degree of civilian control exercised over the armed forces. If this is the case then Russia took a significant step forward with the appointment of Anatolii Serdyukov as Defence Minister in February 2007. Serdyukov is arguably Russia's first genuinely civilian Minister of Defence as his immediate predecessor, Sergei Ivanov, had a background in the Foreign Intelligence Service which diminished his claims to civilian status in the eyes of many analysts. A former furniture salesman and head of Russia's Federal Tax Service, Serdyukov is an outsider who was appointed to deal with corruption in the armed forces. He has made a promising start to this process by selling off some of the Russian army's extensive property holdings and by taking a more aggressive approach to the prosecution of officers suspected of corrupt practices, but corruption within the Ministry of Defence is extensive and deeply entrenched and tackling this problem will require a sustained effort which no Russian political or military leader has so far exhibited.

Determinants of future trends

Throughout his presidency, Vladimir Putin placed a great deal of emphasis upon ensuring Russia's security and on meeting the needs of Russia's defence sector. Early indications suggest that Dmitri Medvedev shares his predecessor's priorities. In the first year of his presidency, Medvedev ordered Russian troops into battle in support of separatists in Georgia and announced a 50 per cent increase in defence spending for the period 2009–11. Russia's ability to continue such a robust approach to security issues will depend to a large extent on two factors. One is the progress of military reform, which will dictate the future size and shape of the armed forces as well as its character. This will in turn provide Russia with a military force that will either improve or restrict its ability to cope with the security challenges of the future. The other factor that will help to determine trends in Russian security is the nature of the relationship between the military, the state and society, which will provide an important context within which future security policy decisions will be taken.

Reform of the armed forces

It is possible that Vladimir Putin's presidency marked the beginning of a serious effort to turn the Russian military into an effective armed force that is capable of defending its territory and its national interests against the threats of the post-Cold War world. The achievement of this task is one of the most important challenges Russia and President Medvedev face in the area of security and defence policy. Russia's defence chiefs have shown that they are not capable of leading significant reform efforts themselves and so the political leaders, especially the president, must provide clear and consistent direction. Tackling the continuing problems of recruitment, retention and morale will require a change in attitude among senior officers towards the soldiers under their command. Measures that are underway, such as the reduction in the term of service for conscripts from 24 months to 12 months from January 2008 and the planned introduction of non-commissioned officers, are likely to contribute to such a change. Such steps, however, are vulnerable to resistance from within the Ministry of Defence, while the campaign against corruption begun by Defence Minister Anatoly Serdyukov will only be effective if it has sustained support from the top political leadership.

President Medvedev also needs to encourage a more realistic assessment of the security threats facing Russia, which will enable much-needed reforms to the structure and organisation of the armed forces. Russia's military leaders have been reluctant to abandon the old certainties of the Cold War, although in this they have been helped by the West, which has treated Russia with a combination of indifference and mistrust. The continued expansion of NATO eastwards, Western support for political change in Ukraine and Georgia, American plans for a national missile defence system as well as the willingness of the United States and its allies to use military force in support of their foreign policy goals (which are often seen as contrary to Russian interests) have all contributed to the perception among Russia's political and military élites that the major Western powers continue to pose a serious military threat. This outdated threat perception has provided support for the continuation of a mass army equipped in the Soviet model, but while Russia's possession of such a force would certainly get the attention of Western governments, there is a real danger that it could prove counter-productive and encourage even more 'anti-Russian' policies.

The preoccupation with potential threats posed by Western forces has also distracted Russian military leaders from devoting serious attention to the more pressing, and rapidly evolving, security threats facing the country. The conflict between Russia and Georgia over South Ossetia in the summer of 2008 provided a vivid demonstration of the volatility of contested territories in Russia's immediate vicinity. Although Russian forces quickly overwhelmed their Georgian counterparts and 'won' the confrontation, accounts suggest that the operation involved a very heavy-handed approach by Russia rather than the more efficient and selective application of force that is the model for modern armies in small-scale conflicts. Even if the situation in South Ossetia is now resolved (which is not certain), there are several other such 'frozen conflicts' in the region that could swiftly develop into hot wars involving Russia. And while the situation in Chechnya has moved into the phase of post-conflict reconstruction, it has left a legacy of low-level terrorist activity which Russia is struggling to combat and which may set a precedent for the use of terror tactics by other disgruntled groups. It is hard to see how a large, standing army which is top-heavy with tanks, nuclear weapons and a fleet of big ships and submarines will be able to adapt to counter-terrorist operations, which require small groups of well-trained and highly disciplined soldiers.

In fact armed force, even in the form of a smaller and more flexible military, will be of little or no use in addressing some of the security threats Russia is likely to face in the near future. For example, the economic prosperity which Russia has enjoyed since 2000 and which has been one of the main outward signs of Russian strength is based primarily on energy exports. The continuation of high levels of Russian energy exports is dependent upon such factors as the prices that international markets are willing to pay for energy, levels of worldwide demand for fossil fuels, the efficiency of Russia's energy production and its ability to gain access to crucial pipeline routes. Russia also faces a serious demographic crisis. The security implications of the long-term decline in the birth rate and the rise in adult and infant mortality rates of ethnic Russians are difficult to predict, but at a minimum these factors are likely to affect the size and composition of Russia's labour force and therefore have consequences for the future of Russia's economic development. Policy makers in Moscow have also expressed concern that portions of the Russian Far East are effectively being lost to large numbers of Chinese settlers occupying the sparsely populated territories on the Russian side of the border. But while Medvedev's statements about the future direction of the Russian military do emphasise the importance of developing an effective and mobile fighting force, they also signal a renewed effort to modernise and expand Russia's nuclear weapons arsenal, which is likely to encourage the great power ambitions of hard-liners and do little to help Russia address internal security threats or those that come from Russia's closest neighbours, especially those threats which can only be addressed using non-military means.

The militarisation of state and society

During Putin's presidency the military and security services gained a higher profile in Russia. This was partly the result of Putin's rhetoric, but it was also a consequence of the appointment of *siloviki* to important official positions as well as policy decisions such as the increase in defence spending and the introduction of military training in secondary schools. The combination of these measures has caused some observers to warn that the Russian state and society are undergoing a process of militarisation – in other words, that the armed forces and its values and priorities are encroaching on and being accepted into everyday life. The responses from Russian society to these developments have been mixed and suggest that militarisation is a complex process which has achieved, at most, only partial success in Russia.

The introduction of military-patriotic education in schools is perhaps the most blatant attempt by the Russian state to bring the military into everyday life. The problems of recruitment and retention of personnel in the armed forces are often blamed by Russian military officials on the rise in social problems among young soldiers which are, in turn, attributed to a malaise in Russian society at large. The remedy in the eyes of many senior military officers is the reintroduction of some form of basic military training in schools. This was a feature of secondary education during much of the Soviet period but had been allowed to lapse after the collapse of the USSR. Such a programme of training would, it is suggested, improve physical fitness and instil a sense of moral purpose and patriotism in young people, together with an appreciation of the work of the armed forces and an eagerness to serve in them.

While still acting President, Vladimir Putin introduced such a course of study, 'Foundation of Military Service', as part of a broader programme of 'Patriotic Education of the Citizens of the Russian Federation'. The military training element was initially an optional subject but it met with a great deal of resistance on the part of both parents and teachers and as a result few schools actually offered the course. It was then made compulsory in 2003, but even this step did not ensure that the programme of patriotic education achieved its aims. Although military training is now a formal part of secondary education in Russia, those with personal experience of the course report that it is not taught effectively or taken seriously by the pupils (Webber and Zilberman 2006: 179–80, 186–7).

The evidence of public opinion polls, however, lends support to the argument that Russia did indeed become a militarised society during the leadership of Vladimir Putin. According to monthly polls conducted by the Russian Public Opinion Research Centre (VCIOM) in 2007, between 41 and 46 per cent of Russians surveyed expressed approval of the army. This compared favourably with a number of other institutions such as law enforcement agencies, political parties and the judiciary, although the media were rated more highly (VCIOM 2007). In February 2008 nearly 75 per cent of Russians surveyed told VCIOM that they regarded the army as capable of protecting Russia from a real, external threat of war, and this figure has been steadily increasing from 60 per cent in 2005 to 67 per cent in 2007 (VCIOM 2008).

But while these surveys indicate that many Russians have an attachment to the idea of the military, perhaps linked to its role as a symbol of a strong Russian state, there is a very large discrepancy between these expressions of support and the unwillingness of young men to join the army and of parents to entrust their sons to its care. Similarly, approval of the armed forces was not sufficient to persuade millions of parents and teachers to devote valuable time during the school day to military training when they were given the choice, and once made compulsory the subject has not proved popular. In other words, while the Russian state exerts pressures on society towards greater acceptance of the military and its values in everyday life, the response of society has been more complex than simple acceptance or rejection.

Chapter 15

Classifying Russia's Politics

STEPHEN WHITE

It was relatively easy to classify a political system of the Soviet type. It had a number of well understood characteristics, not only in the USSR but in all the countries that followed its example. There was a single (or at least dominant) ruling party, normally called a communist or workers' party. There was public ownership of at least the most important sectors of the economy, including natural resources, heavy industry, banking and finance, and in most (but not all) cases agriculture. The party itself was dominated by its leadership, a small group of (usually) elderly men united in a body called the Political Bureau or Politburo. The entire political system was based on 'democratic centralism', which was meant to provide for broad discussion but in fact meant hierarchical subordination; and the party itself played a 'leading role', which meant in practice that its decisions were mandatory in every sphere – in elected institutions, in economic management, and in the wider society.

In fact, a system of this perfectly hierarchical kind was something of an oversimplification even in the Stalin years, and from the early 1950s there were moves towards a greater degree of consultation between regime and society within a framework of 'socialist legality'. The party began to emphasise the 'Leninist norms' that had supposedly been practised in earlier years, the boundaries of debate were widened, and the leadership became a more collective one although a single person, the party leader or General Secretary, was normally dominant. There was still no element of electoral choice, but legislative bodies at all levels began to meet more often, there could occasionally be criticism of the performance of government ministers (the party had nothing to gain from tolerating incompetence), and a developing committee system began to scrutinise legislation more seriously than ever before. The decisive moment in these developments was the 20th Congress of the Communist Party in 1956, with its denunciation of Stalin and the repressive system he had created, and it was the inspiration for a group of 'children of the 20th Congress', including Gorbachev, who believed it had shown there could be a socialism that was also democratic.

In the end, for reasons we explore in this volume, there was no 'third way', and the start of the 1990s saw the repudiation of Marxism–Leninism, the end of communist rule, and the collapse of the USSR itself as all of its fifteen republics gained or restored their independence. But at least in Russia, it was an ambiguous transition. There was no overt rejection of the union itself – at any rate, a 'renewed federation of equal sovereign republics' had overwhelming public support when it was put to the vote in a referendum in March 1991, and the attempted coup in August of that year was followed by a series of attempts to construct a looser form of union among the remaining republics, other than the Baltics (which had formally seceded from the USSR at the start of September). Indeed, a large majority of Russians, according to the survey evidence, still regret the demise of the USSR and are in favour of the closest possible (voluntary) association of all of the former Soviet republics, especially the Slavic ones. Their reasons are not entirely sentimental – the USSR was a human and not just a political union, and when it broke up about 25 million Russians were left outside their 'own' republic. It was also an economic unit, and many believe a heavy cost has been paid for the breakup of long-standing patterns of interaction across what used to be a single market.

There is less regret that communist rule has disappeared – at least, in the sense of a single ruling party with a dominant position in the society – and indeed much of this had already begun to disappear in the Gorbachev years (there were multi-candidate elections from 1989 and by 1990 the party's leading role had been abolished and opposition parties had been fully legalised). By the late summer of 1991 the Communist Party had been banned and its property sequestered; by the end of the year the USSR itself had disappeared, and a new constitution was approved shortly afterwards that committed a newly independent Russia to a whole series of liberal principles including private ownership, multiparty democracy and civil liberties of all kinds. Not just had the USSR been left behind; so too had the elected soviets on which communist rule had been based, and which predated the October revolution itself. Russia was now a 'democratic federal legally based state with a republican form of government'; the constitution even began, in words that appeared to borrow the famous opening of its American counterpart, 'We the multinational people of the Russian Federation ...'

This was hardly 'communist rule', even if many of those in leadership positions had been prominent during the Soviet years – Yeltsin himself had been a member of the Politburo and his prime minister for most of the 1990s, Viktor Chernomyrdin, had been a member of the party's Central Committee; there was no other way to be politically active, and not in prison, during the Soviet period. But at the same time it was hardly 'democracy' in the sense in which it was understood elsewhere, in spite of the optimistic assumptions that were made by Western governments as the Yeltsin administration repudiated Marxism–Leninism and shifted the economy with unprecedented speed into the hands of private owners. Initially, there was broad agreement that the Russian system must be at least 'in transition to democracy' – after all, it had taken Western countries themselves a long period of time to establish a rule of law, extend the franchise and secure the rights of ordinary citizens. But as the Putin leadership consolidated itself, it began to appear that any movement was in the other direction; not only this, the new leadership made clear that it had no intention of establishing a 'second edition' of the political system of the United States or the United Kingdom but rather a system that was closer to Russia's own traditions and circumstances.

All of this left analysts in some difficulty in the early years of the new century, and as Putin was succeeded by Dmitri Medvedev in a presidential election that Western observers regarded as unsatisfactory and yet at the same time a reasonably accurate reflection of the public mood. Was this a variant of democracy – 'hybrid', 'partial', 'defective', or some other kind of 'democracy with adjectives'? Would it not be better, some began to argue, to abandon the assumption that Russia and the other former Soviet republics were best understood in the language of 'democracy' – or even 'transition' – simply because they were no longer under communist rule (the most eloquent statement of this view was Carothers 2002)? Wasn't this just as deterministic and culture-bound as the assumption the Soviet leadership had made in its own time, that the first socialist countries would inevitably be followed by others until the entire world was under communist rule? But if Russia and the other states that it resembled were not 'democracies' or very obviously 'in transition', how were their contemporary politics to be understood?

Issues of institutional design

Formally, at least, the constitution of December 1993 had marked a significant step forward. It was a constitution that committed the new state to 'ideological pluralism', 'political diversity' and 'multiparty politics', and there could be no 'compulsory ideology' of any kind. A whole chapter dealt with the rights and freedoms of the individual, including equality before the law, and equal rights for men and women. There were guarantees of personal inviolability and privacy. There was freedom of conscience, including the right to practise and to 'disseminate religious and other views and act according to them'. The state itself would be a secular one, with a strict separation between the churches and the temporal authorities. There was freedom of movement, within and across national boundaries. Press freedom was guaranteed, and censorship as such was abolished. In the courts, similarly, all had the right to a qualified defence lawyer, and were presumed innocent until proved guilty.

There were some provisions, indeed, that went further than established practices in many of the liberal-democratic countries. There was a commitment to freedom of information that allowed citizens to access whatever information was held about them by any organ of government unless security considerations dictated otherwise. There was a more general commitment to the 'generally recognised principles and norms of international law', and in the event of any disagreement international norms were to have precedence, which was a remarkable qualification of national sovereignty. And there were economic guarantees: the right of private property was protected by law, including the right to hold and to dispose of property and pass it on by inheritance. This included specific recognition of private ownership of land, on a basis to be established by subsequent legislation, and the right of citizens to engage in business. All these rights, moreover, were entrenched: in other words, they could not be amended without a complicated procedure involving a constitutional conference and (normally) a referendum.

At the same time there were grave weaknesses in Russia's new institutional design. For a start, it had been unilaterally imposed, after the order had been given to suppress the Russian parliament in September 1993 and then, in early October, to bomb it into submission. The president had no authority at this time to dissolve parliament, or suspend its sittings; indeed, the constitution as it stood at the time specifically prohibited him from doing so. Yeltsin had taken an oath of allegiance to this constitution when he was inaugurated as Russian president in July 1991. And although he found himself in a difficult position in the early post-communist years, facing a parliament that was hostile to much of what he wanted to do, it was still this parliament that had elected him its chairman in 1990 and then given him extraordinary powers. A more balanced set of proposals was beginning to emerge in the discussions that followed, up to the constitutional conference that met in the summer of 1993 whose outcome was a draft that Yeltsin himself described as 'neither presidential, nor parliamentary'. Indeed there were attempts to mediate even after the president had imposed his own preferences in a television broadcast on the evening of 21 September. But once the parliament had been taken by force and its leadership had been imprisoned, there was little reason to qualify what became an even more strongly presidential final draft.

The new Russian constitution, in the form in which it was adopted in December 1993, was a seriously unbalanced one. Formally, there was a separation of powers. The president had powers in relation to the Duma and the Duma had powers in relation to the president, both of them protected from abuse by an independent judicial system. But the president's powers, it became clear, were extraordinarily extensive in theory and practice: in particular, his power to dismiss the government, as Yeltsin did five times between March 1998 and August 1999, and as Putin did twice (in February 2004 and September 2007), without reference to public or parliamentary opinion. It was because of these far-reaching powers that Russia was often held to have not just a presidential system, but a 'super-presidential' one (see for instance Holmes 1993–4; Colton 1995; Fish 2005). As Yeltsin himself acknowledged after the new constitutional draft had been published, 'I don't deny that the powers of the president in the draft constitution are considerable', he told *Izvestiya* (15 November 1993: 4), 'but what do you expect in a country that is used to tsars and strong leaders?'

The Duma also enjoyed a direct mandate, but its influence over the executive was very limited. Its 'consent' was needed for the appointment of a new prime minister, but if that consent was withheld three times it was automatically dissolved. It could pass a vote of no confidence in the government, but if it did so twice in three months the president could either replace the government or else dissolve the Duma and call new elections. The president, for his own part, could dismiss the entire government at any time, for any reason. And although he could be impeached, it was with a great deal of difficulty. Under the 1993 Constitution an action of this kind could only be taken in the event of treason or a crime of similar gravity, and after the Supreme Court and Constitutional Court had both confirmed that there was a basis for proceeding. Even when the president was unable to exercise his powers effectively because of bad health or other reason, as was occasionally the case under Boris Yeltsin, he remained disproportionately powerful. Presidential elections, inevitably, became a contest for the state itself (although it was only in 1996 that the incumbent faced a serious challenge), the constitution became a set of rules of the game that those who held power found most congenial, and parliamentary elections had only marginal significance – certainly, they had nothing to do with 'winning power'.

On the face of it, a more balanced set of constitutional arrangements came into effect in the spring of 2008 with the formation of the Putin–Medvedev (or was it Medvedev–Putin) 'tandem'. Putin himself, speaking to the foreign press later in the year, pointed out that the prime minister was now the leader of a party that had an overall majority in the Duma, and suggested that this was a sign of the 'increased influence of parliament'. But the 'final word remain[ed] with the President' (*Izvestiya*, 2 June 2008: 2). Medvedev, for his part, insisted that a parliamentary republic was simply not appropriate for Russia, at that time or in the future, although it could be considered again in 'two or three hundred years' time' (ibid. 12 December 2007: 3). Russia, he told interviewers, had 'always developed around a strong executive authority. These lands have been gathered over the centuries, and they can't be governed any other way' (*Versiya* 25 February 2008: 12). For some, the example of Ukraine was instructive: the changes that had taken place since the 'Orange revolution' at the end of 2004 had strengthened the prime minister as against the president, but left it unclear who really determined (for instance) foreign and defence policy. The result was indecision and a continuing struggle for personal ascendancy.

The 'tandem' was in any case some distance from a French semi-presidential system, with a prime minister who could (and sometimes did) represent an oppositional party and who had to command a majority in the assembly as well as the confidence of the president, in a system in which the parties themselves were autonomous and the elections genuinely competitive. So long as the entire process, in Russia, was controlled by the governing authorities, there was little prospect of a parliament that would hold them effectively to account. All that had taken place, from this perspective, was a redistribution of responsibilities within a relatively small and homogeneous ruling group who were all the beneficiaries of a system in which state officials were increasingly involved in the management of the largest companies as well as government itself. It mattered little, in such circumstances, if the constitution was amended in December 2008 to require the government to present an annual report to parliament. It was far more important that the parliament itself would in future be elected for a five-year and the president for a six-year term; on top of the abolition of the single-member constituencies and the direct election of governors, the effect was to open up an even wider gap between ordinary citizens and the government that spoke in their name.

Countervailing forces of all kinds were poorly developed in early postcommunist Russia. There were plenty of political parties, but the authorities regulated them closely under an increasingly restrictive law and made sure that their own 'party of power' – latterly, United Russia – was normally dominant (see Chapter 5). It took a commanding majority of seats in the Russian parliament after the 2003 election, and latterly absorbed other smaller parties as well as individual deputies in a manner that made it even more reminiscent of the Communist Party of the Soviet past. A registration exercise meanwhile reduced the numbers of parties themselves by about half, ostensibly because they had failed to demonstrate a minimum membership of 50,000 but (in the view of those that were disappointed) for political reasons as well. And yet how else, other than by a functioning party system, were Russian voters to be given an organised choice of political alternatives? There were trade unions as well, and they repeatedly made clear that they could bring millions into the streets on 'days of action'. But levels of membership were a fraction of what they had been in the Soviet period, and in any case the trade union leadership had a substantial stake in the *status quo* through the range of properties they managed and the salaries they were able to command.

The press might have represented another check on executive authority, but its circulation had fallen dramatically since the late Soviet years and its ownership was increasingly in the hands of Kremlin-friendly oligarchs (see Chapter 7). A very few titles – for instance, *Novaya gazeta*, a twice-weekly paper supported by ex-President Gorbachev – offered an alternative view; and there were some national dailies that permitted a diversity of opinion, such as the mildly liberal *Nezavisimaya gazeta*, the business paper *Kommersant* and the long-established and serious-minded *Izvestiya*. But their circulations were hardly on the kind of scale that could represent even a potential challenge to Kremlin authority (respectively 40,000, 113,000 and 150,000 copies daily in 2009). Television was a far more potent form of influence, but for this reason it was even more closely controlled; other technologies were available, but their reach was much less than in other developed nations (there were three or four times as many internet users in the United Kingdom and the United States, relative to population, and many more had telephone mainlines, although Russia was ahead of the United States in mobile phone ownership: UNDP 2007b: 273–4). The result was that whole areas of the political agenda remained in partial or total obscurity: such as human rights abuses in the North Caucasus, government corruption, organised crime, and police torture.

It was also clear that independent-minded journalists would be at some risk if they inconvenienced the rich and powerful. The case of Anna Politkovskaya, shot dead in October 2006 in what appeared to be a contract killing, made headlines across the world; her outspoken writings on the Chechen war, and on the Putin system as a whole, had made her a lot of enemies. But she was one of very many examples of attacks on journalists, some of them from her own newspaper, *Novaya gazeta*. In November 2008 a former colleague, now the editor of a local paper in the Moscow suburb of Khimki, was assaulted near his home and left unconscious; he survived in hospital, but lost a leg. He had been a persistent opponent of the local administration, criticising its plans to drive a new road through a local forest and demolish a war memorial that stood in the way (*Guardian*, 18 November 2008: 19). Another casualty was *Kommersant*'s military correspondent, Ivan Safronov, who leapt out of a fifth-floor window of the block of flats in which he lived in an apparent case of suicide, but following his discovery of sensitive information about

Russian arms sales to Iran and Syria that could have embarrassed senior officials (ibid. 10 March 2007: 19).

In early 2009 it was the turn of a human rights lawyer, Stanislav Markelov, who was shot dead in the middle of the afternoon on a busy street in Moscow city centre. Markelov had worked, like Politkovskaya, for *Novaya gazeta*. The killer also shot a trainee journalist, employed by the same paper, who had been walking him to the metro and had tried to give chase when the killer opened fire; she died later in hospital. As well as his work as a journalist Markelov had represented the family of a young Chechen woman who had been raped and then murdered in 2000 by a drunken Russian army colonel, Yuri Budanov, in a case that became something of a cause célèbre. Budanov had been given a ten-year sentence, in the face of fierce opposition from army generals and nationalist groups, but was released early; Markelov had just announced that he would be appealing against the decision to the Russian Supreme Court (*Guardian*, 20 January 2009: 16). Russia was one of the most dangerous countries in the world in which to carry out such duties, according to the Committee to Protect Journalists; between 1992 and the end of 2008 there were 49 deaths, behind only Iraq and Algeria (see www.cpj.org); on other, more inclusive counts there had been more than 200 (see www.ifj.org).

Perhaps most fundamentally, the rule of law remained uncertain (see Chapter 8, which takes a more positive view). Judges, certainly, were 'independent' and 'inviolable' according to the Constitution. But the Constitutional Court, which was supposed to regulate the behaviour of the president as well as of the highest levels of government, was appointed on the nomination of the president himself. Under the previous constitution, up to 1993, the Constitutional Court had been elected by the Congress of People's Deputies and it had countermanded the president's decisions on several important occasions (the fullest study is Trochev 2008). As long as the appointment of judges was (in practice) in the hands of government, it was unlikely that the courts would protect the rights of ordinary citizens if they were infringed by the authorities themselves, and unlikely that individual ministers would be held to account for their decisions and if necessary for any wrongdoing. Perhaps the central theme of President Medvedev's various addresses to the nation, even before his election, was 'legal nihilism': the disregard of law, and the damage that was done to the economy and to public life by its routine violation. But until the administration of justice was more clearly separated from government itself, there would hardly be a qualitative improvement.

The press was certainly full of cases in which the rights of ordinary citizens had been seriously violated by the rich and powerful. Lawyer Inna Yermoshkina, for instance, was not unduly bothered when she found a group of police officers was waiting by the entrance to her apartment building when she returned home one evening in May 2008. But when the plain-clothes officers surrounded Yermoshkina and her husband and a uniformed officer ordered their arrest, she realised that things were rather more serious. She was handcuffed, placed in a police car and assaulted; her husband was meanwhile escorted up to their apartment, where the police confiscated documents she had gathered about relatives of senior city and government officials, supposedly in connection with a fraud investigation. 'That will teach you not to step on the toes of important people', she was told. In practice, Yermoshkina concluded, she was being targeted because of a series of complaints about the corruption that appeared to be widespread in the granting of licences to practise as notaries – relatively few were issued, so that earnings were very high, and Yermoshkina had complained that too many of the licences were being given to the relatives of powerful officials instead of lawyers who were well qualified but politically unconnected (*Moscow Times*, 3 October 2008: 1–2).

Assessing 'democracy'

No political system has yet achieved a perfect balance between the powers that governments need to do their job and the mechanisms that are available to allow citizens to hold them to account. But experience to date has certainly suggested that the rights of individual citizens are more likely to be at risk if the powers of governments are excessive and if the mechanisms that are available to check them are unduly weak. There have been many attempts, since at least the time of Aristotle, to identify the defining characteristics of forms of government on this basis, usually by comparing the degree of authority that rulers are allowed to command and the number of people that are allowed to exercise it. Perhaps the most successful in recent years have been those that have avoided general judgements about 'democracy' and still more so a numerical scale in order to concentrate on a particular set of rights that can be assessed with some degree of objectivity across a range of countries, in all of which the government will ideally have made a formal commitment to the rights in question under international law.

One of the most systematic of these inquiries is conducted by Amnesty International, a non-governmental body established in the 1960s whose particular concern is the treatment of peaceful protest. According to its statute, Amnesty has a 'vision of a world in which every person enjoys all of the human rights enshrined in the Universal Declaration of Human Rights [of 1948] and other international human rights instruments' (see www.amnesty.org.uk). It works through a network of national branches and a much wider network of individual members, drawing for the most part on their subscriptions and taking great care to avoid financial support of any kind that might compromise its independence. It seeks not only to identify and document human rights abuses, particularly the arrest and maltreatment of 'prisoners of conscience' who have refrained from the advocacy of violence, but also to mobilise international opinion so that abuses are quickly remedied and innocent victims released from incarceration. It publishes an annual report as well as a whole series of statements on individual countries and human rights concerns, drawing on a full-time staff and periodic field visits.

Amnesty, deliberately, provides no kind of score or ranking; nor does it assume that the established Western democracies are beyond criticism. In the United Kingdom, for instance, Amnesty was concerned in its 2008 report that individuals continued to be returned to states where they would face a real risk of torture on the strength of unenforceable 'diplomatic assurances'. It also believed that secrecy in the implementation of counter-terrorism measures was leading to 'unfair judicial proceedings'; and there were 'continued failures of accountability for past violations', including 'alleged state collusion in killings in Northern Ireland'. The United States continued to hold hundreds of foreign nationals at its naval base in Guantanamo, the vast majority without charge and without the ability to challenge the legality of their detention. The Central Intelligence Agency continued to follow policies of secret detention and interrogation, and a number of videotapes of these interrogations, which might have provided incriminating evidence, had been destroyed. On top of this there were 'serious failings in state, local and federal measures to address sexual violence against Native American women'; there was evidence of discrimination in a variety of areas, including policing, the operation of the criminal justice system and housing rights; and the death penalty was still applied (see www.thereport.amnesty.org).

But although there was no explicit comparison, it was clear from successive reports that there was much more to worry about in post-communist Russia. The Russian authorities, Amnesty found, were 'increasingly intolerant of dissent or criticism' and increasingly inclined to call it 'unpatriotic'. There had been a 'crackdown on civil and political rights', particularly during the run-up to the December 2007 parliamentary election. Given the strict control that had been established over television and other media, public discontent tended to find an outlet in demonstrations of various kinds; but these 'were the flashpoint during the year for political protests, with police detaining demonstrators, journalists, and human rights activists', some of whom had been beaten. There had been an increase in racially motivated attacks, in which at least 61 people had lost their lives. And all kinds of abuses had been taking place in Chechnya, some of which were being considered by the European Court of Human Rights, which ruled that Russia had been responsible for enforced disappearances, torture and extrajudicial executions in fifteen cases during the year. Serious human rights violations, according to Amnesty, were 'frequent'; detainees were tortured in order to extract 'confessions' as well as for other reasons; and violence against prisoners was widely practised.

The same kinds of concerns appeared in other reports, such as those produced by the New York-based organisation Human Rights Watch (see www.hrw.org). Founded more than thirty years ago, Human Rights Watch is 'dedicated to protecting the human rights of people around the world', aiming to 'prevent discrimination, to uphold political freedom, to protect people from inhumane conduct in wartime, and to bring offenders to justice'. Like Amnesty, it produces an annual report as well as the results of a series of more specific investigations. And like Amnesty, it found much that was troubling as Putin's second presidential term came to an end. Medvedev's election, they found, had not resulted in improvements in the rule of law or the environment for civil society, with the government 'continuing to crack down against independent groups and activists'. Amendments to the law on extremism allowed any politically or ideologically motivated crime to be designated in this way, and the law was itself being used arbitrarily to initiate cases against NGOs, activists and the independent media, including internet sites and blogs. All of this was an 'unmistakable part of the Russian government's efforts to weaken – in some cases beyond recognition – the checks and balances needed for an accountable government'.

Amnesty, Human Rights Watch and (among others) the US State Department in its annual reports on human rights around the world avoid any explicit comparison between one country and another, still more so any attempt to attach a numerical value to their respective performance. A rather different approach is taken by Freedom House of New York, which has been producing its Comparative Survey of Freedom since the early 1970s and which aims at an 'annual evaluation of political rights and civil liberties anywhere in the world' that can be expressed in two seven-point scales (see www.freedomhouse.org). For Freedom House, political rights are the 'extent that the people have a choice in determining the nature of the system and its leaders', and civil liberties are the 'freedoms to develop views, institutions and personal autonomy apart from the state'; both of these are in turn derived from a more detailed and continuously revised checklist of criteria. Based on these scores, countries could be classified as 'free' (if they averaged between 1 and 2.5), 'partly free' (if they averaged between 3 and 5), or 'not free' (if they averaged between 5.5 and 7).

It was clear, on the basis of these criteria, that the end of communist rule had brought about no dramatic or lasting improvement (see Figure 15.1). The USSR, in the Brezhnev years, had been 'not free', but in 1990, while still under communist rule, it was judged to have become 'partly free'. The new union treaty that was under consideration at this time, Freedom House explained, was based on human rights and the creation of a democratic state based on popular representation and the rule of law. All the fifteen republics had declared some form of sovereignty, and the Soviet parliament had adopted laws guaranteeing freedom of the press and freedom of conscience (*Freedom Review*, January–February 1991: 8). Russia, as a Soviet republic, had a higher score, and so did early post-communist Russia, but it never became more than 'partly free' in terms of the Comparative Survey, and its rating was already falling as the decade advanced. In 2004, at the end of Putin's first presidential term, the score fell again, this time into the 'not free' category. By 2009 Russia was still considered 'not free', with a score of 6 for political rights and 5 for civil

Figure 15.1   *Freedom House ratings, selected countries (1980–2008)*

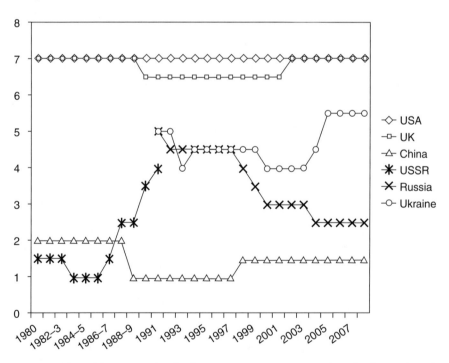

Source: Adapted from www.freedomhouse.org; scores average 'political rights' and 'civil liberties', and have been scaled from 7 = top to 1 = bottom.

liberties; this placed it just above Iran and Iraq, at exactly the same point on the scale as Angola, Cambodia, Egypt, Rwanda and several other Asian or African countries. Of the fifteen former Soviet republics, only the Baltic states and Ukraine were considered to be 'free' at this time. Armenia, Moldova, Georgia and Kyrgyzstan were 'partly free'; and all the others, including Russia, were 'not free'.

Freedom House also produced an annual report, which made clear some of the reasons for this undistinguished showing. The Duma election in December 2007, in its view, had marked a 'new low in the Kremlin's manipulations of the political process'. Access for outside observers had been 'sharply restricted' and the campaign environment had favoured Kremlin-sponsored parties, which had won the 'vast majority of seats'. Not only this, but Putin had announced that he intended to remain on the political stage after his second presidential term came to an end in 2008, advantaging the figures from the security agencies usually known as the *siloviki* that he had appointed to top positions in the government and state-owned enterprises, and setting Russia on a 'firmly authoritarian course'. There were 'strict limits' on opposition political parties, public demonstrations, the media and non-governmental organisations, and no serious attempt had so far been made to address Russia's extensive corruption. The judiciary, meanwhile, suffered from inadequate funding and a lack of qualified personnel, and there were continuing reports of poor prison conditions and the 'widespread use of torture and ill-treatment by law enforcement officials to extract confessions', especially in the North Caucasus. A separate report found the Russian media 'not free', and in further decline.

Democracy and 'sovereign democracy'

All of these, admittedly, were 'Western' judgements. And consciously or otherwise, they reflected the assumptions of Western liberal democracy: in their focus on the individual rather than the collective, in their emphasis on procedural form rather than substantive outcome, and in the priority they attached to formal rights as against social and economic performance. Both East and West (and other countries) had agreed at various times to a common set of criteria, most notably the Universal Declaration of Human Rights that had been approved in 1948. But the Universal Declaration was itself a compromise, embracing both the Western 'liberal' freedoms and the communist world's emphasis on social and economic rights. The classic 'liberal' rights were all there, including equality before the law, freedom of movement, freedom of thought and conscience, freedom of expression and freedom of assembly, based on a government that had been constituted by 'periodic and genuine elections'. But so too were the social and economic rights to which the USSR and its allies attached no less importance, including the right to work, to social security, and to 'a standard of living adequate for the health and wellbeing of himself and of his family'. Predictably, Western countries attached most importance to their comprehensive range of liberal and individual rights; the communist world (and some Catholic and Islamic countries) laid more emphasis on the extent to which they provided full employment and a comprehensive system of social welfare.

At first, it had seemed that Russia and the other post-communist countries would take the same view of these matters as their Western counterparts once they were no longer obliged to commit themselves to Marxism–Leninism. Hadn't the Cold War come to an end? Wasn't this supposed to represent the 'end of history'? But Russia and the other former Soviet republics had developed in rather different ways over long periods of time. For the most part, they had not experienced Roman law, with its insistence on the rights of private property, and they had no more experience of feudalism, which in its 'classic' Western form had provided a framework of reciprocal obligations that could develop into a rule of law. They shared a Christian religion, but it was Eastern or Orthodox Christianity, in which church and state were more closely associated and the individual conscience was less securely protected. In one influential view (Huntington 1993) the Slavic or Orthodox Christian world was a distinct 'civilisation', and one in which it was much less likely that liberal democracy would develop and be sustained than in the Christian West. None of this made it impossible for Russia and the other post-Soviet republics to move in a 'democratic' direction; but it meant that they were likely to do so more slowly and irregularly, or not at all, and in either case it was likely to be in a way that reflected their distinctive values and traditions.

There was accordingly some basis for Putin to insist, from the outset of his presidency, that Russia would and should not attempt to be a

> second edition of, say, the US or Britain, where liberal values have deep historic traditions. Our state and its institutions and structures have always played an exceptionally important role in the life of the country and its people. For Russians, a strong state is not an anomaly to be got rid of. Quite the contrary, it is a source of order and the main driving force of any change.

Russians, Putin explained in his millennium address, had come to value the benefits of democracy, a state based on law, and personal and political freedom. But they were 'alarmed by the obvious weakening of state power' and looked forward to a 'certain restoration of the guiding and regulating role of the state, proceeding from Russia's traditions as well as the current state of the economy' – traditions that were collective rather than individual, and in which it was assumed that improvements in living conditions would come from the state rather than the efforts of individual citizens (*Rossiiskaya gazeta*, 31 December 1999: 5). 'From the very beginning', Putin told a group of journalists shortly afterwards, 'Russia was created as a supercentralised state. That's practically laid down in its genetic code, its traditions, and the mentality of its people' (*First Person* 2000: 186).

Putin was equally clear that Russia was and would remain a democratic country, but one that would choose its own way of realising the democratic ideal. The experience of the 1990s, as he put it in his millennium address, had 'eloquently testifie[d] that a genuinely successful renewal of our homeland without excessive costs [could] not be achieved by the simple transfer to Russian soil of abstract models and schemes taken from foreign textbooks', or by the 'mechanical copying of other nations' experience' (ibid.: 212). Russia, he explained in his 2005 presidential address, had shared the common experience of other European countries, extending human rights, widening the franchise, protecting the weak and emancipating women, sometimes taking the lead in these developments. And Russia had chosen democracy

> for itself, by the will of its own people. It started out on this path itself and, observing all the generally accepted democratic norms, [would] itself decide in what way – taking account of its historical, geopolitical or any other specific features – it [could] guarantee the realisation of the principles of freedom and democracy. As a sovereign country Russia can and will decide for itself on the stages and conditions of any movement along this path. (*Rossiiskaya gazeta*, 26 April 2005: 3–4)

It was a democracy, he told Slovak television, that would 'be adapted to the realities of contemporary Russian life, to our traditions and our history. And we will do this ourselves' (*Nezavisimaya gazeta*, 25 February 2005: 1).

What was perhaps most distinctive in this vision was that the choice of political form should be for Russia alone and that it should avoid anything that weakened the state and allowed it to be manipulated from outside. This was a view that was widely shared across the defence and security officials, collectively known as the *siloviki*, who became an increasingly influential component of the leadership during the Putin years. But it also reflected an understandable reaction, not just in government, to the near-collapse of the state that had taken place during the Yeltsin years, and to the breakup of the Soviet Union that had preceded it.

Communism, Putin explained in his millennium address, had achieved a great deal; but Russians had paid an 'outrageous price' for a social experiment that had left them 'lagging consistently behind the economically advanced countries'. The Soviet state was a different matter, and Putin went as far in his 2005 presidential address as to describe its disintegration as the 'greatest geopolitical catastrophe of the century'. Tens of millions of Russian citizens had found themselves outside their native territory, and an 'epidemic of collapse' had threatened to overwhelm Russia itself. Savings had been devalued; old ideals had been rejected; and many institutions had been dissolved or replaced much too hastily (*Rossiiskaya gazeta*, 26 April 2005: 3).

Concerns of this kind were greatly strengthened when a series of governments in the post-Soviet area were overthrown in the mid-2000s in what became known as the 'coloured revolutions'. Putin and those who shared his thinking were in no doubt that the entire process had been engineered in Washington, and that it was designed to shift as much as possible of the remainder of the Soviet Union into the Western sphere of influence. The 'Orange revolution' in Ukraine at the end of 2004 was particularly important. This was the largest of the other post-Soviet states, with a long common border and a substantial proportion of its citizens who were Russians by language or nationality; but in spite of Putin's open support for his opponent, it was the pro-Western candidate, Viktor Yushchenko, who eventually became president after extended and (as Moscow saw it) externally financed street demonstrations. Putin made clear, shortly afterwards, that he would not allow other countries to turn Russia into an 'amorphous state formation' that could be manipulated from outside in the same kind of way (*Nezavisimaya gazeta*, 25 February 2005: 1). And it was this experience that appears to have been the most direct inspiration for the restrictions that were increasingly imposed on Russian non-governmental organisations, and the attempt that began to be made to develop a coherent narrative of the larger purposes of the Putin presidency.

Gradually, particularly in the writings of presidential advisor Vladislav Surkov, an elaboration of this distinctively Putinist set of objectives began to take shape. It received the name 'sovereign democracy', understood as a form of rule that shared general democratic principles but combined them with the ability to take decisions without deferring to the views of other powers – in other words, real rather than nominal sovereignty. Surkov had already set out his views in a widely noted newspaper interview in late 2004. In the outside world, he told the paper, there were two groups of people: those who wanted a strong and prosperous Russia as a 'good neighbour and reliable ally', and those who were 'still living out the phobias of the cold war', who were trying to build on what they saw as their success in undermining the Soviet Union and whose aim was to 'destroy Russia and fill its enormous territory with numerous unviable quasi-state formations'. The allies of this second group were a 'fifth column of left and right radicals' who had much in common, including their foreign sponsorship and their hostility to their own country (*Komsomol'skaya pravda*, 29 September 2004: 4).

The new term, 'sovereign democracy', came into public use in the spring of 2005, in a journalist's commentary on Putin's presidential address of that year. But there was 'no particular effort to conceal that behind this and many analogous publications stood Surkov and his colleagues' (Ivanov 2008: 236). In at least one authoritative exposition, sovereign democracy was a political regime that satisfied the following conditions (Filippov 2007: 446–7):

1 Responsibility for state decisions is placed by the Constitution in the hands of elected officials.
2 These officials are periodically selected in freely conducted elections that exclude any compulsion.
3 Practically the entire adult population has the right to elect public officials.
4 Practically the entire adult population has the right to seek election to public office.
5 Citizens have the ability to express their opinions without fearing political persecution.
6 Citizens have the right to receive information from alternative sources. Alternative sources of information are protected by the law.
7 Citizens have the right to set up independent associations and organisations, including political parties and associations of like-minded people.
8 The state is wholly sovereign. It has a monopoly on the legitimate use of force and raising of taxes, controls the territory and guarantees security, in other words, is in the full sense of the word a state. It controls the national economy, including strategically important sectors, infrastructure and communications. The significance of various branches may change over time: in the past the key means of communications was the railway, and in the future it may be cosmodromes, but the requirement of national control remains the same. If the national economy is dependent on foreign capital, imports or the fluctuations of the world market, a consuming country is not in a position to defend its interests ... Real sovereignty signifies the ability of a state in reality (and not just in declarations) to conduct its own independent domestic, foreign and defence policy, to conclude and dissolve agreements, to enter or decline to enter relations of strategic partnership, and so forth.

It was clearly this last, eighth point that was the most important and the most controversial.

'Sovereign democracy', as a concept, had opponents as well as supporters. Deputy premier Sergei Ivanov, a figure with a background in defence and security, was one of the most favourable, declaring sovereign democracy the 'quintessence of our internal order', implying the right of citizens to determine their country's policies themselves and to protect that right from outside pressure by any means, including the use of force'. It was one of a 'triad of national values', including a strong economy and military power. There was no democracy in the abstract; all democratic states had their own particular features, and indeed it was one of the main democratic values that states could make these choices for themselves (*Izvestiya* 14 July 2006: 4). Former prime minister Yevgenii Primakov, at the other extreme, was 'categorically opposed' to the use of the term as it could 'lead to the denial of such general human values as the separation of powers, freedom of choice and so on' (*Profil'* no. 27, 2006: 14). Rather more important, Dmitri Medvedev, at this time Ivanov's counterpart as first deputy prime minister, was also opposed to the new orthodoxy. 'Sovereign democracy', he thought, was 'far from an ideal term', as it combined two entirely different concepts; it would have been more correct to speak of 'genuine democracy', or of 'democracy within a comprehensive state sovereignty'. Apart from that it left a 'strange aftertaste' if the term democracy was qualified in any way (*Ekspert* no. 28, 2006: 59).

Surkov, in turn, expressed himself less interested in the term itself and rather more in what it represented. Only a people who had some overall idea of who they were and where they were going could develop organically. And only if they developed their own discourse, their own public philosophy, a national ideology that was acceptable at least to the majority and ideally to all, would they be taken seriously in the wider world. Sovereign democracy was just the first step in this process, and it made no claim to represent the 'truth in the final instance' (*Izvestiya* 31 August 2006: 1). They were 'not in some kind of philology club', he told a United Russia meeting the following month. What was important was the kind of policies that would give Russia back her status as a major world power that was independent not just on paper. Almost all the world's constitutions included a reference to sovereignty; but only a few dozen states were actually independent. The others had neither the military nor the economic capability that would allow them to make their own decisions and not do what someone else told them. 'Do we want to be a self-sufficient country', asked Surkov, 'or should we rely on other, more powerful nations for help? Who said that we should stop trying to be a sovereign people?' (ibid. 13 September 2006: 2).

United Russia was revising its party programme at about this time, and different views were being expressed about whether the concept of sovereign democracy should be included. In the event the party congress adopted a 'programmatic declaration' that called for a 'strategy of qualitative renewal of the country on the principles of sovereign democracy', and went on to define it in terms that were clearly reminiscent of those Surkov had suggested (Ivanov 2008: 249–51). It was also included in United Russia's manifesto for the December 2007 Duma election, in exactly the same words (ibid.: 287). Surkov and Medvedev had meanwhile agreed to bury their differences. As Medvedev explained, they were in complete agreement, with only 'terminological' differences between them. Democracy, as Medvedev put it, 'can be effective only in conditions of full state sovereignty, and sovereignty can achieve results only in conditions of a democratic political regime' (ibid.: 245). Whatever their apparent differences, it was reasonable to conclude that the political class agreed on the fundamentals: that a meaningful democracy was one in which decisions could be taken without being unduly influenced by the outside world; that this was more likely to be achieved in a country that was economically and militarily strong; and that any attempt to articulate an alternative was unhelpful, unpatriotic, and possibly subversive.

Conclusion

In the end, obviously, it was for Russians themselves to decide what kind of 'democracy', or any other political philosophy, they wished to adopt as the basis of their post-communist system. What could less readily be discounted was the accumulating evidence that the distribution of power in the years after Putin's accession had shifted so far towards the central authorities that the achievement of other objectives was in peril. It was understandable, after the near-collapse of the federation during the Yeltsin years, that later presidents would place a heavy emphasis on the effectiveness of government, which meant in practice the powers of the federal authorities in Moscow. It was understandable that they would have popular support in doing so, given the collapse in living standards that had accompanied the years of Yeltsinite 'reform'. And it was predictable that they would continue to have popular support in the years that followed, given high rates of economic growth that in turn were based on record oil prices on world markets.

But the system of government that consolidated during these years was centralised to such a degree that it generated problems of its own. If power was concentrated in the centre, it was the central authorities themselves that would be held responsible for any shortcomings. If institutions were weak, there would be little attachment to the decisions they generated unless they seemed of individual benefit. If the parliament was wholly compliant, laws would be poorly scrutinised and ministerial incompetence would not be exposed in good time. If the courts were unduly influenced by politicians, those who could afford to do so would try to buy the decisions they wanted instead of accommodating themselves to the rule of law. And if political parties were another branch of state power, they would disproportionately recruit careerists. This was certainly true of United Russia, if Putin himself was to be believed. Speaking in November 2007 he complained that the party was 'not an ideal political structure', that it lacked a 'stable ideology [or] principles for which the overwhelming majority of members would be prepared to assert themselves', and that because it was so close to government it attracted 'all kinds of hangers-on' (*Rossiiskaya gazeta*, 14 November 2007: 1).

There had been no resolution of these issues in the early years of the Medvedev presidency. And if there was going to be, it seemed likely that it would make more use of the mechanisms that had been developed in Western liberal democracies to deal with the same kinds of issues. The separation of powers would have to become a real one, so that courts became independent of government. A more even balance would have to be found between an over-powerful executive and an elected parliament. And elections themselves would have to become more genuine contests, without unreasonable barriers to participation and with independent institutions that could conduct them. The Russian tradition was indeed one in which the state had normally been strong, and paternalistic. But it had other elements as well – the city assemblies that had met in medieval Pskov and Novgorod; the self-governing peasant communities that Marx had seen as the harbinger of a communist society; the limited experience of parliamentary government that had accumulated in the early years of the twentieth century. If Russian politics was to be more effective in the future it was likely that it would draw on these indigenous traditions as well as the experience of other countries, and that they would be used to strengthen the accountability of government to those who gave it the authority to rule.

Guide to Further Reading

The listing that follows suggests a number of items that students and others may find useful to consult on the themes that are covered by each chapter of this book. Current developments in Russian politics are regularly considered in several academic journals such as *Europe-Asia Studies* (ten issues annually); the *Journal of Communist Studies and Transition Politics* (quarterly); *Post-Soviet Affairs* (quarterly); *Communist and Post-Communist Studies* (quarterly); and *Problems of Post-Communism* (six issues annually). Legal and constitutional issues across the post-communist countries generally are given particular attention in the *Review of Socialist Law* (quarterly). The *Current Digest of the Post-Soviet Press* (weekly, also available online) is a well organised digest of translations from newspapers and journals. Other electronic resources are considered in the final section.

Chapter 1   Politics in Russia

There are a number of good *overviews of the Soviet system*. These include Gooding (2001), Keep (1996), Kenez (1999), Malia (1994), Marples (2002), Sakwa (1998), Sandle (1997), Service (2005), Suny (1998) and Westwood (2002). The Gorbachev period is covered by Brown (1996, 2007), by Gorbachev himself (1987), and by Sakwa (1990) and White (1994). Arnason (1993) provides a fine analysis of the overall failure of the Soviet system, while Cox's edited book (1998) presents a number of debates about the academic study of the fall. More detailed analyses can be found in Kotkin (2001), Kotz and Weir (1997) and an overview in White (2000). General analyses of contemporary Russian politics can be found in Barany and Moser (2001), Brown (2001), Lane (2002), McFaul, Petrov and Ryabov (2004), Remington (2004) Ross (2004), and Sakwa (2008). Fine biographies of Yeltsin are provided by Aron (2000) and Colton (2008), and his leadership is compared with Gorbachev's by Breslauer (2002), while the Putin period is analysed by Herspring (2003) Sakwa (2008) and Shevtsova (2003), with his own views presented in Putin (2000).

Chapter 2   Semi-presidentialism and the Evolving Executive

Current information on the institutions, personalities, and politics of the Russian *presidency, federal executive, and political system* is most readily found on the internet, especially through gateway sites with specialist service such as those of the Center for Russian and East European Studies at the University of Pittsburgh (www.ucis.pitt.edu/reesweb/) and the Centre for Russian Studies of the Norwegian Institute of International Affairs (www.nupi.no/). Russian governmental websites have both Russian and English language areas, with the official internet site of the Russian presidency (www.president.kremlin.ru/) providing much information. For discussions of the *Putin presidency, policy programme and legacy*, see Åslund (2007), Flikke (2004), Shevtsova (2005), Trenin (2007), Willerton (2007), Sakwa (2008), and Hill and Cappelli (2008). On the development of the Russian presidency up to and including the Yeltsin period, see Huskey (1999), for a discussion of the dynamics of presidential popularity, see Mishler and Willerton (2003), and for an analysis of presidential decree issuance, see Protsyk (2004). For information on the career and legacy of Yeltsin, see Colton (2008), while Karppinen (2006) overviews Russia's political transformation under Yeltsin and Putin. For those fluent in Russian, Zen'kovich (2006) provides an encyclopedic coverage of the Putin regime. Kryshtanovskaya and White (2003) detail the role of security-intelligence officials under Putin. For discussions of Soviet period institutions and policies, see Hough (1979). Brown and Shevtsova (2001) compare the leadership of Gorbachev, Yeltsin, and Putin. A broader comparative discussion of the opportunities and dilemmas of presidential systems is provided in Mainwaring and Shugart (1997), while Wilson (2005) reviews the dilemmas in the crafting of a Russian democracy.

Chapter 3   Parliamentary Politics in Russia

The *Russian Constitution* of 1993 is available in a number of convenient editions, and may be consulted electronically at a number of locations; an easily followed English language version is available at www.departments.bucknell.edu/russian/const/constit.html (note that this and other online and printed versions may not always incorporate amendments, especially the extension of the parliamentary and presidential terms in December 2008). On *representative institutions* since the late Soviet period see McFaul (2001) and Remington (2001b), and on the contemporary Duma and Federation Council see Chaisty (2006), Remington (2006a, 2006b, 2003, 2007, 2008), Troxel (2003), and Smith and Remington (2001).

Chapter 4   Elections and Voters

On the difference between electoral democracies and competitive authoritarian regimes generally, see Diamond (1999, 2002) and Levitsky and Way (2002). On the *evolution of electoral politics* more generally in Russia, see White, Rose and McAllister (1997), McFaul (2001) and McFaul *et al.* (2004).

On specific election outcomes, see the reading suggested in the next section. On the development of Russian political parties, see Hale (2006) and Gel'man (2008) as well as Chapter 5 of this collection. On the Putin era see McFaul and Stoner-Weiss (2008) and Stoner-Weiss (2008).

Chapter 5   Russia's Political Parties and their Substitutes

For analysis of the overall evolution of Russia's *parties* up to and including the Putin presidency, see Gel'man (2005), Hale (2006) and White (2007). Comprehensive discussions of Russia's parties in individual election cycles can be found for 1993 in White, Rose, and McAllister (1997) and Colton and Hough (1998), for 1995–6 in White, Rose and McAllister (1997), Colton (2000) and Belin and Orttung (1997), for 1999–2000 in Colton and McFaul (2003), Hesli and Reisinger (2003), and Rose and Munro (2002), for 2003–4 in Hale, McFaul and Colton (2004), and for December 2007 in McAllister and White (2008). On parties during the late Soviet period and in Russia before the 1993 Duma election, see Fish (1995) and McFaul and Markov (1993). On the rise of United Russia, see Colton and McFaul (2000), Hale (2004a), Smyth, Wilkening and Urasova (2007), and Reuter and Remington (2009). For analysis of the CPRF's origins, see Urban and Solovei (1997) and March (2002). The fate of Russia's liberal parties is discussed in Hale (2004b) and Kullberg and Zimmerman (1999). The virtual parties are explained in Wilson (2005). Smyth (2006) supplies a discussion of Russian party organisation, and Hanson (2003) examines the role of ideology in Russian parties. McFaul (2001) treats the origins of Russia's election system and its effects on parties. On parties in the legislature, see Remington (2001) and the items listed in the recommended reading for Chapter 3.

Chapter 6   Russian Society and the State

Sperling (1999), a well-researched work with revealing insights, is a good starting place for reading on *social organisations in post-communist Russia*. The issues of the journal *Demokratizatsiya* for spring and summer 2002 (vol. 10, nos. 2 and 3) are devoted to the subject of civil society in contemporary Russia. The book edited by Mendelson and Glenn (2002) contains essays on non-governmental organisations in Eastern Europe and the post-Soviet states. Henderson (2003) adds to our knowledge of the impact of Western support on NGOs in Russia. The volume edited by Evans, Henry, and McIntosh Sundstrom (2006) covers the historical background and presents chapters by specialists on various segments of contemporary Russian civil society. The essays by Pyle (2006), Rutland (2006), Yakovlev (2006), and Markus (2007) offer informative analyses of the activity of business groups in Russia. The article by Clément (2008) makes an important contribution to the discussion of changes in civil society in Russia. The web site of the Public Chamber of the Russian Federation gives updates on the work of that body and also includes its reports for 2006, 2007, and 2008 (in Russian); it may be found at http://www.oprf.ru, and the links for the reports appear under 'Itogi raboty'.

Chapter 7   The Media and Political Communication

A wide range of current issues in Russian *media politics* is provided by the various chapters in White (2008). For a more detailed discussion of Russian election campaigns, television and the media audience, see Oates (2006b). On television itself, see most recently Benmers *et al.* (2009) and Hutchings and Rulyova (2009). For eyewitness accounts of how the media and parties behaved in a range of Russian elections, consult the reports from the now-defunct European Institute for the Media, archived online at http://www.media-politics.com/eimreports.htm. For an in-depth analysis of the journalistic profession, see Koltsova (2005). Some reflections on the Russian media and Kursk submarine tragedy can be found in Barany (2004). Both Voltmer (2000) and Pasti (2007) provide useful data and analysis on the workings of post-Soviet journalism; see also the special issue of *Index on Censorship*, no. 1 (2008). Andrei Richter's contributions to the topic of post-Soviet media developments have looked specifically at the ramifications of policy and the lack of it. For example, see the 2007 Post-Soviet Perspective on Censorship and Media Freedom published by UNESCO (available online at http://www.medialaw.ru/e_pages/publications/Rihter_englProtected.pdf) and the 2007 Post-Soviet Perspective on Licensing Television and Radio, published by the European Audiovisual Observatory. On 'media use in Putin's Russia' see Pietiläinen (2008).

Chapter 8   Legal Reform and the Dilemma of Rule of Law

For a comprehensive discussions of the *Russian legal system*, see Butler (2009), Danilenko and Burnham (2000) and Smith (1996). On assessing legal reform in Russia, see Hendley (2006), Solomon (2004), and Kurkchiyan (2003). For detailed analysis of the Russian Constitution and the Constitutional Court, see Trochev (2008), Smith and Sharlet (2008), and Ahdieh (1997). For assessments of the performance of other courts, see Solomon (2004), Trochev (2005) and Hendley (2002). On the reform of laws regulating the economy and commerce, see Oda (2007), Sachs and Pistor (1997) and Hendley (2004). For a further discussion of federalism and efforts to harmonise regional laws with federal laws and the Constitution, see Sharlet and Feldbrugge (2005) and Hahn (2003). On organised crime and corruption, see Serio (2008), Fortescue (2006), and Satter (2004).

Chapter 9   Reforming the Federation

For comparative studies of *federalism* see Burgess and Gagnon (1993), Burgess and Pinder (2007), Elazar (1987, 1991), Filippov, Ordeshook and Shvetsova (2004), and Watts (1999). There are substantial discussions of Russian federalism itself in Kahn (2002), Kempton and Clark (2002), Orttung and Reddaway (2005), Ross (2002a, 2002b), Ross and Campbell (2009), Stoliarov (2001) and Stoner-Weiss (2006). For studies of Russian federalism under Putin see Chebankova (2007a, 2007b), Gel'man (2009), Hahn (2004), Heinemann-Grüder (2002a, 2002b, 2009), Leksin (2004, 2005), Petrov and Slider (2007) and Ross (2005). For excellent overviews of federalism and regional politics in Russia see Sakwa (2008a) and (2008b). Older but still very useful studies are Hahn (2001), Kempton (2001), Stoner-Weiss (1999), and Stepan (2000). For those who read Russian there are particularly authoritative discussions in Turovsky (2006a) and (2006b).

Chapter 10   Politics in the Regions

Economic conditions in the *regions* and regional inequalities are described in detail in UNDP (2007a). Andrew Konitzer (2005) examines Russia's experience with the election of governors from the early 1990s until their suspension in 2004. The development of political parties in Russian regions is explored in Hutcheson (2003), Golosov (2004) and Hale (2006). Many topics connected with regional politics and the reform of local government are discussed in Evans and Gel'man (2004) and Ross and Campbell (2008).

Chapter 11   Managing the Economy

Events have moved so rapidly in Russia that general studies of the *economy and economic policy* can soon seem outdated. One older study of the political economy of reform in Russia, however, remains of interest for its approach: Shleifer and Triesman (2000), who treat reform in Russia as a trial-and-error process in which reformers, usually without a ready-made plan of action, negotiate their way around political obstacles as the latter materialise. This captures well the reform process under Yeltsin and, arguably, in the early Putin years. A slightly later book that is outstanding for balance and perspective is Sutela (2003). For penetrating analyses of policy issues with a wealth of institutional detail, the OECD *Economic Surveys of Russia*, published every two years, are excellent, and accessible to non-economists. A good way of keeping up with economic developments is the *BOFIT Weekly*, put out by the Bank of Finland Institute for Economies in Transition, available without charge at www.bof.fi. The particular issue of oil is well considered in Goldman (2008).

Chapter 12   Social Policy

Russian *social policy* is not as extensively covered in the secondary literature as some other areas covered in this book. A series of three books summarises a wealth of original social survey data and social policy debate: Manning, Shkaratan and Tikhonova (2000); Manning and Tikhonova (2004); and Manning and Tikhonova (2009). The edited collection by Field and Twigg (2000) is also useful. The European Bank for Reconstruction and Development (EBRD) regularly publishes reports on transition countries, and Russia is their biggest client. The specialist *Journal of European Social Policy*, in addition, gives frequent attention to Russian developments.

Chapter 13   Russian Foreign Policy

General accounts of Russian *foreign policy* under Putin may be found in Donaldson and Nogee (2009), Legvold (2007), Rumer (2007), Tsygankov (2006) and Lo (2003). On foreign policy decision making, see White in Allison *et al.* (2006). On Russian policy towards the near abroad, see Jonson (2004), Malfliet *et al.* (2007) and Safranchuk (2008). Russia's relations with the far abroad are covered by Ambrosio (2005), which deals with Russian-US relations, Allison *et al.* (2006), which deals with Russian relations with the EU and NATO, Antonenko and Pinnick (2005), which deals with Russian relations with the EU, and Smith (2006), which covers Russian relations with NATO. Ferdinand (2007) and Lo (2008) examine Sino-Russian relations. A selection of documents, many in English and other languages as well as Russian, may be found on the foreign ministry website www.mid.ru.

Chapter 14   The Military, Security and Politics

For discussions of the condition and readiness of the Russian *military*, see Miller and Trenin (2004), Herspring (2006) and Barany (2007). Webber and Mathers (2006), Betz (2004) and Barany (2008) focus on the links between the armed forces, society and politics. See Daucé and Sieca-Kozlowski (2006) and Webber and Zilberman (2006) on *dedovshchina*. Bukkvoll (2008) provides in-depth discussion of corruption in the military. Cooper (2006) considers many aspects of the defence economy, including secrecy and access to information about the defence budget. For discussions of the phenomenon of Putin and the *siloviki*, see Kryshtanovskaya and White (2003) and Renz (2006).

Chapter 15   Classifying Russia's Politics

The *nature of the Russian system* is regularly considered in the *Journal of Democracy* and in specific respects, in the annual reports of bodies such as Amnesty International (see www.thereport.amnesty.org) and Human Rights Watch (www.hrw.org). The US State Department's 'Country Reports on Human Rights Practices', which is based on the Universal Declaration of Human Rights, may be consulted at http://www.state.gov/g/drl/rls/hrrpt/. The Comparative Survey of Freedom sponsored by Freedom House may be consulted at www.freedomhouse.org; for a further discussion, see for instance White (2003) and Diamond (2008). On the 'end of the transition paradigm' see Carothers (2002); on 'semiauthoritarianism', see for instance Ottaway (2003). On 'sovereign democracy', see Evans (2008a).

Information Resources

Electronic resources may be most conveniently consulted through one of the gateways that provide a specialist service. Particularly comprehensive and well maintained is REESWeb, hosted by the University of Pittsburgh; its services include an annotated link list, a full-text search engine and a central announcement and calendar system (http://www.ucis.pitt.edu/reesweb/). The Library of Congress maintains a 'Portals to the World: Russia' at http://www.loc.gov/rr/international/european/russia/ru.html. Guides to electronic resources are maintained by several other libraries, including the British Library in London ('Guide to Slavonic and East European Internet Resources' at www.bl.uk), the School of Slavonic and East European Studies in London ('Directory of Internet Resources on Central and Eastern Europe and Russia' at www.ssees.ac.uk), and the Bodleian Library at Oxford University ('Guide to Slavonic & East European E-resources' at www.bodley.ox.ac.uk). An inter-university network maintains 'Intute', which provides a comprehensive and (above all) annotated selection of more than two hundred websites from and about the region at http://www.intute.ac.uk/socialsciences/cgi-bin/browse.pl?id=120952.

For *current events*, the Radio Free Europe/Radio Liberty Newsline from 1995 to 2008 may be consulted at http://www.rferl.org/archive/en-newsline/latest/683/683.html, and English-language versions of its broadcast coverage may be found at www.rferl.org. A very useful ongoing collection of journalistic writings on Russian politics and society is *Johnson's Russia List* (website and e-mail newsletter, by subscription, at http://www.cdi.org/russia/johnson/default.cfm). For the Russian government's perspective on current developments, in English, see for instance RIA Novosti (www.en.rian.ru), and Russia Profile (www.russiaprofile.org). The Voice of Russia broadcasts in English (www.ruvr.ru), and so does the television channel Russia Today (www.russiatoday.com). The *Moscow Times* (www.moscowtimes.ru) and *St Petersburg Times* (www.sptimes.ru) are lively and independent; they are available on subscription, but current issues may normally be consulted on their websites without charge.

References

Ahdieh, Robert B. (1997), *Russia's Constitutional Revolution*. University Park PA: Pennsylvania State University Press.

Aldrich, John H. (1995), *Why Parties?* Chicago: University of Chicago Press.

Allison, Roy (2008), 'Russia Resurgent? Moscow's Campaign to "Coerce Georgia to Peace"', *International Affairs*, vol. 84, no. 6 (November), pp. 1145–71.

Allison, Roy, Margot Light and Stephen White (2006), *Putin's Russia and the Enlarged Europe*. Oxford: Blackwell for the Royal Institute of International Relations.

Ambrosio, Thomas (2005), *Challenging America's Global Preeminence: Russia's Quest for Multipolarity*. Aldershot: Ashgate.

Andrews, Josephine T. (2002), *When Majorities Fail: The Russian Parliament, 1990–1993*. Cambridge and New York: Cambridge University Press.

Antonenko, Oksana and Kathryn Pinnick (eds) (2005), *Russia and the European Union: Prospects for a New Relationship*. London, Routledge.

Arnason, Johann P. (1993), *The Future that Failed: Origins and Destinies of the Soviet Model*. London: Routledge.

Arnold, Chloe (2007a), 'Conscript's Prostitution Claims Shed Light on Hazing', *Radio Free Europe/Radio Liberty Report*, 20 March. Available at http://rfe.rferl.org/featuresarticle/2007/03/09d16e9f-0374-4ca2-84f6-88b9b6f2d0e1.html.

Arnold, Chloe (2007b), 'Russia Federation Council Backs Tatarstan Power Sharing Treaty', RFE/RL *Russia Report*, 11 July.

Aron, Leon (2000), *Boris Yeltsin: A Revolutionary Life*. London: HarperCollins.

Article 19 (2006), 'Article 19's Statement on Proposed Amendments to the Russian Extremism Law', London: Article 19. Available online at http://www.article19.org/pdfs/press/russia-extremism-law.pdf.

Åslund, Anders (2007), *Russia's Capitalist Revolution: Why Market Reform Succeeded and Democracy Failed*. New York: Peterson Institute.

Bacon, Edwin and Bettina Renz with Julian Cooper (2006), *Securitising Russia: The Domestic Politics of Putin*. Manchester and New York: Manchester University Press.

Balmforth, R. (2002), 'Russia Sets New Rules for Police Holding Suspects', Reuters News Report, 26 April.

Barany, Z. (2004), 'The Tragedy of the Kursk: Crisis Management in Putin's Russia', *Government and Opposition*, vol. 39, no. 4, pp. 647–50.

Barany, Zoltan (2007), *Democratic Breakdown and the Decline of the Russian Military*. Princeton NJ: Princeton University Press.

Barany, Zoltan (2008), 'Civil-Military Relations and Institutional Decay: Explaining Russian Military Politics', *Europe-Asia Studies*, vol. 60, no. 4, pp. 581–604.

Barany, Zoltan and Robert G. Moser (eds) (2001), *Russian Politics: Challenges of Democratization*. Cambridge: Cambridge University Press.

Barnes, Andrew (2001), 'Property, Power, and the Presidency: Ownership Policy Reform and Russian Executive–Legislative Relations, 1990–1999', *Communist and Post-Communist Studies*, vol. 34, no. 1, pp. 39–61.

Belin, Laura (2005), 'Putin Returns Some Powers to Governors', RFE/RL *Newsline*, vol. 9, no. 127, part 1, 8 July.

Belin, Laura and Robert Orttung (1997), *The Russian Parliamentary Elections of 1995: The Battle for the Duma*. Armonk NY: M.E. Sharpe.

Bessarabov, V. and A. Rybchinsky (2001), 'Prokuratura Rossii: Federalizm i konstitutsionnaya zakonnost'', *Zakonnost*', no. 7, pp. 2–5.

Betz, David J. (2004), *Civil-MilitaryRelations in Russia and Eastern Europe*. London and New York: RoutledgeCurzon.

Beumers, Birgit, Hutchings, Stephen and Rulyova (eds) (2009) *The Post-Soviet Russian Media: Conflicting Signals*. London and New York: Routledge.

Biden, Joseph (2009) Speech in Munich. Consulted at http://halldor2.wordpress.com/2009/02/08/bidens-munich-declaration.

Bigg, Claire (2007), 'Russia: Judicial Reform Underway. But for the Right Reasons?', Radio Free Europe/Radio Liberty Report, 24 October. Available online at www.rferl/org/content/Article/1079013.html.

Bjelakovic, Nebojsa (2008), 'Russian Military Procurement: Putin's Impact on Decision-Making and Budgeting', *Journal of Slavic Military Studies*, vol. 21, no. 3, pp. 527–42.

Blank, Stephen (2008), *The Putin Succession and its Implications for Russian Politics*. Stockholm: Institute for Security and Development Policy.

Bogoslovskaya, Yelizaveta, Ella Polyakova and Yelena Vilenskaya (2001), 'The Soldiers' Mothers of St Petersburg: A Human Rights Movement in Russia', in *The Russian Military into the Twenty-First Century*, edited by Stephen J. Cimbala. London: Cass.

Breslauer, George W. (2002), *Gorbachev and Yeltsin as Leaders*. Cambridge: Cambridge University Press.

Brown, Archie (1996), *The Gorbachev Factor*. Oxford: Oxford University Press.

Brown, Archie (ed.) (2001), *Contemporary Russian Politics: A Reader*. Oxford: Oxford University Press.

Brown, Archie (2007), *Seven Years that Changed the World: Perestroika in Perspective*. Oxford: Oxford University Press.

Brown, Archie, and Lilia Shevtsova (eds) (2001), *Gorbachev, Yeltsin and Putin: Political Leadership in Russia's Transition*. Washington DC: Carnegie Endowment for International Peace.

Bruce, Chloë (2005), 'Fraternal Friction or Fraternal Fiction? The Gas Factor in Russian-Belarusian Relations', Oxford Institute for Energy Studies, NG 8 (March).

Bukkvoll, Tor (2008), 'Their Hands in the Till: Scale and Causes of Russian Military Corruption', *Armed Forces and Society*, vol. 34, no. 2, pp. 259–75.

Bunce, Valerie J. (1995), 'Should Transitologists be Grounded?', *Slavic Review*, vol. 54, no. 1, pp. 111–27.

Bureau of Economic Analysis (1998), *Survey on Economic Policy in Russia in 1997*, Moscow.

Burgess, Michael and A. G. Gaganon (eds) (1993), *Comparative Federalism and Federation*. Hemel Hempstead: Harvester Wheatsheaf.

Burgess, Michael and John Pinder (eds) (2007), *Multinational Federations*. London and New York: Routledge.

Bush, Jason (2007), 'Russian Labor Raises Its Voice', *Business Week*, no. 4062 (10 December), pp. 34–5.

Bush, Jason (2008), 'Russia's Raiders', Spiegel On-Line, 6 June. Available at www.spiegel.de/international/business/0,1518,druck-558096,00.html.

Butler, William E. (2009), *Russian Law*, 3rd edn. Oxford: Oxford University Press.

Carothers, Thomas (2002), 'The End of the Transition Paradigm', *Journal of Democracy*, vol. 13, no. 1 (January), pp. 5–21.

CEFIR (2007), *Monitoring administrativnykh bar"erov na puti razvitiya malogo biznesa v Rossii*. Moscow: Cefir.

Center for Journalists in Extreme Situations (2008), *Second Report on Media Coverage of the 2 December State Duma Elections* (1 October – 22 November 2007). Moscow: Center for Journalists in Extreme Situations.

Center for Journalists in Extreme Situations and the Russian Union of Journalists (2001), *Dangerous Profession: Monitoring of Violations of Journalists' Rights in the CIS*. Moscow: Human Rights Publishers.

Central and East European Law Initiative (2008), Consultation with criminal law experts (oral proceedings), Moscow, 7 May.

Chadwick, Andrew (2006), *Internet Politics: States, Citizens, and New Communication Technologies*. Oxford: Oxford University Press.

Chaisty, Paul (2006), *Legislative Politics and Economic Power in Russia*. New York: Palgrave Macmillan.

Chazan, Guy (2007), 'Spiritual Guidance: In Russia, a Top Rabbi Uses Kremlin Ties to Gain Power', *Wall Street Journal*, 8 May.

Chebankova, Elena (2007a), 'Putin's Struggle for Federalism: Structures, Operation, and the Commitment Problem', *Europe-Asia Studies*, vol. 59, no. 2 (March), pp. 279–302.

Chebankova, Elena (2007b), 'Implications of Putin's Regional and Demographic Policies on the Evolution of Inter-Ethnic Relations in Russia', *Perspectives on European Politics and Society*, vol. 8, no. 4, pp. 439–59.

Chetvernina, T. (1997), 'Forms and Main Features of Hidden Unemployment in Russia' (in Russian), in T. Zaslavskaya (ed.), *Kuda idet Rossiya*. Moscow: Intertsentr.

Clément, Karine (2008), 'New Social Movements in Russia: A Challenge to the "Dominant Model of Power Relationships"?', *Journal of Communist Studies and Transition Politics*, vol. 24, no. 1 (March), pp. 68–89.

Coalson, Robert (2004), 'Analysis: How will Russian Governors Be Appointed?', RFE/RL *Russian Political Weekly*, vol. 4, no. 43, 1 November.

Cohen, Stephen F. (2004), 'Was the Soviet System Reformable?' *Slavic Review*, vol. 63, no. 3 (Fall), pp. 459–88.

Colin Lebedev, Anna (2006), 'The Test of Reality: Understanding Families' Tolerance Regarding Mistreatment of Conscripts in the Russian Army', in *Dedovshchina in the Post-Soviet Military: Hazing of Russian Army Conscripts in a Comparative Perspective*, edited by Françoise Daucé and Elisabeth Sieca-Kozkowski. Stuttgart: ibidem-Verlag.

Colton, Timothy J. (1995), 'Superpresidentialism and Russia's Backward State', *Post-Soviet Affairs*, vol. 11, no. 2 (April–June), pp. 144–8.

Colton, Timothy J. (2000), *Transitional Citizens: Voters and What Influences Them in the New Russia*. Cambridge MA: Harvard University Press.

Colton, Timothy J. (2008), *Yeltsin: A Life*. New York: Basic Books.

Colton, Timothy J. and Jerry F. Hough (eds) (1998), *Growing Pains: Russian Democracy and the Election of 1993*. Washington DC: Brookings.

Colton, Timothy J. and McFaul, Michael (2000), 'Reinventing Russia's Party of Power: "Unity" and the 1999 Duma Election'. *Post-Soviet Affairs*, vol. 16, no. 3 (July–September), pp. 201–24.

Colton, Timothy J. and McFaul, Michael (2003), *Popular Choice and Managed Democracy: The Russian Elections of 1999 and 2000*. Washington DC: Brookings Institution.

Conroy, Mary Schaeffer (2006), 'Civil Society in Late Imperial Russia', in Alfred B. Evans, Jr., Laura A. Henry, and Lisa McIntosh Sundstrom (eds), *Russian Civil Society: A Critical Assessment*. Armonk NY: Sharpe.

Cooper, Julian (2006), 'Society-Military Relations in Russia: The Economic Dimension', in Stephen L. Webber and Jennifer G. Mathers (eds), *Military and Society in Post-Soviet Russia*. Manchester and New York: Manchester University Press.

Cooper, Julian (2008) 'The Internet in Russia – Development, Trends and Research Possibilities', presentation at the CEELBAS Post-Soviet Media Research Methodology Workshop, 28 March, University of Birmingham.

Cox, Gary W. (1997), *Making Votes Count*. Cambridge and New York: Cambridge University Press.

Cox, Michael (ed.) (1998), *Rethinking Soviet Collapse: Sovietology, the Death of Communism and the New Russia*. London: Cassell Academic.

Crowley, Stephen (2002), 'Comprehending the Weakness of Russia's Unions', *Demokratizatsiya*, vol. 10, no. 2 (Spring), pp. 230–55.

Dahl, Robert A. (1971), *Polyarchy, Participation and Opposition*. New Haven and London: Yale University Press.

Danilenko, Gennady M. and Burnham, William (2000), *Law and Legal System of the Russian Federation*, 2nd edn. Huntington NY: Juris.

Daucé, Françoise and Elisabeth Sieca-Kozlowski (eds) (2006), *Dedovshchina in the Post-Soviet Military: Hazing of Russian Army Conscripts in a Comparative Perspective*. Stuttgart: ibidem-Verlag.

Davidova, N. (2007), 'The Interrelationship of Poverty and Health: The Longitudinal Experience', Paper to the International Workshop 'Health,

Health Policy and Poverty in Russia: The Dynamics of the Health Capacities of the Poor and the Social Policy Response', 4–6 May, Helsinki.

Davis, Sue (2006), 'Russian Trade Unions: Where Are They in the Former Workers' State?', in Alfred B. Evans, Jr., Laura A. Henry, and Lisa McIntosh Sundstrom (eds), *Russian Civil Society: A Critical Assessment*. Armonk NY: Sharpe.

Dawisha, Karen and Bruce Parrott (1994), *Russia and the New States of Eurasia: The Politics of Upheaval*. Cambridge and New York: Cambridge University Press.

Diamond, Larry (1999), *Developing Democracy: Toward Consolidation*. Baltimore, MD: Johns Hopkins University Press.

Diamond, Larry (2002), 'Thinking About Hybrid Regimes', *Journal of Democracy*, vol. 13, no. 2 (April), pp. 21–35.

Diamond, Larry (2008), *The Spirit of Democracy: The Struggle to Build Free Societies Throughout the World*. New York: Times Books.

Dininio, Phyllis and Robert Orttung (2005) 'Explaining Patterns of Corruption in the Russian Regions', *World Politics*, vol. 57, no. 4, pp. 500–29.

Donaldson, Robert H. and Joseph L. Nogee (2009), *The Foreign Policy of Russia: Changing Systems, Enduring Interests*, 4th edn. Armonk NY: Sharpe.

Elazar, Daniel J. (1987), *Exploring Federalism*. Tuscaloosa and London: The University of Alabama Press.

Elazar, Daniel J. (1991), *Federal Systems of the World: A Handbook of Federal, Confederal and Autonomy Arrangements*. Harlow: Longman.

Erikson, Robert S., MacKuen, Michael and Stimson, James A. (2002), *The Macro Polity*. Cambridge and New York: Cambridge University Press.

Esping-Andersen, G. (ed.) (1996), *Welfare States in Transition: National Adaptations in Global Economies*. London: Sage.

Esping-Andersen, G. (ed.) (2002), *Why Do We Need a New Welfare State?* Oxford: Oxford University Press.

European Commission (2005), Final Road Maps, available at http://europa.eu.int/comm/external_relations/russia/summit_05_05/index.htm#fsj,

European Institute for the Media (1994), *The Russian Parliamentary Elections: Monitoring of the Election Coverage of the Russian Mass Media*. Düsseldorf: European Institute for the Media. Available online http://www.media-politics.com/eimreports.htm.

European Institute for the Media (February 1996), *Monitoring the Media Coverage of the 1995 Russian Parliamentary Elections*. Düsseldorf: European Institute for the Media. Available online http://www.media-politics.com/eimreports.htm.

European Institute for the Media (September 1996),. *Monitoring the Media Coverage of the 1996 Russian Presidential Elections*. Düsseldorf: European Institute for the Media. Available online http://www.media-politics.com/eimreports.htm.

European Institute for the Media (March 2000), *Monitoring the Media Coverage of the December 1999 Parliamentary Elections in Russia: Final*

Report. Düsseldorf: European Institute for the Media. Available online http://www.media-politics.com/eimreports.htm.

European Institute for the Media (August 2000), *Monitoring the Media Coverage of the March 2000 Presidential Elections in Russia (Final Report)*. Düsseldorf: European Institute for the Media. Available online http://www.media-politics.com/eimreports.htm.

Evans, Alfred B. Jr (2002), 'Recent Assessments of Social Organizations in Russia', *Demokratizatsiya*, vol. 10, no. 3 (Summer), pp. 322–42.

Evans, Alfred B. Jr (2006), 'Civil Society in the Soviet Union?', in Alfred B. Evans, Jr, Laura A. Henry, and Lisa McIntosh Sundstrom (eds), *Russian Civil Society: A Critical Assessment*. Armonk NY: Sharpe.

Evans, Alfred B. Jr (2008a), *Power and Ideology: Vladimir Putin and the Russian Political System*, The Carl Beck Papers in Russian and East European Studies of the University of Pittsburgh, no. 1902.

Evans, Alfred B. Jr (2008b), 'The First Steps of Russia's Public Chamber: Representation or Coordination?', *Demokratizatsiya*, vol. 16, no. 4 (Fall), pp. 345–62.

Evans, Alfred B. Jr and Gel'man, Vladimir (eds) (2004), *The Politics of Local Government in Russia*. Lanham MD: Rowman & Littlefield.

Fajth. G. (2000), 'Social Security in a Rapidly Changing Environments: The Case of the Post-Communist Transformation', in N. Manning and I. Shaw (eds) *New Risks, New Welfare: Signposts for Social Policy*. Oxford: Blackwell.

Federal'naya sluzhba gosudarstvennoi statistiki (2007), *Rossiiskii statisticheskii ezhegodnik*. Moscow: Rosstat.

Ferdinand, Peter (2007), 'Sunset, Sunrise: China and Russia Construct a New Relationship', *International Affairs*, vol. 83, no. 5, pp. 841–67.

Field, Mark G. and Judyth L. Twigg (eds) (2000), *Russia's Torn Safety Nets: Health and Social Welfare During the Transition*. Basingstoke: Palgrave Macmillan.

Filippov, A. V. (2007), *Noveishaya istoriya Rossii 1945–2006 gg. Kniga dlya uchitelya*. Moscow: Prosveshchenie.

Filippov, M., P. C. Ordeshook and O. Shvetsova, (2004), *Designing Federalism: A Theory of Self-Sustainable Federal Institutions*. Cambridge and New York: Cambridge University Press.

Finn, Peter (2005), 'In Russia, Trying Times for Trial by Jury', *Washington Post*, 31 October, p. A12.

Finn, Peter (2006), 'Kremlin Inc. Widening Control over Industry', *Washington Post*, 19 November, pp. A1, A13.

First Person (2000), *First Person: An Astonishingly Frank Self-Portrait by Russia's President Vladimir Putin*, with Nataliya Gevorkyan, Natalya Timakova, and Andrei Kolesnikov, trans. Catherine A. Fitzpatrick. London: Hutchinson and New York: Random House

Fish, M. Steven (1995), *Democracy from Scratch*. Princeton NJ: Princeton University Press.

Fish, M. Steven (2001a), 'Conclusion: Democracy and Russian Politics', in Zoltan Barany and Robert G. Moser (eds), *Russian Politics: Challenges of*

Democratization. Cambridge and New York: Cambridge University Press, pp. 215–51.

Fish, M. Steven (2001b), 'When More Is Less: Superexecutive Power and Political Underdevelopment in Russia', in Victoria E. Bonnell and George W. Breslauer (eds), *Russia in the New Century: Stability or Disorder?* Boulder CO: Westview Press.

Fish, M. Steven (2005), *Democracy Derailed in Russia: The Failure of Open Politics*. Cambridge and New York: Cambridge University Press.

Fitch Ratings. Available at http://www.fitchratings.com/.

Flikke, Geir (ed.) (2004), *The Uncertainties of Putin's Democracy*. Oslo: Norwegian Institute of International Affairs.

Fortescue, Stephen (2006), *Russia's Oil Barons and Metal Magnates: Oligarchs and the State in Transition*. Basingstoke: Palgrave Macmillan.

Fossato, Floriana (2007), 'Television and National Identity in the Russian Regions (1999/2005)', MPhil dissertation, London: University College and School of Slavonic and East European Studies.

Freedom House (2008), 'Freedom of the Press 2008: Table of Global Press Freedom Rankings'. Available for consultation at www.freedomhouse.org.

Gaddy, C. G. and B. W. Ickes (2002), *Russia's Virtual Economy*. Washington DC: Brookings Institution.

Garrard, John and Carol Garrard (2008), *Russian Orthodoxy Resurgent: Faith and Power in the New Russia*. Princeton NJ: Princeton University Press.

Gel'man, Vladimir (2005), 'Political Opposition in Russia: A Dying Species?' *Post-Soviet Affairs*, vol. 21, no. 3 (July–September), pp. 226–46.

Gel'man, Vladimir (2008), 'Russia's Party Politics: Round Table Summary', 6 June, available at http://www.chathamhouse.org.uk/files/11665_060608gelman.pdf).

Gel'man, Vladimir (2009), 'Leviathan's Return: The Policy of Recentralisation in Contemporary Russia', in Cameron Ross and Adrian Campbell (eds), *Federalism and Local Politics in Russia*. London and New York: Routledge, pp. 1–24.

Goble, Paul (2005), 'Putin's Regionalisation Plan Sparks Territorial Disputes', RFE/RL *Newsline*, vol. 9, no. 62, part 1, 4 April.

Goldman, Marshall I. (2008), *Petrostate: Putin, Power, and the New Russia*. Oxford and New York: Oxford University Press.

Golosov, Grigorii (2004), *Political Parties in the Regions of Russia: Democracy Unclaimed*. Boulder CO: Lynne Rienner.

Gooding, John (2001), *Socialism in Russia: Lenin and His Legacy, 1890–1991*. Basingstoke: Palgrave.

Gorbachev, Mikhail (1987), *Perestroika: New Thinking for Our Country and the World*. London: Collins.

Gurvich, E. (2008), 'Dva sroka,' *Gazeta.ru*, 4 March.

Hahn, Gordon M. (2001), 'Putin's Federal Reforms: Integrating Russia's Legal Space or Destabilizing Russian Federalism', *Demokratizatsiya*, vol. 9, no. 4, Fall, pp. 498–530.

Hahn, Gordon M. (2002), *Russia's Revolution from Above, 1985–2000: Reform, Transition, and Revolution in the Fall of the Soviet Communist Regime*. New Brunswick NJ: Transaction Publishers.

Hahn, Gordon M. (2003), 'The Impact of Putin's Federative Reforms on Democratization in Russia', *Post-Soviet Affairs*, vol. 19, no. 2 (April–June), pp. 114–53.

Hahn, Gordon M. (2004), 'Managed Democracy? Building Stealth Authoritarianism in St Petersburg', *Demokratizatsiya: The Journal of Post-Soviet Democratization*, vol. 12, no. 2 (Spring), pp. 195–231.

Hale, Henry E. (2004a), 'The Origins of United Russia and the Putin Presidency: The Role of Contingency in Party-System Development', *Demokratizatsiya: The Journal of Post-Soviet Democratization*, vol. 12, no. 2, pp. 169–94.

Hale, Henry E. (2004b), 'Yabloko and the Challenge of Building a Liberal Party in Russia', *Europe-Asia Studies*, vol. 56, no. 7, pp. 993–1020.

Hale, Henry E. (2006), *Why Not Parties in Russia? Democracy, Federalism, and the State*. Cambridge and New York: Cambridge University Press.

Hale, Henry E. (2008), 'What Makes Dominant Parties Dominant in Hybrid Regimes? The Surprising Importance of Ideas in the Case of United Russia', paper presented at the Annual Meeting of the American Political Science Association, Boston.

Hale, Henry E., Michael McFaul and Timothy J. Colton (2004), 'Putin and the "Delegative Democracy" Trap: Evidence from Russia's 2003–04 Elections', *Post-Soviet Affairs*, vol. 20, no. 4 (October–December), pp.285–319.

Hanson, P. (2006), 'Federalism with a Russian Face: Regional Inequality, Administrative Capacity and Regional Budgets in Russia', *Economic Change and Restructuring*, vol. 39, nos 3–4 (December), pp. 191–211.

Hanson, P. (2007), 'The Russian Economic Puzzle: Going Forwards, Backwards or Sideways?', *International Affairs*, vol. 83, no. 5, pp. 869–89.

Hanson, Stephen E. (2003), 'Instrumental Democracy: The End of Ideology and the Decline of Russian Political Parties', in Vicki L. Hesli and William M. Reisinger (eds), *The 1999–2000 Elections in Russia: Their Impact and Legacy*. Cambridge and New York: Cambridge University Press.

Hausmann, R., L. Pritchett and D. Rodrik (2004), 'Growth Accelerations'. Cambridge MA: National Bureau of Economic Research Working Paper no. 10566.

Heinemann-Grüder, Andreas (ed.) (2002a), *Federalism Doomed: European Federalism Between Integration and Separation*. New York and Oxford: Berghahn Books.

Heinemann-Grüder, Andreas (2002b), 'Is Russia's Federalism Sustainable?', *Perspectives on European Politics and Society*, vol. 3, no. 1, pp. 67–92.

Heinemann-Grüder, Andreas (2009), 'Federal Discourses, Minority Rights, and Conflict Transformation', in Cameron Ross and Adrian Campbell (eds), *Federalism and Local Politics in Russia*. London and New York: Routledge, pp. 54–81.

Heller. P. S. and Keller, C. (2001), 'Social Sector Reform in Transition Countries', *Finance and Development*, vol. 38, no. 3 (September), pp. 2–5.

Henderson, Sarah L. (2003), *Building Democracy in Contemporary Russia: Western Support for Grassroots Organizations*. Ithaca NY: Cornell University Press.

Hendley, Kathryn (2002), 'Suing the State in Russia', *Post-Soviet Affairs*, vol. 18, no. 2 (April–June), pp. 148–81.

Hendley, Kathryn (2004), 'Business Litigation in the Transition: A Portrait of Debt Collection in Russia', *Law and Society Review*, vol. 38, no. 2 (June). pp. 305–47.

Hendley, Kathryn (2006), 'Assessing the Rule of Law in Russia', *Cardozo Journal of International and Comparative Law*, vol. 14, no. 2, pp. 347–91.

Hendley, Kathryn (2007), 'Putin and the Law', in Dale R. Herspring (ed.), *Putin's Russia: Past Imperfect, Future Uncertain*, 3rd edn. Lanham MD: Rowman & Littlefield. pp. 99–124.

Henry, Laura A. (2006a), 'Russian Environmentalists and Civil Society', in Alfred B. Evans, Jr., Laura A. Henry, and Lisa McIntosh Sundstrom (eds), *Russian Civil Society: A Critical Assessment*. Armonk NY: Sharpe.

Henry, Laura A. (2006b), 'Shaping Social Activism in Post-Soviet Russia: Leadership, Organizational Diversity, and Innovation', *Post-Soviet Affairs*, vol. 22, no. 2 (April–June), pp. 99–124.

Herspring, Dale R. (ed.) (2003), *Putin's Russia: Past Imperfect, Future Uncertain*. Oxford: Rowman & Littlefield.

Herspring, Dale R. (2006), 'Undermining Combat Readiness in the Russian Military 1992–2005', *Armed Forces and Society*, vol. 32, no. 4, pp. 513–31.

Hesli, Vicki L. and Reisinger, William M. (eds) (2003), *The 1999–2000 Elections in Russia: Their Impact and Legacy*. Cambridge and New York: Cambridge University Press.

Hill, Fiona (2006), 'Moscow Discovers Soft Power', *Current History*, vol. 105, no. 693 (October), pp. 341–7.

Hill, Ronald J. and Ottorino Cappelli (eds) (2008), 'Putin and Putinism', special issue of the *Journal of Communist Studies and Transition Politics*, vol. 24, no. 4 (December).

Holmes, Stephen (1993–4), 'Superpresidentialism and its Problems', *East European Constitutional Review*, vol. 2, no. 4/vol. 3, no. 1 (Fall/Winter), pp. 123–6.

Hough, Jerry F., and Fainsod, Merle (1979) *How the Soviet Union Is Governed*. Cambridge MA: Harvard University Press.

Huntington, Samuel P. (1968), *Political Order in Changing Societies*. New Haven and London: Yale University Press.

Huntington, Samuel P. (1991), *The Third Wave: Democratization in the Late Twentieth Century*. Norman: University of Oklahoma Press.

Huntington, Samuel P. (1993), 'The Clash of Civilizations', *Foreign Affairs*, vol. 72, no. 3 (Summer), pp. 22–49.

Huskey, Eugene (1999), *Presidential Power in Russia*. Armonk, NY: Sharpe.

Hutcheson, Derek (2003), *Political Parties in the Russian Regions*. New York and London: RoutledgeCurzon.

Hutchings, Stephen and Rulyova, Natalia (eds) (2009), *Television and Culture in Putin's Russia: Remote Control*. London and New York: Routledge.

Il'ina, Irina I. (2000), *Obshchestvennye organizatsii v 1920-kh gody*. Moscow: IRI RAN.

ILO (1999), 'Overcoming Adverse Consequences of the Transition Period in the Russian Federation', Working Paper of International Conference on Social and Labour Issues, Moscow, October.

ILO (2005), 'Social Protection of the Population: Assessing Social Consequences of the Benefit System Monetization'. Moscow: ILO.

International Institute for Strategic Studies (IISS) (1991), *The Military Balance 1991–1992*. London: Brassey's for the IISS.

International Institute for Strategic Studies (IISS) (1993), *The Military Balance 1993–1994*. London: Brassey's for the IISS.

International Institute for Strategic Studies (IISS) (1996), *The Military Balance 1996–1997*. Oxford: Oxford University Press for the IISS.

International Institute for Strategic Studies (IISS) (2008), *The Military Balance 2008*. London: Routledge for the IISS.

IREX (2006), *Survey of Recent Social Policy Studies in Russia*. Moscow.

Ivanenko, Vlad (2007), 'Regional Governors Unclear on How to Stay in Power', *Russia Profile*, vol. 4, issue 3 (April), pp. 11–12.

Ivanitskaya, N., and Yu. Mazneva (2008), 'Nedra pod nadzorom,' *Vedomosti*, 21 February.

Ivanov, Vitalii (2008), *Partiya Putina. Istoriya 'Yedinoi Rossii'*. Moscow: Olma, 2008.

Johnson, Janet Elise (2006), 'Public–Private Permutations: Domestic Violence Centers in Barnaul,' in Alfred B. Evans, Jr, Laura A. Henry, and Lisa McIntosh Sundstrom (eds), *Russian Civil Society: A Critical Assessment*. Armonk NY: Sharpe.

Jonson, Lena (2004), *Vladimir Putin and Central Asia: The Shaping of Russian Foreign Policy*. London: I. B. Tauris.

Kachkaeva, Anna, I. Kiriya and G. Libergal (2006), 'Television in the Russian Federation: Organisational Structure, Programme Production and Audience', a report prepared by Internews Russia for the European Audiovisual Observatory. Moscow: Educated Media, March.

Kahn, Jeff (2002), *Federalism, Democratization and the Rule of Law in Russia*. Oxford: Oxford University Press.

Karppinen, Antti (2006), *The Hammer, Sickle, and Star: Following the Idea of Russia*. Helsinki: Kikimora Publications.

Kaufmann, D., A. Kraay and M. Mastruzzi (2007), *Governance Matters VI: Governance Indicators for 1996–2006*, Washington DC: World Bank.

Kazantsev, Sergei (2008), Consultation, Constitutional Court of the Russian Federation (oral proceedings), Moscow, 8 May.

Keep, John L. H. (1996), *Last of the Empires: A History of the Soviet Union, 1945–1991*. Oxford: Oxford University Press.

Kempton, Daniel (2001), 'Russian Federalism: Continuing Myth or Political Salvation', *Demokratizatsiya*, vol. 9, no. 2 (Spring), pp. 201–42.

Kempton, Daniel R. and Clark, Terry D. (eds) (2002), *Center-Periphery Relations in the Former Soviet Union: Unity or Separation*. Westport CT and London: Praeger.

Kenez, Peter (1999), *A History of the Soviet Union from the Beginning to the End*. Cambridge and New York: Cambridge University Press.

Knox, Zoe (2005), *Russian Society and the Orthodox Church: Religion in Russia after Communism*. London: RoutledgeCurzon.

Kokoshin, Andrei (2006), *Real'nyi suverenitet v sovremennoi miropolitich-eskoi sisteme*, 3rd edn. Moscow: Yevropa.

Koltsova, Olessia (2005), *News Media and Power in Russia*. London: Routledge.

Kommersant (2008), 'Economy Develops Unevenly in Regions', 14 April, reproduced in, *Johnson's Russia List*, no 75, 14 April (no author cited).

Konitzer, Andrew (2005), *Voting for Russia's Governors: Regional Elections and Accountability under Yeltsin and Putin*, Washington DC: Woodrow Wilson Center Press.

Kosachev, Konstantin (2004), 'Russian Foreign Policy Vertical', *Russia in Global Affairs*, vol. 2, no. 3 (July–September), pp. 29–38.

Kotkin, Stephen (2001), *Armageddon Averted: The Soviet Collapse 1970–2000*. Oxford: Oxford University Press.

Kotz, David and Fred Weir (1997), *Revolution from Above: The Demise of the Soviet System*. London: Routledge.

Krainova, Natalya (2008), 'Medvedev Orders Cleanup of Courts', *Moscow News*, 21 May 21, pp. 1–2.

Krasnoboka, Natalya and Holli Semetko (2006), 'Murder, Journalism and the Web: How the Gongadze Case Launched the Internet News Era in Ukraine', in Sarah Oates, Diana Owen and Rachel K. Gibson (eds), *The Internet and Politics: Citizens, Activists and Voters*. London: Routledge, pp. 183–206.

Kryshtanovskaya, Olga and Stephen White (2003), 'Putin's Militocracy', *Post-Soviet Affairs*, vol. 19, no. 4 (October–December), pp. 289–306.

Kulik, Anatolii (2001), 'Perspektivy razvitiya partiino-politicheskoi sistemy v Rossii: kruglyi stol "Ekspertiza"'. Moscow: Gorbachev-Fond, pp. 118–34. Available at http:/www.gorby.ru.

Kullberg, Judith S. and Zimmerman, William (1999), 'Liberal Elites, Socialist Masses, and Problems of Russian Democracy', *World Politics*, vol. 51, no. 3, pp. 323–58.

Kurkchiyan, Marina (2003), 'The Illegitimacy of Law in Post-Soviet Societies', in *Law and Informal Practices: The Post-Communist Experience*, edited by Denis J. Galligan and Marina Kurkchiyan. Oxford: Oxford University Press.

Kusznir, Julia (2007), 'The New Russian-Tatar Treaty and its Implications for Russian Federalism', in *Russian Analytical Digest*, no. 16, (6 March), pp. 2–5.

Kusznir, Julia (2008), 'Russian Territorial Reform: A Centralist Project that Could End Up Fostering Decentralisation?', *Russian Analytical Digest*, no. 43, (17 June), pp. 8–11.

Lane, David (ed.) (2002), *The Legacy of State Socialism and the Future of Transformation*. Oxford: Rowman & Littlefield.

Lavrov, Sergei (2008), 'On the Caucasus Crisis and Russia's Ukrainian Policy,' *2000*, no. 38, 19–25 September, Kyiv. Available on the Russian MFA website at http://www.mid.ru/Brp_4.nsf/arh/7F621FB878AA40 BAC32574CD00209606?OpenDocument.

Legvold, Robert (ed.) (2007), *Russian Foreign Policy in the Twenty-First Century and the Shadow of the Past*. New York: Columbia University Press

Leksin, Vladimir (2004), 'The New Russian Federalism', in Peter H. Solomon, Jr. (ed.), *The Dynamics of 'Real Federalism': Law, Economic Development, and Indigenous Communities in Russia and Canada*. Toronto: Centre for Russian and East European Studies, University of Toronto.

Leksin, Vladimir (2005), 'Federal Statehood in Russia: Legislation and Conflict Resolution' in Peter H. Solomon, Jr (ed.), *Recrafting Federalism in Russia and Canada: Power, Budgets, and Indigenous Governance*. Toronto: Centre for Russian and East European Studies, University of Toronto.

Levitsky, Stephen and Lucan Way (2002), 'The Rise of Competitive Authoritarianism', *Journal of Democracy*, vol. 13, no. 2 (April), pp. 51–65.

Levy, Clifford J. (2008), 'At Expense of All Others, Putin Picks a Church', *New York Times*, 24 April.

Likova, M. V. (2008), 'Tendentsii i perspektivy reformirovaniya otechestvennoi modeli byudgetnovo federalizma', in S. D. Valentei (ed.), *Rossiiskii federalizm: ekonomiko-pravovye problemy*. St Petersburg: Aleteiya.

Lo, Bobo (2003), *Vladimir Putin and the Evolution of Russian Foreign Policy*. London: RIIA and Blackwell.

Lo, Bobo (2008), *Axis of Convenience: Moscow, Beijing and the New Geopolitics*. London: RIIA and Washington DC: Brookings Institution.

Lupis, A. with S. Kishkovsky (2005), 'Rebels and Reporters' in *Dangerous Assignments*. New York: Committee to Project Journalists. Available online at <http://www.cpj.org/Briefings/2005/DA_spring05/DA_spring_05.pdf>.

Mainwaring, Scott, and Matthew Shugart (eds) (1997), *Presidentialism and Democracy in Latin America*. Cambridge and New York: Cambridge University Press.

Makinen, Sirke (2008), *Russian Geopolitical Visions and Argumentation: Parties of Power, Democratic and Communist Opposition on Chechnya and NATO, 1994–2003*. Tampere: Acta Universitatis Tamperensis 1293, Tampere University Press.

Maleva, T., *et al.* (eds) (2007), *Obzor sotsial'noi politiki v Rossii. Nachalo 2000-kh*. Moscow: Independent Institute of Social Policy.

Malfliet, Katlijn, Lien Verpoest and Evgeny Vinokurov (eds) (2007), *The CIS, the EU and Russia: The Challenges of Integration*. Basingstoke and New York: Palgrave Macmillan.

Malia, Martin (1994), *The Soviet Tragedy: A History of Socialism in Russia, 1917–1991*. New York: Free Press.

Manning, N. (1998), 'Social Policy, Labour Markets, Unemployment, and Household Strategies in Russia', *International Journal of Manpower*, vol. 19, nos. 1–2, pp. 48–67.

Manning, N. (2007), 'Inequality in Russia since 1990', in David Lane (ed.), *The Transformation of State Socialism: System Change, Capitalism, or Something Else?* Basingstoke: Palgrave Macmillan.

Manning N. and N. Tikhonova (eds) (2004), *Poverty and Social Exclusion in the New Russia*. Aldershot: Ashgate.

Manning N. and N. Tikhonova (eds) (2009), *Health and Healthcare in the New Russia*. Aldershot: Ashgate.

Manning N., O. Shkaratan and N. Tikhonova (2000), *Work and Welfare in the New Russia*. Aldershot: Ashgate.

March, Luke (2002), *The Communist Party in Post-Soviet Russia*. Manchester: Manchester University Press.

Markus, Stanislav (2007), 'Capitalists of All Russia, Unite! Business Mobilization under Debilitated Dirigisme', *Polity*, vol. 39, no. 3 (July), pp. 277–304.

Marples, David (2002), *Motherland: Russia in the Twentieth Century*. Harlow: Longman.

Mathers, Jennifer G. (2006), 'Women, Society and the Military: Women Soldiers in Post-Soviet Russia', in Stephen L. Webber and Jennifer G. Mathers (eds), *Military and Society in Post-Soviet Russia.*. Manchester and New York: Manchester University Press.

McAllister, Ian and Stephen White (2008), ' "It's the Economy, Comrade!" Parties and Voters in the 2007 Russian Duma Election', *Europe-Asia Studies*, vol. 60, no. 6 (August), pp. 931–57.

McFaul, Michael (1997), *Russia's 1996 Presidential Election: The End of Polarized Politics*. Stanford CA: Hoover Institution Press.

McFaul, Michael (2001), *Russia's Unfinished Revolution: Political Change from Gorbachev to Putin*. Ithaca NY and London: Cornell University Press.

McFaul, Michael and Markov, Sergei (eds) (1993), *The Troubled Birth of Russian Democracy: Parties, Personalities, and Programs*. Stanford CA: Hoover Institution Press.

McFaul, Michael, Nikolai Petrov and Andrei Ryabov (2004), *Between Dictatorship and Democracy: Russian Post-Communist Political Reform*. Washington DC: Carnegie Endowment for International Peace.

McFaul, Michael A. and Stoner-Weiss, Kathryn (2008), 'The Myth of the Authoritarian Model: How Putin's Crackdown Holds Russia Back', *Foreign Affairs*, vol. 87, no. 1 (January–February), pp. 68–84.

McIntosh Sundstrom, Lisa (2006a), *Funding Civil Society: Foreign Assistance and NGO Development in Russia*. Stanford CA: Stanford University Press.

McIntosh Sundstrom, Lisa (2006b), 'Soldiers' Rights Groups in Russia: Civil Society Through Russian and Western Eyes', in Alfred B. Evans, Jr., Laura A. Henry, and Lisa McIntosh Sundstrom (eds), *Russian Civil Society: A Critical Assessment*. Armonk NY: Sharpe.

Medvedev, Dmitri (2008a), Address to a Conference on Judicial Corruption, in Johnson's List, no. 100, 20 May. Available at www.cdi.org/russia/johnson/2008-99-4.cfm.

Medvedev, Dmitri (2008b), Interview to Television Channels Channel One, Rossiya and NTV, 31 August. Available at http://president.kremlin.ru/eng/speeches/2008/08/31/1850_type82912type82916_206003.shtml.

Medvedev, Dmitri (2008c), 'Introductory Remarks at a Meeting on Questions of Farming and Management Cadre Reserve', 23 July, consulted at www.prezident.kremlin.ru.

Mendelson, Sarah E., and John K. Glenn (eds) (2002), *The Power and Limits of NGOs: A Critical Look at Building Democracy in Eastern Europe and Eurasia*. New York: Columbia University Press.

MERT (2008), *Kontseptsiya dolgosrochnogo sotsial'no-ekonomicheskogo razvitiya Rossiiskoi Federatsii (proekt)*, Moscow: Ministry of Economic Development and Trade, March.

Mickiewicz, Ellen (1999), *Changing Channels: Television and the Struggle for Power in Russia*, 2nd edn. Durham NC: Duke University Press

Mickiewicz, Ellen (2008), *Television, Power, and the Public in Russia*. Cambridge and New York: Cambridge University Press.

Miller, Steven E. (2004), 'Moscow's Military Power: Russia's Search for Security in an Age of Transition', in Steven E. Miller and Dmitri Trenin (eds), *The Russian Military: Power and Policy*. Cambridge MA: American Academy of Arts and Sciences.

Miller, Steven E. and Dmitri Trenin (2004), *The Russian Military: Power and Policy*. Cambridge MA: American Academy of Arts and Sciences.

Milov, V. (2008), 'Itogi 2007 goda dlya energetiki Rossii'. Available at www.energypolicy.ru/files/Milov%20Feb-2008.ppt#371.

Ministry of Foreign Affairs (2008), *The Foreign Policy Concept of the Russian Federation*, http://www.kremlin.ru/eng/text/docs/2008/07/204750.shtml), accessed 12 May 2009.

Minpromenergo (2007), *Kontseptsiya energeticheskoi strategii Rossii na period do 2030 g. (proekt)*. Moscow: Minpromenergo.

Mishler, William, and John P. Willerton (2003), 'The Dynamics of Presidential Popularity in Post-Communist Russia: How Exceptional is Russian Politics?', *Journal of Politics*, vol. 65, no. 1 (December), pp. 111–41.

Myagkov, Mikhail and Peter Ordeshook (2008), 'Russian Elections: An Oxymoron of Democracy', *VTP Working Paper #83*. Caltech/MIT Voting Technology Project. Caltech and MIT. Pasadena CA and Cambridge MA.

North, Douglass (1990), *Institutions, Institutional Changes and Economic Performance*. Cambridge and New York: Cambridge University Press.

Oates, Sarah (2006a), 'Comparing the Politics of Fear: The Role of Terrorism News in Election Campaigns in Russia, the United States and Britain', *International Relations*, vol. 20, no. 4, pp. 425–37.

Oates, Sarah (2006b), *Television, Elections and Democracy in Russia*. London: Routledge.

Oates, Sarah (2008), *Introduction to Media and Politics*. London: Sage.

Oates, Sarah and Laure Roselle Helvey (1997), 'Russian Television's Mixed Messages: Parties, Candidates and Control on *Vremya*, 1995–1996', paper presented at the American Political Science Association Annual Meeting, Washington DC.

Oates, Sarah and Laura Roselle (2000), 'Russian Elections and TV News: Comparison of Campaign News on State-Controlled and Commercial Television Channels', *Harvard International Journal of Press/Politics,* vol. 5, no. 2 (Spring), pp. 30–51.

Obshchestvennaya palata Rossiiskoi Federatsii (2007) 'Doklad o sostoyanii grazhdanskogo obshchestva v Rossiiskoi Federatsii'. Moscow: Apparat Obshchestvennoi Palaty Rossiiskoi Federatsii.

Oda, Hiroshi (2007), *Russian Commercial Law*. Leiden: Martinus Nijhoff.

O'Donnell, Guillermo (1993), 'On the State, Democratization and Some Conceptual Problems (A Latin American View with Glances at Some Postcommunist Countries)', *World Development*, vol. 21, no. 8, pp. 1355–69.

O'Donnell, Guillermo (1994), 'Delegative Democracy', *Journal of Democracy*, vol. 5, no. 1, pp. 55–69.

O'Donnell, Guillermo and Philippe C. Schmitter (1986), *Transitions from Authoritarian Rule: Tentative Conclusions about Uncertain Democracies.* Baltimore MD: Johns Hopkins University Press.

O'Donnell, Guillermo, Philippe C. Schmitter and Laurence Whitehead (eds) (1986), *Transitions from Authoritarian Rule*, 4 vols. Baltimore MD: Johns Hopkins University Press.

OECD (2004), *Economic Surveys. Russian Federation,* vol. 2004/11, Paris: OECD.

OECD (2006), *Economic Surveys. Russian Federation*, vol. 2006/17, Paris: OECD.

Open Net Initiative (2005), *Internet Filtering in China in 2004–2005: A Country Study*, 13 April. Available online at http://www.opennetinitiative.net/studies/china/

Organisation for Security and Co-operation in Europe/Office for Democratic Institutions and Human Rights (OSCE/ODIHR) (January 2004), *Russian Federation Elections to the State Duma 7 December 2003 OSCE/ODIHR Election Observation Mission Report*. Warsaw: Office for Democratic Institutions and Human Rights. Available online at http://www.osce.org/item/8051.html.

Organisation for Security and Co-operation in Europe/Office for Democratic Institutions and Human Rights (OSCE/ODIHR) (June 2004), *Russian Federation Presidential Election 14 March 2004 OSCE/ODIHR Election Observation Mission Report*. Warsaw:

Office for Democratic Institutions and Human Rights. Available online at http://www.osce.org/odihr-elections/14520.html.

Orttung, Robert W. and Peter Reddaway (eds) (2005), *The Dynamics of Russian Politics: Putin's Reform of Federal-Regional Relations*, vol. 2. Lanham MD and Oxford: Rowman & Littlefield.

Ottaway, Marina (2003), *Democracy Challenged: The Rise of Semi-Authoritarianism*. Washington DC: Carnegie Endowment.

Ovcharova, L. and A. Pishnyak (2005), 'Social Benefits: What are the Results of Monetization', *SPERO (Social Policy: Expertise, Recommendations, Observations)*, no. 3.

Oxford Analytica Daily Brief (2008), 'Russia: Arms Exports are Set to Decline', 5 May.

Panfilov, Yelena (2008), 'Dmitry Medvedev Began with Corruption', *RBK Daily*, 20 May. Available at www.rbcdaily.ru/2008/05/20/focus/344394.

Pasti, Svetlana (2005), 'Two Generations of Contemporary Russian Journalists', *European Journal of Communication*, vol. 20, no. 1, pp. 89–115.

Pasti, Svetlana (2007), *The Changing Profession of a Journalist in Russia*. Tampere: Tampere University Press.

PBN (The PBN Company) (2007, 2008), *Policy Matters*.

Perechen' (2005), *Perechen' poruchenii po realizatsii osnovnykh polozhenii*, Instruction posted on presidential website www.kremlin.ru on 11 May 2005.

Petrov, Nikolai (2008), 'A Regional Shift in Moscow', *The Moscow Times*, 16 April. Also reproduced on the website of the Carnegie Endowment for International Peace:

Petrov, Nikolai and Slider, Darrell (2007), 'Putin and the Regions', in Dale R. Herspring (ed.), *Putin's Russia: Past Imperfect, Future Uncertain*, 3rd edn. Lanham, MD: Rowman & Littlefield.

Pietiläinen, Jukka (2008), 'Media Use in Putin's Russia', *Journal of Communist Studies and Transition Politics*, vol. 24, no. 3 (September), pp. 365–85.

Pikayev, Alexander A. (2000), 'Moscow's Matrix', *Washington Quarterly*, vol. 23, no. 3 (July), pp. 187–94.

Pleshanova, O. (2008), 'Sud vysshego dostoinstva,' *Kommersant*, 13 May.

Polyakov, L. V. (ed.) (2007), *Pro suverennuyu demokratiyu*. Moscow: Yevropa, 2007.

Preston, Kline (2008), 'Multi-Jurisdictional Developments in Russia Copyright Law', Paper presented at the International Studies Association, 26–29 March, San Francisco.

Protsyk, Oleh (2004), 'Ruling with Decrees: Presidential Decree Making in Russia and Ukraine', *Europe-Asia Studies*, vol. 56, no. 5 (July), pp. 637–60.

Przeworski, Adam (1991), *Democracy and the Market: Political and Economic Reforms in Eastern Europe and Latin America*. Cambridge and New York: Cambridge University Press.

Public Opinion Foundation (2007), 'Russian Courts: Reality and Reality TV', 16 August. Available at http://bd.english.fom.ru/report/map/ed073321.

Public Opinion Foundation (2008), 'Otnoshenie k sudebnoi sisteme', 12 June. Available at www.fom.ru/topics/3241.html.

Putin, Vladimir (1999), 'Russia at the Turn of the Millennium', *Rossiiskaya gazeta*, 31 December. Reprinted in translation in Putin (2000).

Putin, Vladimir (2000) *First Person: An Astonishingly Frank Self-Portrait by Russia's President Vladimir Putin*, with Nataliya Gevorkyan, Natalya

Timakova, and Andrei Kolesnikov, translated by Catherine A. Fitzpatrick. London: Hutchinson.

Putin, Vladimir (2005a), 'Annual Speech to Prosecutors', 21 January. Available at www.cdi.org/russia/johnson/9030-13.cfm.

Putin, Vladimir (2005b), 'Address: "State of the Nation"', 25 April. Available at www.fas.org/irp/news/2005/04/putin042505.html.

Putin, Vladimir (2007a), Transcript of Press Conference with the Russian and Foreign Media. 1 February, Round Hall, Kremlin, Moscow. Available at http://president.kremlin.ru/eng/speeches/2007/02/01/1309_type82915type82917_117609.shtml.

Putin, Vladimir (2007b), Annual Address to the Federal Assembly, 26 April. Available at http://www.kremlin.ru/eng/speeches/2007/04/26/1209_type70029type82912_125670.shtml.

Putin, Vladimir (2008), Transcript of Annual Big Press Conference, 14 February. Available at http://president.kremlin.ru/eng/speeches/2008/02/14/1011_type82915_160266.shtml.

Pyle, William (2006), 'Collective Action and Post-Communist Enterprise: The Economic Logic of Russia's Business Associations', *Europe-Asia Studies*, vol. 58, no. 4 (June), pp. 491–521.

Reddaway, Peter and Dmitri Glinski (2001), *The Tragedy of Russia's Reforms: Market Bolshevism against Democracy*. Washington DC: United States Institute of Peace Press.

Remington, Thomas F. (2001a), 'Putin and the Duma', *Post-Soviet Affairs*, vol. 17, no. 4 (October–December), pp. 285–308.

Remington, Thomas F. (2001b), *The Russian Parliament: Institutional Evolution in a Transitional Regime*. New Haven and London: Yale University Press.

Remington, Thomas F. (2003), 'Majorities without Mandates: The Federation Council since 2000', *Europe-Asia Studies*, vol. 55, no. 5, pp. 667–91.

Remington, Thomas F. (2004) *Politics in Russia*, 3rd edn. London: Pearson Longman.

Remington, Thomas F. (2006a), 'Presidential Support in the Russian State Duma', *Legislative Studies Quarterly*, vol. 31, no. 1, pp. 5–32.

Remington, Thomas F. (2006b), 'Democratization, Separation of Powers, and State Capacity', in Timothy J. Colton and Stephen Holmes (eds), *The State after Communism: Governance in the New Russia.*. Lanham, MD: Rowman & Littlefield, pp. 261–98.

Remington, Thomas F. (2007), 'The Russian Federal Assembly, 1994–2004', *Journal of Legislative Studies*, vol. 13, no. 1, pp. 121–41.

Remington, Thomas F. (2008), 'Patronage and the Party of Power: President-Parliament Relations under Vladimir Putin', *Europe-Asia Studies*, vol. 60, no. 6 (August), pp. 965–93.

Remnick, David (1993), *Lenin's Tomb: The Last Days of the Soviet Empire*. London: Viking.

Renz, Bettina (2006), 'Putin's Militocracy? An Alternative Interpretation of Siloviki in Contemporary Russian Politics', *Europe-Asia Studies*, vol. 58, no. 6, pp. 903–24.

Reuter, Ora John and Thomas F. Remington (2009), 'Dominant Party Regimes and the Commitment Problem: The Case of United Russia', *Comparative Political Studies*, vol. 42, no. 4 (April), pp. 501–26.

RFE/RL *Newsline* (2008a), 'Regional Governors To Serve Two Masters', vol. 12, no. 61, part 1, (1 April) (author cited as LF).

RFE/RL *Newsline,* (2008b), 'Prime Minister Will Be In Charge of Rating Governors', vol. 12, no. 82, part 1, (30 April) (no author cited).

Richter, James (2009), 'Putin and the Public Chamber *Post-Soviet Affairs*, vol. 25, no. 1 (January–March), pp. 39–65.

Rogotsev, Igor (2008), Consultation (oral proceedings), Preston Kline Law Firm, St Petersburg, 5 May.

Rose, Richard and Neil Munro (2002), *Elections Without Order.* Cambridge and New York: Cambridge University Press.

Rose, Richard, William Mishler and Neil Munro (2006), *Russia Transformed: Developing Popular Support for a New Regime.* Cambridge and New York: Cambridge University Press.

Roskomstat (1996), *Rossiiskii statisticheskii yezhegodnik.* Moscow: Logos.

Ross, Cameron (2002a), *Federalism and Democratisation in Russia.* Manchester: Manchester University Press.

Ross, Cameron (ed.) (2002b), *Regional Politics in Russia.* Manchester: Manchester University Press.

Ross, Cameron (ed.) (2004), *Russian Politics under Putin.* Manchester, Manchester University Press.

Ross, Cameron (2005), 'Federalism and Electoral Authoritarianism under Putin', *Demokratizatsiya: The Journal of Post-Soviet Democratization*, vol. 13, no. 3 (Summer), pp. 347–70.

Ross, Cameron (2009a), *Local Politics and Democratization in Russia.* London and New York: Routledge.

Ross, Cameron (2009b), 'Municipal Elections and Electoral Authoritarianism under Putin', in Cameron Ross and Adrian Campbell (eds), *Federalism and Local Politics in Russia.* London and New York: Routledge.

Ross, Cameron and Adrian Campbell (eds) (2009), *Federalism and Local Politics in Russia.* New York: Routledge.

ROSSTAT (2006), *Social Position and Living Standards of Russian Population: Collected Statistics.* Moscow: Rosstat.

Rumer, Eugene (2007), *Russian Foreign Policy Beyond Putin.* Adelphi Papers no. 390, London: International Institute of Strategic Studies.

Russian Federation Council Report (2006), Council of Federation of the Federal Assembly of the Russian Federation 2006 Report, 'On the State of Legislation in the Russian Federation'. Available at www.council.gov.ru/eng/rep/index.html.

Rutland, Peter (2006), 'Business and Civil Society in Russia', in Alfred B. Evans, Jr., Laura A. Henry, and Lisa McIntosh Sundstrom (eds), *Russian Civil Society: A Critical Assessment.* Armonk NY: Sharpe.

Sachs, Jeffrey D. and Katharina Pistor (1997), *The Rule of Law and Economic Reform in Russia.* Boulder CO: Westview Press.

Safranchuk, Ivan (2008), 'The Competition for Security Roles in Central Asia', *Russia in Global Affairs,* vol. 6, no. 1 (January–March), pp. 159–69.

Sakwa, Richard (1990), *Gorbachev and His Reforms, 1985–90.* Hemel Hempstead: Philip Allan.

Sakwa, Richard (1998), *Soviet Politics in Perspective*, 2nd edn. London: Routledge.

Sakwa, Richard (2002), 'Federalism, Sovereignty and Democracy', in Cameron Ross (ed.), *Regional Politics in Russia.* Manchester: Manchester University Press.

Sakwa, Richard (2004, 2nd edn, 2008b), *Putin: Russia's Choice.* London and New York: Routledge.

Sakwa, Richard (2008a), *Russian Politics and Society*, 4th edn. London and New York: Routledge.

Sakwa, Richard (2009), *The Quality of Freedom: Putin, Khodorkovsky and the Yukos Affair.* Oxford and New York: Oxford University Press.

Sandle, Mark (1997), *A Short History of Soviet Socialism.* London, UCL Press.

Satter, David (2004), *Darkness at Dawn: The Rise of the Russian Criminal State.* New Haven and London: Yale University Press.

Schumpeter, Joseph A. (1976), *Capitalism, Socialism and Democracy.* London: George Allen & Unwin.

Serio, Joseph D. (2008), *Investigating the Russian Mafia.* Durham NC: Carolina Academic Press.

Service, Robert (2005), *A History of Modern Russia: From Nicholas II to Vladimir Putin.* Cambridge MA: Harvard University Press.

Shabdurasulov, Igor (2008), 'Otsy-osnovateli', *Novoe Vremya*, 14 April, pp. 18–19.

Sharlet, Robert and Feldbrugge, Ferdinand (eds) (2005), *Public Policy and Law in Russia: In Search of a Unified Legal and Political Space.* Leiden: Martinus Nijhoff.

Shevtsova, Lilia (2003, 2nd edn, 2005), *Putin's Russia.* Washington DC: Carnegie Endowment for International Peace.

Shlapentokh, V. *et al.* (2006), Interview to 'Voice of America', 13 March. Available at http://www.voanews.com.

Shleifer, Andrei and Daniel Treisman (2000), *Without a Map. Political Tactics and Economic Reform in Russia.* Cambridge MA: MIT Press.

Shvaryov, Aleksandr (2003), 'Campaign against a Monster', *Vremya novostei*, 13 March, pp. 1–2.

Smith, Gordon B. (1996), *Reforming the Russian Legal System.* Cambridge and New York: Cambridge University Press.

Smith, Gordon B. and Robert Sharlet (eds) (2008), *Russia and Its Constitution: Promise and Political Reality.* Leiden: Martinus Nijhoff.

Smith, Martin A. (2006), *Russia and NATO since 1991: From Cold War Through Cold Peace to Partnership?* London: Routledge.

Smith, Steven S. and Thomas F. Remington (2001), *The Politics of Institutional Choice: Formation of the Russian State Duma.* Princeton NJ, Princeton University Press.

Smyth, Regina (2006), *Candidate Strategies and Electoral Competition in the Russian Federation: Democracy without Foundation.* Cambridge and New York: Cambridge University Press.

Smyth, Regina, Brandon Wilkening and Anna Urasova (2007), 'Engineering Victory: Institutional Reform, Informal Institutions, and the Formation of a Hegemonic Party Regime in the Russian Federation', *Post-Soviet Affairs*, vol. 23, no. 2 (April–June), pp. 118–37.

Sobyanin, Aleksandr and Vladislav Sukhovol'sky (1995), *Demokratiya, ogranichennaya falsifikatsiyami: vybory i referendum v Rossii v 1991–1993 gg.* Moscow: Yevraziya.

Solomon, Peter H. (2003), 'New Justices of the Peace in the Russian Federation: A Cornerstone of Judicial Reform?', *Demokratizatsiya*, vol. 11, no. 3, pp. 381–96.

Solomon, Peter H. (2004), 'Judicial Power in Russia: Through the Prism of Administrative Justice', *Law and Society Review*, vol. 38, no. 3, pp. 549–81.

Sperling, Valerie (1999), *Organizing Women in Contemporary Russia: Engendering Transition.* Cambridge and New York: Cambridge University Press.

Stack, Graham (2008), 'Equally Distanced Oligarchs,' *Russia Profile*, 22 May, in Johnson's Russia List 2008, no. 102, www.cdi.org/russia/johnson, 23 May.

Standing, G. (1999), *Global Labour Flexibility: Seeking Distributive Justice.* London: Macmillan Press.

State Committee of the Russian Federation on Statistics (1996), *Uroven' zhizni naseleniya Rossii.* Moscow: Goskomstat.

Stepan, A. (2000), 'Russian Federalism in Comparative Perspective', *Post-Soviet Affairs*, vol. 16, no. 2 (April–June), pp. 133–76.

Stoliarov, Mikhail (2001), *Federalism and the Dictatorship of Power.* London and New York: Routledge.

Stoner-Weiss, Kathryn (1999), 'Central Weakness and Provincial Autonomy: Observations on the Devolution Process in Russia', *Post-Soviet Affairs*, vol. 15, no. 1 (January–March), pp. 87–104.

Stoner-Weiss, Kathryn (2006), *Resisting the State: Reform and Retrenchment in Post-Soviet Russia.* Cambridge and New York: Cambridge University Press.

Stoner-Weiss, Kathryn (2008), 'Russia', in *Countries at the Crossroads.* Washington DC: Freedom House.

Suny, Ronald Grigor (1998), *The Soviet Experiment: Russia, The USSR, and the Successor States.* Oxford: Oxford University Press.

Surkov, Vladislav (2006) 'Suverenitet – eto politicheskii sinonim konkurentosposobnosti', in Nikita Garadzha (ed.), *Suverinitet.* Moscow: Yevropa.

Surkov, Vladislav (2007), 'Natsionalizatsiya budushchego', in *Suverennaya demokratiya: Ot idei k doktrine.* Moscow: Yevropa.

Sutela, Pekka (2003), *The Russian Market Economy.* Helsinki: Kikimora.

Sutela, Pekka (2008), 'Economic Growth Remains Surprisingly High,' *Russian Analytical Digest*, vol. 38, (2 April), pp. 2–6.

Teague, Elizabeth (2002), 'Putin Reforms the Federal System', in Cameron Ross (ed.), *Regional Politics in Russia*. Manchester: Manchester University Press.

Teague, Elizabeth (2008), 'Workers' Strikes and Civil Society in Russia,' unpublished manuscript.

Thomas, Timothy L. (1996), 'The Russian Military and the 1995 Duma Elections', *Journal of Slavic Military Studies*, vol. 9, no. 3, pp. 519–47.

Todua, Zurab (2007), 'Russia Must Regain the Initiative in Moldova', *Russia in Global Affairs*, vol. 5, no. 1 (January–March), pp. 196–205.

Trenin, Dmitri (2004), 'Moscow's Realpolitik', *Nezavisimaya gazeta*, 16 February.

Trenin, Dmitri (2007), *Getting Russia Right*. Washington, DC: Carnegie Endowment for Peace.

Treisman, Daniel (1998), 'Dollars and Democratization: The Role and Power of Money in Russia's Transitional Elections', *Comparative Politics*, vol. 31, no. 1 (October), pp. 1–21.

Triesman, Daniel and Vladimir Gimpelson (2001), 'Political Business Cycles and Russian Elections, or the Manipulation of the "Chudar"', *British Journal of Political Science*, vol. 31, no. 2 (April), pp. 225–46.

Trochev, Alexei (2005), 'Distrusted Counts: The Impact of State (In)capacity on Judicial Power in Post-Communist Countries', Paper presented at the Canadian Political Science Association, June, London, Ontario.

Trochev, Alexei (2008), *Judging Russia: Constitutional Court in Russian Politics, 1990–2006*. Cambridge and New York: Cambridge University Press.

Troxel, Tiffany A. (2003), *Parliamentary Power in Russia, 1994–2001: President vs Parliament*. New York: Palgrave Macmillan.

Tsygankov, Andrei P. (2006), *Russia's Foreign Policy: Change and Continuity in National Identity*. Lanham MD: Rowman & Littlefield.

Tucker, Robert C. (1971), *The Soviet Political Mind: Stalinism and Post-Stalin Change*. New York: W. W. Norton.

Turovsky, Rostislav F. (2006a), *Tsentr i regiony: problemy politicheskikh otnoshenii*. Moscow: GU VShE.

Turovsky, Rostislav F. (2006b), *Politicheskaya regionalistika*. Moscow: GU VShE.

UNDP (2007a), *Russia's Regions: Goals, Challenges, Achievements*. Moscow: UNDP.

UNDP (2007b), *Human Development Report 2007/2008. Fighting Climate Change : Human Solidarity in a Divided World*. Houndmills, Basingstoke and New York: Palgrave Macmillan, 2007.

Urban, Joan Barth and Solovei, Valerii D. (1997), *Russia's Communists at the Crossroads*. Boulder: Westview.

US Department of State (2007), 'Russia', in *Country Reports on Human Rights Practices*. Washington: GPO. Available at www.state.gov/g/drl/rls/hrrpt/2007/100581.htm.

VCIOM (Russian Public Opinion Research Center) (2007), 'Russia Has Two Allies: The Army and the Mass Media'. Press Release no. 831. 11 December. Available at http://wciom.com.

VCIOM (Russian Public Opinion Research Center) (2008), 'Will Our Army Protect Us?'. Press Release no. 879. 29 February. Available at http://wciom.com.

Voltmer, Katrin (2000), 'Constructing Political Reality in Russia: Izvestiya – Between Old and New Journalistic Practices', *European Journal of Communication*, vol. 15, no. 4, pp. 469–500.

Watts, Ronald L (1999), *Comparing Federal Systems,* 2nd edn. Montreal and Kingston: McGill-Queen's University Press.

Webber, Stephen L. (2006), 'Introduction: The Society-Military Interface in Russia', in Stephen L. Webber and Jennifer G. Mathers (eds), *Military and Society in Post-Soviet Russia*. Manchester and New York: Manchester University Press.

Webber, Stephen L. and Jennifer G. Mathers (2006), *Military and Society in Post-Soviet Russia*. Manchester and New York: Manchester University Press.

Webber, Stephen L. and Alina Zilberman (2006), 'The Citizenship Dimension of the Society-Military Interface', in Stephen L. Webber and Jennifer G. Mathers (eds), *Military and Society in Post-Soviet Russia*. Manchester and New York: Manchester University Press.

Weber, Max (1990), 'Politics as a Vocation' [1946], in Peter Mair (ed.) *The West European Party System*. Oxford: Oxford University Press, pp. 31–6.

Weber, Max (1995), *The Russian Revolutions*, translated and edited by Gordon C. Wells and Peter Baehr. Cambridge: Polity Press.

Westwood, John (2002), *Endurance and Endeavour: Russian History, 1812–2001*, 5th edn. Oxford: Oxford University Press.

White, Stephen (1994), *After Gorbachev*, revised 4th edn. Cambridge and New York: Cambridge University Press.

White, Stephen (2000), *Communism and its Collapse*. London: Routledge.

White, Stephen (2003), 'Rethinking Postcommunist Transition', *Government and Opposition*, vol. 38, no. 4 (Autumn), pp. 417–35.

White, Stephen (2006), 'The Domestic Management of Russia's Foreign and Security Policy', in Allison, Light and White (2006).

White, Stephen (2007), 'Russia's Client Party System', in Paul Webb and Stephen White (eds), *Party Politics in New Democracies*. Oxford: Oxford University Press.

White, Stephen (ed.) (2008), *Media, Culture and Society in Putin's Russia*. London and New York: Palgrave Macmillan.

White, Stephen, Sarah Oates, and Ian McAllister (2005), 'Media Effects and Russian Elections', *British Journal of Political Science,* vol. 35, no. 2 (April), pp. 191–208.

White, Stephen, Richard Rose and Ian McAllister (1997), *How Russia Votes*. Chatham NJ: Chatham House.

Willerton, John P. (2007), 'The Putin Legacy: Russian-Style Democratization Confronts a "Failing State" ', *The Soviet and Post-Soviet Review*, vol. 34, no. 1, pp. 33–54.

Willerton, John P., Mikhail Beznosov, and Martin Carrier (2005), 'Addressing the Challenge of Russia's "Failing State": The Legacy of Gorbachev and the Promise of Putin', *Demokratizatsiya*, vol. 13, no. 2, pp. 219–39.

Wilson, Andrew (2005), *Virtual Politics: Faking Democracy in the Post-Soviet World*. New Haven and London: Yale University Press.

World Bank (2005), *Growth, Poverty and Inequality. Eastern Europe and the Former Soviet Union*. Washington DC: World Bank. Available at www.worldbank.org.ru.

Yakovlev, Andrei (2006), 'The Evolution of Business-State Interaction in Russia: From State Capture to Business Capture?', *Europe-Asia Studies*, vol. 58, no. 7 (November), pp. 1033–56.

Yasmann, Victor (2006), 'Analysis: The Future of Russia's "Ethnic Republics" ', RFE/RL *Russia Report*, 21 April, pp. 1–3.

Zakaria, Fareed (1997), 'The Rise of Illiberal Democracy', *Foreign Affairs*, vol. 76, no. 6, pp. 22–43.

Zakaria, Fareed (2003), *The Future of Freedom*. New York: W. W. Norton.

Zakatnova, Anna (2001), 'The Prosecutor General's Office on the Eve of Reforms', *Nezavisimaya gazeta*, 12 January, p. 3.

Zen'kovich, Nikolai (ed.) (2006), *Putinskaya entsiklopediya*. Moscow: OLMA-Press.

Index

Rakhimov, Murtaza   164
referendum
    of April 1993   46, 63–4
    of December 1993   46, 64–5
regions, politics in   171–87
    executives in   172–80
    legislatures in   180–3
Right Cause   88
Rogozin, Dmitri   96
Romanov dynasty   2
Russia as 'civilisation'   276
Russia's Choice   87–8
Russian Union of Industrialists and
    Entrepreneurs   108
Russians, outside Russia   8
Rutskoi, Alexander   64, 255

Saakashvili, Mikheil   237
Safronov, Ivan (death of)   269–70
Sajudis (Lithuania)   5
'Secret Speech' (1956)   2–3
semi-presidential political system   27–8
Serdyukov, Anatolii   258–9
Shanghai Cooperation Organisation   233
Shuvalov, Igor   33
siloviki (power brokers)   38, 253, 256, 257,
    275, 277
Single Economic Space   233–4
Sobchak, Anatolii   24
Sobyanin, Sergei   34–5
social policy   206–24
    choices for   222–4
    in Soviet period   206–7
    under Putin   207–22
'social state', concept of   210
'sovereign democracy'   14–15, 278–81
Soviets   43–4
Soviet system   1–7
'St Petersburg' group   35–8
Stabilisation Fund   40, 208–9
Stalin, Joseph   2
State Council   32, 162–3
Stavropol', legislature in   182
strikes   109–10, 191, 201
'super-presidentialism'   267
Surkov, Vladislav   14–15, 197, 278–9, 280
Sychev, Andrei   104

Tajikistan   234
'Tandem' (Putin and Medvedev)   20–1,
    35–42, 267–8

Tatarstan   155, 159, 165–6
television   *see* media
terrorism   140
'third wave'   12
trade unions   *see* Labour unions
Tucker, Ronert C.   115
Tuva, legislature in   182

Ukraine   236–7, 268, 278
    'Orange revolution' in   14
unemployment   216–18
Union of Right Forces   88
United Russia party   52–3, 88, 91–7
    at local level   185
    at regional level   180–3
    in Duma   55–9
    Putin on   53, 282
Unity party   92–3
Universal Declaration of Human Rights
    275–6
Ushakov, Yuri   228
USSR
    attitudes towards   264
    establishment of   1
    Putin on breakup of   10–11, 278

Velikhov, Yevgenii   105
Venezuela   242

women in the armed forces   250
women, violence againsgt   112
women's crisis centres   112
women's organisations   100–12

Yabloko   69, 73, 88
Yakovlev, Alexander   3
Yavlinsky, Grigorii   88
Yeltsin, Boris   5, 8–9
    and Congress of People's Deputies   64,
        87
    and foreign policy   226
    attempted impeachment of   48–9
    'Family' of   37
    rise of (1991–3)   45–7
Yermoshkina, Inna   270–1
Yukos oil company   193, 198–9

Zakaria, Fareed   16
zastoi (stagnation)   3
Zubkov, Viktor   33